come out
FIGHTING

come out
FIGHTING

a century of

essential writing

on gay and lesbian

liberation

edited by CHRIS BULL

• **thunder's mouth press/nation books**
new york

COME OUT FIGHTING: A *Century of Essential Writing on Gay and Lesbian Liberation*

Compilation copyright © 2001 by Chris Bull
Introduction © 2001 by Chris Bull
Foreword © 2001 by Gore Vidal

Published by
Thunder's Mouth Press/Nation Books
161 William St., 16th Floor
New York, NY 10038

Nation Books is a co-publishing venture of the Nation Institute and
Avalon Publishing Group Incorporated.

Library of Congress Cataloging-in-Publication Data

Come out fighting: a century of writing on gay and lesbian liberation / edited by Chris Bull.
    p. cm.
  ISBN 1-56025-325-8
  1. Gay liberation movement—United States—History.
2. Gay men's writings, American.   3. Lesbians' writings,
American.   I. Bull, Chris 1963-

HQ76.8.U5 C66 2001
306.76'6—dc21
                                                2001027051

          9 8 7 6 5 4 3 2 1

Designed by *Pauline Neuwirth, Neuwirth & Associates, Inc.*
Printed in the United States of America
Distributed by Publishers Group West

contents

come out
FIGHTING

foreword

GORE VIDAL

the fact that there is a need for this book is yet another demonstration of how remote the United States is from approaching a civilization that might even get as far as the semi-finals with Rome, Greece or even some of Margaret Mead's Pacific Islanders, imagined or not.

I went into the American army at 17 in 1943 and got out in 1946. During my time there, it did not require much detective work to figure out the essential bisexuality of most men and, presumably, most women. After all, we were largely segregated from another part of the forest that we called, more accurately than we knew, God's country. But what a God! He tells the Jews (or was it Christians?) that he is jealous. Well, he has a lot of time on his hands. Also, by the nature of the monotheism that infected the west at the time of Constantine's vision of the cross—single and double—at the 4th century Milvian Bridge much of the West has been kept in the darkness. The three religions of the so-called book—Jewish, Christian, Islamic—are profoundly totalitarian and patriarchal: one god equals one Pope one king one factory boss one absolute father within the God-blessed family structure. Monotheism has proved to be more deadly to human health—at every level—than AIDS will ever be.

During my three years in the army I came to the conclusion that no people as truly fucked-up in sexual matters—ridden with taboos, superstitions, false assumptions—as the men who comprised The Greatest Generation could ever amount to anything collectively except as manipulated pawns in a highly dangerous totalitarian empire. So I abandoned the family trade of politics (not difficult—hypocrisy on so grand a scale was beyond me) and wrote *The City and the Pillar* whose underlying theme was the naturalness—

even normality—of same-sexuality, an activity for which neither Greek nor wordy Roman had even thought up a proper word to describe as a type, much less a set of hysterical attitudes nurtured by the skygod in his airy absoluteness. Are things better now than during our Great War? Recently, high school boys were polled on what they would most like to be, least like to be. Least, by a hundred percent, was a faggot. All the living contributors to this volume are brave and useful souls but not until monotheism has a stake well and truly run through its black heart will we be free of the life-destroying virus.

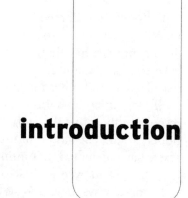

introduction

in his foreword to this volume, Gore Vidal laments the need for a collection of writings on gay and lesbian politics such as this. Vidal's view is consistent with his oft-stated notion that "gay and straight" are "non existent categories...since everyone is a mixture of inclinations," as he puts it in *Pink Triangle and Yellow Stars*, the famous essay included here.

In a perfect world, of course, Vidal could be right. The arbitrary distinction between same- and other-sex eroticism has long afforded bigots an opportunity for cruelty permitted in few other circumstance. But the world, as they say, is what it is. And the ferocious century-long debate over the place of gay men and lesbians in American life has spawned a rich literary tradition of the gay and lesbian political essay, a variety of which I've collected here.

The genre is ideally suited to the historical needs of same-sexers, as Vidal terms gay men and lesbians. Homosexuals have spent the much of the last century as outcasts and pariahs in their own families, communities and nation. These writings, which often appeared first in gay and other underground publications, in many cases were deliberately constructed to form the basis of a political movement that has reached its zenith only in recent years. From belletristic to polemical, from radical to reactionary, from secular to spiritual, the gay political tract made the case for equality in myriad colorful, creative ways. However, these disparate strands of argumentation are united on at least one point: A passionate demand for freedom from disparagement, discrimination, harassment and worse. The second theme to emerge is more pro-active: Why gay men and lesbians should take their rightful place of equality in every America institution, from the military to marriage.

Outsider status forced the construction of a sexual and communal identity, sparking internal and external debates about its merits. This debate, in turn, has changed the nation for the better. America today is far less sadistic and more tolerant place than it was as recently as a decade ago. And it has made inroads far outside the gay community itself, taking a liberating message about personal freedom and responsibility across the globe, a message that the events of Sept. 11 underscored. The gay community is not the only beneficiary: Other-sexers have benefited in innumerable ways, a truth many have begun to concede and even embrace.

In many ways, gays and lesbians have become the exemplars of open societies. In Walt Whitman's *Democratic Vistas*, which kicks off this volume in 1871, the poet predicted (in a footnote no less) the advent of this remarkable movement for change. He also issued a prescient warning about the potential for religious fanaticism and the "glacial purity" of conscience for "devouring, remorseless, like fire and flame" the possibilities of "manly friendship" and "loving com-radeship," which he equated with democracy itself.

Any collection covering as much ground as this one is by defini-tion subjective. I've tried to capture a representative sampling of the great diversity of voices found in this literature. Arranged chronical-ly starting with Whitman, *Come Out Fighting* is intended to provide a flavor of the last century of writings on the topic. I've selected pieces that build on one another. For instance, Freud's "Letter to an American Mother" would not have been possible without the pio-neering work of his friend and colleague Havelock Ellis, included here, which the father of American psychoanalysis gracefully acknowledges. I've relied exclusively upon non-fiction with one exception: Armistead Maupin's "Letter to Mama" from *Tales of the City* because it moved so many. It also dovetailed neatly with Merle Woo's moving non-fiction "Letter to Ma," also published in 1980. Other non-traditional sources—including two passionate pro-gay Supreme Court decisions, one written by a liberal justice in 1986, the other by a conservative in 1995—illustrated how far even some of the most conservative justices had come in less than a decade. As illustrated by Ellis and Freud, and any number of pairings here, the latter could not have happened without the former.

I've also peppered the collection with a healthy dose of an often-overlooked literary form—the personal missive. Two of my favorites are Mike Silverstein's *Letter to Tennessee Williams*, in which the young gay activists implores the writer to use his celebrity to further gay causes. Another is Marvin Liebman's brave coming-out letter to his longtime conservative friend William F. Buckley, reprinted alongside Buckley's response. In entreaties like these, the personal truly becomes the political.

On a personal note, I'd like acknowledge my editor Daniel O'Connor, without whom this collection would never have been published. Thanks also to Matthew Lore, Jeffrey Escoffier, John Gallagher, Michael Bronski and Hans Johnson, inspirations all to the volume and the tradition it seeks to uphold.

—Chris Bull
November 2001

democratic vistas
WALT WHITMAN
1871

. . **let** us survey America's works, poems, philosophies, fulfilling prophecies, and giving form and decision to best ideals. Much that is now undream'd of, we might then perhaps see establish'd, luxuriantly cropping forth, richness, vigor of letters and of artistic expression, in whose products character will be a main requirement, and not merely erudition or elegance.

Intense and loving comradeship, the personal and passionate attachment of man to man—which, hard to define, underlies the lessons and ideals of the profound saviours of every land and age, and which seems to promise, when thoroughly develop'd, cultivated and recognized in manners and literature, the most substantial hope and safety of the future of these States, will then be fully express'd . . . [1]

. . . Offsetting the material civilization of our race, our nationality, its wealth, territories, factories, population, products, trade, and military and naval strength, and breathing breath of life into all these, and more, must be its moral civilization—the formulation, expression, and aidancy whereof, is the very highest height of literature. The climax of this loftiest range of civilization, rising above all the gorgeous shows and results of wealth, intellect, power, and art, as such—above even theology and religious fervor—is to be its development, from the eternal bases, and the fit expression, of absolute Conscience, moral soundness, Justice. Even in religious fervor there is a touch of animal heat. But moral conscientiousness, crystalline, without flaw, not Godlike only, entirely human, awes and enchants forever. Great is emotional love, even in the order of the rational universe. But, if we must make gradations, I am clear there is something greater. Power, love, veneration, products, genius, esthetics,

tried by subtlest comparisons, analyses, and in serenest moods, somewhere fail, somehow become vain. Then noiseless, with flowing
steps, the lord, the sun, the last ideal comes. By the names right, justice, truth, we suggest, but do not describe it. To the world of men it
remains a dream, an idea as they call it. But no dream is it to the
wise—but the proudest, almost only solid, lasting thing of all. Its
analogy in the material universe is what holds together this world,
and every object upon it, and carries its dynamics on forever sure and
safe. Its lack, and the persistent shirking of it, as in life, sociology, literature, politics, business, and even sermonizing, these times, or any
times, still leaves the abysm, the mortal flaw and smutch, mocking
civilization to-day, with all its unquestion'd triumphs, and all the civilization so far known . . . [2]

[1.] It is to the development, identification, and general prevalence of that fervid comradeship,
(the adhesive love, at least rivaling the amative love hitherto possessing imaginative literature,
if not going beyond it,) that I look for the counterbalance and offset of our materialistic and vulgar American democracy, and for the spiritualization thereof. Many will say it is a dream, and
will not follow my inferences: but I confidently expect a time when there will be seen, running
like a half-hid warp through all the myriad audible and visible worldly interests of America,
threads of manly friendship, fond and loving, pure and sweet, strong and life-long, carried to
degrees hitherto unknown—not only giving tone to individual character, and making it
unprecedently emotional, muscular, heroic, and refined, but having the deepest relations to
general politics. I say democracy infers such loving comradeship, as its most inevitable twin or
counterpart, without which it will be incomplete, in vain, and incapable of perpetuating itself.

[2.] I am reminded as I write that out of this very conscience, or idea of conscience, of intense
moral right, and in its name and strain'd construction, the worst fanaticisms, wars, persecu-
tions, murders, etc., have yet, in all lands, in the past, been broach'd, and have come to their
devilish fruition. Much is to be said—but I may say here, and in response, that side by side with
the unflagging stimulation of the elements of religion and conscience must henceforth move
with equal sway, science, absolute reason, and the general proportionate development of the
whole man. These scientific facts, deductions, are divine too—precious counted parts of moral
civilization, and, with physical health, indispensable to it, to prevent fanaticism. For abstract
religion, I perceive, is easily led astray, ever credulous, and is capable of devouring, remorseless, like fire and flame. Conscience, too, isolated from all else, and from the emotional nature,
may but attain the beauty and purity of glacial, snowy ice. We want, for these States, for the
general character, a cheerful, religious fervor, endued with the ever-present modifications of
the human emotions, friendship, benevolence, with a fair field for scientific inquiry, the right
of individual judgment, and always the cooling influences of material Nature.

letter to dr. hirschfeld

EMMA GOLDMAN
1923

dear dr. hirschfeld:

I have been acquainted with your great works on sexual psychology for a number of years now. I have always deeply admired your courageous intervention on behalf of the rights of people who are by their natural disposition unable to express their sexual feelings in what is customarily called the "normal" way. Now that I have had the pleasure of making your personal acquaintance and observing your efforts at first hand, I feel more strongly than ever the impress of your personality and the spirit which has guided you in your difficult undertaking. Your willingness to place your periodical at my disposal, giving me the opportunity to present a critical evaluation of the essay by Herr von Levetzow on the alleged homosexuality of Louise Michel, is proof—if such proof were ever required—that you are a man with a deep sense of justice and interested only in the truth. Permit me to express my sincere appreciation both for this gesture and for your brave and courageous stand in the service of enlightenment and humaneness in opposition to ignorance and hypocrisy.

Above all, I feel obliged to preface my response to the statements of the above-mentioned author with a few brief comments. In challenging what I regard as erroneous presuppositions on the part of Herr von Levetzow. I am in no way motivated by any prejudice against homosexuality itself or any antipathy towards homosexuals in general. Had Louise Michel ever manifested any type of sexual feelings in all those relationships with people whom she loved and who were devoted to her, I would certainly be the last to seek to cleanse her of this "stigma." It is a tragedy, I feel, that people of a different sexual type are caught in a world which shows so little understanding for homosexuals, is so crassly indifferent to the various gradations and variations of gender and their great significance in life. Far be it for me to seek to evaluate these people as inferior, less moral, or incapable of higher feelings and actions. I am the last person to whom it would occur to "protect" Louise Michel, my great teacher and comrade, from the charge of homosexuality. Louise Michel's service to humanity and her great work of social liberation are such that they can be neither enlarged nor reduced, whatever her sexual habits were.

Years ago, before I knew anything about sexual psychology and when my sole acquaintance with homosexuals was limited to a few women I had met in prison (where I was held because of my political convictions), I spoke up in no uncertain terms on behalf of Oscar Wilde. As an anarchist, my place has always been on the side of the persecuted. The entire persecution and sentencing of Wilde struck me as *an act of cruel injustice and repulsive hypocrisy* on the part of the society which condemned this man. And this alone was the reason which prompted me to stand up for him.

Later I came to Europe, where I became acquainted with the works of Havelock Ellis, Kraft-Ebing, Carpenter, and some others, which first made me fully aware of the crime which had been perpetrated upon Oscar Wilde and his kind. From then on I defended in the spoken and written word those whose entire nature is different in regard to sexual feelings and needs. It was primarily your works, dear Doctor, which helped me to illuminate the extremely complex problems of sexual psychology and to mold the entire position of my audience in a more humane way toward these questions.

From all of this, your readers may recognize that any prejudice or antipathy towards homosexuals is totally foreign to me. On the contrary! Among my male and female friends, there are a few who are of either a completely Uranian or a bisexual disposition. I have found these individuals far above average in terms of intelligence, ability, sensitivity, and personal charm. I empathize deeply with them, for I know that their sufferings are of a larger and more complex sort than those of ordinary people. But there exists among very many homosexuals a predominant intellectual outlook which I must seriously challenge. I am speaking here of the practice of claiming every possible prominent personality as one of their own, attributing their own feelings and character traits to these people.

To be sure, this is not a homosexual peculiarity but instead a psychological characteristic of *all* those who are publicly held in disdain. Such people are always inclined to cite the most prominent individuals of all ages in support of their cause. *Misery seeks company.* One notes, for example, that Jews are almost inclined to attribute Jewish origins, or at least Jewish character traits, to all the significant men and women in the world. A similar practice is to be found among the Irish: the people of India will always tell us that theirs is the greatest civilization, etc., etc. We encounter the same phenomenon among political outcasts. Socialists like to claim men like Walt Whitman and Oscar Wilde as advocates of the theories of Karl Marx, while anarchists see kindred spirits in Nietzsche, Wagner, Ibsen, and others. Many-sidedness has always been a sign of true greatness, no doubt; but I have always felt it rather importunate to claim great creative personalities for my ideas *so long as they themselves have not expressed their agreement with them.*

If one were to believe the assurances and claims of many homosexuals, one would be forced to the conclusion that no truly great person is or ever was to be found outside the circle of persons of a different sexual type. Social ostracism and persecution inevitably spawn sectarianism; but this outlook, narrow in its perspective, often renders people unjust in their praise of others. Without wishing to offend Herr von Levetzow in any way, I must say that he seems to be strongly influenced by the sectarian spirit of many homosexuals, perhaps unconsciously so. Beyond that, he has an antiquated conception of the essence of womanhood. He sees in woman a being meant by nature solely to delight man with her attractiveness, bear his children, and otherwise figure as a domestic and general household slave. Any woman who fails to meet these shopworn requirements of womanhood is promptly taken as a Uranian by this writer. In light of the accomplishments of women to date in every sector of human intellectual life and in efforts for social change, this traditional male conception of womanhood scarcely deserves regard any longer. I nonetheless feel compelled to pursue the outmoded views of this writer concerning Louise Michel to some extent, if only to show the reader what nonsensical conclusions can be reached if one proceeds from nonsensical presuppositions . . .

Modern woman is no longer satisfied to be the beloved of a man: she looks for understanding, comradeship; she wants to be treated as a human being and not simply as an object for sexual gratification. And since man in many cases cannot offer her this, she turns to her sisters.

She represented *a new type of womanhood* which is nonetheless as old as the race, and she had a soul which was permeated by an all-encompassing and all-understanding love for humanity. In short, Louise Michel was a complete woman, free of all the prejudices and traditions which for centuries held women in chains and degraded them to household slaves and objects of sexual lust. The new woman celebrated her resurrection in the figure of Louise, the woman capable of heroic deeds but one who remains a woman in her passion and in her love.

sexual inversion

HAVELOCK ELLIS
1933

when the sexual impulse is directed towards persons of the same sex we are in the presence of an aberration variously known as "sexual inversion," "contrary sexual feeling," "uranism," or, more generally, "homosexuality," as opposed to normal heterosexuality. "Homosexuality" is the best general term for all forms of the anomaly, in distinction from normal heterosexuality, while "sexual inversion" is best reserved for apparently congenital and fixed forms. It is the most clearly defined of all sexual deviations, for it presents an impulse which is completely and fundamentally transferred from the normal object to an object which is normally outside the sphere of sexual desire, and yet possesses all the attributes which in other respects appeal to human affection. It is a highly abnormal aberration, and yet it seems to supply a greater satisfaction than any other aberration can furnish. It is probably this characteristic of sexual inversion which renders it so important. This importance is manifested in three ways: (1) its wide diffusion and the large place it has played in various epochs of culture; (2) its frequency in civilization today, and (3) the large number of distinguished persons who have manifested the aberration.

The fundamental and what may be called "natural" basis of homosexuality is manifested by its prevalence among animals. It is common among various mammals, and, as we should expect, is especially found among the Primates most nearly below Man. G. V. Hamilton, studying monkeys and baboons, states that "the immature male monkey typically passes through a period during which he is overtly and almost exclusively homosexual, and that this period is terminated at sexual maturity by an abrupt turning to heterosexual ways." Zuckerman has closely observed the homosexual behavior of baboons and chimpanzees, sometimes finding it more pronounced in the females than in the males, and he is even inclined to assimilate homosexual and heterosexual behavior among the apes, finding no pronounced differences.

Among many savage and barbarous peoples homosexuality has been conspicuous and sometimes treated with reverence. This was so even among the ancient civilizations on which our own is founded. It was known to the Assyrians, and the Egyptians, nearly four thousand years ago, attributed paederasty to their gods Horus and Set. It has been associated not only with religion but with military virtues, and was in this way cultivated among the ancient Carthaginians, Dorians, and Scythians, as it was later by the Normans. Among the ancient Greeks, finally, it was idealized not merely in association with military virtue, but with intellectual, aesthetic, and even ethical qualities, and was by many regarded as more noble than normal heterosexual love. After the coming of Christianity it still held its ground, but it fell into disrepute, while as a psychological anomaly consisting in an idealization of persons of the same sex even apart from homosexual acts it was forgotten or unknown. It was only recognized after Justinian's time as sodomy, that is to say as a vulgar vice, or rather as a crime, deserving of the most severe secular and ecclesiastical penalties, even burning at the stake.

In the Middle Ages it is probable that sexual inversion flourished not only in camps but also in cloisters, and it is constantly referred to in the Penitentials. It is not, however, until the Renaissance that it plays a conspicuous part in the world; Latini, Dante's teacher, was inverted, and Dante refers to the frequency of this perversion among men of intellect and fame. The distinguished French humanist Muret was from this cause in danger of death throughout his life; Michaelangelo, the greatest sculptor of the Renaissance, cherished homosexual ideals and passions, although there is no reason to suppose that he had physical relations with the men he was attracted to; Marlowe, one of the chief poets of the Renaissance in England, was clearly of the same way of feeling, as also, there is ground for believing, was Bacon.

It is quite true that the invert seldom places himself under a physician's hands. He usually has no wish to be different from what he is, and as his intelligence is generally quite up to the average level, if not above it, he is careful to avoid discovery and seldom attracts the attention of the police. In this way the prevalence of inversion is unknown to those who do not know where to look for it or how to detect it. In Germany Hirschfeld, whose knowledge of homosexuality is unrivaled, has shown that a large number of separate estimates among different classes of the population reveal a proportion of inverted and bisexual persons varying between one and five per cent. In England my own independent observations, though of a much less thorough and extensive character, indicate a similar prevalence among the educated middle class, while among the lower social classes homosexuality is certainly not rare, and even if not innate there often appears to be among them a remarkable absence of repulsion to homosexual relations; many inverts have referred to this point. Among women, though less easy to detect, homosexuality appears to be scarcely less common than among men, in this respect unlike nearly all other aberrations; the pronounced cases are, indeed, perhaps less frequently met with than among men, but less marked and less deeply rooted cases are probably more frequent than among men. Some professions show a higher proportion of inverts than others. Inversion is not specially prevalent among scientific and medical men; it is more frequent among literary and artistic people, and in the dramatic profession it is often found. It is also specially common among hairdressers, waiters, and waitresses Artistic aptitude of one kind or another, and a love of music, are found among a large proportion of educated inverts, in my experience as much as sixty-eight per cent.

In America among the educated and professional classes, M.W. Peck among 60 college men in Boston, representing all departments of the University and College life, found 7 who were definitely homosexual, six of them admitting adult overt experiences. Two others were clearly though unconsciously homosexual; he considers that 10 per cent college men are homosexual, whether or not there are overt practices. G. V. Hamilton found that only 44 of his 100 married men could deny all memory of homosexual play in early life; while 46 men and 23 women owned to friendship with their own sex involving stimulation of the sexual organs. Katharine Davis found that 31.7 per cent of women admitted "intense emotional relations with other women," and 27.5 per cent of unmarried women admitted homosexual play in childhood, 48.2 per cent of them dropping it after adolescence.

The importance of homosexuality is, again, shown by the prevalence of homosexual prostitution. This has been specially studied in Berlin where the police tolerate it, on the same basis as female prostitution, in order to be able to control and limit its manifestations.

Hirschfeld considers the number of male prostitutes in Berlin to be about twenty thousand; more recently and more cautiously Werner Picton estimates it as six thousand. More than one third are judged to be psychopathic, less than a quarter of them to be homosexual themselves. Unemployment is a commonly assigned cause, as of female prostitution, but probably various other elements enter into the causation.

Although sexual inversion is thus so important a phenomenon it is only in recent times that it has received scientific study, or even recognition. This first took place in Germany. At the end of the eighteenth century two cases were published in Germany of men showing a typical emotional sexual attraction towards their own sex. But although Hössli, Caspar, and especially Ulrichs (who invented for it the term "uranism") further prepared the way, it was not until 1870 that Westphal published a detailed history of an inverted young woman, and clearly showed that the case was congenital and not acquired, so that it could not be termed a vice, and was also, though neurotic elements were present, not a case of insanity. From that moment the scientific knowledge of sexual inversion rapidly increased. Krafft-Ebing, who was the first great clinician of sexual inversion, brought together a large number of cases in his *Psychopathia Sexualis*, which was the earliest scientific book dealing with abnormal sexuality to attract general attention. Moll, with a more critical mind than was Krafft-Ebing's, and a wider scientific culture, followed with an admirable treatise on sexual inversion. Then Magnus Hirschfeld, with an unrivaled and most sympathetic personal knowledge of inverts, greatly contributed to our knowledge, and his book, *Der Homosexualität* (1914), not yet translated into English, is an encyclopedia of the whole subject. In Italy, where the term "inversione sessuale" seems to have originated, cases were from an early period brought forward by Ritti, Tamassia, Lombroso, and others. In France, where Charcot and Magnan first took up this study in 1882, a series of distinguished investigators, including Féré, Sérieux, and Saint-Paul (writing under the pen-name of "Dr. Laupts") have elucidated our knowledge of sexual inversion. In Russia Tarnowsky first investigated the phenomena. In England, John Addington Symonds, son of a distinguished physician and himself a brilliant man of letters, privately published two notable pamphlets, one on sexual inversion in ancient Greece and another on the modern problem of homosexuality. Edward Carpenter (also at first privately) printed a pamphlet on the subject and later a book (first published in German) on *The Intermediate Sex*. Raffalovich published a notable book in French, and my own book on sexual inversion was published first in Germany (*Das Konträre Geschlechtsgefühl*, 1896), and then in England and America, where also, at an earlier date, Kiernan and Lydston had given attention to the facts and theory of sexual inversion. The most notable recent book (1932) is Marañón's, translated from the Spanish.

The amount of study lately devoted to the subject has not yet resulted in complete unanimity. The first and most fundamental difficulty lay in deciding whether sexual inversion is congenital or acquired. The prevailing opinion, before Krafft-Ebing's influence began to be felt, was that homosexuality is acquired, that it is, indeed, simply a "vice," generally the mere result of masturbation or sexual excesses, having produced impotence in normal coitus, or else (with Binet and Schrenck-Notzing) that it is the result of suggestion in early life. Krafft-Ebing accepted both the congenital and the acquired varieties of homosexuality, and the subsequent tendency has been towards minimizing the importance of acquired homosexuality. This tendency was well marked in Moll's treatise. Hirschfeld and Marañón consider that there is always a congenital element in homosexuality, and Bloch, Aletrino, etc., separated off the non-congenital homosexual persons who, for some reason or another, indulge in homosexual practices, as belonging to a group of "pseudo-homosexuality"; this was also the view of Näcke who considered that we have to distinguish not between congenital and acquired inversion, but between true and false, and who regarded homosexuality appearing late in life as not acquired, but "retarded" or delayed homosexuality on a congenital basis. Some authorities who started with the old view that sexual inversion is exclusively or chiefly an acquired condition (like Näcke and Bloch) later adopted the more modern view. Many psycho-analysts still cherish the belief that homosexuality is always acquired, but as at the same time they also recognize that it is frequently fixed, and therefore presumably constitutional, the difference of opinion becomes unimportant.

Another fundamental point in regard to which opinion has changed is the question as to whether sexual inversion, even if congenital, should be considered a morbid or "degenerate" state. On this matter Krafft-Ebing at first ranged himself with the ancient view and regarded inversion as the manifestation of a neuropathic or psychopathic state, but in his latest writings he judiciously modified this position and was content to look on inversion as an anomaly and not a disease or a "degeneration." This is the direction in which modern opinion has steadily moved. Inverts may be healthy, and normal in all respects outside their special aberration. This has always been my own standpoint, though I regard inversion as frequently in close relation to minor neurotic conditions. We may agree with Hirschfeld (who finds hereditary taint in not more than 25 per cent inverts) that even if there is a neuropathic basis in inversion the morbid element is usually small.

We are thus brought to what may be regarded as the fundamental basis in biological constitution on which, when we go outside the psychological field, homosexuality can be said to rest. It may seem easy to say that there are two definitely separated distinct and immutable sexes, the male that bears the sperm-cell and the female that bears the ovum or egg. That statement has, however, long ceased to be, biologically, strictly correct. We may not know exactly what sex is; but we do know that it is mutable, with the possibility of one sex being changed into the other sex, that its frontiers are often uncertain, and that there are many stages between a complete male and a complete female. In some forms of animal life, indeed, it is not easy to distinguish which is male and which female. In all these cases sex may be regarded as one of the devices (for there are other devices in Nature) for securing reproduction, though we are justified in studying the phenomena of sex apart from the question of reproduction. However true it may be that reproduction is Nature's primary aim, it is equally true that sexual reproduction is only one of several devices for attaining that end.

We are bound to assume that in every sex-chromosome, whether XX or XY, resides the physical basis of an impulse which tends to impose the male type or the female type on the developing individual. When two individuals of different races, as of some moths (in which the phenomena have been specially studied) are bred together, the offspring often ceases to be normal, and the male offspring may show a tendency in the direction of femaleness, or, under other circumstances, the female offspring shows a tendency to maleness, the strain thus able to give an impress being termed "strong" and the other "weak." Here we see already, in a low zoölogical form, the condition of *inter-sexuality* which when we proceed to Man and enter the psychological field has sometimes been considered (though incorrectly) to constitute an "intermediate" sex. It is, more strictly, the result of a quantitative disharmony between the male and female sex-determining factors. Being part of the hereditary constitution of the individual, it is inborn, likely to become more pronounced as development proceeds, and, in the higher mammals, to manifest itself in the psychic sphere.

When dealing with moths, it is found that this intersexuality, more simple than when occurring higher in the zoölogical scale, may be produced by mixing different races of the same species. When we approach nearer to Man, the forms of intersexuality differ, are less pronounced, or not at all, in the external physical aspect, and are due less to mixture of different races than to varied individual deviations from the normal, while sometimes at all stages external factors may be influential.

We begin to come closer to the actual mechanism by which intersexuality is produced when we turn again to the action of the hormones. We may view these as taking up the guidance of the sex process after the influence of the initial sex-chromosomes, XX or XY, has been exhausted. The somatic, or general, tissues of the body possess the potency of developing the characters of either sex under the stimulus of the special complex of sex-hormones which they receive. The ovary, indeed, it is believed, does not at any early stage exert any marked influence upon the soma, the female development being seemingly innate, though the developed female sex-equipment depends on the sex-hormones for its maintenance. Male differentiation, on the other hand, requires the male testicular hormone for its development. Thus the female, it is held, represents the neutral form which the soma assumes in the absence of the male sex hormone. When the male hormone appears later than usual some form of intersexuality thus results, and the later its appearance the more femaleness there is in the result. "The degree of abnormality," as Crew puts it, "will be determined by the time at which the male sex-hormone becomes operative." That helps to explain why an individual who appears female in early life assumes male characters at sexual maturity.

To the adrenal cortex is specially attributed the formation of a hormone which exerts a masculinizing influence in the same direction as that of the testes. This result, "virilism" as it is now sometimes termed (formerly "adreno-genital syndrome"), is associated with hypertrichosis and in males with precocious sexual and somatic development, while in females there is atrophy of the uterus, with changes in the ovaries, under-development of the labia and over-growth of the clitoris, atrophy of the mammæ, narrowing of the hips, broadening of the shoulders, with either marked muscular development or adiposity. There are disturbances of sexual function and even complete sterility. Four types of virilism have been described, depending on the time of onset: (1) *Congenital type* (with feminine pseudo-hermaphroditism, the sexual glands remaining female while the secondary sex characters are male); (2) *Puberty type* (beginning near puberty, with hirsutism and menstrual disturbances predominating); (3) *Adult type* (rather similar but less marked); (4) *Obstetrical type* (after the menopause with obesity, excess or loss of hair, psychic disturbances and asthenia). The exact method in which the adrenal hormone acts is still a matter of dispute.

When we deal with homosexuality we are still in the intersexual sphere, and we are no doubt still largely concerned with the action of the hormones, but we are in a psychic sphere where physical syndromes are usually difficult to trace. There is no doubt that in a slight degree, and occasionally in a marked degree, they still exist, but they are unimportant, though many years ago Weil and others have sought to demonstrate the presence of slight but measurable physical differentia of congenital origin in the homosexual. Apart from such measurable differences, there can be little doubt that certain individuals, in organic constitution, and probably as a result of unusual hormonic balance, possess a special aptitude to experience sexual satisfaction with persons of their own sex. There are a larger number, as is well known, presumably normal, both in Man and among lower animals, who when deprived of the presence of individuals of the opposite sex can find temporary sexual satisfaction in their own sex.

It may seem hazardous to assert that every individual is made up of mixed masculine and feminine elements, variously combined, and that the male invert is a person with an unusual proportion of female elements, the female invert a person with an unusual proportion of male elements; it is a schematic view which will scarcely account altogether for the phenomena. But when we put aside occasional homosexuality in presumably normal persons, we seem justified in looking upon inversion as a congenital anomaly—or, to speak more accurately, an anomaly based on congenital conditions—which if it is pathological, is only so in Virchow's sense that pathology is the science not of diseases but of anomalies, so that an inverted person may be as healthy as a color-blind person. Congenital sexual inversion is thus akin to a biological variation. It is a variation doubtless due to imperfect sexual differentiation, but often having no traceable connection with any morbid condition in the individual himself.

This view of sexual inversion now tends to prevail and has gained much force recently. But it may be traced some way back. Ulrichs, so long ago as 1862, declared that inversion is "a species of hermaphroditism." Kiernan in America in 1888 insisted on the significance of the fact that the ancestors of the human species were originally bisexual; Chevalier in 1893 put forward a theory of inversion based on fœtal bisexuality. Letamendi of Madrid in 1894 set forth a theory of panhermaphroditism according to which there are always latent female germs in the male, and latent male germs in the female. Finally, about 1896, Krafft-Ebing, Hirschfeld, and I (all, it seems, more or less independently) adopted a somewhat similar explanation.

The prevalence of these general views of sexual inversion has influenced the clinical classification of its varieties. Krafft-Ebing accepted four different varieties of congenital inversion and four different varieties of the acquired form. Moll rejected this elaborate classification, recognizing only psychosexual hermaphroditism (or, as it is now usually termed, bisexuality) and complete inversion. This corresponds to the division now recognized by most authorities. That is to say that when we have put aside the people who are exclusively attracted to the opposite sex, we have those who are exclusively attracted to the same sex, and those who are attracted to both sexes. When we go beyond this simple and elementary classification we encounter an endless number of individual variations, but they do not easily admit of being arranged in definite groups. Even the bisexual class is not rigidly uniform, for it certainly contains many individuals who are congenital inverts with an acquired heterosexuality.

When we consider well-marked cases of sexual inversion we find certain characteristics which frequently tend to recur. While a considerable proportion (in my experience over fifty per cent) belong to reasonably healthy families, in about forty per cent there is in the family some degree of morbidity or abnormality—eccentricity, alcoholism, neurasthenia or nervous disease—of slight or greater degree. The heredity inversion is well-marked, though it has sometimes been denied; sometimes a brother and sister, a mother and son, an uncle and nephew, are both inverted even unknown to each other; I find this family or hereditary inversion in thirty-five per cent cases, and von Römer has found exactly the same proportion. It is alone sufficient to show that inversion may be inborn. The general personal health is in about two-thirds of the cases good and sometimes very good; among the remainder there is often a tendency to nervous trouble or to a more or less unbalanced temperament; only a small proportion (about eight per cent in my experience) are markedly morbid.

In the great majority the inverted tendency appears in early life, often at puberty, but frequently there are indications of it before puberty. Sexual precocity appears to be marked in a large proportion, and there is often a tendency to sexual hyperaesthesia. Many inverts describe themselves as "sensitive" or "nervous." The influence of suggestion can be not infrequently traced, but in these cases there is usually also evidence of predisposition. Masturbation has been practiced in a large proportion of cases, but masturbation is also common among the heterosexual and there is no reason to suppose that it is a factor in the causation of inversion. The erotic dreams of inverts are usually inverted, but this is by no means invariably the case, and even inverts who appear to be such congenitally sometimes have normal dreams, just as normal persons occasionally have homosexual dreams.

The satisfaction of the inverted sexual impulse is effected in a variety of ways. Among my cases nearly twenty per cent had never had any kind of sexual relationship. In thirty to thirty-five per cent the sexual relationship rarely goes beyond close contact, or at most mutual masturbation. In the others inter-crural connection or occasionally *fellatio* is the method practiced. In woman gratification is obtained by kissing, close contact, mutual masturbation, and in some cases *cunnilinctus*, which is usually active rather than passive. The proportion of male inverts who desire *paedicatio* (more often active than passive) is not large. Hirschfeld places it at eight per cent cases; I have found it to be nearer fifteen percent

In male inverts there is a frequent tendency to approximate to the feminine type and in female inverts to the masculine type; this occurs both in physical and in psychic respects, and though it may be traced in a considerable number of respects it is by no means always obtrusive. Some male inverts, however, insist on their masculinity, while many others are quite unable to say whether they feel more like a man or a woman. Among female inverts, there is usually some approximation to the masculine attitude and temperament though this is by no means always conspicuous. Various minor anamolies of structure or function may occur in inverts. The sexual organs in both sexes are sometimes overdeveloped or, perhaps more usually, underdeveloped, in a slight approximation to the infantile type; gynecomasty is at times observed; in women there may be a somewhat masculine development of the larynx, as well as some degree of hypertrichosis. (Marañón finds that male traits tend to appear on the right side of the body, female on the left.) Male inverts are sometimes unable to whistle. In both sexes a notable youthfulness of appearance is often preserved into adult age. The love of green (which is normally a preferred color chiefly by children and especially girls) is frequently observed. A certain degree of dramatic aptitude is not uncommon, as well as some tendency to vanity and personal adornment, and occasionally a feminine love of ornament and jewelry. Many of these physical and psychic characteristics may be said to indicate some degree of infantilism, and this is in agreement with the view of inversion which traces it to a fundamental bisexual basis, for the further back we go in the life-history of the individual the nearer we approach to the bisexual stage.

Morally, inverts usually apply to themselves the normal code, and seek to justify their position. Those who fight against their instincts, or permanently disapprove of their own attitude, or even feel doubtful about it, are a small minority, less than twenty per cent. This is why so few inverts seek medical advice. They are fortified in their self-justification by the fact that not only in France but in several other countries (Italy, Belgium, Holland, etc.) which have been influenced by the Code Napoléon homosexual practices *per se* are not touched by the law provided there has been no violence, no outrage on a minor, and no offense against public decency. England and the United States are probably the chief countries in which the ancient ecclesiastical jurisdiction against homosexuality still retains an influence. In these countries, however, the law in this matter causes much difficulty and dispute; it is difficult to decide what homosexual actions amount to a criminal offense; it is only in a few cases that the culprits are detected, or even sought, for, as a rule, the police carefully avoid pursuing their traces; and there is not the slightest reason to suppose that the countries which legislate against inversion possess a smaller, or even less prominent, proportion of inverts. In France, for instance, under the ancient monarchy, when an invert was, according to the law, liable to be burned, inversion was sometimes fashionable and conspicuous; at the present day the reverse is the case. In view of these facts there is today a movement, which finds support alike in medical and in legal quarters, in favor of abolishing the punishment of homosexual acts except when the circumstances under which the acts are committed give them an anti-social character. It is a powerful argument in favor of such abolition that it at once puts a stop to the movement of agitation, and the tendency to the glorification of homosexuality—which is undesirable and even in many respects harmful—prevailing in those countries which still regard homosexuality as a crime.

letter to an american mother

SIGMUND FREUD
1935

dear mrs. . . .

I gather from your letter that your son is a homosexual. I am most impressed by the fact that you do not mention this term yourself in your information about him. May I question you, why you avoid it? Homosexuality is assuredly no advantage, but it is nothing to be ashamed of, no vice, no degradation, it cannot be classified as an illness; we consider it to be a variation of the sexual function produced by a certain arrest of sexual development. Many highly respectable individuals of ancient and modern times have been homosexuals, several of the greatest men among them (Plato, Michelangelo, Leonardo da Vinci, etc.). It is a great injustice to persecute homosexuality as a crime, and cruelty, too. If you do not believe me, read the books of Havelock Ellis.

By asking me if I can help, you mean, I suppose, if I can abolish homosexuality and make normal heterosexuality take its place. The answer is, in a general way, we cannot promise to achieve it. In a certain number of cases we succeed in developing the blighted germs of heterosexual tendencies which are present in every homosexual, in the majority of cases it is no more possible. It is a question of the quality and the age of the individual. The result of treatment cannot be predicted.

What analysis can do for your son runs in a different line. If he is unhappy, neurotic, torn by conflicts, inhibited in his social life, analysis may bring him harmony, peace of mind, full efficiency whether he remains a homosexual or gets changed. . . .

Sincerely yours with kind wishes,
Freud

the homosexual in society

ROBERT DUNCAN
1944

something in James Agee's recent approach to the Negro
pseudo-folk (*Partisan Review*, Spring 1944) is the background of the
notes which I propose in discussing yet another group whose only
salvation is in the struggle of all humanity for freedom and individual integrity; who have suffered in modern society persecution,
excommunication; and whose "intellectuals," whose most articulate members, have been willing to desert that primary struggle, to
beg to gain at the price, if need be, of any sort of prostitution, privilege for themselves, however ephemeral; who have been willing,
rather than to struggle toward self-recognition, to sell their product,
to convert their deepest feelings into marketable oddities and senti-
mentalities.

Although in private conversation, at every table, at every editorial
board, one knows that a great body of modern art is cheated by what
almost amounts to a homosexual cult: although hostile critics have
opened fire in a constant attack as rabid as the attack of Southern sen-
ators upon "niggers"; critics who might possibly view the homosexual
with a more humane eye seem agreed that it is better that nothing be
said. Pressed to the point, they may either, as in the case of such an
undeniable homosexual as Hart Crane, contend that they are great
despite their "perversion"[1]—much as my mother used to say how
much better a poet Poe would have been had he not taken dope; or
where it is possible they have attempted to deny the role of the homosexual in modern art, the usual reply to unprincipled critics like
Craven and Benton in painting being to assert that modern artists
have not been homosexual. (Much as PM goes to great length to
prove that none of the Communist leaders have been Jews—as if, if

all the leaders were Jews, it would be that that would make the party suspect.)

But one cannot, in face of the approach taken to their own problem by homosexuals, place any weight of criticism upon the liberal body of critics. For there are Negroes who have joined openly in the struggle for human freedom, made articulate that their struggle against racial prejudice is part of the struggle for all; while there are Jews who have sought no special privilege of recognition for themselves as Jews, but have fought for *human* recognition and rights. But there is in the modern scene no homosexual who has been willing to take in his own persecution a battlefront toward human freedom. Almost co-incident with the first declarations for homosexual rights was the growth of a cult of homosexual superiority to the human race; the cultivation of a secret language, the *camp*, a tone and a vocabulary that is loaded with contempt for the human. They have gone beyond, let us say, Christianity, in excluding the pagan world.

Outside the ghetto the word "goy" disappears, wavers and dwindles in the Jew's vocabulary. But in what one would believe the most radical, the most enlightened "queer" circles the word "jam" remains, designating all who are not homosexual, filled with an unwavering hostility and fear, gathering an incredible force of exclusion and blindness. It is hard (for all the sympathy which I can bring to bear) to say that this cult plays any other than an evil role in society.

But names cannot be named, I cannot, like Agee, name the nasty little midgets, the entrepreneurs of this vicious market, the pimps of this special product. There are critics whose cynical, back-biting joke upon their audience is no other than this secret special superiority; there are poets whose nostalgic picture of special worth in suffering, sensitivity and magical quality is no other than this intermediate "sixth sense"; there are new cult leaders whose special divinity, whose supernatural and visionary claim is no other than this mystery of sex. The law has declared homosexuality secret, non-human, unnatural (and why not then supernatural?). The law itself sees in it a crime, not in the sense that murder, thievery, seduction of children or rape is seen as a crime—but in an occult sense. In the recent Lonergan case it was clear that murder was a *human* crime, but homosexuality was non-human. It was not a crime against man but a crime against "the way of nature," as defined in the Christian religion, a crime against "God."[2] It was lit up and given an awful and lurid attraction such as witchcraft (I can think of no other immediate example) was given in its time.

Like early witches, the homosexual propagandists have rejected any struggle toward recognition in social equality and, far from seeking to undermine the popular superstition, have accepted the charge of Demonism. Sensing the fear in society that is generated in ignorance of their nature, they have sought not to bring about an understanding, to assert their equality and their common aims with mankind, but they have sought to profit by that fear and ignorance, to become witch doctors in the modern chaos.

To go about this they have had to cover with mystery, to obscure, the work of all these who have viewed homosexuality as but one of the many facets, one of the many eyes through which the human being may see and who, admitting through which eye they saw, have had primarily in mind as they wrote (as Melville, Proust, or Crane had) mankind and its liberation. For these great early artists their humanity was the source, the sole source, of their work. Thus in *Remembrance of Things Past* Charlus is not seen as the special disintegration of a homosexual but as a human being in disintegration, and the forces that lead to that disintegration, the forces of pride, self-humiliation in love, jealousy, are not special forces but common to all men and women. Thus in Melville, though in *Billy Budd* it is clear that the conflict is homosexual, the forces that make for that conflict, the guilt in passion, the hostility rising from subconscious sources, and the sudden recognition of these forces as it comes to Vere in that story; these are forces which are universal, which rise in other contexts, which in Melville's work have risen in other contexts.

It is, however, the body of Crane that has been most ravaged by these modern ghouls and, once ravaged, stuck up cult-wise in the mystic light of their special cemetery literature. The live body of Crane is there, inviolate; but in the window display of modern poetry, of so many special critics and devotees, is a painted mummy, deep sea green. One may tiptoe by, as the visitors to Lenin's tomb tiptoe by and, once outside, find themselves in a world in his name that has celebrated the defeat of all that he was devoted to. One need only point out in all the homosexual imagery of Crane, in the longing and vision of love, the absence, for instance, of the "English" specialty, the private world of boys' schools and isolate sufferings that has been converted into the poet's intangible "nobility," into the private[3] sensibility that colors so much of modern writing. Where the Zionists of homosexuality have laid claim to a Palestine of their own, asserting in their miseries their nationality, Crane's suffering, his rebellion, and his love are sources of poetry for him not because they are what make him different from, superior to, mankind, but because he saw in them his link with mankind: he saw in them his sharing in universal human experience.

What can one do in the face of this, both those critics and artists, not homosexuals, who, however, are primarily concerned with all inhumanities, all forces of convention and law that impose a tyranny upon man, and those critics and artists who, as homosexuals, must face in their own lives both the hostility of society in that they are "queer" and the hostility of the homosexual cult of superiority in that they are human?

For the first group the starting point is clear, that they must recognize homosexuals as equals and as equals allow them neither more nor less than can be allowed any human being. For the second group the starting point is more difficult; the problem is more treacherous.

In the face of the hostility of society which I risk in making even the acknowledgement explicitly in this statement, in the face of the "crime" of my own feelings, in the past I publicized those feelings as private and made no stand for their recognition but tried to sell them disguised, for instance, as conflicts rising from mystical sources. I colored and perverted simple and direct emotions and realizations into a mysterious realm, a mysterious relation to society. Faced by the inhumanities of society I did not seek a solution in humanity but turned to a second out-cast society as inhumane as the first. I joined those who, while they allowed for my sexual nature, allowed for so little of the moral, the sensible and creative direction which all of living should reflect. They offered a family, outrageous as it was, a community in which one was not condemned for one's homosexuality, but it was necessary there for one to desert one's humanity for which one would be suspect, "out of key." In drawing rooms and in little magazines I celebrated the cult with a sense of sanctuary such as a Medieval Jew must have found in the ghetto; my voice taking on the modulations which tell of the capitulation to snobbery and the removal from the "common sort"; my poetry exhibiting the objects made divine and tyrannical as the Catholic church has made bones of saints, and bread and wine, tyrannical.

After an evening at one of those salons where the whole atmosphere was one of suggestion and celebration, I returned recently experiencing again the after-shock, the desolate feeling of wrongness, remembering in my own voice and gestures the rehearsal of unfeeling. Alone, not only I, but, I felt, the others who had appeared as I did so mocking, so superior to feeling, had known, knew still, those troubled emotions, the deep and integral longings that we as human beings feel, holding us from violate action by the powerful sense of humanity that is their source, longings that lead us to love, to envision a creative life. "Towards something far," as Hart Crane wrote, "now farther away than ever."

Among those who should understand those emotions which society condemned, one found that the group language did not allow for any feeling at all other than this self-ridicule, this gaiety (it is significant that the homosexual's word for his own kind is "gay"), a wave surging forward, breaking into laughter and then receding, leaving a wake of disillusionment, a disbelief that extended to one-self, to life itself. What then, disowning this career, can one turn to?

What I think can be asserted as a starting point is that only one devotion can be held by a human being as a creative life and expression, and that is a devotion to human freedom, toward the liberation of human love, human conflicts, human aspirations. To do this one must disown *all* the special groups (nations, religions, sexes, races) that would claim allegiance. To hold this devotion every written word, every spoken word, every action, every purpose, must be examined and considered. The old fears, the old specialties will be there, mocking and tempting; the old protective associations will be there, offering for a surrender of one's humanity congratulations upon one's special nature and value. It must be always recognized that the others, those who have surrendered their humanity, are not less than oneself. It must be always remembered that one's own honesty, one's battle against the inhumanity of his own group (be it against patriotism, against bigotry, against, in this specific case, the homosexual cult) is a battle that cannot be won in the immediate scene. The forces of inhumanity are overwhelming, but only one's continued opposition can make any other order possible, can give an added strength for all those who desire freedom and equality to break at last those letters that seem now so unbreakable.

1. *Critics of Crane, for instance, consider that his homosexuality is the cause of his inability to adjust to society. Another school feels that inability to adjust to society causes homosexuality. What seems fairly obvious is that what society frustrated in Crane was his effort to write poetry and to write what he wanted to in the way he wanted to. He might well have adjusted his homosexual desires within society as many have done by "living a lie." It was his desire for truth that society condemned.*

2. *Just as certain judges assume and are more inclined to pardon murder in inverts and treason in Jews for reasons derived from original sin and racial predestination." Sodome et Gomorrhe, Proust.*

3. *My private I in no sense mean personal.*

homosexual play

ALFRED C. KINSEY, WARDELL B. POMEROY, CLYDE E. MARTIN

1948

homosexual Play. On the whole, the homosexual child play is found in more histories, occurs more frequently, and becomes more specific than the pre-adolescent heterosexual play. This depends, as so much of the adult homosexual activity depends, on the greater accessibility of the boy's own sex. In the younger boy, it is also fostered by his socially encouraged disdain for girls' ways, by his admiration for masculine prowess, and by his desire to emulate older boys. The anatomy and functional capacities of male genitalia interest the younger boy to a degree that is not appreciated by older males who have become heterosexually conditioned and who are continuously on the defensive against reactions which might be interpreted as homosexual.

About half of the older males (48%), and nearer two-thirds (60%) of the boys who were pre-adolescent at the time they contributed their histories, recall homosexual activity in their pre-adolescent years. The mean age of the first homosexual contact is about nine years, two and a half months (9.21 years).

The order of appearance of the several homosexual techniques is: exhibition of genitalia, manual manipulation of genitalia, anal or oral contacts with genitalia, and urethral insertions. Exhibition is much the most common form of homosexual play (in 99.8 per cent of all the histories which have any activity). It appears in the sex play of the youngest children, where much of it is incidental, definitely casual, and quite fruitless as far as erotic arousal is concerned. The most extreme development of exhibitionism occurs among the older pre-adolescents and the younger adolescent males who have discovered the significance of self masturbation and may have acquired proficiency in effecting orgasm. By that time there is a social value in establishing one's ability, and many a boy exhibits his masturbatory techniques to lone companions or to whole groups of boys. In the latter case, there may be simultaneous exhibition as a group activity. The boy's emotional reaction in such a performance is undoubtedly enhanced by the presence of the other boys. There are teenage boys who continue this exhibitionistic activity throughout their high school years, some of them even entering into compacts with their closest friends to refrain from self masturbation except when in the presence of each other. In confining such social performances to self masturbation, these boys avoid conflicts over the homosexual. By this time, however, the psychic reactions may be homosexual enough, although it may be difficult to persuade these individuals to admit it.

Exhibitionism leads naturally into the next step in the homosexual play, namely the mutual manipulation of genitalia. Such manipulation occurs in the play of two-thirds (67.4%) of all the pre-adolescent males who have any homosexual activity. Among younger pre-adolescents the manual contacts are still very incidental and casual and without any recognition of the emotional possibilities of such experience. Only a small portion of the cases leads to the sort of manipulation which does effect arousal and possibly orgasm in the partner. Manual manipulation is more likely to become so specific if the relation is had with a somewhat older boy, or with an adult. Without help from more experienced persons, many pre-adolescents take a good many years to discover masturbatory techniques that are sexually effective.

Anal intercourse is reported by 17 per cent of the pre-adolescents who have any homosexual play. Anal intercourse among younger boys usually fails of penetration and is therefore primarily femoral. Oral manipulation is reported by nearly 16 per cent of the boys (Table 27). Among younger boys, erotic arousal is less easily effected by oral contacts, more easily effected by manual manipulation. The anal and oral techniques are limited as they are because even at these younger ages there is some knowledge of the social taboos on these activities; and it is, in consequence, probable that the reported data are considerable understatements of the activities which actually occur.

Pre-adolescent homosexual play is carried over into adolescent or adult activity in something less than half of all the cases. There are differences between social levels. In lower educational levels, the chances are 50–50 that the pre-adolescent homosexual play will be continued into adolescence or later. For the group that will go to college, the chances are better than four to one that the pre-adolescent activity will not be followed by later homosexual experience. In many cases, the later homosexuality stops with the adolescent years, but many of the adults who are actively and more or less exclusively homosexual date their activities from pre-adolescence.

preservation of innocence *from*

JAMES BALDWIN
1949

the problem of the homosexual, so vociferously involved with good
and evil, the unnatural as opposed to the natural, has its roots in the
nature of man and woman and their relationship to one another.
While at one time we speak of nature and at another of the nature of
man, we speak on both occasions of something of which we know
very little, and we make the tacit admission that they are not one and
the same. Between nature and man there is a difference; there is,
indeed, perpetual war. It develops when we think about it, that not
only is a natural state perversely indefinable outside of the womb or
before the grave, but that it is *not* on the whole a state which is altogether desirable. It is just as well that we cook our food and are not
baffled by water-closets and do not copulate in the public thorough-
fare. People who have not learned this are not admired as natural but
are feared as primitive or incarcerated as insane.

We spend vast amounts of our time and emotional energy in learning how not to be natural and in eluding the trap of our own nature
and it therefore becomes very difficult to know exactly what is meant
when we speak of the unnatural. It is not possible to have it both
ways, to use nature at one time as the final arbiter of human conduct
and at another to oppose her as angrily as we do. As we are being
inaccurate, perhaps desperately defensive and making, inversely, a
most damaging admission when we describe as inhuman, some rep-
rehensible act committed by a human being, so we become hope-
lessly involved in paradox when we describe as unnatural something
which is found in nature. A cat torturing a mouse to death is not
described as inhuman for we assume that it is being perfectly natural;
nor a table condemned as being unnatural for we know that it has

nothing to do with nature. What we really seem to be saying when we speak of the inhuman is that we cannot bear to be confronted with that fathomless baseness shared by all humanity and when we speak of the unnatural that we cannot imagine what vexations nature will dream up next.

We have, in short, whenever nature is invoked to support our human divisions, every right to be suspicious, nature having betrayed only the most perplexing and untrustworthy interest in man and none whatever in his institutions. We resent this indifference and we are frightened by it; we resist it; we ceaselessly assert the miracle of our existence against this implacable power. Yet we know nothing of birth or death except that we remain powerless when faced by either. Much as we resent or threaten or cajole nature, she refuses absolutely to relent; she may at any moment throw down the trump card she never fails to have hidden and leave us bankrupt. In time, her ally and her rather too explicit witness, suns rise and set and the face of the earth changes; at length the limbs stiffen and the light goes out of her eyes.

And nothing 'gainst time's scythe may make defense
Save breed to brave him when he takes thee hence.

We arrive at the oldest, the most insistent and the most vehement charge faced by the homosexual: he is unnatural because he has turned from his life-giving function to a union which is sterile. This may, in itself, be considered a heavy, even an unforgivable, crime, but since it is not so considered when involving other people, the unmarried or the poverty-stricken or the feeble, and since his existence did not always invoke that hysteria with which he now contends, we are safe in suggesting that his present untouchability owes its motive power to several other sources. Let me suggest that his present debasement and our obsession with him corresponds to the debasement of the relationship between the sexes; and that his ambiguous and terrible position in our society reflects the ambiguities and terrors which time has deposited on that relationship as the sea piles seaweed and wreckage along the shore.

For, after all, I take it that no one can be seriously disturbed about the birth-rate; when the race commits suicide, it will not be in Sodom. Nor can we continue to shout unnatural whenever we are confronted by a phenomenon as old as mankind, a phenomenon, moreover, which nature has maliciously repeated in all of her domain. If we are going to be natural then this is a part of nature; if we refuse to accept this, then we have rejected nature and must find other criterion.

Instantly the Deity springs to mind, in much the same manner, I suspect, that He sprang into being on the cold, black day when we discovered that nature cared nothing for us. His advent, which alone had the power to save us from nature and ourselves, also created a self-awareness and, therefore, tensions and terrors and responsibilities with which we had not coped before. It marked the death of innocence; it set up the duality of good-and-evil; and now Sin and Redemption, those mighty bells, began that crying which will not cease until, by another act of creation, we transcend our old morality. Before we were banished from Eden and the curse was uttered. "I will put enmity between thee and the woman," the homosexual did not exist; nor, properly speaking, did the heterosexual. We were all in a state of nature.

We are forced to consider this tension between God and nature and are thus confronted with the nature of God because He is man's most intense creation and it is not in the sight of nature that the homosexual is condemned, but in the sight of God. This argues a profound and dangerous failure of concept, since an incalculable number of the world's humans are thereby condemned to something less than life; and we may not, of course, do this without limiting ourselves. Life, it is true, is a process of decisions and alternatives, the conscious awareness and acceptance of limitations. Experience, nevertheless, to say nothing of history, seems clearly to indicate that it is not possible to banish or to falsify any human need without ourselves undergoing falsification and loss. And what of murder? A human characteristic surely. Must we embrace the murderer? But the question must be put another way: is it possible not to embrace him? For he is in us and of us. We may not be free until we understand him.

The nature of man and woman and their relationship to one another fills seas of contecture and an immense proportion of the myth, legend, and literature of the world is devoted to this subject. It has caused, we gather, on the evidence presented by any library, no little discomfort. It is observable that the more we imagine we have discovered, the less we know and that, moreover, the necessity to discover and the effort and self-consciousness involved in this necessity makes their relationship more and more complex.

Men and women seem to function as imperfect and sometimes unwilling mirrors for one another; a falsification or distortion of the nature of the one is immediately reflected in the nature of the other. A division between them can only betray a division within the soul of each. Matters are not helped if we thereupon decide that men must recapture their status as then and that women must embrace their function as women; not only does the resulting frigidity of attitude put to death any possible communion, but, having once listed the bald physical facts, no one is prepared to go further and decide, of our multiple human attributes, which are masculine and which are feminine. Directly we say that women have finer and more delicate sensibilities we are reminded that she is insistently, mythically, and even historically treacherous. If we are so rash as to say that men have greater endurance, we are reminded of the procession of men who have long gone to their long home while women walked about the streets—mourning, we are told, but no doubt, gossiping and shopping at the same time.

We can pick up no novel, no drama, no poem; we may examine no fable nor any myth without stumbling on this merciless paradox in the nature of the sexes. This is a paradox which experience alone is able to illuminate and this experience is not communicable in any language that we know. The recognition of this complexity is the signal of maturity; it marks the death of the child and the birth of the man.

the society we envisage

DONALD WEBSTER CORY
1951

what does the homosexual want? He cries out against the injustice of society, yet offers no alternative. He finds the discrimination and the calumnies a manifestation of the grossest intolerance, but he fails to offer the world at large a pattern for a better social organization in which he could be integrated.

This is not at all surprising, for the development of such a plan would, by its very nature, imply freedom of discussion. It is only from the exchange of opinion in a free press and by all other methods of communication that a subject of this type, wrought with so many unknowns and paradoxes, can reach adequate solution.

What does the homosexual want? The question cannot be answered because each person can speak only for himself, and his reply will be prejudiced by his religious and ethical background, by his philosophy of life, and by the degree of happiness he has been able to achieve. The actress whose predilections are almost public knowledge and are no impediment to her stardom and public acceptance is hardly likely to feel the same need for social reorganization as the lonely, the wretched, and the frustrated. A deeply religious Roman Catholic invert who professes that there is no justification for any sexual pleasure outside of the sacrament of marriage can hardly share aspirations for social change with two men who are living together in a happy physical and spiritual union.

The homosexual society, such as it is and to the extent that it exists at all, reflects differences of opinion on the social solution of this question just as does any other group of people on any problem confronting them. There is no single, quasi-official, universally accepted version of the social organization envisaged by homosexuals, any more than there could be a single opinion of college professors on loyalty oaths, of university students on the accomplishments of education, of physicians on socialized medicine.

But the homosexual viewpoint is less well-developed than that of other groups on other questions because of the virtual impossibility of having an exchange of opinion through the usual channels of thought expression. First, the facts themselves on which an opinion must be based are difficult to obtain and, once found, are difficult to communicate to others. There are very few reliable statistics, and even the words of experts are usually based on the most atypical homosexuals, namely those who fall into the hands of the law or who are seeking help from a psychiatrist.

Even were the facts more readily available, an expression of opinion requires a free and open debate, and American society is hardly more advanced in this respect that the totalitarian lands. There is, of course, no interference with the effort to discuss the subject by word of mouth, provided the discussion remains within the homosexual group. It is almost impossible to have, except in a few and rare circles, a full interchange of opinion between people of all sexual temperaments in which each viewpoint is defended ably and each argument refuted honestly.

Homosexuals have had little opportunity for the development of a well-defined outlook. Within the homosexual group, there is little uniformity of opinion, and perhaps even less so than would be found in another minority group. One person can therefore do little more than express his personal viewpoint, reflecting only what he himself envisions for the homosexual group in the supposedly Utopian situation, but in this reflection there are distilled the arguments, viewpoints, contradictions, and philosophies of many others with whom discussions have been held over a period of many years.

There is probably only one thing on which homosexuals would in general agree with regard to the attitude of society, and that is that the present situation is unjust and that change is necessary. The injustice is not so much before the bar, nor in the effort to obtain employment, but is found above all in the general social attitude of the heterosexual society. No one can prevent an individual from expressing hostility toward another, provided he stays within the law and neither libels nor physically harms his enemy, but when this hostile attitude is officially sponsored by all possible means among the entire population, it is no longer the private affair of a single person.

The homosexual, first and foremost, wants recognition of the fact that he is doing no one any harm. He wants to live and let live, to punish and be punished when there are transgressions, and to go about the ordinary and everyday pursuits of life, unhindered either by law or by an unwritten hostility which is even more effectual than the written law.

This is a far-reaching program, requiring the modification of attitudes over a period of generations, and it is only natural that it must fall upon those most concerned with this problem—the inverts—to take the initiative in remolding public opinion.

However, the invert is not alone in feeling that the present situation is unsatisfactory. The dominant group in our society tacitly understands and is ready to concede that it has no proposal for bettering a situation which is obviously unjust. It would like—in a manner similar to the attitude of many white persons on the color question—to "wish" the problem out of existence. It dreams of a world in which the problem does not exist, hopes that the problem will not touch the lives of individuals personally related to oneself, and just does not think, talk, or write about it. But its dreams are in vain.

The dominant society cannot offer a cure for homosexuality. It urges in a weak, ineffectual, and ignorant manner that willpower be exerted, but willpower solves nothing. It talks of suppression and sublimation, while its own scientists scoff at such a proposal. It damns in the harshest of terms in the hope that damnation will be a deterrent, but again there is failure. It passes laws that make felons of homosexuals, but ignores its own laws and admits that it cannot put homosexuals behind bars. It concedes that homosexuals must earn a living, and banishes them from employment. And, as society always does when it is in a blind alley, tied by tradition and folkways to a system which is unreasonable and which does not answer the needs of the people, it uses silence as the answer. It hides its head in the sand, pretends that the problem does not exist, and forbids discussion, save in professional circles.

But the problem does exist, and it will be discussed. Furthermore, is not a problem created by the homosexuals. A sociologist writing on racial minorities—and again the parallel is inescapable—has stated that there are no minority problems. There are only majority problems. There is no Negro problem except that created by whites; no Jewish problem except that created by Gentiles. To which I add: and no homosexual problem except that created by the heterosexual society.

There would be no economic dilemma for the invert were he not excluded from practically all jobs unless he hides his identity. There would be no blackmail problem for the homosexual except that he cannot live happily after exposure, because the world which has learned of his temperament will inflict severe sanctions. There would be no ethical problem of being a lawbreaker except that the laws have been codified in such manner that he cannot be a homosexual without at least aspiring to break them. And thus the problems of the homosexual could be enumerated, and it could be seen that they are majority problems—not minority ones!

Even the psychological aspects of the homosexual's dilemma primarily involve adjustment to a hostile world. There would be no need for the invert to feel guilty, to suffer remorse, to be forced to suppress hatred toward his love-object, if society did not condemn so bitterly. He would not be faced with the paradoxical problem of attempting on the one hand to be proud of himself and on the other to deny his temperament, if it were not so difficult to live in a world that demanded such denial.

It is a majority problem, but only the minority is interested in solving it. The fundamental dilemma is that it must rest primarily upon the homosexuals, being the most interested party, to take the initiative in bringing about change, but until such change is effected, anyone taking such initiative is open to pillory and contumelious scorn.

The homosexual is thus locked in his present position. If he does not rise up and demand his rights, he will never get them, but until he gets those rights, he cannot be expected to expose himself to the martyrdom that would come if he should rise up and demand them. It is a vicious circle, and what the homosexual is seeking, first and foremost, is an answer to this dilemma.

It is an answer that I contend can be found and one which happens, by the most fortunate of coincidences, to be identical with the needs of society at large and with the historic task of the democratic forces of our generation. The answer is to be found in the liberalization of our newspapers, radio, and theater, so that homosexuality can be discussed as freely as any other subject and within the confines that circumscribe any other type of discussion. Already a beginning has been made in the very large interest shown in the subject by novelists, and in the occasional portrayal of homosexuality on the stage. A few popular magazines in the United States have at least mentioned it. In the larger cities serious articles have appeared even in the newspapers, and in one case an entire series of articles, written in a penetrating and not unsympathetic manner and without any evasion of terms, appeared in a New York newspaper.

This discussion may prove to be an opening wedge. There will be more articles, books, and further utilization of other means of thought communication, and out of this will come the interchange of opinion, the conflict and the controversy, which alone can establish truth.

And all of this is good for society, good particularly in this era, when no greater threat to the democratic way of life and to everything that has evolved in modern civilization, both Western and Eastern, appears than the suppression of all differences of opinion, the repression of all controversy. At this moment in history, when the forces of totalitarianism seek to extend the conspiracy of silence and the distortions of truth to all phases of life—to science and politics and human relations—the homosexuals (including even those few who are mistakenly in the camp of the totalitarians) are seeking to extend freedom of the individual, of speech, press, and thought to an entirely new realm. While others wish to narrow the confines of allowable differences of opinion and permissible discussion, the homosexual seeks to broaden them. This is not because he is a greater lover of liberty, but because he is fortunately placed in that historic position where his liberties have been denied and he seeks to regain them.

Thus, as the first answer to the society we homosexuals envisage, we seek freedom of thought and expression on this question. This involves not only the right to publish books and magazines without interference from the police, but the right to employ the main channels of communication, the leading newspapers, magazines, and the air for the expression of a viewpoint in the spirit and traditions of American freedoms. It may be the right of one editor or publisher to express his own viewpoint, as he does on things political, and to exclude the opposition from his press, but when his outlook coincides with that of all of the major editors, and when those who differ fear to open their pages because of reprisals by church, government, or advertisers, then there is a totalitarian control of the press by a particular group and hence a denial of freedom to the other. This is indubitably the situation so far as the rights of homosexuals are concerned today.

If the day of free and open discussion arrives, and if, during the course of such discussion, the struggle for it, and as a consequence of it, the social stigma attached to being a homosexual begins to be lifted, there will automatically come about a happier milieu in which the individual can live, love, thrive, and work. Part of that happier relationship will be found in the dropping of the disguise.

Many homosexuals consider that their greatest fortune, their one saving grace, has been the invisibility of the cross which they have had to bear. The ease with which they were able to hide their temperaments from the closest friends and business associates, from their parents, wives, and children, made it possible to partake of the full benefits and material and spiritual advantages life offers to the heterosexual. Many such people—and I include myself—have constantly striven to perfect their technique of concealment.

Actually, the inherent tragedy—not the saving grace—of homosexuality is found in the ease of concealment. If the homosexual were as readily recognizable as are members of certain other minority groups, the social condemnation could not possibly exist. Stereotype thinking on the part of the majority would, in the first instance, collapse of its own absurdity if all of us who are gay were known for what we are. Secondly, our achievements in society and our contributions to all phases of culture and social advancement would become well-known, and not merely the arsenal of argument in the knowledge of a few. The laws against homosexuality could not be sustained if it were flagrantly apparent that millions of human beings in all walks of life were affected. Blackmail, naturally enough, would be non-existent as a problem facing the invert.

It is a chimera, but worthy of speculation. If only all of the inverts, the millions in all lands, could simultaneously rise up in our full strength! For the fact is that we homosexuals are defeated by the self-perpetuation of the folkways which inflict severe punishment on those who protest against these folkways. Again, the circle is vicious.

We need freedom of expression to achieve freedom of inversion, but only the free invert is in a position to demand and to further freedom of expression. And what are we to do in the meantime?

A few individuals, well-placed because of their position in society, their economic freedom, their universally acknowledged attainments, can speak up and further their cause. Others can, with discretion, spread enlightenment to a few intimate and trustworthy friends. And still others can utilize their knowledge or talents by disseminating truthful information and by bringing the subject before the public, but behind the veil of pseudonymity.

But once there is freedom of expression and once the invert is fully accepted and is an object neither of calumny nor sneer, an object neither to scorn nor to pity, how will he fit into our social and family life? Is it proposed that society recognize and sanction marriages in which both "bride" and "groom" are of the same sex and in which the two parties to such a union have the same rights and obligations as in any other marriage?

Most of the problems concomitant with being homosexual would be automatically solved if there were no discriminatory attitudes on the part of society. Many homosexuals would marry and have children, attracted by the family life which such a prospect offers, but there would be no shame of the homosexuality, no concealment from wife or from offspring. Others would form unions with males, as they do today, but without social ostracism; they would bring their friends to social functions and might adopt an orphan child or a nephew of an overcrowded and overburdened family. Others would live the lives of bachelors, perhaps have many loves or few, and as the years pass would probably show less interest in the pursuit of the sexual object than in cultural activities.

In all such matters the homosexual's life would parallel that of the heterosexual. Some people require a mate; others do not. Some pursue sex relentlessly; others organize a life in which the physical gratification of their impulses plays a rather minor rôle.

What the homosexual wants is freedom—not only freedom of expression, but also sexual freedom. By sexual freedom is meant the right of any person to gratify his urges when and how he sees fit, without fear of social consequences, so long as he does not use the force of either violence, threat, or superior age; so long as he does not inflict bodily harm or disease upon another person; so long as the other person is of sound mind and agrees to the activity. This means that both on the statute books and in the realm of public opinion all sexual activity is accepted as equally correct, right, and proper so long as it is entered into voluntarily by the parties involved; they are perfectly sane and above a reasonable age of consent, free of communicable disease, and no duress or misrepresentation is employed.

This is, for our society, a radical proposal. It has been expounded in the remarkable works of Guyon,[1] among others, and its full exposition would be beyond the realm of this book. But it is radical only to expound and defend this theory, for sexual freedom is actually being

[1] René Guyon, *The Ethics of Sexual Acts* (New York: Alfred A. Knopf, 1934 and 1948) and *Sexual Freedom* (New York: Alfred A. Knopf, 1950).

practiced on a very wide scale in modern life, despite its being condemned by school, church, newspapers, and government. Adultery,
fellatio between husband and wife, homosexuality, premarital fornication—all are so common that it is rare to find the individual who has
not indulged in one or several of these forms of sexual activity quite frequently.

However, on the law books these are punishable acts, and in the
realm of public opinion even more so. The result is that modern civilization adopts a hypocritical attitude and attempts to force an
extreme feeling of shame upon the individuals who live what to them
is a normal and natural life.

The homosexual often feels that the source of his difficulty lies in
the fact that he is born into a hostile world, and this hostility is inherent, he believes, in that he lives in a heterosexual society. He is, in
my opinion, entirely wrong in this concept. The root of the homosexual difficulty is that he lives, not in a heterosexual world, but in an
anti-sexual world.

The anti-sexual nature of modern civilization is apparent wherever
one turns. In the description of the virgin birth, the term "immaculate
conception" is used, and thus an inference is made that all concep-
tions that take place by means of sexual intercourse are not immaculate and are therefore unclean. Any humor pertaining to sex is called
a "dirty joke." It is "lewd" to fail to conceal the sexual organs, and the
strongest epithets in the English language—and in many other languages—are synonymous with having sexual intercourse. Even the
more progressive educators teach the children about birds and flowers
and something about the physiology of sex, but skirt the fact that the
higher animals, and particularly man, indulge in sex for the pure joy
of the thing. In modern anti-sexual society, the heterosexual is tolerated only because he is necessary for the propagation of the species,
but the virgin and the chaste are glorified as pristine purity. If we
homosexuals lived in a predominantly heterosexual and not an anti-
sexual society—as witness the American Indians and the South Sea
Islanders—we would not be in constant conflict with our fellowmen
nor with ourselves.

Some will object that there is a basic contradiction. Have I not,
throughout this book, decried the attitudes of the heterosexual society, of
the heterosexual-dominated society? Is the reader now to be informed
that that heterosexual society is non-existent? The fact is that it is only
apparently a heterosexual society. The anti-sexual culture pretends that it
is heterosexual, in order the better to suppress all sex for pleasure!

The heterosexual's conflicts in our society are also deep; sexual maladjustment is by no means the sole property of the homosexual in modern life. But the lesser stigma attached to adultery and premarital relationships, the ease of concealment of fellatio when it takes place with the opposite sex, and, finally, society's acceptance (albeit reluctantly) of sex in the conjugal relationships—these facts place the heterosexual in a preferred position in the anti-sexual setup.

The homosexual then, to summarize, desires freedom of expression, aspires to recognition of his temperament without discriminatory attitudes or punishment, and will find all of this possible only when he is able to proclaim his true nature. Such a program will be possible only in a culture that proclaims sexual freedom—the right of adults to enter into any voluntary sexual arrangement with each other without fear of reprisal by society. At the same time the embracing of such a guiding policy of sexual freedom will hasten the liberation of the homosexual from concealment and from silence.

The homosexual, thus, has two historic missions to perform. Whether he is a democrat or a totalitarian by political conviction, he is historically forced to enter the struggle for the widening of freedom of expression. And, whether his religious and ethical convictions are those of the continent or the libertarian, he is historically compelled to enlist in the legions fighting for liberalization of the sexual mores of modern civilization.

It is interesting and heartening to note that in the two greatest totalitarian regimes of our century veritable reigns of terror against homosexuality were instituted, despite the collaboration of certain homosexuals in the establishment of these regimes. The purge of Roehm by Hitler can be understood only in this light—that no free, deviating, unassimilable viewpoint was tolerable in Nazi Germany, no matter how obsequious it might be to the Hitler regime.

After the Russian Revolution, the laws against homosexuality were repealed. These Tsarist laws were denounced as the remnants of the bourgeois concept of sex, and a new era of sexual freedom was foreseen. In the years that followed, as the totalitarian stranglehold on all channels of thought expression was strengthened, the old bourgeois and Tsarist laws were restored. Abortion was illegalized, divorce made increasingly difficult to obtain, and the law restoring homosexuality to a crime, placing it in the same category as other social crimes, was signed by Kalinin in March, 1934. This is a significant date, for it was the period of the heightened struggle against the Old Bolsheviks, the last great effort of the Stalin regime to bring about a complete system of thought and action control. "The mass arrests of homosexuals," writes Wilhelm Reich, "led to a panic . . . It is said that there were numerous suicides in the army."[2] Since that time, there have been several reports that homosexuals have been involved in anti-Stalinist conspiracies.

Today, Russia is much more backward than the rest of Europe and America in its attitudes toward the sexual non-conformist, just as it is in the attitude toward all non-conformists. There is no room except for orthodoxy, and that includes things sexual as much as things political. In the socialist state the homosexual lives in dread. Even the few channels open to him in the United States are closed in Russia. With medieval severity he can be seized and pilloried.

How can one account for Russian and Nazi cruelty on this question? Only in this way—that in a totalitarian state, there was no room for a group of people who, by their very sexual temperaments, could never be assimilated, must always remain apart with their own ways of life, their own outlooks, their own philosophies.

And it is this inherent lack of assimilability that is the greatest historic value of homosexuality. Any minority which does not commit anti-social acts, which is not destructive of the life, property, or culture of the majority or of other minority groups, is a pillar of democratic strength. So long as there are such minorities in our culture, whether of a sexual or religious or ethnic character, there will be many broths in the melting pot, many and variegated waves in the seas. No force will be able to weave these groups into a single totalitarian unity which is the unanimity of the graveyard.

Thus on three scores, homosexuality—fortunately but unwittingly—must inevitably play a progressive rôle in the scheme of things. It will broaden the base for freedom of thought and communication, will be a banner-bearer in the struggle for liberalization of our sexual conventions, and will be a pillar of strength in the defense of our threatened democracy.

[2] Wilhelm Reich, *The Sexual Revolution*. (New York: Orgone Institute Press. 1945), p. 209.

advertisement for "the homosexual villain"

NORMAN MAILER
1954

some time back in the early fifties, a group of young men in Los Angeles started a homosexual magazine called One. To attract attention they sent free copies of the magazine and a personal letter out to a horde of big and little celebrities including Bishop Fulton Sheen, Eleanor Roosevelt, Tennessee Williams, Arthur Miller, and fifty-eight others including myself. It was an arresting idea. The top of the letterhead flared the legend: One—the Homosexual Magazine, and like a pile of chips on the left margin, we worthies had our names banked, as if we were sponsors. "Dear Norman Mailer" went my letter. "On the left you will see your name listed. You are one of those prominent Americans whom we are seeking to interest in our magazine, so that you might help us to dispel public ignorance and hostility on the subject." And the letter went on to invite us to contribute to the magazine. (I quote it from memory.) About a month later, this letter was followed by a phone call—the New York secretary of the organization called me up to say that he didn't know just what I had to do with all this, but out on the West Coast they had asked him to get in touch with me because I might be able to write for them.

I didn't know the first thing about homosexuality I hurried to tell him.

Well, the secretary assured me (he had a high-pitched folksy voice) he could understand how I felt about the whole matter, but he could assure Mr. Mailer it was really a very simple matter, Mr. Mailer could say what he wished to say under a pseudonym.

"I told you," I said, "I don't know anything about the subject. I hardly even know any homosexuals."

"Well, Lordy-me," said the secretary, "I could introduce you to a

good many of us, Mr. Mailer, and you would see what interesting problems we have."

"No . . . now look."

"Mr. Mailer, wouldn't you at least say that you're sympathetic to
the aims of the magazine?"

"Well, I suppose the police laws against homosexuals are bad, and
all that. I guess homosexuality is a private matter."

"Would you say that for us?"

"It's not a new idea."

"Mr. Mailer, I can understand that a man with your name and reputation wouldn't want to get mixed up with such dangerous ideas."

He was right. I was ready to put my name to any radical statement,
my pride was that I would say in print anything I believed, and yet I
was not ready to say a word in public defense of homosexuals.

So I growled at the New York secretary of One magazine, "If I were
to write something about homosexuality, I would sign my name to it."

"You would, Mr. Mailer? Listen, I must tell you, by the most conservative statistics, we estimate there are ten million homosexuals in this
country. We intend to get a lobby and in a few years we expect to be
able to elect our own Congressman. If you write an article for us, Mr.
Mailer, why then you might become our first Congressman!"

I cannot remember the secretary's name, but he had a small knife-
like talent—he knew the way to me: mate the absurd with the apoca-
lyptic, and I was a captive. So before our conversation was over, I had
promised to write an article for One magazine.

It is printed here. I delayed for months getting down to it, my mood
would be depressed whenever I remembered my promise, I writhed at
what the gossip would be—for every reader who saw my piece there
would be ten or a hundred who would hear that Mailer was writing for
a faggot magazine. It would be taken for granted I was homosexual—
how disagreeable! I used to wish that One magazine would fail, and
be gone forever.

Then the New York secretary had a fight with the West Coast. He
wrote me a letter in which he advised me not to write the piece after all.
Since he was my connection to the magazine, I was set free from my
promise. Yet I took the step of writing to the editors to ask them if they
still wanted an article from me. Not surprisingly, they did. I got their
answer in Mexico, and in a flat dutiful mood I sat down and wrote
"The Homosexual Villain." It is beyond a doubt the worst article I
have ever written, conventional, empty, pious, the quintessence of the
Square. Its intellectual level would place it properly in the pages of the

Reader's Digest, *and if the* Reader's Digest *had a desire to be useful at its doubtfully useful level it would have scored a Square coup by reprinting it, for the article has a satisfactory dullness of thought which comes from writing in a state of dull anxiety.*

Now, it is easier to understand why I did this piece. The Deer Park *was then in galleys at Rinehart, and I was depressed about it. Apart from its subject, I thought it a timid, inhibited book. I must have known that my fear of homosexuality as a subject was stifling my creative reflexes, and given the brutal rhythms of my nature, I could kill this inhibition only by jumping into the middle of the problem without any clothes. Done gracefully this can stop the show, but I was clumsy and constipated and sick with the bravery of my will, and so "The Homosexual Villain," while honorable as a piece of work, is dressed in the gray of lugubrious caution.*

Yet it was important for my particular growth. The gray prose in "The Homosexual Villain" was the end of easy radical rhetoric—I knew I had nothing interesting to say about homosexuality because the rational concepts of socialism, nicely adequate to writing about the work of David Riesman, were not related to the ills of the homosexual. No, for that one had to dig—deep into the complex and often foul pots of thought where sex and society live in their murderous dialectic. Writing "The Homosexual Villain" showed me how barren I was of new ideas, and so helped to blow up a log jam of accumulated timidities and restraints, of caution for my good name. Later when I was back in New York, my mind running wild in the first fevers of self-analysis, I came to spend some months and some years with the endless twists of habit and defeat which are latent homosexuality for so many of us, and I came to understand myself, and become maybe a little more of a man, although it's too soon to brag on it, for being a man is the continuing battle of one's life, and one loses a bit of manhood with every stale compromise to the authority of any power in which one does not believe. Which is a part of the explanation for the tenacity of organized faith, patriotism and respect for society. But that is another essay, and here is "The Homosexual Villain."

the homosexual villain

those readers of *One* who are familiar with my work may be somewhat surprised to find me writing for this magazine. After all, I have been as guilty as any contemporary novelist in attributing unpleasant, ridiculous, or sinister connotations to the homosexual (or more accurately, bisexual) characters in my novels. Part of the effectiveness of General Cummings in *The Naked and The Dead*—at least for those people who thought him well-conceived as a character—rested on the homosexuality I was obviously suggesting as the core of much of his motivation. Again, in *Barbary Shore*, the "villain" was a secret police agent named Leroy Hollingsworth whose sadism and slyness were essentially combined with his sexual deviation.

At the time I wrote those novels, I was consciously sincere. I did believe—as so many heterosexuals believe—that there was an intrinsic relation between homosexuality and "evil," and it seemed perfectly natural to me, as well as *symbolically* just, to treat the subject in such a way.

The irony is that I did not know a single homosexual during all those years. I had met homosexuals of course, I had recognized a few as homosexual, I had "suspected" others, I was to realize years later that one or two close friends were homosexual, but I had never known one in the human sense of knowing, which is to look at your friend's feelings through his eyes and not your own. I did not *know* any homosexual because obviously I did not want to. It was enough for me to recognize someone as homosexual, and I would cease to consider him seriously as a person. He might be intelligent or courageous or kind or witty or virtuous or tortured—no matter. I always saw him as at best ludicrous and at worst—the word again—sinister.

(I think it is by the way significant that just as many homosexuals feel forced and are forced to throw up protective camouflage, even boasting if necessary of women they have had, not to mention the thousand smaller subtleties, so heterosexuals are often eager to be so deceived for it enables them to continue friendships which otherwise their prejudices and occasionally their fears might force them to terminate.)

Now, of course, I exaggerate to a certain degree. I was never a roaring bigot, I did not go in for homosexual-baiting, at least not face to face, and I never could stomach the relish with which soldiers would describe how they had stomped some faggot in a bar. I had, in short, the equivalent of a "gentleman's anti-Semitism."

The only thing remarkable about all this is that I was hardly living in a small town. New York, whatever its pleasures and discontents, is not the most uncivilized milieu, and while one would go too far to say that its attitude toward homosexuals bears correspondence to the pain of the liberal or radical at hearing someone utter a word like "nigger" or "kike," there is nonetheless considerable tolerance and considerable propinquity. The hard and fast separations of homosexual and heterosexual society are often quite blurred. Over the past seven or eight years I had had more than enough opportunity to learn something about homosexuals if I had wanted to, and obviously I did not.

It is a pity I do not understand the psychological roots of my change of attitude, for something valuable might be learned from it. Unfortunately, I do not. The process has seemed a rational one to me, rational in that the impetus apparently came from reading and not from any important personal experiences. The only hint of my bias mellowing was that my wife and I had gradually become friendly with a homosexual painter who lived next door. He was pleasant, he was thoughtful, he was a good neighbor, and we came to depend on him in various small ways. It was tacitly understood that he was homosexual, but we never talked about it. However, since so much of his personal life was not discussable between us, the friendship was limited. I accepted him the way a small-town banker fifty years ago might have accepted a "good" Jew.

About this time I received a free copy of *One* which was sent out by the editors to a great many writers. I remember looking at the magazine with some interest and some amusement. Parts of it impressed me unfavorably. I thought the quality of writing generally poor (most people I've talked to agree that it has since improved), and I questioned the wisdom of accepting suggestive ads in a purportedly serious magazine. (Indeed, I still feel this way no matter what the problems of revenue might be.) But there was a certain militancy and honesty to the editorial tone, and while I was not sympathetic, I think I can say that for the first time in my life I was not unsympathetic. Most important of all, my curiosity was piqued. A few weeks later I asked my painter friend if I could borrow his copy of Donald Webster Cory's *The Homosexual in America.*

Reading it was an important experience. Mr. Cory strikes me as being a modest man, and I think he would be the first to admit that while his book is very good, closely reasoned, quietly argued, it is hardly a great book. Nonetheless, I can think of few books which cut so radically at my prejudices and altered my ideas so profoundly. I resisted it, I argued its points as I read, I was often annoyed, but what I could not overcome was my growing depression that I had been acting as a bigot in this matter, and "bigot" was one word I did not enjoy applying to myself. With that came the realization I had been closing myself off from understanding a very large part of life. This thought is always disturbing to a writer. A writer has his talent, and for all one knows, he is born with it, but whether his talent develops is to some degree responsive to his use of it. He can grow as a person or he can shrink, and by this I don't intend any facile parallels between moral and artistic growth. The writer can become a bigger hoodlum if need be, but his alertness, his curiosity, his reaction to life must not diminish. The fatal thing is to shrink, to be interested in less, sympathetic to less, desiccating to the point where life itself loses its flavor, and one's passion for human understanding changes to weariness and distaste.

So, as I read Mr. Cory's book, I found myself thinking in effect, *My God, homosexuals are people, too.* Undoubtedly, this will seem incredibly naïve to the homosexual readers of *One* who have been all too painfully aware that they are indeed people, but prejudice is wed to naïveté, and even the sloughing of prejudice, particularly when it is abrupt, partakes of the naïve. I have not tried to conceal that note. As I reread this article I find its tone ingenuous, but there is no point in trying to alter it. One does not become sophisticated overnight about a subject one has closed from oneself.

At any rate I began to face up to my homosexual bias. I had been a libertarian socialist for some years, and implicit in all my beliefs had been the idea that society must allow every individual his own road to discovering himself. Libertarian socialism (the first word is as important as the second) implies inevitably that one have respect for the varieties of human experience. Very basic to everything I had thought was that sexual relations, above everything else, demand their liberty, even if such liberty should amount to no more than compulsion or necessity. For, in the reverse, history has certainly offered enough examples of the link between sexual repression and political repression. (A fascinating thesis on this subject is *The Sexual Revolution* by Wilhelm Reich.) I suppose I can say that for the first time I understood homosexual persecution to be a political act and a reactionary act, and I was properly ashamed of myself.

On the positive side, I found over the next few months that a great deal was opening to me—to put it briefly, even crudely, I felt that I understood more about people, more about life. My life-view had been shocked and the lights and shadows were being shifted, which is equal to saying that I was learning a great deal. At a perhaps embarrassingly personal level, I discovered another benefit. There is probably no sensitive heterosexual alive who is not preoccupied at one time or another with his latent homosexuality, and while I had no conscious homosexual desires, I had wondered more than once if really there were not something suspicious in my intense dislike of homosexuals. How pleasant to discover that once one can accept homosexuals as real friends, the tension is gone with the acceptance. I found that I was no longer concerned with latent homosexuality. It seemed vastly less important, and paradoxically enabled me to realize that I am actually quite heterosexual. Close friendships with homosexuals had become possible without sexual desire or even sexual nuance—at least no more sexual nuance than is present in all human relations.

However, I had a peculiar problem at this time. I was on the way to finishing *The Deer Park*, my third novel. There was a minor character in it named Teddy Pope who is a movie star and a homosexual. Through the first and second drafts he had existed as a stereotype, a figure of fun; he was ludicrously affected and therefore ridiculous. One of the reasons I resisted Mr. Cory's book so much is that I was beginning to feel uneasy with the characterization I had drawn. In life there are any number of ridiculous people, but at bottom I was saying that Teddy Pope was ridiculous because he was homosexual. I found myself dissatisfied with the characterization even before I read *The Homosexual in America*; it had already struck me as being compounded too entirely of malice, but I think I would probably have left it that way. After Mr. Cory's book, it had become impossible. I no longer believed in Teddy Pope as I had drawn him.

Yet a novel which is almost finished is very difficult to alter. If it is at all a good book, the proportions, the meanings, and the inter-relations of the characters have become integrated, and one does not violate them without injuring one's work. Moreover, I have developed an antipathy to using one's novels as direct expressions of one's latest ideas. I, therefore, had no desire to change Teddy Pope into a fine, virtuous character. That would be as false, and as close to propaganda, as to keep him the way he was. Also, while a minor character, he had an important relation to the story, and it was obvious that he could not be transformed too radically without recasting much of the novel. My decision, with which I am not altogether happy, was to keep Teddy Pope more or less intact, but to try to add dimension to him. Perhaps I have succeeded. He will never be a character many readers admire, but it is possible that they will have feeling for him. At least he is no longer a simple object of ridicule, nor the butt of my malice, and I believe *The Deer Park* is a better book for the change. My hope is that some readers may possibly be stimulated to envisage the gamut of homosexual personality as parallel to the gamut of heterosexual personality even if Teddy Pope is a character from the lower half of the spectrum. However, I think it is more probable that the majority of homosexual readers who may get around to reading *The Deer Park* when it is published will be dissatisfied with him. I can only say that I am hardly satisfied myself. But this time, at least, I have discovered the edges of the rich theme of homosexuality rather than the easy symbolic equation of it to evil. And to that extent I feel richer and more confident as a writer. What I have come to realize is that much of my homosexual prejudice was a servant to my aesthetic needs. In the variety and contradiction of American life, the difficulty of finding a character who can serve as one's protagonist is matched only by the difficulty of finding one's villain, and so long as I was able to preserve my prejudices, my literary villains were at hand. Now, the problem will be more difficult, but I suspect it may be rewarding too, for deep down I was never very happy nor proud of myself at whipping homosexual straw-boys.

A LAST REMARK. If the homosexual is ever to achieve real social equality and acceptance, he, too, will have to work the hard row of shedding his own prejudices. Driven into defiance, it is natural if regrettable, that many homosexuals go to the direction of assuming that there is something intrinsically superior in homosexuality, and carried far enough it is a viewpoint which is as stultifying, as ridiculous, and as anti-human as the heterosexual's prejudice. Finally, heterosexuals are people too, and the hope of acceptance, tolerance, and sympathy must rest on this mutual appreciation.

letter to the members of the u.s. house of representatives

FRANKLIN KAMENY
1962

hon.___,
house of representatives, washington, d.c.

DEAR___,: Enclosed, for your interest and information, is a formal statement of the purposes of the Mattachine Society of Washington, a newly formed organization, devoted to the improvement of the status of our country's 15 million homosexuals.

Included, also, is a copy of our news release, which was submitted to the Washington newspapers and others, and to the various press services.

The question of homosexuality, and the prejudice against it, both personal and official, is a serious one, involving, as it does more than 1 out of every 10 American citizens, including roughly a quarter-million in, each, the Federal civil service, the Armed Forces, and security-sensitive positions in private industry, and at least 10 percent of your constituents.

We feel that the Government's approach is archaic, unrealistic, and inconsistent with basic American principles. We feel, in addition, that it is inexcusably and unnecessarily wasteful of trained manpower and of the taxpayers' money.

We realize that this area presents you with many potential problems, some of them quite subtle and touchy ones of politics and public relations, and that they are not always subject to easy solution, but policies of repression, persecution, and exclusion will not prove to be workable ones in the case of this minority, any more than they have, throughout history, in the case of other minorities. This is a problem which must be worked with, constructively, not worked against, destructively, as is now the case. A fresh approach by the Federal Government is badly needed.

We welcome any comments which you may have on this subject.

We will be pleased to meet with you personally, at your convenience, to discuss these and related matters.

Thank you for your consideration of our position.

Sincerely yours,
FRANKLIN E. KAMENY
President

notes on "camp"

SUSAN SONTAG
1964

many things in the world have not been named; and many things, even if they have been named, have never been described. One of these is the sensibility—unmistakably modern, a variant of sophistication but hardly identical with it—that goes by the cult name of "Camp."

A sensibility (as distinct from an idea) is one of the hardest things to talk about; but there are special reasons why Camp, in particular, has never been discussed. It is not a natural mode of sensibility, if there be any such. Indeed, the essence of Camp is its love of the unnatural: of artifice and exaggeration. And Camp is esoteric— something of a private code, a badge of identity even, among small urban cliques. Apart from a lazy two-page sketch in Christopher Isherwood's novel *The World in the Evening* (1954), it has hardly broken into print. To talk about Camp is therefore to betray it. If the betrayal can be defended, it will be for the edification it provides, or the dignity of the conflict it resolves. For myself, I plead the goal of self-edification, and the goad of a sharp conflict in my own sensibility. I am strongly drawn to Camp, and almost as strongly offended by it. That is why I want to talk about it, and why I can. For no one who wholeheartedly shares in a given sensibility can analyze it; he can only, whatever his intention, exhibit it. To name a sensibility, to draw its contours and to recount its history, requires a deep sympathy modified by revulsion.

Though I am speaking about sensibility only—and about a sensibility that, among other things, converts the serious into the frivolous—these are grave matters. Most people think of sensibility or taste as the realm of purely subjective preferences, those mysterious attractions, mainly sensual, that have not been brought under the sovereignty of reason. They *allow* that considerations of taste play a part in their reactions to people and to works of art. But this attitude is naïve. And even worse. To patronize the faculty of taste is to patronize oneself. For taste governs every free—as opposed to rote—human response. Nothing is more decisive. There is taste in people, visual taste, taste in emotion—and there is taste in acts, taste in morality. Intelligence, as well, is really a kind of taste: taste in ideas. (One of the facts to be reckoned with is that taste tends to develop very unevenly. It's rare that the same person has good visual taste *and* good taste in people *and* taste in ideas.)

Taste has no system and no proofs. But there is something like a logic of taste: the consistent sensibility which underlies and gives rise to a certain taste. A sensibility is almost, but not quite, ineffable. Any sensibility which can be crammed into the mold of a system, or handled with the rough tools of proof, is no longer a sensibility at all. It has hardened into an idea . . .

To snare a sensibility in words, especially one that is alive and powerful,[1] one must be tentative and nimble. The form of jottings, rather than an essay (with its claim to a linear, consecutive argument), seemed more appropriate for getting down something of this particular fugitive sensibility. It's embarrassing to be solemn and treatise-like about Camp. One runs the risk of having, oneself, produced a very inferior piece of Camp.

These notes are for Oscar Wilde.

> One should either be a work of art, or wear a work of art.
>
> —PHRASES & PHILOSOPHIES
> FOR THE USE OF THE YOUNG

1. To start very generally: Camp is a certain mode of aestheticism. It is one way of seeing the world as an aesthetic phenomenon. That way, the way of Camp, is not in terms of beauty but in terms of the degree of artifice, of stylization.

2. To emphasize style is to slight content, or to introduce an attitude which is neutral with respect to content. It goes without saying

---

1. The sensibility of an era is not only its most decisive but also its most perishable aspect. One may capture the ideas (intellectual history) and the behavior (social history) of an epoch without ever touching upon the sensibility or taste which informed those ideas, that behavior. Rare are those historical studies—like Huizinga on the late Middle Ages, Febvre on sixteenth-century France—which do tell us something about the sensibility of the period.

that the Camp sensibility is disengaged, depoliticized—or at least apolitical.

3. Not only is there a Camp vision, a Camp way of looking at things. Camp is as well a quality discoverable in objects and the behavior of persons. There are "campy" movies, clothes, furniture, popular songs, novels, people, buildings ... This distinction is important. True, the Camp eye has the power to transform experience. But not everything can be seen as Camp. It's not *all* in the eye of the beholder.

4. Random examples of items which are part of the canon of Camp:

Zuleika Dobson
Tiffany lamps
Scopitone films
The Brown Derby restaurant on Sunset Boulevard in L.A.
The Enquirer, headlines and stories
Aubrey Beardsley drawings
Swan Lake
Bellini's operas
Visconti's direction of *Salome* and *'Tis Pity She's a Whore*
certain turn-of-the-century picture postcards
Schoedsack's *King Kong*
the Cuban pop singer La Lupe
Lynn Ward's novel in woodcuts, *God's Man*
the old Flash Gordon comics
women's clothes of the twenties (feather boas, fringed and beaded
    dresses, etc.)
the novels of Ronald Firbank and Ivy Compton-Burnett
stag movies seen without lust

5. Camp taste has an affinity for certain arts rather than others. Clothes, furniture, all the elements of visual décor, for instance, make up a large part of Camp. For Camp art is often decorative art, emphasizing texture, sensuous surface, and style at the expense of content. Concert music, though, because it is contentless, is rarely Camp. It offers no opportunity, say, for a contrast between silly or extravagant content and rich form ... Sometimes whole art forms become saturated with Camp. Classical ballet, opera, movies have seemed so for a long time. In the last two years, popular music (post rock-'n'-roll, what the French call yé-yé) has been annexed. And

movie criticism (like lists of "The 10 Best Bad Movies I Have Seen") is probably the greatest popularizer of Camp taste today, because most people still go to the movies in a high-spirited and unpretentious way.

6. There is a sense in which it is correct to say "It's too good to be Camp." Or "too important," not marginal enough. (More on this later.) Thus, the personality and many of the works of Jean Cocteau are Camp, but not those of André Gide; the operas of Richard Strauss, but not those of Wagner; concoctions of Tin Pan Alley and Liverpool, but not jazz. Many examples of Camp are things which, from a "serious" point of view, are either bad art or kitsch. Not all, though. Not only is Camp not necessarily bad art, but some art which can be approached as Camp (example: the major films of Louis Feuillade) merits the most serious admiration and study.

> The more we study Art, the less we care for Nature.
> THE DECAY OF LYING

7. All Camp objects, and persons, contain a large element of artifice. Nothing in nature can be campy . . . Rural Camp is still man-made, and most campy objects are urban. (Yet they often have a serenity—or a naïveté—which is the equivalent of pastoral. A great deal of Camp suggests Empson's phrase, "urban pastoral.")

8. Camp is a vision of the world in terms of style—but a particular kind of style. It is the love of the exaggerated, the "off," of things-being-what-they-are-not. The best example is in Art Nouveau, the most typical and fully developed Camp style. Art Nouveau objects, typically, convert one thing into something else: the lighting fixtures in the form of flowering plants, the living room which is really a grotto. A remarkable example: the Paris Metro entrances designed by Hector Guimard in the late 1890s in the shape of cast-iron orchid stalks.

9. As a taste in persons, Camp responds particularly to the markedly attenuated and to the strongly exaggerated. The androgyne is certainly one of the great images of Camp sensibility. Examples: the swooning, slim, sinuous figures of pre-Raphaelite painting and poetry; the thin, flowing, sexless bodies in Art Nouveau prints and posters, presented in relief on lamps and ashtrays; the haunting androgynous vacancy behind the perfect beauty of Greta Garbo. Here Camp taste draws on a mostly unacknowledged truth of taste: the most refined form of sexual attractiveness (as well as the most

refined form of sexual pleasure) consists in going against the grain of one's sex. What is most beautiful in virile men is something feminine; what is most beautiful in feminine women is something masculine . . . Allied to the Camp taste for the androgynous is something that seems quite different but isn't: a relish for the exaggeration of sexual characteristics and personality mannerisms. For obvious reasons, the best examples that can be cited are movie stars. The corny flamboyant femaleness of Jayne Mansfield, Gina Lollobrigida, Jane Russell, Virginia Mayo; the exaggerated he-manness of Steve Reeves, Victor Mature. The great stylists of temperament and mannerism, like Bette Davis, Barbara Stanwyck, Tallulah Bankhead, Edwige Feuillère.

10. Camp sees everything in quotation marks. It's not a lamp, but a "lamp"; not a woman, but a "woman." To perceive Camp in objects and persons is to understand Being-as-Playing-a-Role. It is the furthest extension, in sensibility, of the metaphor of life as theater.

11. Camp is the triumph of the epicene style. (The convertibility of "man" and "woman," "person" and "thing.") But all style, that is, artifice, is, ultimately, epicene. Life is not stylish. Neither is nature.

12. The question isn't "Why travesty, impersonation, theatricality?" The question is, rather, "When does travesty, impersonation, theatricality acquire the special flavor of Camp?" Why is the atmosphere of Shakespeare's comedies (As You Like It, etc.) not epicene, while that of Der Rosenkavalier is?

13. The dividing line seems to fall in the eighteenth century; there the origins of Camp taste are to be found (Gothic novels, Chínoiserie, caricature, artificial ruins, and so forth). But the relation to nature was quite different then. In the eighteenth century, people of taste either patronized nature (Strawberry Hill) or attempted to remake it into something artificial (Versailles). They also indefatigably patronized the past. Today's Camp taste effaces nature, or else contradicts it outright. And the relation of Camp taste to the past is extremely sentimental.

14. A pocket history of Camp might, of course, begin further back—with the mannerist artists like Pontormo, Rosso, and Caravaggio, or the extraordinarily theatrical painting of Georges de La Tour, or euphuism (Lyly, etc.) in literature. Still, the soundest starting point seems to be the late seventeenth and early eighteenth century, because of that period's extraordinary feeling for artifice, for surface, for symmetry; its taste for the picturesque and the thrilling, its elegant conventions for representing instant feeling and the total presence of

character—the epigram and the rhymed couplet (in words), the flourish (in gesture and in music). The late seventeenth and early eighteenth century is the great period of Camp: Pope, Congreve, Walpole, but not Swift; *les précieux* in France; the rococo churches of Munich; Pergolesi. Somewhat later: much of Mozart. But in the nineteenth century, what had been distributed throughout all of high culture now becomes a special taste; it takes on overtones of the acute, the esoteric, the perverse. Confining the story to England alone, we see Camp continuing wanly through nineteenth-century aestheticism (Burne-Jones, Pater, Ruskin, Tennyson), emerging full-blown with the Art Nouveau movement in the visual and decorative arts, and finding its conscious ideologists in such "wits" as Wilde and Firbank.

15. Of course, to say all these things are Camp is not to argue they are simply that. A full analysis of Art Nouveau, for instance, would scarcely equate it with Camp. But such an analysis cannot ignore what in Art Nouveau allows it to be experienced as Camp. Art Nouveau is full of "content," even of a political moral sort; it was a revolutionary movement in the arts, spurred on by a utopian vision (somewhere between William Morris and the Bauhaus group) of an organic politics and taste. Yet there is also a feature of the Art Nouveau objects which suggests a disengaged, unserious, "aesthete's" vision. This tells us something important about Art Nouveau—and about what the lens of Camp, which blocks out content, is.

16. Thus, the Camp sensibility is one that is alive to a double sense in which some things can be taken. But this is not the familiar split-level construction of a literal meaning, on the one hand, and a symbolic meaning, on the other. It is the difference, rather, between the thing as meaning something, anything, and the thing as pure artifice.

17. This comes out clearly in the vulgar use of the word Camp as a verb, "to camp," something that people do. To camp is a mode of seduction—one which employs flamboyant mannerisms susceptible of a double interpretation; gestures full of duplicity, with a witty meaning for cognoscenti and another, more impersonal, for outsiders. Equally and by extension, when the word becomes a noun, when a person or a thing is "a camp," a duplicity is involved. Behind the "straight" public sense in which something can be taken, one has found a private zany experience of the thing.

To be natural is such a very difficult pose to keep up.

AN IDEAL HUSBAND

18. One must distinguish between naïve and deliberate Camp. Pure Camp is always naïve. Camp which knows itself to be Camp ("camping") is usually less satisfying.

19. The pure examples of Camp are unintentional; they are dead-serious. The Art Nouveau craftsman who makes a lamp with a snake coiled around it is not kidding, nor is he trying to be charming. He is saying, in all earnestness: Voilà! the Orient! Genuine Camp—for instance, the numbers devised for the Warner Brothers musicals of the early thirties (*42nd Street; The Golddiggers of 1933;... of 1935;... of 1937;* etc.) by Busby Berkeley—does not *mean* to be funny. Camping—say, the plays of Noël Coward—does. It seems unlikely that much of the traditional opera repertoire could be such satisfying Camp if the melodramatic absurdities of most opera plots had not been taken seriously by their composers. One doesn't need to know the artist's private intentions. The work tells all. (Compare a typical nineteenth-century opera with Samuel Barber's *Vanessa*, a piece of manufactured, calculated Camp, and the difference is clear.)

20. Probably, intending to be campy is always harmful. The perfection of *Trouble in Paradise* and *The Maltese Falcon*, among the greatest Camp movies ever made, comes from the effortless smooth way in which tone is maintained. This is not so with such famous would-be Camp films of the fifties as *All About Eve* and *Beat the Devil*. These more recent movies have their fine moments, but the first is so slick and the second so hysterical; they want so badly to be campy that they're continually losing the beat . . . Perhaps, though, it is not so much a question of the unintended effect versus the conscious intention, as of the delicate relation between parody and self-parody in Camp. The films of Hitchcock are a showcase for this problem. When self-parody lacks ebullience but instead reveals (even sporadically) a contempt for one's themes and one's materials—as in *To Catch a Thief, Rear Window, North by Northwest*—the results are forced and heavy-handed, rarely Camp. Successful Camp—a movie like Carné's *Drôle de Drame;* the film performances of Mae West and Edward Everett Horton; portions of the Goon Show—even when it reveals self-parody, reeks of self-love.

21. So, again, Camp rests on innocence. That means Camp discloses innocence, but also, when it can, corrupts it. Objects, being objects, don't change when they are singled out by the Camp vision. Persons, however, respond to their audiences. Persons begin "camping": Mae West, Bea Lillie, La Lupe, Tallulah Bankhead in *Lifeboat*,

Bette Davis in *All About Eve*. (Persons can even be induced to camp without their knowing it. Consider the way Fellini got Anita Ekberg to parody herself in *La Dolce Vita*.)

22. Considered a little less strictly, Camp is either completely naïve or else wholly conscious (when one plays at being campy). An example of the latter: Wilde's epigrams themselves.

> It's absurd to divide people into good and bad. People are either charming or tedious.
>
> LADY WINDEMERE'S FAN

23. In naïve, or pure, Camp, the essential element is seriousness, a seriousness that fails. Of course, not all seriousness that fails can be redeemed as Camp. Only that which has the proper mixture of the exaggerated, the fantastic, the passionate, and the naïve.

24. When something is just bad (rather than Camp), it's often because it is too mediocre in its ambition. The artist hasn't attempted to do anything really outlandish. ("It's too much," "It's too fantastic," "It's not to be believed," are standard phrases of Camp enthusiasm.)

25. The hallmark of Camp is the spirit of extravagance. Camp is a woman walking around in a dress made of three million feathers. Camp is the paintings of Carlo Crivelli, with their real jewels and *trompe-l'oeil* insects and cracks in the masonry. Camp is the outrageous aestheticism of Sternberg's six American movies with Dietrich, all six, but especially the last, *The Devil Is a Woman* . . . In Camp there is often something *démesuré* in the quality of the ambition, not only in the style of the work itself. Gaudi's lurid and beautiful buildings in Barcelona are Camp not only because of their style but because they reveal—most notably in the Cathedral of the Sagrada Familia—the ambition on the part of one man to do what it takes a generation, a whole culture to accomplish.

26. Camp is art that proposes itself seriously, but cannot be taken altogether seriously because it is "too much." *Titus Andronicus* and *Strange Interlude* are almost Camp, or could be played as Camp. The public manner and rhetoric of de Gaulle, often, are pure Camp.

27. A work can come close to Camp but not make it because it succeeds. Eisenstein's films are seldom Camp because, despite all exaggeration, they do succeed (dramatically) without surplus. If they were a little more "off," they could be great Camp—particularly *Ivan the Terrible I & II*. The same for Blake's drawings and paintings,

weird and mannered as they are. They aren't Camp; though Art Nouveau, influenced by Blake, is.

What is extravagant in an inconsistent or an unpassionate way is
not Camp. Neither can anything be Camp that does not seem to
spring from an irrepressible, a virtually uncontrolled sensibility.
Without passion, one gets pseudo-Camp—what is merely decorative,
safe, in a word, chic. On the barren edge of Camp lie a number of
attractive things: the sleek fantasies of Dali, the haute-couture preciosity of Albicocco's *The Girl with the Golden Eyes*. But the two
things—Camp and preciosity—must not be confused.

28. Again, Camp is the attempt to do something extraordinary. But
extraordinary in the sense, often, of being special, glamorous. (The
curved line, the extravagant gesture.) Not extraordinary merely in the
sense of effort. Ripley's Believe-It-Or-Not items are rarely campy.
These items, either natural oddities (the two-headed rooster, the egg-
plant in the shape of a cross) or else the products of immense labor
(the man who walked from here to China on his hands, the woman
who engraved the New Testament on the head of a pin), lack the
visual reward—the glamour, the theatricality—that marks off certain
extravagances as Camp.

29. The reason a movie like *On the Beach*, books like *Winesburg,
Ohio* and *For Whom the Bell Tolls* are bad to the point of being
laughable, but not bad to the point of being enjoyable, is that they
are too dogged and pretentious. They lack fantasy. There is Camp in
such bad movies as *The Prodigal* and *Samson and Delilah*, the series
of Italian color spectacles featuring the super-hero Maciste, numerous Japanese science-fiction films (*Rodan, The Mysterians, The
H-Man*), because, in their relative unpretentiousness and vulgarity,
they are more extreme and irresponsible in their fantasy—and therefore touching and quite enjoyable.

30. Of course, the canon of Camp can change. Time has a great
deal to do with it. Time may enhance what seems simply dogged or
lacking in fantasy now because we are too close to it, because it
resembles too closely our own everyday fantasies, the fantastic nature
of which we don't perceive. We are better able to enjoy a fantasy as
fantasy when it is not our own.

31. This is why so many of the objects prized by Camp taste are
old-fashioned, out-of-date, *démodé*. It's not a love of the old as such.
It's simply that the process of aging or deterioration provides the necessary detachment—or arouses a necessary sympathy. When the
theme is important, and contemporary, the failure of a work of art

may make us indignant. Time can change that. Time liberates the work of art from moral relevance, delivering it over to the Camp sensibility . . . Another effect: time contracts the sphere of banality. (Banality is, strictly speaking, always a category of the contemporary.) What was banal can, with the passage of time, become fantastic. Many people who listen with delight to the style of Rudy Vallee revived by the English pop group The Temperance Seven would have been driven up the wall by Rudy Vallee in his heyday.

Thus, things are campy, not when they become old—but when we become less involved in them, and can enjoy, instead of be frustrated by, the failure of the attempt. But the effect of time is unpredictable. Maybe Method Acting (James Dean, Rod Steiger, Warren Beatty) will seem as Camp someday as Ruby Keeler's does now—or as Sarah Bernhardt's does, in the films she made at the end of her career. And maybe not.

32. Camp is the glorification of "character." The statement is of no importance—except, of course, to the person (Loie Fuller, Gaudf, Cecil B. De Mille, Crivelli, de Gaulle, etc.) who makes it. What the Camp eye appreciates is the unity, the force of the person. In every move the aging Martha Graham makes she's being Martha Graham, etc., etc. . . . This is clear in the case of the great serious idol of Camp taste, Greta Garbo. Garbo's incompetence (at the least, lack of depth) as an *actress* enhances her beauty. She's always herself.

33. What Camp taste responds to is "instant character" (this is, of course, very eighteenth century); and, conversely, what it is not stirred by is the sense of the development of character. Character is understood as a state of continual incandescence—a person being one, very intense thing. This attitude toward character is a key element of the theatricalization of experience embodied in the Camp sensibility. And it helps account for the fact that opera and ballet are experienced as such rich treasures of Camp, for neither of these forms can easily do justice to the complexity of human nature. Wherever there is development of character, Camp is reduced. Among operas, for example, *La Traviata* (which has some small development of character) is less campy than *Il Trovatore* (which has none).

> Life is too important a thing ever to talk seriously about it.
>
> VERA, OR THE NIHILISTS

34. Camp taste turns its back on the good-bad axis of ordinary aesthetic judgment. Camp doesn't reverse things. It doesn't argue that

the good is bad, or the bad is good. What it does is to offer for art (and life) a different—a supplementary—set of standards.

35. Ordinarily we value a work of art because of the seriousness and dignity of what it achieves. We value it because it succeeds—in being what it is and, presumably, in fulfilling the intention that lies behind it. We assume a proper, that is to say, straightforward relation between intention and performance. By such standards, we appraise *The Iliad*, Aristophanes's plays, The Art of the Fugue, *Middlemarch*, the paintings of Rembrandt, Chartres, the poetry of Donne, *The Divine Comedy*, Beethoven's quartets, and—among people—Socrates, Jesus, St. Francis, Napoleon, Savonarola. In short, the pantheon of high culture: truth, beauty, and seriousness.

36. But there are other creative sensibilities besides the seriousness (both tragic and comic) of high culture and of the high style of evaluating people. And one cheats oneself, as a human being, if one has *respect* only for the style of high culture, whatever else one may do or feel on the sly.

For instance, there is the kind of seriousness whose trademark is anguish, cruelty, derangement. Here we do accept a disparity between intention and result. I am speaking, obviously, of style of personal existence as well as of a style in art; but the examples had best come from art. Think of Bosch, Sade, Rimbaud, Jarry, Kafka, Artaud, think of most of the important works of art of the twentieth century, that is, art whose goal is not that of creating harmonies but of overstraining the medium and introducing more and more violent, and unresolvable, subject matter. This sensibility also insists on the principle that an *oeuvre* in the old sense (again, in art, but also in life) is not possible. Only "fragments" are possible . . . Clearly, different standards apply here than to traditional high culture. Something is good not because it is achieved but because another kind of truth about the human situation, another experience of what it is to be human—in short, another valid sensibility—is being revealed.

And third among the great creative sensibilities is Camp: the sensibility of failed seriousness, of the theatricalization of experience. Camp refuses both the harmonies of traditional seriousness and the risks of fully identifying with extreme states of feeling.

37. The first sensibility, that of high culture, is basically moralistic. The second sensibility, that of extreme states of feeling, represented in much contemporary "avant-garde" art, gains power by a tension between moral and aesthetic passion. The third, Camp, is wholly aesthetic.

38. Camp is the consistently aesthetic experience of the world. It incarnates a victory of "style" over "content," "aesthetics" over "morality," of irony over tragedy.

39. Camp and tragedy are antitheses. There is seriousness in Camp (seriousness in the degree of the artist's involvement) and, often, pathos. The excruciating is also one of the tonalities of Camp; it is the quality of excruciation in much of Henry James (for instance, *The Europeans, The Awkward Age, The Wings of the Dove*) that is responsible for the large element of Camp in his writings. But there is never, never tragedy.

40. Style is everything. Genet's ideas, for instance, are very Camp. Genet's statement that "the only criterion of an act is its elegance"[2] is virtually interchangeable, as a statement, with Wilde's "in matters of great importance, the vital element is not sincerity, but style." But what counts, finally, is the style in which ideas are held. The ideas about morality and politics in, say, *Lady Windemere's Fan* and *Major Barbara* are Camp, but not just because of the nature of the ideas themselves. It is those ideas, held in a special playful way. The Camp ideas in *Our Lady of the Flowers* are maintained too grimly, and the writing itself is too successfully elevated and serious, for Genet's books to be Camp.

41. The whole point of Camp is to dethrone the serious. Camp is playful, anti-serious. More precisely, Camp involves a new, more complex relation to "the serious." One can be serious about the frivolous, frivolous about the serious.

42. One is drawn to Camp when one realizes that "sincerity" is not enough. Sincerity can be simple philistinism, intellectual narrowness.

43. The traditional means for going beyond straight seriousness—irony, satire—seem feeble today, inadequate to the culturally oversaturated medium in which contemporary sensibility is schooled. Camp introduces a new standard: artifice as an ideal, theatricality.

44. Camp proposes a comic vision of the world. But not a bitter or polemical comedy. If tragedy is an experience of hyper-involvement, comedy is an experience of under-involvement, of detachment.

I adore simple pleasures, they are the last refuge of the complex.

A WOMAN OF NO IMPORTANCE

2. Sartre's gloss on this in *Saint Genet* is: "Elegance is the quality of conduct which transforms the greatest amount of being into appearing."

45. Detachment is the prerogative of an elite; and as the dandy is the nineteenth century's surrogate for the aristocrat in matters of culture, so Camp is the modern dandyism. Camp is the answer to the problem: how to be a dandy in the age of mass culture.

46. The dandy was overbred. His posture was disdain, or else ennui. He sought rare sensations, undefiled by mass appreciation. (Models: Des Esseintes in Huysmans's *A Rebours, Marius the Epicurean*, Valéry's *Monsieur Teste*.) He was dedicated to "good taste."

The connoisseur of Camp has found more ingenious pleasures. Not in Latin poetry and rare wines and velvet jackets, but in the coarsest, commonest pleasures, in the arts of the masses. Mere use does not defile the objects of his pleasure, since he learns to possess them in a rare way. Camp—Dandyism in the age of mass culture—makes no distinction between the unique object and the mass-produced object. Camp taste transcends the nausea of the replica.

47. Wilde himself is a transitional figure. The man who, when he first came to London, sported a velvet beret, lace shirts, velveteen knee breeches and black silk stockings could never depart too far in his life from the pleasures of the old-style dandy; this conservatism is reflected in *The Picture of Dorian Gray*. But many of his attitudes suggest something more modern. It was Wilde who formulated an important element of the Camp sensibility—the equivalence of all objects—when he announced his intention of "living up" to his blue-and-white china, or declared that a doorknob could be as admirable as a painting. When he proclaimed the importance of the necktie, the boutonniere, the chair, Wilde was anticipating the democratic *esprit* of Camp.

48. The old-style dandy hated vulgarity. The new-style dandy, the lover of Camp, appreciates vulgarity. Where the dandy would be continually offended or bored, the connoisseur of Camp is continually amused, delighted. The dandy held a perfumed handkerchief to his nostrils and was liable to swoon; the connoisseur of Camp sniffs the stink and prides himself on his strong nerves.

49. It is a feat, of course. A feat goaded on, in the last analysis, by the threat of boredom. The relation between boredom and Camp taste cannot be overestimated. Camp taste is by its nature possible only in affluent societies, in societies or circles capable of experiencing the psychopathology of affluence.

What is abnormal in Life stands in normal relations to Art. It is the only thing in Life that stands in normal relations to Art.
A FEW MAXIMS FOR THE INSTRUCTION OF THE OVER-EDUCATED

50. Aristocracy is a position vis-à-vis culture (as well as vis-à-vis power), and the history of Camp taste is part of the history of snob taste. But since no authentic aristocrats in the old sense exist today to sponsor special tastes, who is the bearer of this taste? Answer: an improvised self-elected class, mainly homosexuals, who constitute themselves as aristocrats of taste.

51. The peculiar relation between Camp taste and homosexuality has to be explained. While it's not true that Camp taste *is* homosexual taste, there is no doubt a peculiar affinity and overlap. Not all liberals are Jews, but Jews have shown a peculiar affinity for liberal and reformist causes. So, not all homosexuals have Camp taste. But homosexuals, by and large, constitute the vanguard—and the most articulate audience—of Camp. (The analogy is not frivolously chosen. Jews and homosexuals are the outstanding creative minorities in contemporary urban culture. Creative, that is, in the truest sense: they are creators of sensibilities. The two pioneering forces of modern sensibility are Jewish moral seriousness and homosexual aestheticism and irony.)

52. The reason for the flourishing of the aristocratic posture among homosexuals also seems to parallel the Jewish case. For every sensibility is self-serving to the group that promotes it. Jewish liberalism is a gesture of self-legitimization. So is Camp taste, which definitely has something propagandistic about it. Needles to say, the propaganda operates in exactly the opposite direction. The Jews pinned their hopes for integrating into modern society on promoting the moral sense. Homosexuals have pinned their integration into society on promoting the aesthetic sense. Camp is a solvent of morality. It neutralizes moral indignation, sponsors playfulness.

53. Nevertheless, even though homosexuals have been its vanguard, Camp taste is much more than homosexual taste. Obviously, its metaphor of life as theater is peculiarly suited as a justification and projection of a certain aspect of the situation of homosexuals. (The Camp insistence on not being "serious," on playing, also connects with the homosexual's desire to remain youthful.) Yet one feels that if homosexuals hadn't more or less invented Camp, someone else would. For the aristocratic posture with relation to culture cannot die, though it may persist only in increasingly arbitrary and ingenious ways. Camp is (to repeat) the relation to style in a time in which the adoption of style—as such—has become altogether questionable. (In the modern era, each new style, unless frankly anachronistic, has come on the scene as an anti-style.)

One must have a heart of stone to read the death of Little Nell without laughing.

IN CONVERSATION

54. The experiences of Camp are based on the great discovery that the sensibility of high culture has no monopoly upon refinement. Camp asserts that good taste is not simply good taste; that there exists, indeed, a good taste of bad taste. (Genet talks about this in *Our Lady of the Flowers*.) The discovery of the good taste of bad taste can be very liberating. The man who insists on high and serious pleasures is depriving himself of pleasure; he continually restricts what he can enjoy; in the constant exercise of his good taste he will eventually price himself out of the market, so to speak. Here Camp taste supervenes upon good taste as a daring and witty hedonism. It makes the man of good taste cheerful, where before he ran the risk of being chronically frustrated. It is good for the digestion.

55. Camp taste is, above all, a mode of enjoyment, of appreciation—not judgment. Camp is generous. It wants to enjoy. It only seems like malice, cynicism. (Or, if it is cynicism, it's not a ruthless but a sweet cynicism.) Camp taste doesn't propose that it is in bad taste to be serious; it doesn't sneer at someone who succeeds in being seriously dramatic. What it does is to find the success in certain passionate failures.

56. Camp taste is a kind of love, love for human nature. It relishes, rather than judges, the little triumphs and awkward intensities of "character" . . . Camp taste identifies with what it is enjoying. People who share this sensibility are not laughing at the thing they label as "a camp," they're enjoying it. Camp is a tender feeling.

(Here one may compare Camp with much of Pop Art, which—when it is not just Camp—embodies an attitude that is related, but still very different. Pop Art is more flat and more dry, more serious, more detached, ultimately nihilistic.)

57. Camp taste nourishes itself on the love that has gone into certain objects and personal styles. The absence of this love is the reason why such kitsch items as *Peyton Place* (the book) and the Tishman Building aren't Camp.

58. The ultimate Camp statement: it's good because it's awful . . . Of course, one can't always say that. Only under certain conditions, those which I've tried to sketch in these notes.

a gay manifesto

CARL WITTMAN
1969

san Francisco is a refugee camp for homosexuals. We have fled here from every part of the nation, and like refugees elsewhere, we came not because it is so great here, but because it was so bad there. By the tens of thousands, we fled small towns where to be ourselves would endanger our jobs and any hope of a decent life; we have fled from blackmailing cops, from families who disowned or "tolerated" us; we have been drummed out of the armed services, thrown out of schools, fired from jobs, beaten by punks and policemen.

And we have formed a ghetto, out of self-protection. It is a ghetto rather than a free territory because it is still theirs. Straight cops patrol us, straight legislators govern us, straight employers keep us in line, straight money exploits us. We have pretended everything is OK, because we haven't been able to see how to change it—we've been afraid.

In the past year there has been an awakening of gay liberation ideas and energy. How it began we don't know; maybe we were inspired by black people and their freedom movement; we learned how to stop pretending from the hip revolution. Amerika in all its ugliness has surfaced with the war and our national leaders. And we are revulsed by the quality of our ghetto life.

Where once there was frustration, alienation, and cynicism, there are new characteristics among us. We are full of love for each other and are showing it; we are full of anger at what has been done to us. And as we recall all the self-censorship and repression for so many years, a reservoir of tears pours out of our eyes. And we are euphoric, high with the initial flourish of a movement.

We want to make ourselves clear: our first job is to free ourselves;

that means clearing our heads of the garbage that's been poured into them. This article is an attempt at raising a number of issues, and presenting some ideas to replace the old ones. It is primarily for ourselves, a starting point of discussion. If straight people of good will find it useful in understanding what liberation is about, so much the better.

It should also be clear that these are the views of one person, and are determined not only by my homosexuality, but my being white, male, middle-class. It is my individual consciousness. Our group consciousness will evolve as we get ourselves together—we are only at the beginning.

I. On Orientation
1. *What homosexuality is:* Nature leaves undefined the object of sexual desire. The gender of that object is imposed socially. Humans originally made homosexuality taboo because they needed every bit of energy to produce and raise children: survival of the species was a priority. With overpopulation and technological change, that taboo continued only to exploit us and enslave us.

As kids we refused to capitulate to demands that we ignore our feelings toward each other. Somewhere we found the strength to resist being indoctrinated, and we should count that among our assets. We have to realize that our loving each other is a good thing, not an unfortunate thing, and that we have a lot to teach straights about sex, love, strength, and resistance.

Homosexuality is *not* a lot of things. It is not a makeshift in the absence of the opposite sex; it is not hatred or rejection of the opposite sex; it is not genetic; it is not the result of broken homes except inasmuch as we could see the sham of American marriage. *Homosexuality is the capacity to love someone of the same sex.*

2. *Bisexuality:* Bisexuality is good; it is the capacity to love people of either sex. The reason so few of us are bisexual is because society made such a big stink about homosexuality that we got forced into seeing ourselves as either straight or non-straight. Also, many gays got turned off to the ways men are supposed to act with women and vice-versa, which is pretty fucked-up. Gays will begin to turn on to women when 1) it's something that we do because we want to, and not because we should, and 2) when women's liberation changes the nature of heterosexual relationships.

We continue to call ourselves homosexual, not bisexual, even if we do make it with the opposite sex also, because saying "Oh, I'm Bi" is a copout for a gay. We get told it's OK to sleep with guys as long as we sleep with women, too, and that's still putting homosexuality down. We'll be gay until everyone has forgotten that it's an issue. Then we'll begin to be complete.

3. *Heterosexuality:* Exclusive heterosexuality is fucked up. It reflects a fear of people of the same sex, it's anti-homosexual, and it is fraught with frustration. Heterosexual sex is fucked up, too; ask women's liberation about what straight guys are like in bed. Sex is aggression for the male chauvinist; sex is obligation for the traditional woman. And among the young, the modern, the hip, it's only a subtle version of the same. For us to become heterosexual in the sense that our straight brothers and sisters are is not a cure, it is a disease.

II. On Women

1. *Lesbianism:* It's been a male-dominated society for too long, and that has warped both men and women. So gay women are going to see things differently from gay men; they are going to feel put down as women, too. Their liberation is tied up with both gay liberation and women's liberation.

This paper speaks from the gay male viewpoint. And although some of the ideas in it may be equally relevant to gay women, it would be arrogant to presume this to be a manifesto for lesbians.

We look forward to the emergence of a lesbian liberation voice. The existence of a lesbian caucus within the New York Gay Liberation Front has been very helpful in challenging male chauvinism among gay guys, and anti-gay feelings among women's liberation.

2. *Male chauvinism:* All men are infected with male chauvinism — we were brought up that way. It means we assume that women play subordinate roles and are less human than ourselves. (At an early gay liberation meeting one guy said, "Why don't we invite women's liberation — they can bring sandwiches and coffee.") It is no wonder that so few gay women have become active in our groups.

Male chauvinism, however, is not central to us. We can junk it much more easily than straight men can. For we understand oppression. We have largely opted out of a system which oppresses women daily — our egos are not built on putting women down and having them build us up. Also, living in a mostly male world we have become used to playing different roles, doing our own shit-work. And finally, we have a common enemy: the big male chauvinists are also the big anti-gays.

But we need to purge male chauvinism, both in behavior and in thought among us. Chick equals nigger equals queer. Think it over.

3. *Women's liberation:* They are assuming their equality and dignity and in doing so are challenging the same things we are: the roles, the exploitation of minorities by capitalism, the arrogant smugness of straight white male middle-class Amerika. They are our sisters in the struggle.

Problems and differences will become clearer when we begin to work together. One major problem is our own male chauvinism. Another is uptightness and hostility to homosexuality that many women have—that is the straight in them. A third problem is differing views on sex: sex for them has meant oppression, while for us it has been a symbol of our freedom. We must come to know and understand each other's style, jargon and humor.

III. On Roles

1. *Mimicry of straight society:* We are children of straight society. We still think straight: that is part of our oppression. One of the worst of straight concepts is inequality. Straight (also white, English, male, capitalist) thinking views things in terms of order and comparison. A is before B, B is after A; one is below two is below three; there is no room for equality. This idea gets extended to male/female, on top/on bottom, spouse/not spouse, heterosexual/homosexual, boss/worker, white/black, and rich/poor. Our social institutions cause and reflect this verbal hierarchy. This is Amerika.

We've lived in these institutions all our lives. Naturally we mimic the roles. For too long we mimicked these roles to protect ourselves—a survival mechanism. Now we are becoming free enough to shed the roles which we've picked up from the institutions which have imprisoned us.

"Stop mimicking straights, stop censoring ourselves."

2. *Marriage:* Marriage is a prime example of a straight institution fraught with role playing. Traditional marriage is a rotten, oppressive institution. Those of us who have been in heterosexual marriages too often have blamed our gayness on the breakup of the marriage. No. They broke up because marriage is a contract which smothers both people, denies needs, and places impossible demands on both people. And we had the strength, again, to refuse to capitulate to the roles which were demanded of us.

Gay people must stop gauging their self-respect by how well they mimic straight marriages. Gay marriages will have the same problems as straight ones except in burlesque. For the usual legitimacy and pressures which keep straight marriages together are absent, e.g. kids, what parents think, what neighbors say.

To accept that happiness comes through finding a groovy spouse and settling down, showing the world that "we're just the same as you" is avoiding the real issues, and is an expression of self-hatred.

3. *Alternatives to marriage:* People want to get married for lots of good reasons, although marriage won't often meet those needs or desires. We're all looking for security, a flow of love, and a feeling of belonging and being needed.

These needs can be met through a number of social relationships and living situations. Things we want to get away from are: 1) exclusiveness, propertied attitudes toward each other, a mutual pact against the rest of the world; 2) promise about the future, which we have no right to make and which prevent us from, or make us feel guilty about, growing; 3) inflexible roles, roles which do not reflect us at the moment but are inherited through mimicry and inability to define equalitarian relationships.

We have to define for ourselves a new pluralistic, role-free social structure for ourselves. It must contain both the freedom and physical space for people to live alone, live together for awhile, live together for a long time, either as couples or in larger numbers; and the ability to flow easily from one of these states to another as our needs change.

Liberation for gay people is defining for ourselves how and with whom we live, instead of measuring our relationship in comparison to straight ones, with straight values.

4. *Gay "stereotypes":* The straights' image of the gay world is defined largely by those of us who have violated straight roles. There is a tendency among "homophile" groups to deplore gays who play visible roles—the queens and the nellies. As liberated gays, we must take a clear stand. 1) Gays who stand out have become our first martyrs. They came out and withstood disapproval before the rest of us did. 2) If they have suffered from being open, it is straight society whom we must indict, not the queen.

5. *Closet queens:* This phrase is becoming analagous to "Uncle Tom." To pretend to be straight sexually, or to pretend to be straight socially, is probably the most harmful pattern of behavior in the ghetto. The married guy who makes it on the side secretly; the guy who will go to bed once but who won't develop any gay relationships; the pretender at work or school who changes the gender of the friend

he's talking about; the guy who'll suck cock in the bushes but who won't go to bed.

If we are liberated we are open with our sexuality. Closet queenery must end. *Come out.*

But in saying come out, we have to have our heads clear about a few things: 1) Closet queens are our brothers, and must be defended against attacks by straight people; 2) The fear of coming out is not paranoia; the stakes are high: loss of family ties, loss of job, loss of straight friends—these are all reminders that the oppression is not just in our heads. It's real. Each of us must make the steps toward openness at our own speed and on our own impulses. Being open is the foundation of freedom: it has to be built solidly; 3) "Closet queen" is a broad term covering a multitude of forms of defense, self-hatred, lack of strength, and habit. We are all closet queens in some ways, and all of us had to come out—very few of us were "flagrant" at the age of seven! We must afford our brothers and sisters the same patience we afforded ourselves. And while their closet queenery is part of our oppression, it's more a part of theirs. They alone can decide when and how.

IV. On Oppression

It is important to catalog and understand the different facets of our oppression. There is no future in arguing about degrees of oppression. A lot of "movement" types come on with a line of shit about homosexuals not being oppressed as much as blacks or Vietnamese or workers or women. We don't happen to fit into their ideas of class or caste. Bull! When people feel oppressed, they act on that feeling. We feel oppressed. Talk about the priority of black liberation or ending imperialism over and above gay liberation is just anti-gay propaganda.

1. *Physical attacks:* We are attacked, beaten, castrated and left dead time and time again. There are half a dozen known unsolved slayings in San Francisco parks in the last few years. "Punks," often of minority groups who look around for someone under them socially, feel encouraged to beat up on "queens," and cops look the other way. That used to be called lynching.

Cops in most cities have harassed our meeting places: bars and baths and parks. They set up entrapment squads. A Berkeley brother was slain by a cop in April when he tried to split after finding out that the trick who was making advances to him was a cop. Cities set up "pervert" registration, which if nothing else scares our brothers deeper into the closet.

One of the most vicious slurs on us is the blame for prison "gang rapes." These rapes are invariably done by people who consider themselves straight. The victims of these rapes are us and straights who can't defend themselves. The press campaign to link prison rapes with homosexuality is an attempt to make straights fear and despise us, so they can oppress us more. It's typical of the fucked-up straight mind to think that homosexual sex involves tying a guy down and fucking him. That's aggression, not sex. If that's what sex is for a lot of straight people, that's a problem they have to solve, not us.

2. *Psychological warfare*: Right from the beginning we have been subjected to a barrage of straight propaganda. Since our parents don't know any homosexuals, we grow up thinking that we're alone and different and perverted. Our school friends identify "queer" with any non-conformist or bad behavior. Our elementary school teachers tell us not to talk to strangers or accept rides. Television, billboards and magazines put forth a false idealization of male/female relationships, and make us wish we were different, wish we were "in." In family living class we're taught how we're supposed to turn out. And all along the best we hear about homosexuality is that it's an unfortunate problem.

3. *Self-oppression*: As gay liberation grows, we will find our uptight brothers and sisters, particularly those who are making a buck off our ghetto, coming on strong to defend the status quo. This is self-oppression: "don't rock the boat"; "things in SF are OK"; "gay people just aren't together"; "I'm not oppressed." These lines are right out of the mouths of the straight establishment. A large part of our oppression would end if we would stop putting ourselves and our pride down.

4. *Institutional oppression*: Discrimination against gays is blatant, if we open our eyes. Homosexual relationships are illegal, and even if these laws are not regularly enforced, they encourage and enforce closet queenery. The bulk of the social work/psychiatric field looks upon homosexuality as a problem, and treats us as sick. Employers let it be known that our skills are acceptable only as long as our sexuality is hidden. Big business and government are particularly notorious offenders.

The discrimination in the draft and armed services is a pillar of the general attitude toward gays. If we are willing to label ourselves publicly not only as homosexual but as sick, then we qualify for deferment; and if we're not "discreet" (dishonest) we get drummed out of the service. Hell, no, we won't go, of course not, but we can't let the army fuck over us this way, either.

V. On Sex

1. *What sex is*: It is both creative expression and communication: good when it is either, and better when it is both. Sex can also be aggression, and usually is when those involved do not see each other as equals; and it can also be perfunctory, when we are distracted or preoccupied. These uses spoil what is good about it.

I like to think of good sex in terms of playing the violin: with both people on one level seeing the other body as an object capable of creating beauty when they play it well; and on a second level the players communicating through their mutual production and appreciation of beauty. As in good music, you get totally into it—and coming back out of that state of consciousness is like finishing a work of art or coming back from an episode of an acid or mescaline trip. And to press the analogy further: the variety of music is infinite and varied, depending on the capabilities of the players, both as subjects and as objects. Solos, duets, quartets (symphonies, even, if you happen to dig Romantic music!) are possible. The variations in gender, response, and bodies are like different instruments. And perhaps what we have called sexual "orientation" probably just means that we have not yet learned to turn on to the total range of musical expression.

2. *Objectification*: In this scheme, people are sexual objects, but they are also subjects, and are human beings who appreciate themselves as object and subject. This use of human bodies as objects is legitimate (not harmful) only when it is reciprocal. If one person is always object and the other subject, it stifles the human being in both of them. Objectification must also be open and frank. By silence we often assume or let the other person assume that sex means commitments: if it does. OK: but if not, say it. (Of course, it's not all that simple: our capabilities for manipulation are unfathomed—all we can do is try.)

Gay liberation people must understand that women have been treated exclusively and dishonestly as sexual objects. A major part of their liberation is to play down sexual objectification and to develop other aspects of themselves which have been smothered so long. We respect this. We also understand that a few liberated women will be appalled or disgusted at the open and prominent place that we put sex in our lives; and while this is a natural response from their experience, they must learn what it means for us.

For us, sexual objectification is a focus of our quest for freedom. It is precisely that which we are not supposed to share with each other.

Learning how to be open and good with each other sexually is part of our liberation. And one obvious distinction: objectification of sex for us is something we choose to do among ourselves, while for women it is imposed by their oppressors.

3. *On positions and roles:* Much of our sexuality has been perverted through mimicry of straights, and warped from self-hatred. These sexual perversions are basically anti-gay:

"I like to make it with straight guys"
"I'm not gay, but I like to be 'done' "
"I like to fuck, but don't want to be fucked"
"I don't like to be touched above the neck"

This is role playing at its worst; we must transcend these roles. We strive for democratic, mutual, reciprocal sex. This does not mean that we are all mirror images of each other in bed, but that we break away from roles which enslave us. We already do better in bed than straights do, and we can be better to each other than we have been.

4. *Chickens and studs:* Face it, nice bodies and young bodies are attributes, they're groovy. They are inspiration for art, for spiritual elevation, for good sex. The problem arises only in the inability to relate to people of the same age, or people who don't fit the plastic stereotypes of a good body. At that point, objectification eclipses people, and expresses self-hatred: "I hate gay people, and I don't like myself, but if a stud (or chicken) wants to make it with me. I can pretend I'm someone other than me."

A note on exploitation of children: kids can take care of themselves, and are sexual beings way earlier than we'd like to admit. Those of us who began cruising in early adolescence know this, and we were doing the cruising, not being debauched by dirty old men. Scandals such as the one in Boise, Idaho—blaming a "ring" of homosexuals for perverting their youth—are the fabrications of press and police and politicians. And as for child molesting, the overwhelming amount is done by straight guys to little girls: it is not particularly a gay problem, and is caused by the frustrations resulting from anti-sex puritanism.

5. *Perversion:* We've been called perverts enough to be suspect of any usage of the word. Still many of us shrink from the idea of certain kinds of sex: with animals, sado/masochism, dirty sex (involving piss or shit). Right off, even before we take the time to learn any more, there are some things to get straight:

1. we shouldn't be apologetic to straights about gays whose sex lives we don't understand or share;

2. it's not particularly a gay issue, except that gay people probably are less hung up about sexual experimentation;

3. let's get perspective: even if we were to get into the game of deciding what's good for someone else, the harm done in these "perversions" is undoubtedly less dangerous or unhealthy than is tobacco or alcohol;

4. while they can be reflections of neurotic or self-hating patterns, they may also be enactments of spiritual or important phenomena: *e.g.* sex with animals may be the beginning of interspecies communication: some dolphin-human breakthroughs have been made on the sexual level: *e.g.* one guy who says he digs shit during sex occasionally says it's not the taste or texture, but a symbol that he's so far into sex that those things no longer bug him; *e.g.* sado/masochism, when consensual, can be described as a highly artistic endeavor, a ballet the constraints of which are the thresholds of pain and pleasure.

VI. On Our Ghetto

We are refugees from Amerika. So we came to the ghetto—and as other ghettos, it has its negative and positive aspects. Refugee camps are better than what preceeded them, or people never would have come. But they are still enslaving, if only that we are limited to being ourselves there and only there.

Ghettos breed self-hatred. We stagnate here, accepting the status quo. The status quo is rotten. We are all warped by our oppression, and in the isolation of the ghetto we blame ourselves rather than our oppressors.

Ghettos breed exploitation. Landlords find they can charge exorbitant rents and get away with it, because of the limited area which is safe to live in openly. Mafia control of bars and baths in NYC is only one example of outside money controlling our institutions for their profit. In San Francisco the Tavern Guild favors maintaining the ghetto, for it is through ghetto culture that they make a buck. We crowd their bars not because of their merit but because of the absence of any other social institution. The Guild has refused to let us collect defense funds or pass out gay liberation literature in their bars—need we ask why?

Police or con men who shake down the straight gay in return for not revealing him; the bookstores and movie makers who keep raising prices because they are the only outlet for pornography; heads of "modeling" agencies and other pimps who exploit both the hustlers and the johns—these are the parasites who flourish in the ghetto.

San Francisco—ghetto or free territory: Our ghetto certainly is more beautiful and larger and more diverse than most ghettos, and is certainly freer than the rest of Amerika. That's why we're here. But it isn't ours. Capitalists make money off us, cops patrol us, government tolerates us as long as we shut up, and daily we work for and pay taxes to those who oppress us.

To be a free territory, we must govern ourselves, set up our own institutions, defend ourselves, and use our own energies to improve our lives. The emergence of gay liberation communes and our own paper is a good start. The talk about a gay liberation coffee shop/dance hall should be acted upon. Rural retreats, political action offices, food cooperatives, a free school, unalienating bars and after hours places—they must be developed if we are to have even the shadow of a free territory.

VII. On Coalition

Right now the bulk of our work has to be among ourselves—self educating, fending off attacks, and building free territory. Thus basically we have to have a gay/straight vision of the world until the oppression of gays is ended.

But not every straight is our enemy. Many of us have mixed identities, and have ties with other liberation movements: women, blacks, other minority groups; we may also have taken on an identity which is vital to us: ecology, dope, ideology. And face it: we can't change Amerika alone.

Who do we look to for coalition?

1. *Women's liberation:* Summarizing earlier statements, 1) they are our closest ally; we must try hard to get together with them; 2) a lesbian caucus is probably the best way to attack gay guys' male chauvinism, and challenge the straightness of women's liberation; 3) as males we must be sensitive to their developing identities as women, and respect that; if we *know what our* freedom is about, *they* certainly know what's best for *them.*

2. *Black liberation:* This is tenuous right now because of the uptightness and supermasculinity of many black men (which is understandable). Despite that, we must support their movement, particularly when they are under attack from the establishment; we must show them that we mean business; and we must figure out who our common enemies are: police, city hall, capitalism.

3. *Chicanos:* Basically the same problem as with blacks: trying to overcome mutual animosity and fear, and finding ways to support them. The extra problem of super up-tightness and machismo among Latin cultures, and the traditional pattern of Mexicans beating up "queers," can be overcome: we're both oppressed, and by the same people at the top.

4. *White radicals and ideologues:* We're not, as a group, Marxist or Communist. We haven't figured out what kind of political/economic system is good for us as gays. Neither capitalist or socialist countries have treated us as anything other than *non grata* so far.

But we know we are radical, in that we know the system that we're under now is a direct source of oppression, and it's not a question of getting our share of the pie. The pie is rotten.

We can look forward to coalition and mutual support with radical groups if they are able to transcend their anti-gay and male chauvinist patterns. We support radical and militant demands when they arise, *e.g.* Moratorium, People's Park; but only as a group; we can't compromise or soft-peddle our gay identity.

Problems: because radicals are doing somebody else's thing, they tend to avoid issues which affect them directly, and see us as jeopardizing their "work" with other groups (workers, blacks). Some years ago a dignitary of SDS on a community organization project announced at an initial staff meeting that there would be no homosexuality (or dope) on the project. And recently in New York, a movement group which had a coffee-house get-together after a political rally told the gays to leave when they started dancing together. (It's interesting to note that in this case, the only two groups which supported us were women's liberation and the Crazies.)

Perhaps most fruitful would be to broach with radicals their stifled homosexuality and the issues which arise from challenging sexual roles.

5. *Hip and street people:* A major dynamic of rising gay liberation sentiment is the hip revolution within the gay community. Emphasis on love, dropping out, being honest, expressing yourself through hair and clothes, and smoking dope are all attributes of this. The gays who are the least vulnerable to attack by the establishment have been the freest to express themselves on gay liberation.

We can make a direct appeal to young people, who are not so up tight about homosexuality. One kid, after having his first sex with a male, said, "I don't know what all the fuss is about; making it with a girl just isn't that different."

The hip/street culture has led people into a lot of freeing activities: encounter/sensitivity, the quest for reality, freeing territory for the people, ecological consciousness, communes. These are real points of agreement and probably will make it easier for them to get their heads straight about homosexuality, too.

6. *Homophile groups:* 1) Reformist or pokey as they sometimes are, they are our brothers. They'll grow as we have grown and grow. Do not attack them in straight or mixed company. 2) Ignore their attack on us. 3) Cooperate where cooperation is possible without essential compromise of our identity.

Conclusion: An Outline of Imperatives for Gay Liberation

1. Free ourselves: come out everywhere; initiate self defense and political activity; initiate counter community institutions.

2. Turn other gay people on: talk all the time; understand, forgive, accept.

3. Free the homosexual in everyone: we'll be getting a good bit of shit from threatened latents: be gentle, and keep talking and acting free.

4. We've been playing an act for a long time, so we're consummate actors. Now we can begin to be, and it'll be a good show!

the politics of being queer

PAUL GOODMAN
1969

in essential ways, my homosexual needs have made me a nigger. Most obviously, of course, I have been subject to arbitrary brutality from citizens and the police; but except for being occasionally knocked down, I have gotten off lightly in this respect, since I have a good flair for incipient trouble and I used to be nimble on my feet. What makes me a nigger is that it is not taken for granted that my out-going impulse is my right. Then I have the feeling that it is not my street.

I don't complain that my passes are not accepted; nobody has a claim to be loved (except small children). But I am degraded for making the passes at all, for being myself. Nobody likes to be rejected, but there is a way of rejecting some one that accords him his right to exist and is the next best thing to accepting him. I have rarely enjoyed this treatment.

Allen Ginsberg and I once pointed out to Stokely Carmichael how we were niggers, but he blandly put us down by saying that we could always conceal our disposition and pass. That is, he accorded us the same lack of imagination that one accords to niggers; we did not really exist for him. Interestingly, this dialogue was taking place on (British) national TV, that haven of secrecy. More recently, since the formation of the Gay Liberation Front, Huey Newton of the Black Panthers has welcomed homosexuals to the revolution, as equally oppressed.

In general in America, being a queer nigger is economically and professionally not such a disadvantage as being a black nigger, except for a few areas like government service, where there is considerable fear and furtiveness. (In more puritanic regimes, like present-day

Cuba, being queer is professionally and civilly a bad deal. Totalitarian regimes, whether communist or fascist, seem to be inherently puritanic.) But my own experience has been very mixed. I have been fired three times because of my queer behavior or my claim to the right to it, and these are the only times I have been fired. I was fired from the University of Chicago during the early years of Robert Hutchins; from Manumit School, an offshoot of A. J. Muste's Brookwood Labor College; and from Black Mountain College. These were highly liberal and progressive institutions, and two of them prided themselves on being communities. — Frankly, my experience of radical community is that it does not tolerate my freedom. Nevertheless, I am all for community because it is a human thing, only I seem doomed to be left out.

On the other hand, so far as I know, my homosexual acts and the overt claim to them have never disadvantaged me much in more square institutions. I have taught at half a dozen State universities. I am continually invited, often as chief speaker, to conferences of junior high school superintendents, boards of Regents, guidance counsellors, task forces on delinquency, etc., etc. I say what I think is true — often there are sexual topics; I make passes if there is occasion: and I seem to get invited back. I have even sometimes made out — which is more than I can say for conferences of S.D.S. or the Resistance. Maybe the company is so square that it does not believe, or dare to notice, my behavior; or more likely, such professional square people are more worldly (this is our elderly word for "cool") and couldn't care less what you do, so long as they don't have to face anxious parents and yellow press.

As one grows older, homosexual wishes keep one alert to adolescents and young people more than heterosexual wishes do, especially since our society strongly discountenances affairs between older men and girls or older women and boys. And as a male, the homosexual part of one's character is a survival of early adolescence anyway. But needless to say, there is a limit to this bridging of the generation gap. Inexorably I, like other men who hang around campuses, have found that the succeeding waves of freshmen seem more callow and incommunicable and one stops trying to rob the cradle. Their music leaves me cold. After awhile my best contact with the young has gotten to be with the friends of my own grown children, as an advisor in their politics, rather than by my sexual desires. (The death of my son estranged me from the young world altogether.)

On the whole, although I was desperately poor up to a dozen years ago — I brought up a family on the income of a share-cropper — I don't attribute this to being queer but to my pervasive ineptitude, truculence, and bad luck. In 1945, even the Army rejected me as "Not Military Material" (they had such a stamp) not because I was queer but because I made a nuisance of myself with pacifist action at the examination and also had bad eyes and piles.

Curiously, however, I have been told by Harold Rosenberg and the late Willie Poster that my sexual behavior used to do me damage in precisely the New York literary world. It kept me from being invited to advantageous parties and making contacts to get published. I must believe Harold and Willie because they were unprejudiced observers. What I myself noticed in the 30's and 40's was that I was excluded from the profitable literary circles dominated by Marxists in the 30's and ex-Marxists in the 40's because I was an anarchist. For example, I was never invited to P.E.N. or the Committee for Cultural Freedom. — When C.C.F. finally got around to me at the end of the 50's, I had to turn them down because they were patently tools of the C.I.A. (I said this in print in '61, but they lied their way out.)

To STAY MORALLY alive, a nigger uses various kinds of spite, which is the vitality of the powerless. He may be randomly destructive, since he feels he has no world to lose, and maybe he can prevent the others from enjoying their world. Or he may become an in-group fanatic, feeling that only his own kind are authentic and have soul. There are queers and blacks belonging to both these parties. Queers are "artistic," blacks have "soul." (This is the kind of theory, I am afraid, that is self-disproving; the more you believe it, the stupider you become; it is like trying to prove that you have a sense of humor.) In my own case, however, being a nigger seems to inspire me to want a more elementary humanity, wilder, less structured, more variegated, and where people pay attention to one another. That is, my plight has given energy to my anarchism, utopianism, and Gandhianism. There are blacks in this party too.

My actual political stance is a willed reaction-formation to being a nigger. I act that "the society I live in is mine," the title of one of my books. I regard the President as my public servant whom I pay, and I berate him as a lousy employee. I am more Constitutional than the Supreme Court. And in the face of the gross illegitimacy of the Government—with its Vietnam War, military-industrial cabal, and C.I.A.—I come on as an old-fashioned patriot, neither supine nor more revolutionary than is necessary for my modest goals. This is a quixotic position. Sometimes I sound like Cicero.

In their in-group, Gay Society, homosexuals can get to be fantastically snobbish and a-political or reactionary. This is an understandable ego-defense: "You gotta be better than somebody," but its payoff is very limited. When I give talks to the Mattachine Society, my invariable sermon is to ally with all other libertarian groups and liberation movements, since freedom is indivisible. What we need is not defiant pride and self-consciousness, but social space to live and breathe. The Gay Liberation people have finally gotten the message of indivisible freedom, but they have the usual fanaticism of the Movement.

BUT THERE IS a positive side. In my observation and experience, queer life has some remarkable political values. It can be profoundly democratizing, throwing together every class and group more than heterosexuality does. Its promiscuity can be a beautiful thing (but be prudent about V.D.)

I have cruised rich, poor, middle class, and petit bourgeois; black, white, yellow, and brown; scholars, jocks, Gentlemanly C's, and dropouts; farmers, seamen, railroad men, heavy industry, light manufacturing, communications, business, and finance; civilians, soldiers and sailors, and once or twice cops. (But probably for Oedipal reasons, I tend to be sexually anti-semitic, which is a drag.) There is a kind of political meaning, I guess, in the fact that there are so many types of attractive human beings; but what is more significant is that the many functions in which I am professionally and economically engaged are not altogether cut and dried but retain a certain animation and sensuality. H.E.W. in Washington and I.S. 201 in Harlem are not total wastes, though I talk to the wall in both. I have something to occupy me on trains and buses and during the increasingly long waits at airports. At vacation resorts, where people are idiotic because they are on vacation, I have a reason to frequent the waiters, the boatmen, the room clerks, who are working for a living. I have something to do at peace demonstrations—I am not inspirited by guitar music—though no doubt the TV files and the FBI with their little cameras have pictures of me groping somebody. The human characteristics that are finally important to me and can win my lasting friendship are quite simple: health, honesty, not being cruel or resentful, being willing to come across, having either sweetness or character on the face. As I reflect on it now, only gross stupidity, obsessional cleanliness, racial prejudice, insanity, and being habitually drunk or high really put me off.

In most human societies, of course, sexuality has been one more area in which people can be unjust, the rich buying the poor, males abusing females, sahibs using niggers, the adults exploiting the young. But I think this is neurotic and does not give the best satisfaction. It is normal to befriend and respect what gives you pleasure. St. Thomas, who was a grand moral philosopher though a poor metaphysician, says that the chief human use of sex—as distinguished from the natural law of procreation—is to get to know other persons intimately. That has been my experience.

A common criticism of homosexual promiscuity, of course, is that, rather than democracy, it involves an appalling superficiality of human conduct, so that it is a kind of archetype of the inanity of mass urban life. I doubt that this is generally the case, though I don't know; just as, of the crowds who go to art-galleries, I don't know who are being spoken to by the art and who are being bewildered further—but at least some are looking for something. A young man or woman worries, "Is he interested in me or just in my skin? If I have sex with him, he will regard me as nothing": I think this distinction is meaningless and disastrous; in fact I have always followed up in exactly the opposite way and many of my lifelong personal loyalties had sexual beginnings. But is this the rule or the exception? Given the usual coldness and fragmentation of community life at present, my hunch is that homosexual promiscuity enriches more lives than it desensitizes. Needless to say, if we had better community, we'd have better sexuality too.

I cannot say that my own promiscuity (or attempts at it) has kept me from being possessively jealous of some of my lovers—more of the women than the men, but both. My experience has not borne out what Freud and Ferenczi seem to promise, that homosexuality diminishes this voracious passion, whose cause I do not understand. But the ridiculous inconsistency and injustice of my attitude have sometimes helped me to laugh at myself and kept me from going overboard.

Sometimes it is sexual hunting that brings me to a place where I meet somebody—e.g., I used to haunt bars on the waterfront; sometimes I am in a place for another reason and incidentally hunt—e.g., I go to the TV studio and make a pass at the cameraman; sometimes these are both of a piece—e.g., I like to play handball and I am sexually interested in fellows who play handball. But these all come to the same thing, for in all situations I think, speak, and act pretty much the same. Apart from ordinary courteous adjustments of vocabulary—but not of syntax, which alters character—I say the same say and do not wear different masks or find myself suddenly with a different personality. Perhaps there are two opposite reasons why I can maintain my integrity: on the one hand, I have a strong enough intellect to see how people are for real in our only world, and to be able to get in touch with them despite differences in background; on the other hand, I am likely so shut in my own preconceptions that I don't even notice glaring real obstacles that prevent communication.

How I do come on hasn't made for much success. Since I don't use my wits to manipulate the situation, I rarely get what I want out of it. Since I don't betray my own values, I am not ingratiating. My aristocratic egalitarianism puts people off unless they are secure enough in themselves to be also aristocratically egalitarian. Yet the fact I am not phony or manipulative has also kept people from disliking or resenting me, and I usually have a good conscience. If I happen to get on with some one, there is not a lot of lies and bullshit to clear away.

Becoming a celebrity in the past few years, however, seems to have hurt me sexually rather than helped me. For instance, decent young collegians who might like me and who used to seek me out, now keep a respectful distance from the distinguished man. Perhaps they are now sure that I *must* be interested in their skin, not in them. And the others who seek me out just because I am well known seem to panic when it becomes clear that I don't care about that at all, and I come on as myself. Of course, a simpler explanation of my worsening luck is that I'm growing older every day, probably uglier, and certainly too tired to try hard.

AS A RULE I don't believe in poverty and suffering as a way of learning anything, but in my case the hardship and starvation of my inept queer life have usefully simplified my notions of what a good society is. As with any other addict who cannot get an easy fix, they have kept me in close touch with material hunger. So I cannot take the Gross National Product very seriously, nor status and credentials, nor grandiose technological solutions, nor ideological politics, including ideological liberation movements. For a starving person, the world has got to come across in kind. It doesn't. I have learned to have very modest goals for society and myself: things like clean air, green grass, children with bright eyes, not being pushed around, useful work that suits one's abilities, plain tasty food, and occasional satisfying nookie.

A happy property of sexual acts, and perhaps especially of homosexual acts, is that they are dirty, like life: as Augustine said, *Inter urinas et feces nascimur*, we're born among the piss and shit. In a society as middle class, orderly, and technological as ours, it's good to break down squeamishness, which is an important factor in what is called racism, as well as in cruelty to children and the sterile exiling of the sick and aged. And the illegal and catch-as-catch-can nature of much homosexual life at present breaks down other conventional attitudes. Although I wish I could have had my parties with less apprehension and more unhurriedly, yet it has been an advantage to learn that the ends of docks, the backs of trucks, back alleys, behind the stairs, abandoned bunkers on the beach, and the washrooms of trains are all adequate samples of all the space there is. For both bad and good, homosexual life retains some of the alarm and excitement of childish sexuality.

It is damaging for societies to check any spontaneous vitality. Sometimes it is necessary, but rarely; and certainly not homosexual acts which, so far as I have heard, have never done any harm to anybody. A part of the hostility, paranoia, and automatic competitiveness of our society comes from the inhibition of body contact. But in a very specific way, the ban on homosexuality damages and depersonalizes the educational system. The teacher-student relation is almost aways erotic.—The only other healthy psychological motivations are the mother-hen relevant for small children and the professional who needs apprentices, relevant for graduate schools.—If there is fear and to-do that erotic feeling might turn into overt sex, the teacher-student relation lapses or, worse, becomes cold and cruel. And our culture sorely lacks the pedagogic sexual friendships, homosexual, heterosexual, and lesbian, that have starred other cultures. To be sure, a functional sexuality is probably incompatible with our mass school systems. This is one among many reasons why they should be dismantled.

I recall when *Growing Up Absurd* had had a number of glowing reviews, finally one irritated critic, Alfred Kazin, darkly hinted that I wrote about my Puerto Rican delinquents (and called them "lads") because I was queer for them. News. How could I write a perceptive book if I didn't pay attention, and why should I pay attention to something unless, for some reason, it interested me? The motivation of most sociology, whatever it is, tends to produce worse books. I doubt that anybody would say that my observations of delinquent adolescents or of collegians in the Movement have been betrayed by infatuation. But I do care for them.—Of course, *they* might say, "With such a friend, who needs enemies?"

Yet it is true that an evil of the hardship and danger of queer life in our society, as with any situation of scarcity and starvation, is that we become obsessional and one-track-minded about it. I have certainly spent far too many anxious hours of my life fruitlessly cruising, which I might have spent sauntering for other purposes or for nothing at all, pasturing my soul. But I trust that I have had the stamina, or stubbornness, not to let my obsession cloud my honesty. So far as I know, I have never praised a young fellow's bad poem because he was attractive. But, of course, I am then especially pleased if it is good and I can say so. And best of all, of course, if he is my lover and he shows me something that I can be proud of and push with an editor. Yes, since I began these reflections on a bitter note, let me end them with a happy poem that I like, from *Hawkweed*:

> We have a crazy love affair
> it is wanting each other to be happy.
> Since nobody else cares for that
> we try to see to it ourselves.
>
> Since everybody knows that sex
> is part of love, we make love.
> When that's over, we return
> to shrewdly plotting the other's advantage.
>
> Today you gazed at me, that spell
> is why I choose to live on.
> God bless you who remind me simply
> of the earth and sky and Adam.
>
> I think of such things more than most
> but you remind me simply. Man,
> you make me proud to be a workman
> of the Six Days, practical.

On balance, I don't know whether my choice, or compulsion, of a bisexual life has made me especially unhappy or only averagely unhappy. It is obvious that every way of life has its hang-ups, having a father or no father, being married or single, being strongly sexed or rather sexless, and so forth; but it is hard to judge what other people's experience has been, to make a comparison. I have persistently felt that the world was not made for me, but I have had good moments. And I have done a lot of work, have brought up some beautiful children, and have gotten to be 58 years old.

manifesto issued by the black panthers

HUEY NEWTON
1970

during the past few years, strong movements have developed among women and among homosexuals seeking their liberation. There has been some uncertainty about how to relate to these movements.

Whatever your personal opinions and your insecurities about homosexuality and the various liberation movements among homosexuals and women (and I speak of the homosexuals and women as oppressed groups), we should try to unite with them in a revolutionary fashion. I say "whatever your insecurities are" because, as we very well know sometimes our first instinct is to want to hit a homosexual in the mouth and want a woman to be quiet. We want to hit the homosexual in the mouth because we're afraid we might be homosexual; and we want to hit the woman or shut her up because we're afraid that she might castrate us, or take the nuts that we might not have to start with.

We must gain security in ourselves and therefore have respect and feelings for all oppressed people. We must not use the racist type attitude like the White racists use against people because they are Black and poor. Many times the poorest White person is the most racist, because he's afraid that he might lose something, or discover something that he doesn't have; you're some kind of threat to him. This kind of psychology is in operation when we view oppressed people and we're angry with them because of their particular kind of behavior, or their particular kind of deviation from the established norm.

Remember, we haven't established a revolutionary value system; we're only in the process of establishing it. I don't remember us ever constituting any value that said that a revolution must say offensive things towards homosexuals, or that a revolutionary should make sure that women do not speak out about their own particular kind of oppression. Matter of fact, it's just the opposite: we say that we recognize the women's right to be free. We haven't said much about the homosexual at all, and we must relate to the homosexual movement because it's a real thing. And I know through reading and through my life experience, my observations, that homosexuals are not given freedom and liberty by anyone in the society. Maybe they might be the most oppressed people in the society.

And what made them homosexual? Perhaps it's a whole phenomena that I don't understand entirely. Some people say that it's the decadence of capitalism. I don't know whether this is the case; I rather doubt it. But whatever the case is, we know that homosexuality is a fact that exists, and we must understand it in its purest form: That is, a person should have freedom to use his body in whatever way he wants to. That's not endorsing things in homosexuality that we wouldn't view as revolutionary. But there's nothing to say that a homosexual cannot also be a revolutionary.

And maybe I'm now injecting some of my prejudice by saying that "even a homosexual can be a revolutionary." Quite on the contrary, maybe a homosexual could be the most revolutionary.

When we have revolutionary conferences, rallies and demonstrations there should be full participation of the gay liberation movement and the women's liberation movement. Some groups might be more revolutionary than others. We shouldn't use the actions of a few to say that they're all reactionary or counterrevolutionary, because they're not.

We should deal with the factions just as we deal with any other group or party that claims to be revolutionary. We should try to judge somehow, whether they're operating sincerely, in a revolutionary fashion, from a really oppressed situation. (And we'll grant that if they're women, they're probably oppressed.) If they do things that are un-revolutionary or counter-revolutionary, then criticize that action. If we feel that the group in spirit means to be revolutionary in practice, but they make mistakes in interpretation of the revolutionary philosophy, or they don't understand the dialectics of the social forces in operation, we should criticize that and not criticize them because they're women trying to be free. And the same is true for homosexuals. We should never say a whole movement is dishonest, when in fact they're trying to be honest, they're just making honest mistakes. Friends are allowed to make mistakes. The enemy is not allowed to make mistakes because his whole existence is a mistake, and we suffer from it. But the women's liberation front and gay liberation front are our friends, they are potential allies; and we need as many allies as possible.

We should be willing to discuss the insecurities that many people have about homosexuality. When I say "insecurities," I mean the fear that they're some kind of threat to our manhood. I can understand this fear. Because of the long conditioning process which builds insecurity in the American male, homosexuality might produce certain hangups in us. I have hangups myself about male homosexuality. Where, on the other hand, I have no hangup about female homosexuality. And that's phenomenal in itself. I think it's probably because male homosexuality is a threat to me, maybe, and the females are no threat.

We should be careful about using those terms that might turn our friends off. The terms "faggot" and "punk" should be deleted from our vocabulary, and especially we should not attach names normally designed for homosexuals to men who are enemies of the people, such as Nixon or Mitchell. Homosexuals are not enemies of the people.

We should try to form a working coalition with the Gay liberation and Women's liberation groups. We must always handle social forces in the most appropriate manner. And this is really a significant part of the population—both women, and the growing number of homosexuals that we have to deal with.

an open letter to tennessee williams

MIKE SILVERSTEIN

1971

dear tennessee,

First of all, I love you. I love you because when my own parents were
strangers to me, and didn't know who I was, you were one of the few
people who told me I was beautiful, and showed me how to be courageous and endure. I want you to know this. I also want you to know I
never believed the lies they told me about you. I never believed you
were how they said you were: "the notorious Tennessee Williams, tal-
ented, but a little weird. Insightful, in a sick sort of a way. Interesting,
but never forget how distorted—perverted—his point of view is." The
artist as an item of gossip, and slightly risque story.

This is what my parents told me you were—a queer—when they
deemed I was old enough to know about such things. This is what
the straight critics have always told you you are, and still tell you you
are. Someone who is interesting just to the extent that the people
you write about have nothing to do with them, the human experiences you describe have nothing to do with theirs, and above all,
you are not like them at all, since you are obviously doomed to self-
destruction.

But I knew that what you said did have to do with me, I knew I was
a queer, too—long before my parents deemed I was old enough to
know about such things. I looked to you, because you were a queer,
to tell me about myself, who I was. You, and a few other people, Allen
Ginsberg, Christopher Isherwood, were the only queers I knew, and
the only people who would tell me anything of my humanity.

I'm writing to you now because what you told me wasn't enough.
What you told me I was, what you told me I could be, what you told

me you are, are still too close to what my parents told me I was, what your critics tell you you are. You helped me free myself, but I can see you are not free, because you still tell me we can never be free.

This is what happened: my parents, my friends, my teachers told me that I was a victim, a loser. I must lose in a world where only the winner is a Man, a human being. I was not a real Man. I was a queer, a half-Man, a pseudo-Man, like a woman. I could never aspire to the dignity accorded only to the conqueror, the Man on top. Men fought and won, they fought other Men for the ownership of the rest of creation, lesser peoples, the losers, women, the Third World, as well as the natural environment. I could never be a real Man. I didn't want to own women. I didn't want to fight other men. I wanted to love them, and I can only stand in awe before the material world, not own it. This made me obscene in this society, a dirty joke, contemptuous, the worst thing a Man can be, a loser, a victim.

You were one of the few that contradicted this. You told me to love myself, told me I was of infinite worth, holy. You taught me that only the victims still cling to their humanity. You taught me that the courage the victims show when they endure is the true human courage, and the true expression of our human beauty. You taught me that humanity is destroyed by the fight with Men for the ownership of other people, mastery, the despoilation of the world. You taught me to honor my beauty and courage as a victim, as the real expression of humanity.

You also taught me a sense of acceptance and resignation. Because you also taught that my fate was unavoidable, that because the source of my humanity lies in the endurance of my victimization, the price of my humanity is my submission to the strong and soulless, the Men, who have sold their soul for mastery.

And you spoke not only to me, not only to queers, but to other victims as well, especially to women. I had been taught that women are wild animals, to be hunted, tamed, and used—screwed, fucked, made to serve. You were among the first to teach me that women are my sisters, fellow-victims. Blanche DuBois, Hannah Jelkes, above all the Gnadiges Fraulein—who was all of us—these were the first sisters I had encountered, the first people who shared my victimization, and my humanity. You were the first to teach me to love my sisters. (The critics, those liars, say you hate women.)

But to my sisters and myself, you taught that solace lies in the inevitability of our hopelessness. When I was 16, in 1957, I clung to this teaching, it kept me sane, and gave me courage, because it seemed the only hope, the only humanity I was capable of.

Now I see you being destroyed by the teaching that was the beginning of my liberation. By finding your humanity in your victimization, you have been trapped by your critics into accepting self-destruction as the price of your continued humanity. You have accepted that you must be the loser, the victim they want you to be. Now they have made you a success, a "celebrity," so in order for you to retain the victimhood that is your humanity you must destroy yourself. They have tricked you. They can make you drink—their old weapon against us—so they can call you a drunkard, and show how different you are from them. They want you to join the legion of gay brothers drinking themselves to death in the bars they have set up for us. The straight man's whole world is a conspiracy to destroy you, and they even have your complicity in it, because you believe them when they call you a paranoid for seeing this.

But I will no longer follow that way. Once I learned from you the courage of my humanity. I could no longer accept my victimization. It was still too much like what the straight world said I should be. You are still not free of the straight world, especially your critics. You still believe your humanity must be linked to your victimization, so you still tell us victims, queers, women, too much of what they want us to be told. You tell us that we must submit to their mastery.

Tennessee, what you taught was perhaps the best hope you could offer. Perhaps you spoke for a whole generation of gay men, expressing their humanity in the only way allowed to them. But now we can and must do more, we must refuse to be victims, losers, queers. I will be free. I, only I, will say who I am. I will be gay, I will not accept that I must submit. I will not accept that I am doomed. I will not destroy myself.

You were right in many things, and I must not forget the things you taught me that are true. We must not give up our humanity to become like the Man. We must not seek to conquer, to become the master. Our gayness, our ability to love one another, is our humanity, and it must not be sold for the Man's mastery over others. And if the straight Man's revolution is based on mastery and conquest we will have no part on it.

But we are going to make a gay revolution, a revolution that will be an assertion of humanity. And remembering what you taught us of our humanity, we gay men, together with women, and all the other victims, those who don't seek to be masters, can create it.

And we will fight and even hate if we have to. It is part of one's humanity to hate one's oppressors. If an oppressor has taken from you the ability to hate him, he's taken part of your humanity from you. And here, too, they tricked you into telling us only to endure, not to fight back. We can fight back, struggle and hate, and as long as we are not seduced by the man's victory, conquest, as long as we avoid his love of the fight, the hatred, the revolution will be in the name of humanity, and for the creation of a truly human society without conquest, mastery, winners, or hatred.

This is what I want to tell you. You and I, we need not be victims, queers, in order to be human. You are being destroyed by your oppressors. They are making you kill yourself, as they have made generations of gay men, the best of us, kill ourselves. Stop and fight them. They are lying to you when they tell you you must destroy yourself not to be like them.

And we have discovered something else you must know. They are also lying to you when they tell you that you must be alone. This is another lie they have tricked you into repeating to us. It is they who must always be alone, the Man, the master, whose mastery keeps him apart and afraid of humanity. Join us! We don't have to be alone. We still have the ability to love one another. It is very hard. We have been so corrupted by them. We have learned so much of their mistrust, their will for power, their aloneness. But we are struggling to trust one another, to open ourselves up to one another, to love one another. And before our love; the world will look and wonder. Our love will be a humanity new under the sun, and a new world will be born from it.

Tennessee, look, an army of lovers is beginning to arise. It is being born from among the victims, the queers, the women you were among the first to love. We were queer like you, victims like you. But now we are gay, no longer accepting our victimization, and proudly proclaiming our humanity. We can give you back your love. The world will tremble, fall and be reborn before the love we former losers have for one another. An army of lovers cannot lose.

Love,
MIKE SILVERSTEIN
July 23, 1971

on being different

MERLE MILLER
1971

edward Morgan Forster was a very good writer and a very gutsy
man. In the essay "What I Believe," he said:

> I hate the idea of causes, and if I had to choose between betraying
> my country and betraying my friend, I hope I would have the guts
> to betray my country. Such a choice may scandalize the modern
> reader, and he may stretch out his patriotic hand to the telephone
> at once and ring up the police. It would not have shocked Dante,
> though. Dante places Brutus and Cassius in the lowest circle of
> Hell because they had chosen to betray their friend Julius Caesar
> rather than their country Rome.

It took courage to write those words, just as it does, at times, for
anyone else to repeat them. In the early 1950s, when I wanted to use
them on the title page of a book on blacklisting in television that I
wrote for the American Civil Liberties Union, officials of the
A.C.L.U. advised against it. Why ask for more trouble, they said.
Being against blacklisting was trouble enough. Those were timorous
days. "What I Believe" was included in a book of essays used in secondary schools, but it disappeared from the book around 1954 and
was replaced by something or other from *Reader's Digest*. When I
protested to the publisher, he said—it was a folk saying of the time—
"You have to roll with the tide." The tide was McCarthyism, which
had not then fully subsided—assuming it ever has or will.

Forster was not a man who rolled with the tide. I met him twice,
heard him lecture several times, was acquainted with several of his
friends, and knew that he was homosexual, but I did not know that he

had written a novel, *Maurice*, dealing with homosexual characters, until it was announced last November. On top of the manuscript he wrote: "Publishable—but is it worth it?" The novel, completed in 1915, will, after fifty-five years and the death of Forster, at last be published.

Is it worth it? Even so outspoken a man as Forster had to ask himself that question. It is one thing to confess to political unorthodoxy but quite another to admit to sexual unorthodoxy. Still. Yet. A homosexual friend of mine has said, "Straights don't want to know for sure, and they can never forgive you for telling them. They prefer to think it doesn't exist, but if it does, at least keep quiet about it." And one Joseph Epstein said in *Harper's* in September, 1970:

> . . . however wide the public tolerance for it, it is no more acceptable privately than it ever was . . . private acceptance of homosexuality, in my experience, is not to be found, even among the most liberal-minded, sophisticated, and liberated people. . . . Nobody says, or at least I have never heard anyone say, "Some of my best friends are homosexual." People do say—I say—"fag" and "queer" without hesitation—and these words, no matter who is uttering them, are put-down words, in intent every bit as vicious as "kike" or "nigger."

Is it true? Is that the way it is? Have my heterosexual friends, people I thought were my heterosexual friends, been going through an elaborate charade all these years? I would like to think they agree with George Weinberg, a therapist and author of a book on therapy called *The Action Approach*, who says, "I would never consider a person healthy unless he had overcome his prejudice against homosexuality." But even Mr. Weinberg assumes that there is a prejudice, apparently built-in, a natural part of the human psyche. And so my heterosexual friends had it, maybe still have it? The late Otto Kahn, I think it was, said, "A kike is a Jewish gentleman who has just left the room." Is a fag a homosexual gentleman who has just stepped out? Me?

I can never be sure, of course, will never be sure. I know it shouldn't bother me. That's what everybody says, but it does bother me. It bothers me every time I enter a room in which there is anyone else. Friend or foe? Is there a difference?

When I was a child in Marshalltown, Iowa, I hated Christmas almost as much as I do now, but I loved Halloween. I never wanted to take off the mask; I wanted to wear it everywhere, night and day, always. And I suppose I still do. I have often used liquor, which is another kind of mask, and, more recently, pot.

Then, too, I suppose if my friends have been playing games with me, they might with justice say that I have been playing games with them. It took me almost fifty years to come out of the closet, to stop pretending to be something I was not, most of the time fooling nobody.

But I guess it is never easy to open the closet door. When she talked to the Daughters of Bilitis, a Lesbian organization, late in the summer of 1970, Kate Millett, author of *Sexual Politics*, said, "I'm very glad to be here. It's been kind of a long trip. . . . I've wanted to be here, I suppose, in a surreptitious way for a long time, and I was always too chicken. . . . Anyway, I'm out of the closet. Here I am."

Not surprisingly, Miss Millett is now being attacked more because of what she said to the Daughters of Bilitis than because of what she said in her book. James Owles, president of Gay Activists' Alliance, a militant, nonviolent organization concerned with civil rights for homosexuals, says, "We don't give a damn whether people like us or not. We want the rights we're entitled to."

I'm afraid I want both. I dislike being despised, unless I have done something despicable, realizing that the simple fact of being homosexual is all by itself despicable to many people, maybe, as Mr. Epstein says, to everybody who is straight. Assuming anybody is ever totally one thing sexually.

Mr. Epstein says, "When it comes to homosexuality, we know, or ought to know, that we know next to nothing"—and that seems to me to be true. Our ignorance of the subject is almost as great now as it was in 1915 when Forster wrote *Maurice*—almost as great as it was in 1815 or, for that matter, 1715. Freud did not add much knowledge to the subject, nor have any of his disciples, none that I have read or listened to, none that I have consulted. I have spent several thousand dollars and several thousand hours with various practitioners, and while they have often been helpful in leading me to an understanding of how I got to be the way I am, none of them has ever had any feasible, to me feasible, suggestion as to how I could be any different.

And that includes the late Dr. Edmund Bergler, who claimed not only that he could "cure" me but get rid of my writer's block as well. He did neither. I am still homosexual, and I have a writer's block every morning when I sit down at the typewriter. And it's too late now to change my nature. At fifty, give or take a year or so, I am afraid I will have to make do with me. Which is what my mother said in the beginning.

Nobody seems to know why homosexuality happens, how it happens, or even what it is that does happen. Assuming *it* happens in any one way. Or any thousand ways. We do not even know how prevalent it is. We were told in 1948 by Dr. Alfred C. Kinsey in *Sexual Behavior in the Human Male* that thirty-seven percent of all males have had or will have at least one homosexual experience between adolescence and old age. And last year a questionnaire answered by some twenty thousand readers of *Psychology Today* brought the same response. Thirty-seven percent of the males said that they had had one homosexual experience. (I will be speaking in what follows largely of male homosexuality, which has been my experience.)

Voltaire is said to have had one such experience, with an Englishman. When the Englishman suggested that they repeat it, Voltaire is alleged to have said, "If you try it once, you are a philosopher; if twice, you are a sodomite."

The National Institute of Mental Health says that between three and four million Americans of both sexes are predominantly homosexual, while many others display what the institute delicately calls occasional homosexual tendencies.

But how do they know? Because the closets are far from emptied; there are more in hiding than out of hiding. That has been my experience anyway. And homosexuals come in all shapes and sizes, sometimes in places where you'd least expect to find them. If Jim Bouton is to be believed, in big league baseball and, if we are to go along with Dave Meggysey, in the National Football League. Nobody knows. The question as to who is and who isn't was not asked in the 1970 census.

A Harris survey indicates that sixty-three percent of the American people feel that homosexuals are "harmful" to American society. One wonders—I wondered anyway—how those thirty-seven percent of the males with one admitted homosexual experience responded to the question. After how many such experiences does one get to be harmful? And harmful in what way? The inquisitive Mr. Harris appears not to have asked. Harmful. Feared. Hated. What do the hardhats find objectionable in the young? Their lack of patriotism and the fact that they are all faggots. Aren't they? We're in the midst of a "freaking fag revolution," said the prosecutor in the Chicago conspiracy trial. At least that seems to be the politically profitable thing to say in Chicago.

In the 1950s, McCarthy found that attacking homosexuals paid off almost as well as attacking the Communists, and he claimed they were often the same. Indeed, the District of Columbia police set up a special detail of the vice squad "to investigate links between homosexuality and Communism."

The American Civil Liberties Union recently has been commendably active in homosexual cases, but in the early fifties, when homosexuals and people accused of homosexuality were being fired from all kinds of Government posts, as they still are, the A.C.L.U. was notably silent. And the most silent of all was a closet queen who was a member of the board of directors, myself.

Epstein, a proclaimed liberal, said in *Harper's*:

> If a close friend were to reveal himself to me as being a homosexual, I am very uncertain what my reaction would be — except to say that it would not be simple. . . . If I had the power to do so, I would wish homosexuality off the face of this earth.

I could not help wondering what Epstein, who is, I believe, a literary critic, would do about the person and the work of W. H. Auden, homosexual and generally considered to be the greatest living poet in English. "We must love one another or die." Except for homosexuals?

> Beleaguered by the same
> Negation and despair,
> Show an affirming flame.

The great fear is that a son will turn out to be homosexual. Nobody seems to worry about a Lesbian daughter; nobody talks about it anyway. But the former runs through every level of our culture. In the song Peggy Lee recently made popular, "Love Story," part of the lyric has to do with the son she and her husband will have, *He's got to be straight/We don't want a bent one*. In the Arpège ad this Christmas: "Promises, husbands to wives, 'I promise to stop telling you that our youngest is developing effeminate tendencies.' "

And so on, and on. I should add that not all mothers are afraid that their sons will be homosexuals. Everywhere among us are those dominant ladies who welcome homosexuality in their sons. That way the mothers know they won't lose them to another woman.

And, of course, no television writer would feel safe without at least one fag joke per script. Carson, Cavett, and Griffin all give their audiences the same knowing grin when *that* subject is mentioned, and audiences always laugh, though somewhat nervously.

Is homosexuality contagious? Once again, nobody seems to know for sure. The writer Richard Rhodes reports that those tireless and tedious investigators Dr. William Masters and Mrs. Virginia Johnson of St. Louis have got into the subject of homosexuality. And Masters *hinted* to Rhodes that his clinical work had shown that "homosexual seduction in adolescence is generally the predetermining factor in later homosexual choice."

One should not hold the indefatigable doctor to a "hint," but the Wolfenden Committee set up by the British Government in the fifties to study homosexuality and prostitution found the opposite:

> It is a view widely held, and one which found favor among our police and legal witnesses, that seduction in youth is the decisive factor in the production of homosexuality as a condition, and we are aware that this condition has done much to alarm parents and teachers. We have found no convincing evidence in support of this contention. Our medical witnesses unanimously held that seduction has little effect in inducing a settled pattern of homosexual behavior, and we have been given no grounds from other sources which contradict their judgment. Moreover, it has been suggested to us that the fact of being seduced often does less harm to the victim than the publicity which attends the criminal proceedings against the offender and the distress which undue alarm sometimes leads parents to show.

Martin Hoffman, a San Francisco psychiatrist who has written a book about male homosexuality called *The Gay World*, said in a recent issue of *Psychology Today*:

> Until we know about the mechanisms of sexual arousal in the central nervous system and how learning factors can set the triggering devices for those mechanisms, we cannot have a satisfactory theory of homosexual behavior. We must point out that heterosexual behavior is as much of a scientific puzzle as homosexual behavior. . . . We assume that heterosexual arousal is somehow natural and needs no explanation. I suggest that to call it natural is to evade the whole issue; it is as if we said it's natural for the sun to come up

in the morning and left it at that. Is it possible that we know less about human sexuality than the medieval astrologers knew about the stars?

I know this. Almost the first words I remember hearing, maybe the first words I choose to remember hearing, were my mother's, saying, "We ordered a little girl, and when you came along, we were somewhat disappointed." She always claimed that I came from Montgomery Ward, and when I would point out that there was no baby department in the Monkey Ward catalogue, she would say, "This was special."

I never knew what that meant, but I never asked. I knew enough. I knew that I was a disappointment. "But we love you just the same," my mother would say, "and we'll have to make do."

We had to make do with a great many things in those days. The Depression came early to our house, around 1927, when my father lost all his money in the Florida land boom, and once we got poor, we stayed poor. "You'll have the wing for supper, because this is a great big chicken and will last for days, and tomorrow you can take a whole leg to school in your little lunch pail and have it all to yourself." Day-old bread, hand-me-down clothes that had once belonged to more prosperous cousins, holes in the soles of my shoes—all of it. I was a combination of Oliver Twist and Little Nell.

They say that the Depression and the World War were the two central experiences of my generation, and that may be. I certainly had more than enough of both, but I was never really hungry for food. It was love I craved, approval, forgiveness for being what I could not help being. And I have spent a good part of my life looking for those things, always, as a few psychologists have pointed out, in the places I was least likely to find them.

My baby blankets were all pink, purchased before the disaster, my birth. The lace on my baby dress was pink; my bonnet was fringed with pink, and little old ladies were forever peering into the baby buggy and crib, saying, "What an adorable little girl." They kept on saying that until I got my first butch haircut, at four, just before I started kindergarten. Until then I had long, straight hair, mouse-brown, lusterless, and long hair was just as unpopular in Marshall-town then as it is now.

Not until college did I read that Oscar Wilde's mother started him down the garden path by letting his hair grow and dressing him as a little girl. As Oscar said, "Children begin by loving their parents; as they grow older they judge them; sometimes they forgive them."

I was four years old when I started school. My mother had told them I was five; I was somewhat precocious, and she may just have wanted to get me out of the house. But butch haircut or not, some boys in the third grade took one look at me and said, "Hey, look at the sissy," and they started laughing. It seems to me now that I heard that word at least once five days a week for the next thirteen years, until I skipped town and went to the university. Sissy and all the other words—pansy, fairy, nance, fruit, fruitcake, and less printable epithets. I did not encounter the word faggot until I got to Manhattan. I'll tell you this, though. It's not true, that saying about sticks and stones; it's words that break your bones.

They used to call my friend Sam G. a kike, but that was behind his back. The black boy and black girl in my high school class were "jigs" or "coons," but that, too, was behind their backs. Some Catholic boys were "mackerel snappers," but to their faces only if they were much younger and weaker.

I was the only one they looked right at when they said the damning words, and the only thing I can think of to my credit is the fact that I almost never ran away; I almost always stared them down; I almost never cried until later, when I was alone.

I admit I must have been a splendid target, undersized always, the girlish voice, the steel-rimmed glasses, always bent, no doubt limp of wrist, and I habitually carried a music roll. I studied both piano and violin all through school, and that all by itself was enough to condemn one to permanent *sissydom*.

When I was doing a television documentary of Harry Truman's life, he said at one point, "I was never what you'd call popular when I went to school. The popular boys were the athletes with their big, tight fists, and I was never like that. . . . I always had a music roll and wore thick glasses; I was wall-eyed, you know. . . . I stopped playing the piano when I was fourteen years old. Where I come from, playing the piano wasn't considered the proper thing for a boy to do."

I said, "Mr. President, did they ever call you 'four-eyes' when you were a little boy?"

"Oh, yes," he said, " 'four-eyes,' 'sissy,' and a lot of other things. When that happens, what you have to do is, you have to work harder than they do and be smarter, and if you are, things usually turn out all right in the end."

As a child I wanted to be the girl my mother had had in mind— or else the All-American boy everybody else so admired. Since sex changes were unheard of in those days, I clearly couldn't be a girl;

so I tried the other. I ate carloads of Wheaties, hoping I'd turn into another Jack Armstrong, but I still could neither throw nor catch a baseball. I couldn't even see the thing; I'd worn glasses as thick as plate-glass windows since I was three. ("You inherited your father's eyes, among other weaknesses.") I sold enough *Liberty* magazines to buy all the body-building equipment Charles Atlas had to offer, but it did no good. I remained an eighty-nine-pound weakling year after year. And when the voices of all the other boys in my class had changed into a very low baritone, I was still an uncertain soprano, and remained that until I got to the University of Iowa in Iowa City and, among other disguises, lowered my voice at least two octaves so that I could get a job as a radio announcer on the university station.

I also became city editor of *The Daily Iowan* and modeled myself after a character out of *The Front Page*, wearing a hat indoors and out, talking out of the corner of my mouth, never without a cigarette, being folksy with the local cops, whom I detested, one and all. I chased girls, never with much enthusiasm I'm afraid, and denounced queers—I hadn't yet come on the word fag—with some regularity in the column I wrote for the *Iowan*. Most of those odd people were in the university theater, or so I chose to pretend, and while I never came right out and said they were sexually peculiar, I hinted at it. They wore what was by the standards of the time long hair, and I denounced that as well. What a fink I was—anything to avoid being called a sissy again.

I was afraid I would never get into the army, but after the psychiatrist tapped me on the knee with a little hammer and asked how I felt about girls, before I really had a chance to answer, he said, "Next," and I was being sworn in. For the next four years as an editor of *Yank*, first in the Pacific and then in Europe, I continued to use my deepest city-editor's-radio-announcer's voice, ordered reporters and photographers around and kept my evenings to myself, especially in Paris.

After the war, I became as much a part of the Establishment as I had ever been, including servitude as an editor of *Time*. I remember in particular a long discussion about whether to use the picture of a British composer on the cover because a researcher had discovered that he was . . . I am sure if there was a vote, I voted against using the picture.

A little later, after finishing my first successful novel, *That Winter*, which became a best seller, I decided there was no reason at all why

I couldn't be just as straight as the next man. I might not be able to play baseball, but I could get married.

Peter Ilyich Tchaikovsky had the same idea. Maybe marriage would cure him of what he called "The." But, afterwards, in a letter to his friend Nadejda von Meck, he wrote:

> ... I saw right away that I could never love my wife and that the *habit* on which I had counted would never come. I fell into despair and longed for death. ... My mind began to go. ...

Peter Ilyich's marriage lasted only two weeks. My own lasted longer and was not quite so searing an experience, but it could not have succeeded.

Lucy Komisar says in *Washington Monthly* that this country is obsessed by what she calls "violence and the masculine mystique," which is certainly true enough. "The enemies of national 'virility' are called 'effete,' a word that means 'sterile, spent, worn-out,' and conjures up the picture of an effeminate panty-waist." Also true, but Americans are certainly not the first people to get uptight about "virility."

Philip of Macedon was forever fussing at Olympias because he claimed she was making their son Alexander effeminate. And, to be sure, Alexander turned out to be at least bisexual, maybe totally homosexual. How else could one explain his grief at the death of his lover, Hephaestion? According to Plutarch:

> Alexander was so beyond all reason transported that, to express his sorrow, he immediately ordered the manes and tails of all his horses and mules cut, and threw down the battlements of the neighboring cities. The poor physician he crucified, and forbade playing on the flute or any other musical instrument in the camp a great while. ...

Gore Vidal has been quoted as saying, "The Italians are sexual opportunists. Anything that feels good, they're for it." Which may be true, but I cannot imagine an Italian father who would not be devastated if he found that his son was homosexual. Or, for that matter, a father in any country in Western society. In England, where the Sexual Offenses Act has been on the law books since 1967, ten years after the recommendations of the Wolfenden Committee, Anthony Gray, director of an organization that helps sexual minorities, says that even today "... the briefest experience is enough to convince one that discrimination against known homosexuals is still the rule rather than the exception." Gray notes that homosexuals still cannot belong to the Civil Service and are still likely to lose their jobs if "found out."

Most members of the Gay Liberation Front appear to believe that Marxism is the answer, which is odd because in Communist China homosexuals are put in prisons for brainwashing that are called "hospitals for ideological reform." Chairman Mao has said, "Our object in exposing errors and criticizing short-comings is like that of a doctor in curing a disease." In Cuba homosexuals have been placed in concentration camps.

Still, as Huey P. Newton, Supreme Commander of the Black Panther Party, has said, there is no reason to think a homosexual cannot be a revolutionary. In late summer of 1970, shortly after the New York chapter of the Gay Liberation Front gave a $500 donation to the Panthers, Newton, in a rambling, rather tortured statement said, "What made them homosexuals? Some people say that it's the decadence of capitalism. I don't know whether this is the case; I rather doubt it. . . . But there's nothing to say that a homosexual cannot also be a revolutionary. . . . Quite the contrary, maybe a homosexual could be the most revolutionary."

On the other hand, Eldridge Cleaver in *Soul on Ice* gives what I am sure is a more prevalent view among the Panthers: "Homosexuality is a sickness, just as are baby-rape or wanting to become head of General Motors."

Of course, the Soviet Union claims not to have any homosexuals. I cannot comment on the validity of that claim, never having been there, but I do know that when one of the Russian ballet companies is in town, you can hear a great many Russian accents on West 42d Street and in various gay bars.

Growing up in Marshalltown, I was allowed to take as many books as I wanted from the local library, and I always wanted as many as I could carry, eight or ten at a time. I read about sensitive boys, odd boys, boys who were lonely and misunderstood, boys who really didn't care all that much for baseball, boys who were teased by their classmates, books about all of these, but for years nobody in any of the books I read was ever tortured by the strange fantasies that tore at me every time, for instance, my mother insisted I go to the "Y" to learn how to swim. They swam nude at the "Y," and I never went. Lead me not into temptation. In gym—it was required in high school—I always tried to get in and out of the locker room before anybody else arrived.

And in none of the books I read did anybody feel a compulsion, and compulsion it surely was, to spend so many hours, almost as many as I spent at the library, in or near the Minneapolis & St. Louis railroad station, where odd, frightening things were written on the walls of the men's room. And where in those days, there were always boys in their teens and early twenties who were on their way to and from somewhere in freight cars. Boys who were hungry and jobless and who for a very small amount of money, and sometimes none at all, were available for sex; almost always they were. They needed the money, and they needed someone to recognize them, to actually see them.

That was the way it happened the first time. The boy was from Chicago, and his name was Carl. He was seventeen, and I was twelve and the aggressor. I remember every detail of it; I suppose one always does. Carl hadn't eaten, said he hadn't eaten for two days. His father was a plumber, unemployed, and his mother was, he said rather vaguely, "away, hopefully forever." I remember once I said, "But why don't you go home anyway?" And he said, "Where would that be?"

Years later a boy I met on West 42d Street said it best, about the boys in my childhood and the boys on all the streets of all the cities where they wait. He was the next-to-youngest child in a very poor family of nine, and once he ran away from home for two days and two nights, and when he got back, nobody knew that he had been gone. Then, at nineteen, he discovered The Street, and he said, "All of a sudden here were all these men, and they were looking at me."

The boys who stopped by at the M. and St. L. in Marshalltown all had stories, and they were all anxious to tell them. They were all lonely and afraid. None of them ever made fun of me. I was never beaten up. They recognized, I guess, that we were fellow aliens with no place to register.

Like my three friends in town. They were aliens, too: Sam, whose father ran a grocery store my mother wouldn't patronize. ("Always buy American, Merle, and don't you forget it. We don't know *where* the Jews send the money you spend in one of their stores.") A girl in a wheelchair, a polio victim; we talked through every recess in school. And there was the woman with a clubfoot who sold tickets at the Casino, a movie house, and let me in for free—tickets couldn't have been a dime then, but they were—until I was sixteen, and, as I say, skipped town.

The black boy and the black girl in my high school class never spoke to me, and I never spoke to them. That was the way it was. It never occurred to me that that was not necessarily the way it was meant to be.

There were often black boys on the freight trains, and we talked and had sex. Their stories were always sadder than anybody else's. I never had any hangups about the color of somebody's skin. If you were an outcast, that was good enough for me. I once belonged to twenty-two organizations devoted to improving the lot of the world's outcasts. The only group of outcasts I never spoke up for publicly, never donated money to or signed an ad or petition for were the homosexuals. I always used my radio announcer's voice when I said "No."

I was fourteen when I happened on a book called *Winesburg, Ohio.* I don't know how. Maybe it was recommended by the librarian, a kind and knowing woman with the happy name of Alice Story. Anyway, there at last, in a story called "Hands," were the words I had been looking for. I was not the only sissy in the world:

> Adolf Myers was meant to be a teacher . . . In their feeling for the
> boys under their charge such men are not unlike the finer sort of
> women in their love of men.

Sherwood Anderson's story ended unhappily. Of course. How else could it end?

> And then the tragedy. A half-witted boy of the school becomes
> enamored of the young master. In his bed at night he imagined
> unthinkable things and in the morning went forth to tell his dreams
> as facts. Strange, hideous accusations fell from his loose-hung lips.
> Through the Pennsylvania town went a shiver. Hidden, shadowy
> doubts that had been in men's minds concerning Adolf Myers were
> galvanized into beliefs.

I must have read "Hands" more than any story before or since. I can still quote it from beginning to end:

> They had intended to hang the schoolmaster, but something in his
> figure, so small, white, and pitiful, touched their hearts and they let
> him escape.

Naturally. If you were *that way*, what else could you expect? Either they ran you out of town or you left before they got around to it. I decided on the latter. I once wrote that I started packing to leave Marshalltown when I was two years old, which is a slight exaggeration.

> As he ran into the darkness, they repented of their weakness and ran after him, swearing and throwing sticks and great balls of soft mud at the figure that screamed and ran faster into the darkness.

Winesburg was published in 1919, and one of the terrifying things is that the people in any town in the United States, quite likely any city, too, would react very much the same way today, wouldn't they?

Look what happened only fifteen years ago, in 1955, in Boise, Idaho, when a "homosexual underworld" was uncovered. The "upright" citizens panicked, and some people left town, some were run out of town, and others were sentenced to long prison terms.

In a perceptive and thorough account of what happened, *The Boys of Boise*, John Gerassi reports that a lawyer told him that during the height of the hysteria the old American custom of a night on the town with the boys disappeared entirely:

> You never saw so many men going out to the bars at night with their wives and girl friends . . . we used to have a poker game once a week. Well, for a few weeks we canceled them. Then one of the guys got an idea: "We'll invite a girl to play with us. You know, it's not very pleasant to play poker with women, not when you're in a serious game. But that's what we had to do."

I have been back to Marshalltown only briefly in all the years since my escape, but a few years ago I did return to a reunion of my high school class. I made the principal speech at the banquet, and at the end there was enough applause to satisfy my ego temporarily, and various of my classmates, all of whom looked depressingly middle-aged, said various pleasant things, after which there was a dance.

I have written about that before, but what I have not written about, since I was still not ready to come out of the closet, is that a little while after the dance began, a man whose face had been only vaguely familiar and whose name I would not have remembered if he had not earlier reminded me came up, an idiot grin on his face, his wrists limp, his voice falsetto, and said, "How about letting me have this dance, sweetie?" He said it loud enough for all to hear.

I said, "I'm terribly sorry, but my dance card is all filled up." By no means the wittiest of remarks, but under the circumstances it was the best I could manage.

Later, several people apologized for what he had said, but I wondered (who would not?) how many of them had been tempted to say the same thing. Or would say something of the kind after I had gone. Fag, faggot, sissy, queer. A fag is a homosexual gentleman who has just left the room.

And the man who said it was a successful newspaper executive in Colorado, in his mid-forties, a father of five, I was told, a grandfather. After all those years, twenty-seven of them, was he still . . . what? Threatened by me? Offended? Unsettled? Challenged? No children or grandchildren around to be perverted. Was his own sexual identity so shaky that . . . ? A closet queen at heart? No, that's too easy. And it's too easy to say that he's the one who needs treatment, not me. George Weinberg says:

> The "homosexual problem," as I have described it here, is the problem of condemning *variety* in human existence. If one cannot enjoy the fact of this variety, at the very least one must learn to become indifferent to it, since obviously it is here to stay.

The fear of it simply will not go away, though. A man who was once a friend, maybe my best friend, the survivor of five marriages, the father of nine, not too long ago told me that his eldest son was coming to my house on Saturday: "Now, please try not to make a pass at him."

He laughed. I guess he meant it as a joke; I didn't ask.

And a man I've known, been acquainted with, let's say, for twenty-five years, called from the city on a Friday afternoon before getting on the train to come up to my place for the weekend. He said, "I've always leveled with you, Merle, and I'm going to now. I've changed my mind about bringing—[his sixteen-year-old son]. I'm sure you understand.

I said that, no, I didn't understand. Perhaps he could explain it to me.

He said, "———is only an impressionable kid, and while I've known you and know you wouldn't, but suppose you had some friends in, and . . . ?"

I suggested that he not come for the weekend. I have never molested a child my whole life through, never seduced anybody, assuming that word has meaning, and, so far as I know, neither have any of my homosexual friends. Certainly not in my living room or bedroom. Moreover, I have known quite a few homosexuals, and I have listened to a great many accounts of how they got that way or think they got that way. I have never heard anybody say that he (or she) got to be homosexual because of seduction.

But, then, maybe it is contagious, floating in the air around me, like a virus. Homosexuals themselves often seem to think so. How else can you explain the self-pitying *The Boys in the Band?*

Martin Hoffman, the San Francisco therapist I mentioned earlier, says:

> Self-condemnation pervades the homosexual world and, in concert with the psychodynamic and biological factors that lead toward promiscuity, makes stable relationships a terrific problem. In spite of the fact that so many homosexuals are lonely and alone, they can't seem to find someone with whom to share even part of their lives. This dilemma is the core problem of the gay world and stems in large measure from the adverse self-definitions that society imprints on the homosexual mind. Until we can change these ancient attitudes, many men—including some of our own brothers, sons, friends, colleagues and children yet unborn—will live out their lives in the quiet desperation of the sad gay world.

Perhaps. None of my homosexual friends are any too happy, but then very few of my heterosexual friends—supposed friends, I should say—are exactly joyous, either. And as for the promiscuity and short-term relationships, neither of those has been quite true in my case, and only recently I attended an anniversary party of two homosexuals who had been together for twenty-five years, reasonably constant, reasonably happy. They still hold hands, though not in public, and they are kind to each other, which is rare enough anywhere these days.

Late in October, 1970, members of the Gay Activists Alliance staged an all-day sit-in at *Harper's* to protest the Epstein article, surely the first time in the 120-year history of the magazine that that has happened. And as Peter Fisher, a student at Columbia who helped organize the sit-in, kept saying, "What you don't understand is that there's been a revolution."

I'm not sure it's a full-scale revolution yet, but there's been a revolt, and for thousands of young homosexuals, and some not so young, the quiet desperation that Hoffman talks about is all over. They are neither quiet nor desperate.

The whole thing began with an event that has been compared to the Boston Tea Party or the firing on Fort Sumter: the Stonewall Rebellion. On June 28, 1969, the police started to raid a gay bar in the West Village, the Stonewall Inn. The police are forever raiding gay bars, especially around election time, when they also move in on West 42d Street. And in the past, what you did was, you took the cops' abuse, and sometimes you went off with only a few familiar epithets or a hit on the head. And sometimes you were taken to the station on one charge or another and, usually, released the next morning.

But that is not what happened on June 28, 1969. A friend of mine who was there said, "It was fantastic. The crowd was a fairly typical weekend crowd, your usual queens and kids from the sticks, and the people that are always around the bars, mostly young. But this time instead of submitting to the cops' abuse, the sissies fought back. They started pulling up parking meters and throwing rocks and coins at the cops, and the cops had to take refuge in the bar and call for reinforcements. . . . It was beautiful."

That was the beginning, and on the anniversary last summer between five thousand and fifteen thousand gay people of both sexes marched up Sixth Avenue from Sheridan Square to the Sheep Meadow in Central Park for a "gay-in." Other, smaller parades took place in Chicago and Los Angeles, and all three cities survived the sight and sound of men with their arms around men and women kissing women, chanting, "Shout it loud, gay is proud," "Three-five-seven-nine, Lesbians are mighty fine," carrying signs that said, "We Are the People Our Parents Warned Us Against," singing "We Shall Overcome."

And something else perhaps even more important happened during the 1970 elections. When Arthur J. Goldberg, running for Governor of New York, paid what was to have been a routine campaign visit to the intersection of 85th and Broadway, more than three dozen members of the G.A.A. were waiting for him. They shook his hand and asked if he was in favor of fair employment for homosexuals and of repeal of the state laws against sodomy. Goldberg's answer to each question was, "I think there are more important things to think about."

But before the election Goldberg had issued a public statement answering yes to both questions, promising as well to work against police harassment of homosexuals. The candidates for senator, Richard Ottinger and Charles Goodell, also issued statements supporting constitutional rights for homosexuals. Of course, Governor Rockefeller and Senator Buckley, the winners, remained silent on those issues, but Representative Bella Abzug, one of the earliest supporters of G.A.A., won, and so did people like State Assemblyman Antonio Olivieri, the first Democrat elected in the 66th Assembly District in fifty-five years. Olivieri took an ad in a G.A.A. benefit program that served to thank the organization for its support.

Marty Robinson, an extremely vocal young man, a carpenter by profession, who was then in charge of political affairs for G.A.A., said that "this election serves notice on every politician in the state and nation that homosexuals are not going to hide any more. We're becoming militant, and we won't be harassed or degraded any more."

John Paul Hudson, one of the alliance's founders, said: "G.A.A. is a political organization. Everything is done with an eye toward political effect. . . . G.A.A. adopted this policy because all oppression of homosexuals can only be ended by means of a powerful political bloc."

For an organization only a little more than a year old and with only 180 paid-up members, G.A.A. has certainly made itself heard. And that, according to Arthur Evans, another fiery member, is just the beginning. He said, "At the end of June we had a statement that gay is good. We had a joyous celebration, as is right. But today we know not only that gay is good, gay is angry. We are telling all the politicians and elected officials of New York State that they are going to become responsible to the people. We will make them responsible to us, or we will stop the conduct of the business of government." Well.

Small wonder that the Mattachine Society, which for twenty years has been trying to educate straight people to accept homosexuals, is now dismissed by some members of G.A.A. and the Gay Liberation Front as "the N.A.A.C.P. of our movement."

Laws discriminating against homosexuals will almost surely be changed. If not this year, in 1972; if not in 1972, in 1976; if not in 1976 . . .

Private acceptance of homosexuals and homosexuality will take somewhat longer. Most of the psychiatric establishment will continue to insist that homosexuality is a disease, and homosexuals, unlike the blacks, will not benefit from any guilt feelings on the part of liberals. So far as I can make out, there simply aren't any such feelings. On the contrary, most people of every political persuasion seem to be too uncertain of their own sexual identification to be anything but defensive. Fearful. And maybe it is contagious. Prove it isn't.

I have never infected anybody, and it's too late for the head people to do anything about me now. Gay is good. Gay is proud. Well, yes, I suppose. If I had been given a choice (but who is?), I would prefer to have been straight. But then, would I rather not have been me? Oh, I think not, not this morning anyway. It is a very clear day in late December, and the sun is shining on the pine trees outside my studio. The air is extraordinary clear, and the sky is the color it gets only at this time of year, dark, almost navy-blue. On such a day I would not choose to be anyone else or any place else.

take a lesbian to lunch

RITA MAE BROWN
1972

women's tragedy is that we are not defeated by hybris, gods or our own passion but by society, a society controlled by insensitive men. We are not the masters of that social organization and so it towers over us just as Moira, fate, towered over the mythical chauvinist, Oedipus. Women began to fight that corrupting, anti-human, anti-life structure. This beginning is known as the Women's Liberation Movement.

However, before there was a WLM there were always a number of women who questioned the system and found it destructive to themselves. Those women became women-identified. The male culture's word for this kind of women is lesbian. This is a narrow definition so typical of the male culture's vulgar conceptual limitations—the term applies only to sexual activity between women. To us, to be a lesbian means much more. It means you move toward women and are capable of making a total commitment to women.

The male party line concerning lesbians is that women became lesbians out of reaction to men. This is a pathetic illustration of the male ego's inflated proportions. I became a lesbian because of women, because women are beautiful, strong and compassionate. Secondarily, I became a lesbian because the culture that I live in is violently anti-woman. How could I, a woman, participate in a culture that denies me my humanity? How can any woman in touch with herself participate in this culture? To give a man support and love before giving it to a sister is to support that culture, that power system, for men receive the benefits of sexism regardless of race or social position. The higher up they are on the color line and the salary line the more benefits they receive from society but all men benefit from sexism.

Proof of the pudding is that the most rabid man-haters are heterosexual women, and with good reason, for they are directly oppressed
by individual men. The contradiction of supporting the political system that oppresses you and the individuals who benefit by that system, men, is much more intense for the heterosexual woman than
for the homosexual woman. Lesbians are oppressed by the male
power system but not by individual men in the same intimate, insid-
ious fashion. Therefore, we lesbians are the ultimate insult to the sexist male and the world he has built up around his weaknesses. Why?
Because we ignore him. Heterosexual women are still caught up in
reacting to him. Because we ignore him, because we are the ultimate
insult, we pay and we pay heavily. Following are some instances of
how a woman pays for lesbianism in America. The examples are
from my direct experience.

In 1962, when I was sixteen, a schoolmate's father threatened to
shoot me on sight. He had found love letters that I had written to his
daughter. He literally locked the girl up. He drove her to and from
school. She couldn't go out at night, and she couldn't receive phone
calls unless he screened them. He went so far as to go to the administration of the school and have her transferred out of the classes we
had together. I also got kicked off the student council, thanks to his
moral purity. Naturally, our classmates were surprised at my getting
bounced and at the sudden ending of my friendship with this girl.
Many of them vaguely figured out what was happening. The result of
this sleuthing was that our friends split over whether we were lesbians
or whether we weren't. Our closest friends hotly defended us by saying we weren't lesbians—that we couldn't possibly be such horrible
creatures. Our not-so-close friends smacked their lips over the scan-
dal, and in a short time it was all over our high school as well as every
other high school in the city.

The gossip was short-lived as I flatly stated that I did love the girl
and if that was lesbianism I was damn glad of it. The gossip stopped
and so did the friendships. My closest friends nearly trampled each
other in the rush for the door. My civics teacher and student council
advisor, a pompous, pasty-faced asshole who proudly proclaimed his
membership in the John Birch Society, declared as he canned me,
that I was unhealthy. I was sick all right, but not in the way they imagined—I was sick of all those dirty looks, snickers and outright fights I
was having with everyone who crossed my path.

The next year I went to the state university. I had won a scholarship, which was a good thing because my family's total income for

1962 was $2,300. The university had around 15,000 students, if not from the state itself, from neighboring Southern states. Everything was fine until I became mildly involved in the just-beginning civil rights movement. I had been seen on the black side of town. One of my friends called me into her room to talk about my sudden change for the worse. I told her I thought just the opposite about my behavior. She upbraided me for mixing with those people—blacks and Jews (who were behind it all, of course—can you believe it?) I told her I didn't give a flying fuck about race or sex. As far as I was concerned, it was the person that counted, not pigment, not sex. At that time, I believed that.

Within three hours of that conversation I was called into the office of the Dean of Women, guardian of morals and the flowers of Southern womanhood. This cheery-faced, apple-cheeked, ex-Marine sergeant offered me a cigarette with a tight-lipped smile and then blasted me with, "Now what's this I hear about your relationships with other women?" She went on to accuse me of seducing the president of Delta Delta Delta, of seducing numerous innocents in the dorms and, sin of sins, of sleeping with black men. She threw in a few black women for good measure. If I had kept such a busy schedule, I think I would have been too exhausted to walk into her office.

She hinted in heavy tones that in addition to my numerous sexual perversions that I was also a communist and was "stirring up the nigras." In a burst of anger I cracked her with: "How dare you accuse me of lesbianism when you are a lesbian yourself? You persecute me to protect yourself, you broad-assed sow." Rational discourse collapsed. She put me under house arrest, and I couldn't leave the dorms at night. I was also checked out hourly by the resident counselor in the dorm and had the pleasure of reporting to the university psychiatrist once a day, and if I didn't, the campus guards went out looking for me. My psychiatrist couldn't speak good English, but he was a whiz at Turkish. I couldn't speak Turkish. He had, however, perfected one English phrase with remarkable enunciation: "You sleep with women?" He had a habit of embracing me after our half hour of international exchange. I question whether those embraces were part of my therapy since he always had a hard-on.

All of this happened during exam period. One night I was busy cramming for a physics exam when a self-appointed contingent of physical education majors burst into my room. It was quite a shock since no one had been speaking to me since the beginning of this mess, but they didn't exactly speak to me, either. Frightened past reason, these wild-eyed women informed me that if I even hinted that they were lesbians or that any of their beloved faculty fell into that damned category—they would kill me. Nothing like a little melodrama to spice my misery.

The next day, I was treated to an example of how sexism kills minds. I walked into my exam, and silence fell over the crowded auditorium. When I would try to sit in an empty seat, the student next to it would inform me that it was taken, that I should drop dead, that it was broken—plus a few I don't remember. I took my exam sitting on the floor, and I know I got an "A." I had a 99 percent average before the exam, and the exam itself was easy. When the grades were reported, my average was 61 percent. No explanation, just 61 percent.

Southern hospitality does not apply if you are a lesbian, and if you dared to wink an eye at civil rights. I couldn't get a job. My scholarships were suspended, so I couldn't go back to school. In other words, I couldn't go home again. And so, after a long series of adventures, I arrived in New York City. I felt as though I were in the hanging gardens of neon. Home now was an abandoned red-and-black Hudson automobile near Washington Square. I lived in the back seat, with another orphan, a kitten named Baby Jesus. The front seat was inhabited by Calvin, a South Carolina homosexual. Calvin had suffered many beatings from his heterosexual black brothers because of his homosexuality. Our pain was a common bond: Nobody wants their queers. We stayed together a short time until Calvin found someone to keep him.

Eventually, I got a job as a waitress. I had to wear demeaning clothes, and put up with passes that ranged from the tragically transparent to the truly creative. I saved money by living in a cold-water flat, without stove or heat. I wore few clothes and saved money until I could enroll in New York University. Finally, I earned a scholarship and finished my education.

During the week I would sometimes go into gay bars. To avoid paying for drinks, I grabbed the first empty glass in sight and went to the bathroom where I filled it with water. If anyone asked me what I was drinking, I said "gin." The women I met were interesting. Many were tied into establishment jobs and others were secretaries trying to look like the women tied into the establishment jobs.

New York's old gay lesbian world has as many rules as the tsarina's court. Most often I was struck by the isolation the women enforced upon each other. Oppression runs deep, and among our own we act it out on each other with as much viciousness (sometimes) as the very culture which produced the oppression. It was in gay bars that I learned that a world of women can only work if we destroy the male value system, the male pattern for human relationship (if you can call it human). These methods employ role play, economic exploitation, dominance and passivity, and material proof of your social rank—they can only keep people apart and fighting with each other. As long as you work within that system you can never really know anyone—least of all, yourself.

When the rumblings of the just-born women's liberation movement reached me, I was filled with hope. I thought women's liberation could conquer sexism once and for all, but what I found was that sexism exists even between women in the movement and is just as destructive as the sexism between men and women.

I came to women's liberation via a political homosexual group, the Student Homophile League, which was male-dominated. Homosexual men (with few exceptions) are like heterosexual men in that they don't give a damn about the needs of women. So I left the group for the National Organization for Women. I went to a few business meetings where the women conducted themselves in a parliamentary manner and generally behaved like good, white, middle-class ladies are supposed to behave. I was hardly enamored of the bejeweled and well-dressed women. I heard vaguely of more radical groups, but I couldn't get in touch with any of them. It was almost like prohibition days—you had to know somebody who knew somebody in those groups. I didn't know anybody, so I gritted my teeth and stuck it out with the golden girls. I sat at the general meeting and said nothing. Eventually a woman did talk to me. I questioned her on the lesbian issue, and she bluntly told me that the word "lesbian" was never to be uttered. "After all, that is exactly what the press wants to say we are, a bunch of lesbians." She then went on to say patronizingly: "What are you doing worrying about lesbians; you must have lots of boyfriends." OK, sister, have it your way!

Finally NOW had a rap session for new women, and I attended. The women bitched about job discrimination, the pill, and so on. Although I had been silent until now, I am not generally a silent, retiring woman. I had kept silent up until this meeting because I was unfamiliar with the organization, because I was born poor, and because now I was surrounded by privileged, well-spoken women, who took food, housing, and education for granted. Lastly, I did not want to jeopardize other lesbians.

By this time I had had a few months to review the political issues at stake and to come up with the firm conclusion that NOW was, to make a long story short, full of shit. A women's movement is for women. Its actions and considerations should be for women, not for what the white, male media finds acceptable. In other words, lesbianism definitely was an important issue and should be out in the open.

I stood up and said something that went like this: "All I've heard about tonight and in the other meetings was you women complaining about men, in one form or another. I want to know why you don't speak about other women? Why you deliberately avoid lesbianism and why you can't see anything but men? I think lesbians are ahead of you." (At that time I believed the lesbian politically superior to the heterosexual woman. I still do although now I recognize there are such gaps as apolitical lesbians and political heterosexuals.) What followed my short remarks resembled a mass coronary. One woman jumped up and declared that lesbians want to be men and that NOW only wants "real" women. This kind of thing went on for awhile. Then the second wave set in—the sneaky, sly curiosity that culminates in: "Well, what do you do in bed?" (I paint myself green and hang from the rafters.)

After approximately one hour of being the group freak and diligently probed, poked, and studied, these ladies bountiful decided that, yes, I was human. I even looked like what young women in their early twenties were supposed to look like. (I had long hair and was in a skirt. Now I have short hair, and if I wear pants, I'm told I look like a young boy. You figure it out.) There were other lesbians in the room, and they too looked like what women are supposed to look like. The difference between them and me was that I opened my mouth and fought the straight ladies. I was even angrier at my silent lesbian sisters than at these incredibly rude, peering, titillated heterosexual wonders. Lesbian silence is nothing new to me, but it never fails to piss me off. I know all the reasons to be quiet in front of the straight enemy. They cut no ice with me. Every time you keep your mouth shut you make life that much harder for every lesbian in this country. Our freedom is worth you losing your job and your friends. If you keep your mouth shut, you are a coward. The women in that room were cowards. They thought they would pass for straight, but in the last three years since that meeting, every one of them has been brutally purged from NOW!

In that room somehow, a few women got past the label "lesbian" and tried to see me as a person. At the next general meeting, some of them came over and talked. They were trying to break down the barriers between us. The NOW leadership was another story. They would in no way recognize the issue of lesbianism as relevant to the movement. Secretly, a few of them called me and "confessed" to being lesbians themselves. They were ashamed of their silence, but their logic was, when in Rome, do as the Romans do. They were very busy playing straight because they didn't want to lose their positions in the leadership. They asked me not to reveal them, and there were hints that I could have a place in the leadership if I would play my cards right (shut up). This kind of buy-off is commonly known as being the token nigger. They got a real bargain with me, because not only was I a lesbian, I was poor, I was an orphan (adopted) without knowledge of my racial/ethnic origins.

At the time, I saw the co-optation, but I had nowhere else to go, and it didn't occur to me then to start a whole new movement. I became editor of New York NOW's newsletter. From that I moved up to being the administrative coordinator for the national organization—an appointed post. It sounds good if you care about titles, but what it really means is that you do lots of boring labor, like collating, stapling, and mailing.

Everything was fine as long as I did not bring up the lesbian issue. After all, the issue was solved because I was in the power structure, and I was a lesbian. Being the token lesbian, I also helped take the heat off the hidden lesbians. It wasn't right, but I couldn't figure out how to fight it. I still couldn't get in touch with the radical groups, and when I mentioned my interest in these groups, a woman on the executive board told me they were all a gang of unclean girls who hated lesbians and who talked about their personal hang-ups. I asked her if she had ever been to a meeting and she said that she hadn't. However, she assured me that she had heard this on very good authority.

As women began to be comfortable with me and see that I was a fairly decent human being with no obvious defects, they began to turn on to me. It was very painful for me because when they experienced warm, or sexual feelings, they began to treat me as a man. All these women knew was men, and I was getting the old seduction game we learn in preschool sex-role training. I can't respond to that kind of thing anymore. Some of the women were hurt, some angry, and some vicious. Then there was the most manipulative woman of all, the one who was going to liberate herself on my body. She could then pass herself off as right on, new-wave feminist because she had slept with a woman. It was pretty confusing.

As you can see, the women still thought of lesbianism as a sexual activity only. This is the way in which men define it. The women couldn't understand that lesbianism means a different way of living. It means, for me, that you dump all roles as much as possible, that you fight the male power system, and that you give women primacy in your life—emotionally, personally, politically. It doesn't mean that you look at girlie magazines or pinch the bottoms of passers-by.

Difficult as all this was, worse events were to follow. A NOW national officer of much fame made a clumsy pass at me. Not only do I not want to make passes at other women, I don't want women to make passes at me. It all sounds like a football game. Needless to say, I did not respond to the woman. Within an amazingly short time I was relieved of my duties at the national office for lack of funds. While the leadership was nervously casting its eyes about for someone to take on the burden of the newsletter, I decided to go down fighting. I put out the January, 1970 issue of the newsletter with a blast at the leadership for its sexist, racist, and class-biased attitudes. Two other NOW officers who were fed up with the back-room politicking and high-powered prison guarding helped with the issue and also publicly resigned their offices.

By this time, I had discovered some of the other groups. I went to Redstockings, an organization which pushed consciousness-raising and the pro-woman line. Redstockings was not too pro-woman when it came to lesbians. They could empathize with the prostitute, support the housewife, encourage the single woman, and seek child care for the mother, but they wouldn't touch the lesbian. I became the token lesbian once more, and I became more and more depressed. At least I had enough insight to reliaze that this was not my personal problem. It was and still is the crucial political issue, and the first step toward a coherent, all-woman ideology. But when there is just one person pushing an issue, that one person becomes the issue until others see it; she becomes a Cassandra of sorts.

Lesbianism is the one issue that deals with women reacting positively to other women. All other issues deal with men and the society they have built to contain us. The real questions are: Why are women afraid of one another? Why does the straight woman throttle the lesbian? Why do women keep insisting this is a bedroom issue and not a political issue, when in fact, this issue is at the bottom of our self-image? If we cannot look at another woman and see a human being worth making a total commitment to—politically, emotion-ally, physically—then where the hell are we? If we can't find another woman worthy of our deepest emotions, then can we find ourselves worthy of our own emotions, or are all commitments reserved for men, those that benefit by our oppression? It is clear that men are not reserving their deepest commitments for women. Otherwise, we couldn't be raped, butchered on abortionists' tables, jeered at in the public streets, and denied basic rights under a government that preaches equality. We are taunted in the streets, in the courts, in the homes—as though we are nothing more than walking sperm recepta-cles.

A few Redstockings tried to deal with these issues. They received no support from the other women. By this time I was too tired and too wise to spend much energy on the straight ladies. I left the group with recriminations and blow-ups. Those women from the group who have become lesbians have also left.

The next move was to the Gay Liberation Front. It supposedly is for men and women, but I was wary because of my previous experi-ence in the SHL. Some of the women there had gay consciousness but little women's consciousness, and I thought that introducing the idea of consciousness-raising to them would be a positive step for them as well as me, as I needed to be among other lesbians. If these lesbians could connect their two oppressions, it would be a new ball game.

There are good reasons why many lesbians have no political con-sciousness of woman oppression. One of the ways in which many les-bians have protected themselves from the pain of woman oppression is to refuse to see themselves as traditional women. Society encour-ages this view because if you are not a traditional woman, then you must be some kind of man. Some lesbians do assume a male role (become imitation men) but never get the man's political and eco-nomic privileges. Other lesbians feel themselves to be women, know intensely that they are not imitation men but stay away from women's liberation: They know from direct experience that straight women cannot be trusted with lesbian sensibilities and sensitivities.

Many of the women in GLF fell into that group. They would rather work with male homosexuals and endure the chauvinism than expose themselves to a more obviously hostile element—the hetero-sexual woman, who is more hostile because lesbianism forces her to face herself with no social props, more hostile because inside she knows and hates herself for her fears.

When I suggested consciousness-raising to the women in GLF, they were suspicious. They thought I was a Pied Piper, wooing them into women's liberation instead of fighting homosexual oppression by working through GLF. They didn't bother to ask me much: if they had, they would have found out that I went that route in 1967–68.

In spite of their suspicions, they did form consciousness-raising groups. A sense of woman oppression was developed, and many were well along the way because of their increasing anger over how the gay men mistreated them. They saw that lesbian oppression and male homosexual oppression have less in common than they formerly thought. What we have in common is that heterosexuals of both sexes hate and fear us. The similarity stops there because that hate and fear take on vastly different forms for the lesbian and the male homosexual. As the months rolled by, a few of the homosexual women began to see that, yes, I was human, etc. Through the work of those original consciousness-raising groups, a new phase was started in the war against sexism. Women who love women came together. We are no longer willing to be token lesbians in the women's liberation movement nor are we willing to be the token women in the Gay Liberation Front.

The first explosion from this new growth came at the Second Congress to Unite Women when the lesbians (40 in number) confronted the women there. For the first time, straight women were forced to face their own sexism and their complicity with the male power structure. The lesbians are moving and have grown enormously since the Congress, which was in the spring of 1970. As the lesbians have grown in number and in revolutionary ideology, the backlash has increased until it has become clear to all revolutionary lesbians that straight women work for The Man and are not to be trusted. They don't want to lose the privilege they gain by being heterosexual. Out of the lesbian/heterosexual split has come a clearer politics, and the terms heterosexual and lesbian mark the difference between reform and revolution. It is the woman who loves women who will make the revolution. It is the woman who sells out to men who will betray her. And time decides who wins. Or will we all be destroyed by The Man's next filthy war?

I'd like to be expansive and say that the last four years in the Woman's Liberation Movement weren't all that bad. I'd like to be generous and say that I didn't resent the reaction of the women in the Gay Liberation Front. I'd like to close this article with glowing phrases of sisterhood and coalition fronts. But I can't. My experience has taught me that sisterhood is for straight women to use to cover up their dirt. My experience taught me that straight women do not love other women. It taught me not to trust the straight woman because she cannot build a solid politics. I have learned from my experience and will build on the bones of my life rather than phrases snatched from former revolutions, revolutions made by heterosexual males that fucked the women over who gave themselves to those revolutions. I know there can be a revolution, and I know it will be made by women who are women-identified.

This article is critical of a movement that has already been co-opted by the media: I mean women's liberation. Co-opted because greedy reformists and egotistical writers have used it to advance themselves in the white male world. For those who build toward a new world, women's liberation is a dead movement twitching its limbs in the vulgar throes of establishment recognition. It can now join hands with the male left and black capitalism as the unholy trio of sell-outs—take what goodies you can from The Man and let the people fend for themselves.

Women-identified women will not sell out. Neither will we go around making loud noises about killing pigs and blowing up the Capitol. Talk is cheap, and violent talk is the cheapest of all. We are not taken in by the easy politics of violence just as we are not taken in by the more clever politics of reform. We have no instant formula that will dazzle reporters and media vultures. We have mountains to move, and we have, today, only our hands to move them with. But every day there are more hands.

lesbians in revolt

CHARLOTTE BUNCH
1972

the development of lesbian-feminist politics as the basis for the liberation of women is our top priority; this article outlines our present ideas. In our society, which defines all people and institutions for the benefit of the rich, white male, the lesbian is in revolt. In revolt because she defines herself in terms of women and rejects the male definitions of how she should feel, act, look, and live. To be a lesbian is to love oneself, woman, in a culture that denegrates and despises women. The lesbian rejects male sexual/political domination; she defies his world, his social organization, his ideology, and his definition of her as inferior. Lesbianism puts women first while the society declares the male supreme. Lesbianism threatens male supremacy at its core. When politically conscious and organized, it is central to destroying our sexist, racist, capitalist, imperialist system.

Lesbianism is a Political Choice

Male society defines lesbianism as a sexual act, which reflects men's limited view of women: they think of us only in terms of sex. They also say lesbians are not real women, so a real woman is one who gets fucked by men. We say that a lesbian is a woman whose sense of self and energies, including sexual energies, center around women—she is woman-identified. The woman-identified-woman commits herself to other women for political, emotional, physical, and economic support. Women are important to her. She is important to herself. Our society demands that commitment from women be reserved for men.

The lesbian, woman-identified-woman, commits herself to women not only as an alternative to oppressive male/female relationships but primarily because she *loves* women. Whether consciously or not, by her actions, the lesbian has recognized that giving support and love to men over women perpetuates the system that oppresses her. If women do not make a commitment to each other, which includes sexual love, we deny ourselves the love and value traditionally given to men. We accept our second-class status. When women do give primary energies to other women, then it is possible to concentrate fully on building a movement for our liberation.

Woman-identified lesbianism is, then, more than a sexual preference; it is a political choice. It is political because relationships between men and women are essentially political: they involve power and dominance. Since the lesbian actively rejects that relationship and chooses women, she defies the established political system.

Lesbianism, By Itself, is Not Enough

Of course, not all lesbians are consciously woman-identified, nor are all committed to finding common solutions to the oppression they suffer as women and lesbians. Being a lesbian is part of challenging male supremacy, but not the end. For the lesbian or heterosexual woman, there is no individual solution to oppression.

The lesbian may think that she is free since she escapes the personal oppression of the individual male/female relationship. But to the society she is still a woman, or worse, a visible lesbian. On the street, at the job, in the schools, she is treated as an inferior and is at the mercy of men's power and whims. (I've never heard of a rapist who stopped because his victim was a lesbian.) This society hates women who love women, and so, the lesbian, who escapes male dominance in her private home, receives it doubly at the hands of male society; she is harassed, outcast, and shuttled to the bottom. Lesbians must become feminists and fight against woman oppression, just as feminists must become lesbians if they hope to end male supremacy.

U.S. society encourages individual solutions, apolitical attitudes, and reformism to keep us from political revolt and out of power. Men who rule, and male leftists who seek to rule, try to depoliticize sex and the relations between men and women in order to prevent us from acting to end our oppression and challenging their power. As the question of homosexuality has become public, reformists define it as a private question of whom you sleep with in order to sidetrack our understanding of the politics of sex. For the lesbian-feminist, it is not private; it is a political matter of oppression, domination, and power. Reformists offer solutions that make no basic changes in the system that oppresses us, solutions that keep power in the hands of the oppressor. The only way oppressed people end their oppression is by seizing power: people whose rule depends on the subordination of others do not voluntarily stop oppressing others. Our subordination is the basis of male power.

Sexism is the Root of All Oppression

The first division of labor, in prehistory, was based on sex: men hunted, women built the villages, took care of children, and farmed. Women collectively controlled the land, language, culture, and the communities. Men were able to conquer women with the weapons that they developed for hunting when it became clear that women were leading a more stable, peaceful, and desirable existence. We do not know exactly how this conquest took place, but it is clear that the original imperialism was male over female: the male claiming the female body and her service as his territory (or property).

Having secured the domination of women, men continued this pattern of suppressing people, now on the basis of tribe, race, and class. Although there have been numerous battles over class, race, and nation during the past three thousand years, none has brought the liberation of women. While these other forms of oppression must be ended, there is no reason to believe that our liberation will come with the smashing of capitalism, racism, or imperialism today. Women will be free only when we concentrate on fighting male supremacy.

Our war against male supremacy does, however, involve attacking the latter-day dominations based on class, race, and nation. As lesbians who are outcasts from every group, it would be suicidal to perpetuate these man-made divisions among ourselves. We have no heterosexual privileges, and when we publicly assert our Lesbianism, those of us who had them lose many of our class and race privileges. Most of our privileges as women are granted to us by our relationships to men (fathers, husbands, boyfriends) whom we now reject. This does not mean that there is no racism or class chauvinism within us, but we must destroy these divisive remnants of privileged behavior among ourselves as the first step toward their destruction in the society. Race, class, and national oppressions come from men, serve ruling-class white male interests, and have no place in a woman-identified revolution.

Lesbianism is the Basic Threat to Male Supremacy

Lesbianism is a threat to the ideological, political, personal, and economic basis of male supremacy. The lesbian threatens the ideology of male supremacy by destroying the lie about female inferiority, weakness, passivity, and by denying women's "innate" need for men. Lesbians literally do not need men, even for procreation.

The lesbian's independence and refusal to support one man undermines the personal power that men exercise over women. Our rejection of heterosexual sex challenges male domination in its most individual and common form. We offer all women something better than submission to personal oppression. We offer the beginning of the end of collective and individual male supremacy. Since men of all races and classes depend on female support and submission for practical tasks and feeling superior, our refusal to submit will force some to examine their sexist behavior, to break down their own destructive privileges over other humans, and to fight against those privileges in other men. They will have to build new selves that do not depend on oppressing women and learn to live in social structures that do not give them power over anyone.

Heterosexuality separates women from each other; it makes women define themselves through men; it forces women to compete against each other for men and the privilege that comes through men and their social standing. Heterosexual society offers women a few privileges as compensation if they give up their freedom: for example, mothers are "honored," wives or lovers are socially accepted and given some economic and emotional security, a woman gets physical protection on the street when she stays with her man, etc. The privileges give heterosexual women a personal and political stake in maintaining the status quo.

The lesbian receives none of these heterosexual privileges or compensations since she does not accept the male demands on her. She has little vested interest in maintaining the present political system since all of its institutions—church, state, media, health, schools—work to keep her down. If she understands her oppression, she has nothing to gain by supporting white rich male America and much to gain from fighting to change it. She is less prone to accept reformist solutions to women's oppression.

Economics is a crucial part of woman oppression, but our analysis of the relationship between capitalism and sexism is not complete. We know that Marxist economic theory does not sufficiently consider the role of women or lesbians, and we are currently working on this area.

However, as a beginning, some of the ways that lesbians threaten the ecônomic system are clear: in this country, women work for men in order to survive, on the job and in the home. The lesbian rejects this division of labor at its roots; she refuses to be a man's property, to submit to the unpaid labor system of housework and child care. She rejects the nuclear family as the basic unit of production and consumption in capitalist society.

The lesbian is also a threat on the job because she is not the passive/part-time woman worker that capitalism counts on to do boring work and be part of a surplus labor pool. Her identity and economic support do not come through men, so her job is crucial and she cares about job conditions, wages, promotion, and status. Capitalism cannot absorb large numbers of women demanding stable employment, decent salaries, and refusing to accept their traditional job exploitation. We do not understand yet the total effect that this increased job dissatisfaction will have. It is, however, clear that as women become more intent upon taking control of their lives, they will seek more control over their jobs, thus increasing the strains on capitalism and enhancing the power of women to change the economic system.

Lesbians Must Form Our Own Movement to Fight Male Supremacy

Feminist-lesbianism, as the most basic threat to male supremacy, picks up part of the women's liberation analysis of sexism and gives it force and direction. Women's liberation lacks direction now because it has failed to understand the importance of heterosexuality in maintaining male supremacy, and because it has failed to face class and race as real differences in women's behavior and political needs. As long as straight women see lesbianism as a bedroom issue, they hold back the development of politics and strategies that would put an end to male supremacy, and they give men an excuse for not dealing with their sexism.

Being a lesbian means ending identification with, allegiance to, dependence on, and support of heterosexuality. It means ending your personal stake in the male world so that you join women, individually and collectively, in the struggle to end your oppression. Lesbianism is the key to liberation and only women who cut their ties to male privilege can be trusted to remain serious in the struggle against male dominance. Those who remain tied to men, individually or in political theory, cannot always put women first. It is not that heterosexual women are evil or do not care about women. It is because the very essence, definition, and nature of heterosexuality is men first. Every woman has experienced that desolation when her sister puts her man first in the final crunch: heterosexuality demands that she do so. As long as women still benefit from heterosexuality, receive its privileges and security, they will at some point have to betray their sisters, especially lesbian sisters who do not receive those benefits.

Women in women's liberation have understood the importance of having meetings and other events for women only. It has been clear that dealing with men divides us and saps our energies, and that it is not the job of the oppressed to explain our oppression to the oppressor. Women also have seen that collectively, men will not deal with their sexism until they are forced to do so. Yet, many of these same women continue to have primary relationships with men individually and do not understand why lesbians find this oppressive. Lesbians cannot grow politically or personally in a situation which denies the basis of our politics: that lesbianism is political, that heterosexuality is crucial to maintaining male supremacy.

Lesbians must form our own political movement in order to grow. Changes that will have more than token effects on our lives will be led by woman-identified lesbians who understand the nature of our oppression and are therefore in a position to end it.

indiscriminate promiscuity as an act of revolution

CHARLEY SHIVELY

1974

choosing homosexuality is in itself an act of rebellion, a revolutionary stance. Becoming a homosexual meant I rejected the boyfriend/girlfriend, jock/homecoming queen, auto mechanic/cooking class, dirty joke/purity, science/poetry divisions that were everything in Hamilton, Ohio. I refused to become a "man." I was (and am) "queer as a three-dollar bill."

I am [1974] also thirty-six years old and am part of a movement not more than twenty (really no more than five) years old. Why have we waited so many centuries to act on the revolutionary core, potential, voice deep within us? Notwithstanding Walt Whitman, Oscar Wilde, Paul Verlaine, or Magnus Hirschfeld—why have faggots been so slow to rebel?

The answer partly rests in the massive drains of energy put into surviving, the co-optation by the ruling class and other causes common to oppressed groups. But there is, I think, a unique potentiality among faggots to break away from the existing power structure and search out new alternatives. The nuclear family is the foundation stone of all that is established. Because we are so radically opposed to the breeding family unit with reproduction as its ultimate aim, our sexuality makes us revolutionary.

Everywhere people belittle our practice. In the spring of 1971, I wrote the first part of my "Cocksucking as an Act of Revolution" (*Fag Rag* #1, June 1971), and got little comment except people saying surely you don't mean that *just* sucking cocks or taking it up the ass can be revolutionary. If you do, you're wrong (or stupid) not to notice it's been done for centuries without much change. Aren't you just "wishfully thinking about our sex habits as though they *were* revolutionary"? If sucking cocks would do, then "given the number of numbers making it every night in bushes from Boston to Bulgaria, the state would [long ago] have exploded."

I have always refused to concede the point here because I believe there is an implicit denigration of sexuality and of the body. Our bodies are real, they are not some social theory, some utopian proposal; their relationship to labor, the state, the economy and consciousness is no less fundamental than the other way around. We still wince at taking our bodies and sexuality seriously. Certainly I do. Doing child care at a conference recently, I was just stunned at the "innocent" sexuality of the "children." They had not learned yet how much more important thought and consciousness was then their bodies or the bodies of those they love. They simply did it.

Getting back into, back to our bodies, our sexuality can be a revolutionary perspective for ourselves. How much less utopian can I be? to rest everything on the "flesh," "lust"—prevailing practice instead of magisterial theories? Why can't our bodies, commonplace things found in every home—why can't they be the source of change and revolution? Do we have to sail to Byzantium, the Kremlin, Hanoi, Havana, Santiago or Zanzibar to find *the revolution?* If so, there ain't many'll be able to afford the trip.

Obviously there is decadence, cruelty and exploitation everywhere in faggotland. But I say that decadence comes not from our bodies or our sexual practices; decadence comes from accepting the straight, white-man values. Believing that we are sick, inferior, cursed, bad, spoiled, wrong, wretched; believing "they" are always right; wanting to be them; not wanting to be ourselves. It is so easy to wander from sensation—to go away from what we feel into what they want us to feel, believe, think, and experience. Maybe, I'd do better to say "Revolutionary Sensuality" is intended to be a revolutionary perspective for ourselves—the antithesis to bourgeois decadence. But I prefer to talk of "Cocksucking as an Act of Revolution." When the ass is licked clean, then come to me talking of "revolutionary sensuality." Then I will kiss your sweet tongue.

Because our sexuality is not only strange, but dangerous and lethal, to the existing powers, they have invented peculiar and unique ways of talking about and conceptualizing us. Ruling-class men associate faggots with effeteness. Their projection is oddly perverted from their normal way of fantasizing about "oppressed" groups. Generally the administrators equate inferiority with sexuality and subjectivity (both being base, sensual) and their own superiority with thought and objectivity. This holds true of every group *except* faggots. We are considered animal/sexual/base because our only defining characteristic is sexual; at the same time we are paradoxically seen as an effete part of the ruling class—given over to music, philosophy, decoration, poetry and other intellectual pursuits. The accepted wisdom is that (unlike other oppressed groups) we are rich or nearly so. By one count, 80 percent of all U.S. homosexuals *as* homosexuals are living affluent lives or struggling to do so.

I don't accept such counts, nor the fantasy about our being an effete part of the ruling class. Quite the contrary, I think faggots suffer all the existing discriminations of our class/race-bound society plus those of sexual oppression. We need a more real understanding of our social standing—how it is a part of a class society—and from that I think we can find real strategies out of the existing, collapsing society.

To begin with, we need to understand that the idea of faggots being only a small group of decadent ruling-class parasites is nothing but a fantasy. Ruling-class faggots (of which there are plenty) are more visible and freer, but that doesn't mean they are necessarily more numerous. There are not fewer faggots in the working class, there are only more closets there. Manliness is really a mark of class oppression, and the lower class you are, the more manly you are expected and required to be—both by your peers and the society in general. Thus sports—i.e. baseball, football, hockey, boxing, etc.—are primarily an interest of young and lower-class men. Almost a social necessity that declines as you rise on the class scale.

In the gay community, these marks of class are visible everywhere. The young, virile, beautiful, educated—usually white—form a circle of beautiful people, who as a group enjoy more fun and privilege than the old, ugly, poor, uneducated. All faggots carry in their heads a computer system/switchboard in which they weigh each other. On the grid we process such factors as height, penis size, ass shape, eyes, clothing, personality, smile, weight, age, skin/hair color, virility, education, intelligence, sun sign, birthplace and so forth. The inexorable computer says: Meet my Fantasy or be gone, what do you think this is, some kind of charity?

Too many protests against the horrors of this computer system have been against the values being processed rather than the process itself. That is, someone with a short penis will argue that technique should count more. Or someone will want to substitute personality, intelligence and education for those areas in which he would get a lower score. And isn't the demand for counting personality similar? A friend writes: "i have my best luck meeting people on the streets, just talking, and many times, through the beginnings of compassion or intimacy, the other person (who might have refused my advances in a bar or the fens) sees that i am a *person* and responds. in fact, i think i can say that i have luck *only* when i can get myself across as a decent, interesting human being."

I don't deny this heartfelt cry in any way; just typing it makes me want to stop and cry—search the faggot out and embrace. Yet I can't help feeling some failure to recognize the goodness in anonymity. Plenty has been said of its shortcomings; it's supposed to be the breakdown of the family and civilization according to some sociologists. (They put it in French, *anomie*, to make their observation seem even profound.)

Faggots live *anomie* more than virtually any other group of people I know; despite the pitfalls, maybe we're onto something good. Because sometimes it does help the old, ugly, poor, uneducated and generally "unfortunate." Since the computer of each faggot is "fussy" to some degree about who they'll copulate with, the more casual the encounter the less particular they are likely to be. In the baths or bushes, a faggot will more likely make it with someone he will not have to live with the next day. The Trucks in New York City are one example of a very unfamilial rendezvous—where words are seldom spoken, names are unknown, the whole body may never be seen. Unlike the baths and bars, they are also cheap (no cover charge).

As the stakes go up in the relationship, the standards go up. You might trick with someone in the bushes who has a score of 25, but require a score of 50 before you'd take him home to bed; 65 before you'd fix him breakfast; 69 before you'd actually make it again with him; 75 before you'd live with him; 85 before you'd become his lover; 95 before you'd live with him the rest of your life.

Thus the denunciations of tea-room sex or the baths or one-night stands are denunciations of victims. The typical bourgeois morality; people are bad because they are poor, less successful, less happy; they have done poorly in the economy, they are to blame. An *Advocate* poll asks the question: "Do you think that tearoom and park 'queens' are a disgrace and discredit to Gays?" A recent front page story in the Boston *Gay Community News* condemns such sex because it might alienate the Massachusetts state legislature. Laud Humphreys in *Tea Room Trade* found that many more lowerclass men (often married) used the tea rooms than went to bars. More older men likewise. The baths or the bushes are similar. For instance, in Boston for many years you would not see more than one or two black faggots in the Punch Bowl (loud, brassy) or Sporters (collegiate) or Napoleon (high church)—but in the subway tea rooms or along the Esplanade, the proportion was greater.

Our computer/capitalist wiring grades not only people and places for cruising; more deviously it also controls our sexual practice. We carry around a control board indicating just what we can and will do in bed. Some people are wired only to suck; others only to fuck; some to sex only with black men; some only with white men; some only 69; some only in chains. Both as a group and as individuals, faggots have suffered from tightly delineated sex roles. Breaking these, building new wider, better circuits, is our most important task. Each person should be free to choose a role if he wants and to live without roles if he wants, but the freedom and potentiality should be wired in, available.

Least freedom probably exists in prison; here the roles tend to be most tightly defined. You either fuck or get fucked, and if you are fucked, you fit into an inescapable and undesirable category. When I went to visit the Billerica House of Correction, the prison master arranged an interview with two older trustees in order to intimidate any gay people coming to visit the prison. A lot of what they said was lies (like we were in danger of being raped and stabbed there), but one thing stood out in my mind. The trustee said, don't you understand, they've taken everything from us; we've only got one thing to hold onto, our manhood. Having to be a man is a mark of oppression; the more wretched your position, the more manly you're expected to be and the harder it is for you to be a faggot. The more you have to stay in the closet. The less freedom you have to be gay.

The situation with femininity or transvestism among men is similar—both in prison and in general "society." If you relinquish the role of straight man, then you have no other choice but to accept the role of woman—which brings a loss of freedom, money and independence. My own experience of cross-dressing is not great but that little has been educational. I remember wearing a robe at one gay "pride" celebration. In workshops, the lunch room and around the campus—everyone tended to ignore me and everything I said. Pantalooned men might open a few doors but for them I had otherwise ceased to exist. In themselves, roles are not evil but what is wrong is the fact that some people are involuntarily forced into certain definitely inferior roles and others fit into superior roles by their birthright as it were.

The idea of freedom seems particularly middle class; children of the working class are taught that you must either dominate someone or be dominated. And these roles appear in sexual relations. Anal sex is much more common among men in the third world or in rural areas than in the ruling parts of the empire (big cities for instance). The mouth is closer to the mind, personality above the rectum. Generally one is either dominant or dominated. The more middle-class a group of faggots, the more likely they will be into oral sex and the more likely it will be mutual. An interesting study shows that college students active in gay groups tend more toward oral sex than those outside gay groups who tend more toward anal sex. (No report on relative tooth decay.)

Whatever the shortcomings of the gay liberation fronts, they really tried to break down roles. Admittedly they could be freer because so many were from the middle class. The luxury and possibilities of freedom were hard to come to and to understand, but that insight is perhaps our single most precious heritage. It doesn't always make things easier; Phyllis Sawyer's "After Women's Liberation" says it in two lines: "Hurting more/enjoying it less." But occasionally the vision, luxury, even ecstasy of a mutual faggot sexuality can be found. A few days ago, I felt it in Lindhurst Butte, Oregon: when I was fucking and couldn't tell whether I was inside him or he was inside me. And later I couldn't remember which way it was. Maybe everyone feels that all the time but it was a revelation to me.

Everything boils down to *inequality*. We live in a culture/economy where all things are measured and sold; any inequality is counted and counts against you. Even the drug culture is a rat race of competition and selling and enslavement where the "superior" or those who have an edge either use it or have the potential for using it, and thus rule, prevail, while those without the edge fall to one side. Inequality cannot be dealt with on an individual philanthropic level: the unequal resent philanthropy, fear the loss of largesse. For instance, if a beautiful trick decides to befriend a "dirty old man," love him, go home with him, and become his lover, the economy dictates that the D.O.M. should live in constant jeopardy; he knows that he lives at the mercy of the other who has enough points to make different choices; the D.O.M. resents inevitably the disparity. Or the inequality could be money; someone might be rich and able to buy lovers. The poor lover will inevitably resent the inequality, where riches can be denied or granted him by reasons beyond his control.

Billie Holiday sings that "Them that's got, gets; them that's not, lose, that's what the Bible says—and it still is news." Matthew 25:29, "For the man who has will always be given more, till he has enough and to spare; and the man who has not will forfeit even what he has." An Arab proverb says, "If you are a peg, endure the knocking; if you are a mallet, strike." That's the conventional wisdom of centuries against which we now speak.

I believe early clues to a new direction can be found in my own experiences in tea rooms, parks, trucks, baths and other untalked of corners of this land. I don't want to make comparisons (such as faggots have made immemorially) about which faggots are good, better, best. Nor would I want to suggest the best bar or argue that monogamous marriage is the only respectable way. What I want to defend is the proposition that there is a whole body of experience within the existing promiscuity of faggots that (if accepted for the good it is) is revolutionary. I don't say there aren't "bad" sides to faggot behavior, the way we treat and mistreat each other. I offer some generalizations not as a utopian fantasy, but as a way for making change, a way rooted in the actual social experience of faggots—a way tied deeply into centuries of suffering and experience. You could label it "revolutionary sensuality," but I prefer *Indiscriminate Promiscuity*. People (particularly menpeople) have tended to classify love as changeless, timeless, natural, and as unavoidable or indefinite as death. This mystification is a fraud meant to prevent any questioning or change in the so-called "reality." Why should there not be a socialism of love and sex no less than of work and money? Should not equality and freedom extend to our bodies and their physical relationships as well as to the economy?

We need to be *indiscriminate*. No one should be denied love because they are old, ugly, fat, crippled, bruised, of the wrong race, color, creed, sex or country of national origin. We need to copulate with anyone who requests our company; set aside all the false contraptions of being hard to get, unavailable—that is, costly on the capitalist market. We need to leave behind the whole mentality of measurement; it is a massive tool of social control. We all measure ourselves against some standard, find ourselves wanting, and feel inferior, guilty, wrong, weak—in need of authority, direction, correction, ruling and enslavement.

Discriminating and distinguishing involves more than recognizing differences. Differences can indeed be precious, but they need to be understood as that—precious differences, not marketable qualities that have to be counted, compared and graded. Indeed, discrimination presumes a scale in which one perfection is taken as standard; everything short of achieving that goal is substandard and inferior on a particular scale.

Beauty, for instance, tends to cluster around a few ruling imperial standards—blond, blue-eyed, Nordic, etc. But even if different standards were set—"Black is beautiful," for instance—that would not be enough unless the competitive, measuring, rewarding, punishing system were junked. We are crippled by the pursuit of a false social ideal in sex—generally that of an Anglo-Saxon man. In fact, beauty is not one ideal; it is in men everywhere. Beauty needs to be appreciated in its multiplicity and many manifestations; it also needs to be freed from its market value, its power, its usefulness in getting what you want (a lover, money, love, attention, customers, etc.).

Actually the greatest impediment to indiscriminacy is probably not so much ugliness as familiarity. I learned early about the incest tabu. I had this understanding faggot friend, who could see through my soul and perhaps me likewise. He made it with lots of people, some not that different from me. So once I said, "Why don't we try it together?" "Oh no," he answered, "that would be too much like incest." A faggot is more likely to be attracted to some stranger—hitchhiker, new-in-town, transient—than to a close friend. Part of this is the simple desire to keep social relations and sex separated; the latter being considered dirty and unworthy. But even those who overcome this prejudice, who can accept their sexuality for the joy, dignity and beauty that it can be—they still lose some ardor and passion after a few years' acquaintance with another faggot. I've noticed this with my lover of nearly ten years; as he has come to be like my family to me, he has lost interest in me sexually.

Being indiscriminate would not only break down the hesitations about "ugliness" and undesirability but also break tabus between those who work and live closely together. A meeting would never be for "business" alone; every contact could be sexual as well. Our whole social system could become eroticized, sexualized, changed, revolutionized. The alienation most of us feel most of the time is most pronounced in our most intimate institutions—the "family" of social units in which we live. As David Cooper maintains in *Death of the Family*, these units are "the ultimately perfected form of non-meeting" of "anonymized people."

We need to be more *promiscuous* as well as less discriminating. Promiscuous in every way with our bodies. Release all the armors and shackles, open all the pores and holes up for sexual communication.

No restraint in any way. Multiple loves—amoeba-like as in orgies at the baths—single couplings, perhaps between subway stops or between classes or on the way shopping. We must be open at all times for sexual activity; in fact, not make it an in-between action, but make every action sexual. Unlike capitalist decadence, our sexuality would not be separated from our business, our sexuality would not "drag" us down or wear us out for the tasks of building a totally free society. Our sexuality would be that society.

Promiscuity among faggots is not some dream or fantasy; it is a real social experience in many parts of our community. The present shortcomings of the baths, bushes, trucks, tea rooms and other libidinous areas is partly the discrimination that still goes on there. But it is more in the failure to provide for our lovers once we have been with them. Without a society in which everyone can make it (as well as make out), there will continue to be the question of "taking care of" each other—that is inequality, where the superior must provide for the inferior. Much of the fears and possessiveness in our present families comes from the way people are measured and sold on the love market as property. In our economy of scarcity, everyone continuously fears poverty and abandonment. Everyone is constantly hoarding people and love. Each relationship is curdled by the tendency to cling to someone else, to hold on for fear that there will be no more love after this. And the more marketable the love object and the less marketable the lover, the more desperate the clinging and the more terrifying the loss of a love object.

I think this may be my own greatest fantasy and fear—that of loss and abandonment. I've always worried about loss, what happens when the lover goes away, what if he leaves me, where then will I be? Such fear leads one to shut off, to be closed to loving, to protect oneself for fear of being wounded. And even coming to love the wound too dearly. Doubtless my own fantasy is my own particular one and cannot be exactly imposed on others, certainly not all faggots nor all society. Yet, I offer my humble solution, Indiscriminate Promiscuity, and wonder if it wouldn't allow for a society in which each person could be free to provide for themselves without dependency.

This would, I believe, be the essence of a socialist economy: where each individual would become a person, be free, be an independent, unique agent, where they might explore the voice deep within. A humane socialism must move beyond trade-union economism; it must lose its prudery, and find sexuality. In calling for a socialist society, we do not ask some party or state to suddenly give something to us—like legalize homosexuality.

We don't want something, we want everything. Not half a loaf, but the whole thing; not for some but for everyone. Our desires are not false, nor an expression of hunger, appetite, want: our desires—to suck cock for instance—are creative, they are the road to creation, to the modification of reality. Our bodies themselves are real; our sexual organs are not separate from our persons; they should be an expression of our individuality. "Capitalism," a friend of mine writes, "keeps the desires in the frame of its limits, it enlarges these limits to contain the desires, it co-opts. There is hope, though, because no one knows where the new eruption is going to come from, and desire is more and more coming from unexpected places, so that capitalism has a harder time to prevent revolution. While the capitalists are reading Mao, Castro, Che, to prevent a surprise attack, the marginals invent revolutionary strategies, unheard of, unread before."

it is the lesbian in us . . .

ADRIENNE RICH
1976

I was born in 1929. In that year, Virginia Woolf was writing of the necessity for a literature that would reveal "that vast chamber where nobody has been"—the realm of relationships between women.

Whatever is unnamed, undepicted in images, whatever is omitted from biography, censored in collections of letters, whatever is misnamed as something else, made difficult-to-come-by, whatever is buried in the memory by the collapse of meaning under an inadequate or lying language—this will become, not merely unspoken, but *unspeakable*.

Two women, one white, one black, were the first persons I loved and who I knew loved me. Both of them sang me my first songs, told me my first stories, became my first knowledge of tenderness, passion, and, finally, rejection. Each of them, over time, surrendered me to the judgment and disposition of my father and my father's culture: white and male. My love for the white woman and the black woman became blurred with anger, contempt, and guilt. I did not know which of them had injured me; they became merged together in my inarticulate fury. I did not know that neither of them had had a choice. Nor did I know that what had happened between—and among—the three of us was important. It was *unspeakable*.

My father's library I felt as the source and site of his power. I was right. It contained Plutarch and Havelock Ellis, Ovid and Spinoza, Swinburne and Emerson. In that library I came to believe—a child's belief, but also a poet's—that language, writing, those pages of print, could teach me how to live, could tell me *what was possible*. But on the subject of woman-to-woman relationships, in Emily Dickinson's words: "My Classics veiled their faces." (And still, in most literature courses, most libraries, syllabi, curricula, young women are handed classics that veil, not only what might be possible, but what has been going on all along.)

In a striking essay, the novelist Bertha Harris has written of the silence surrounding the lesbian:

> The lesbian, without a literature, is without life. Sometimes porno-graphic, sometimes a mark of fear, sometimes a sentimental flour-ish, she . . . floats in space . . . without that attachment to earth where growth is composed.[1]

Reading her essay, I found she had described to me for the first time my own searches through literature in the past, in pursuit of a flickering, often disguised reality which came and went throughout women's books. That reality was nothing so simple and dismissible as the fact that two women might go to bed together. It was a sense of desiring oneself; above all, of choosing oneself; it was also a primary intensity between women, an intensity which in the world at large was trivialized, caricatured, or invested with evil.

Even before I wholly knew I was a lesbian, it was the lesbian in me who pursued that elusive configuration. And I believe it is the lesbian in every woman who is compelled by female energy, who gravitates toward strong women, who seeks a literature that will express that energy and strength. It is the lesbian in us who drives us to feel imag-inatively, render in language, grasp, the full connection between woman and woman. It is the lesbian in us who is creative, for the dutiful daughter of the fathers in us is only a hack.

It was the lesbian in me, more than the civil libertarian, or even the feminist, that pursued the memory of the first black woman I loved before I was taught whiteness, before we were forced to betray each other. And that relationship—mutual knowledge, fear, guilt, jealousy, anger, longing—between black and white women, I did not find, have not yet found, in literature, except perhaps, as a beginning, in Alice Walker's *Meridian*, and in some of Audre Lorde's poems. I found no black women at all in literature, only fantasies of them by whites, or by black men. But some women writers are now beginning

[1.] Quoted from an unpublished paper, "The Purification of Monstrosity: The Lesbian as Liter-ature," given at the MLA forum on "The Homosexual in Literature," 1974. For a further explo-ration of these themes, see Harris's article, "Notes toward Defining the Nature of Lesbian Literature," in *Heresies: A Feminist Publication on Art and Politics*, vol. 1, no. 3, fall 1977; avail-able from *Heresies*, P.O. box 766, Canal St. Station, New York, N.Y. 10013.

to dare enter that particular chamber of the "unspeakable" and to breathe word of what we are finding there.

I go on believing in the power of literature, and also in the politics of literature. The experience of the black woman *as woman,* of the white and black woman cast as antagonists in the patriarchal drama, and of black and white women as lesbians, has been kept invisible for good reason. Our hidden, yet omnipresent lives have served some purpose by remaining hidden: not only in the white patriarchal world but within both the black and feminist communities, on the part both of black male critics, scholars, and editors, and of institutions like the Feminist Press. Both black studies and women's studies have shied away from this core of our experience, thus reinforcing the very silence out of which they have had to assert themselves. But it is the subjects, the conversations, the facts we shy away from, which claim us in the form of writer's block, as mere rhetoric, as hysteria, insomnia, and constriction of the throat.

a reply to a review

TENNESSEE WILLIAMS
1977

the reason that I am replying to your review of *Memoirs* is not to express and assuage outraged feelings but for two other reasons: that the review appears in the only completely literate and serious Gay journal with which I'm acquainted [*Gay Sunshine*]—and because I sense that your shocking misapprehension of my plays is something that touches upon a subject, a point, that might become current among "Gay Lib" attitudes toward creative writing and art. This would be almost, if not altogether, as dreadful a thing as the chauvinistic put-downs which are delivered by 'macho' critics to all artists associated with the gay world. We must not imitate the conscious or unconscious mistakes of our opposites: right?

At the end of your review of my *Memoirs* (mostly dedicated to an attempt to annihilate my work for the theatre), you make these extravagant charges. You call my plays 'lies' and 'lies not like truth' but 'complicated misreprentations of reality' and you really blast off about this in a very militant vehemently self-righteous way.

I hardly hope to dissuade you from this attitude but I think I must point out your misapprehensions to other critics in the Gay-Lib movement.

Now, surely, Mr. Dvosin, you don't believe that the precise sexual orientation of a character in a play is what gives validity to the play. Is there such a thing as precise sexual identity in life? I've never encountered it in my sixty-five years of living and getting about widely. Nearly every person I've known has either two or three sexual natures, that of the male, the female and that of the androgyne which is far from being a derogatory classification to my way of feeling and thinking. Now a confession. I contain all three. The reason that I have no difficulty at all in creating female characters is because, in my psyche, there is a little congregation of panicky ladies and/or tramps. Why panicky? Because they are confined there. I've never been at all attracted to the idea of wearing 'drag,' at least not in the occidental world or at any time preceding the time when I am absolutely convinced that I am close to death. Maybe then, in a place such as Singapore or Hong Kong or Bangkok, I might appear in black widow's weeds with a very thick veil: I might bear a black sequin handbag and pause in a ricksha or cab or samlor to display an enticing bill in the local currency.

(Black Joke, I suppose.)

Now let's get back quickly to the main topic. I believe that I have not only created authentic ladies for the stage but authentic gentlemen and also some quite credible good, plain males—and also a number of androgynes that seemed quite believable to audiences beside my own of one. But I have always had something to say in my plays which was more important to the play, to me, to the audiences, than the non-existent thing, a precise sexual identity of a character. Have you read my plays, have you seen them performed in the theatre as well as in the usually distorted film-versions? I doubt it, somehow.

Of course, it is perfectly true—to take a case in point—that Blanche was a daemonic lady. But I assure you that there are such ladies. The same could be said of 'Miss Alma,' especially in 'The Eccentricities of a Nightingale.'

But please believe me, there are no lies in the creation of these characters. Nothing repels me more than untruth and nothing attracts me more strongly than honesty—I mean on the spiritual level.

At the time when my most successful theatre-work was produced—never mind the films—naturally there were some differences of character-interpretation between myself and the director—who wisely opted for the more important thematic truth of the play and couldn't exercise more control. Only Jose Quintero—among the film-directors—went for broke in avoiding all distortion—in *The Roman Spring of Mrs. Stone*.

Well, things are different now, for the better.

Finally, can you really think of a reason why a person like myself—one of divided (psychic) gender—should find it difficult or at all disagreeable to write about love, sexual or spiritual, between woman and man? I tell you honestly, it was always to me as natural as a duck taking to water or a bird to the air.

I could say what I needed to say as easily through love-scenes between a man and woman as I could have between two Gays: that I swear.

So where's the lie?

I feel that it would be more profitable for you to look for rigidities and repressions in your own attitude as a reviewer, in this instance.

With All Best Wishes,
TENNESSEE WILLIAMS,
New York City

the meaning of our love for women is what we have constantly to expand

ADRIENNE RICH
1977

I want to talk about some connections which I believe it is urgent for us to make at this time—connections which demand of us, not only pride, anger, and courage, but the willingness to think, and to face our own complexity.

A concerted attack is now being waged against homosexuality, by the church, by the media, by all the forces in this country that need a scapegoat to divert attention from racism, poverty, unemployment, and utter, obscene corruption in public life.[1] It is not a bit surprising that this attack has created a new popular and infamous image of feminine evil: Anita Bryant. It should be obvious to us all that no woman in male-dominated society can wield the public influence ascribed to Anita Bryant unless men say she shall do so, and unless male power networks give her, as they have given Phyllis Schlafly of the anti-ERA campaign, access to the media, free publicity, and financial support.

Last weekend in Los Angeles, these forces joined to attempt a take-over of the International Women's Year Conference in the state of California. Only a mass turnout of feminists prevented the passing of resolutions for the essential overturn of every gain made by the feminist movement over the past eight years. It should be clear that Anita Bryant and Phyllis Schlafly are the masks behind which the system of male dominance is attacking, not just lesbians, or "gay" men, but women, and the feminist movement even in its most moderate form; that the attack is being fueled and fostered by the only people in America with the resources to do so: men.

[1.] And, of course, from the psychic and physical destruction of thousands of women by institutionalized heterosexuality, in marriage and the pursuit of "normal" sexuality.

We also know that in the rhetoric of Anita Bryant, as in the rhetoric of the male "gay" movement, "homosexuality" is viewed through a male lens, as a male experience. I have stopped believing that this is because lesbians are simply perceived as "not threatening." Much as the male homophobe hates the male homosexual, there is a far deeper—and extremely well-founded—dread in patriarchy of the mere existence of lesbians. Along with persecution, we have met with utter, suffocating silence and denial: the attempt to wipe us out of history and culture altogether. This silence is part of the totality of silence about women's lives. It has also been an effective way of obstructing the intense, powerful surge toward female community and woman-to-woman commitment, which threatens patriarchy far worse than the bonding of male homosexuals does, or the plea for equal rights. And finally, there is an even deeper threat now being posed by lesbian/feminism, which is a wholly new force in history.

Before any kind of feminist movement existed, or could exist, lesbians existed: women who loved women, who refused to comply with the behavior demanded of women, who refused to define themselves in relation to men. Those women, our foresisters, millions of whose names we do not know, were tortured and burned as witches, slandered in religious and later in "scientific" tracts, portrayed in art and literature as bizarre, amoral, destructive, decadent women. For a long time, the lesbian has been a personification of feminine evil. At the same time, as male homosexual culture developed, the lives of men have, as ever, been seen as the "real" culture. Lesbians have never had the economic and cultural power of homosexual men; and those parts of our lives which homosexual men could not relate to— our faithful and enduring relationships, our work as social activists on behalf of women and children, our female tenderness and strength, our female dreams and visions—have only begun to be portrayed, in literature and scholarship, by lesbians.

Lesbians have been forced to live between two cultures, both male-dominated, each of which has denied and endangered our existence. On the one hand, there is the heterosexist, patriarchal culture, which has driven women into marriage and motherhood through every possible pressure—economic, religious, medical, and legal—and which has literally colonized the bodies of women. Heterosexual, patriarchal culture has driven lesbians into secrecy and guilt, often to self-hatred and suicide.

On the other hand, there is homosexual patriarchal culture, a culture created by homosexual men, reflecting such male stereotypes as dominance and submission as modes of relationship, and the separation of sex from emotional involvement—a culture tainted by profound hatred for women. The male "gay" culture has offered lesbians the imitation role-stereotypes of "butch" and "femme," "active" and "passive," cruising, sado-masochism, and the violent, self-destructive world of "gay" bars. Neither heterosexual nor "gay" culture has offered lesbians a space in which to discover what it means to be self-defined, self-loving, woman-identified, neither an imitation man nor his objectified opposite. In spite of this, lesbians throughout history have survived, worked, supported each other in community, and passionately loved.

There have been self-conscious, political feminists for nearly two hundred years;[2] there has been a homophile movement for nearly a century; and many of the most uncompromising and heroic activists in all movements for social change have been lesbians. We are now for the first time at a point of fusing lesbianism and feminism. And this is precisely the thing that patriarchy has most to dread, and will do all in its power to keep us from grasping.

I believe that a militant and pluralistic lesbian/feminist movement is potentially the greatest force in the world today for a complete transformation of society and of our relation to all life. It goes far beyond any struggle for civil liberties or equal rights—necessary as those struggles continue to be. In its deepest, most inclusive form it is an inevitable process by which women will claim our primary and central vision in shaping the future.

We can, however, be turned aside by the same strategy that has kept us powerless for centuries. The strategy takes many forms but its purpose is always the same: to divide us from each other, to tell us we may not work and love together. Patriarchy has always split us into virtuous women and whores, mothers and dykes, madonnas and medusas. The present-day male Left has steadily refused to work on women's issues, to deal with sexual oppression in any but the most shallow, hypocritical terms, to confront its own fear and hatred of women. Instead, it continues to attempt to divide lesbians and "straight"-identified women, black and white women, to represent lesbianism as bourgeois decadence and feminism as counterrevolutionary, middle-class trivia, just as men in the black movement have

<hr />

[2.] A cautious estimate. The witch-burnings of the fourteenth-seventeenth centuries in Europe were undoubtedly a form of antifeminist backlash; and as we unbury female history in earlier centuries we find more and more individual female-identified, politically conscious women.

tried to define lesbianism as a "white woman's problem." (In this connection, I love to think of the independent women silk-workers of China, whom Agnes Smedley described in the 1930s, who refused to marry, lived in female communities, celebrated the births of daughters with joy, formed secret women's unions in the factories, and were openly attacked as lesbians.)[3] The male-defined "sexual revolution" of pornography, a multi-billion-dollar industry which asserts rape as pleasurable, humiliation as erotic, is also a message to women who relate sexually to men, that they can still be "normal" whatever degradations they may undergo in the name of heterosexuality. Better to collaborate in male fantasies of sexual violence than be a lesbian; better to be battered than queer.

Today, lesbians are being urged by the male "gay" movement to bond with men against a common enemy, symbolized by a "straight" woman; to forget that we are women and define ourselves again as "gay." It is important for lesbian voices to be heard there, insisting on our lesbian reality; we cannot afford to reject or dismiss our sisters who are attending the "gay" rally today, although we *can* hope that they are insisting that the "gay" movement confront its own vicious sexism, if it shall continue to expect even occasional support from lesbians. For without a pervasive, insistent feminist consciousness, the "gay" movement is as little a source of change as the Socialist Workers party.

There is another appeal, coming not from men but out of the most intense pain, rage, and frustration that we have experienced—the appeal to a simplistic dyke separatism: the belief that to withdraw from the immense, burgeoning diversity of the global women's movement will somehow provide a kind of purity and energy that will advance our freedom. All lesbians know the anger, grief, disappointment, we have suffered, politically and personally, from homophobia in women we hoped were too aware, too intelligent, too feminist, to speak, write, or act, or to remain silent, out of heterosexual fear and blindness. The gynephobia of men does not touch us nearly so deeply or shatteringly as the gynephobia of women. Many times I have touched the edge of that pain and rage, and comprehended the impulse to dyke separatism. But I believe it is a temptation into sterile "correctness," into powerlessness, an escape from radical complexity. When abortion—a right which the Supreme

[3.] See Agnes Smedley, *Portraits of Chinese Women in Revolution* (Old Westbury, N. Y.: Feminist Press, 1976).

Court has just effectively denied, most effectively to poor women—when abortion can be labeled a "straight" issue, we are simply not dealing with the fact that thousands of women are still forced, by rape or economic necessity, to have sex with men; that among these women there are an unquantifiable number of lesbians; that *whatever* their sexual orientation, freedom of reproduction is an issue urgently affecting the lives of poor and nonwhite women, and that to turn our backs upon millions of our sisters in the name of loving women is to deceive ourselves most grievously. Racism is not a "straight" issue, motherhood and childcare are not "straight" issues, while there is one black or Third World lesbian, or one lesbian mother, in the world. Violence against women takes no note of class, color, age, or sexual preference. Lesbians and straight-identified women alike are victims of enforced sterilization, indiscriminate mastectomy and hysterectomy, the use of drugs and electroshock therapy to tame and punish our anger. There is no way we can withdraw from these issues by calling them "man-connected problems." There is no way we can afford to narrow the range of our vision.

In this country, as in the world today, there is a movement of women going on like no other in history. Let us have no doubt: it is being fueled and empowered by the work of lesbians. Lesbians are running presses, starting magazines and distribution systems, setting up crisis centers and halfway houses for rape victims and battered women; creating political dialogues; changing our use of language; making a truly lesbian and female history available for us for the first time; doing grassroots organizing and making visionary art. I want to name just a few institutions that exist in this city alone thanks to lesbian/feminists: the journal *13th Moon*; Out & Out Books, a publishing house; Virginia Woolf House, a collective now raising funds to open a center for lesbians in stress, which will also provide referrals for straight-identified women; the Lesbian Herstory Archives, the first library devoted entirely to documenting our lives, past and present; the magazine *Conditions*, publishing writing by women "with an emphasis on writing by lesbians." These women, and many like them, are trying to reveal and express and support our female complexity, acting *towards* rather than reacting *against*; moving us forward. These projects are not "reformist." We are engaged today in trying to change not one or two, but every aspect of women's lives.

We need much, much more: we need women's centers and coffeehouses throughout the five boroughs, not just one or two spaces where women can seek community away from the bars; we need women's places of healing, shelters for old women now roaming the streets, shelters for battered women, whether housewives or prostitutes; halfway houses for women in transition from prison; self-health clinics, childcare centers, counselling and therapy that is genuinely lesbian and feminist, yet trained and experienced and not a rip-off. We need the brains, the hands, the backbone of every lesbian, in all her love, skill, courage, and anger.

We come from many pasts: out of the Left, out of the ghetto, out of the holocaust, out of the churches, out of marriage, out of the "gay" movement, out of the closet, out of the darker closet of long-term suffocation of our love of women. To the historic feminist demand for equal humanity, for a world free of domination through violence, lesbian/feminism has joined the more radical concept of woman-centered vision, a view of society whose goal is not equality but utter transformation. In the last few years, lesbian/feminism has taken enormous strides, and it has done so because lesbian/feminists have steadily taken leadership and responsibility in issues which affect all women. When we are totally, passionately engaged in working and acting and communicating with and for women, the notion of "withdrawing energy from men" becomes irrelevant: we are already cycling our energy among ourselves.[4] We must remember that we have been penalized, vilified, and mocked, not for hating men, but for loving women. The meaning of our love for women is what we have constantly to expand.

Thinking about today and its significance has forced me to place myself and my feelings absolutely on the line. This rally and some of

4. The danger of some ironic forms of "false transcendence" should be noted here. True separatism has yet to be adequately defined. Some "separatists" expend a major portion of energy on fantasies of violence against men, while actively trashing women who work in male-dominated institutions, publish in the male-controlled media, or even hold meetings and cultural events in spaces open to men. The "separatism" expressed in psychic and physical harassment of women who have not severed all ties with men (including their male children) may be a diversion from the more serious and difficult problem, the lifelong process of separating ourselves from the patriarchal elements in our own thinking, such as the use of phallic language and the fear of any difference from our own "correct" positions. The woman whose psyche is still heavily involved with a father, brother, teacher, or other male figures out of her past, and who denies the power these figures still exert in her, may refuse to sleep, eat, or speak with men, yet still be psychically enthralled to maleness. The movement of the self away from male-identification, dependence on male ideology, involves genuine psychic struggle. Therefore it is continually being reduced to and dealt with as a rigid political position, a program, an act of will.

A. R., 1978: A separatism which is neither simplistic nor rigid is beginning to be defined, e.g., by Mary Daly in *Gyn/Ecology: The Metaethics of Radical Feminism*, and by such writers as Marilyn Frye in "Some Thoughts on Separatism and Power," in *Sinister Wisdom*, no. 6, summer 1978.

my sisters, women I love, have created the conditions in which I have had to try and think my way through the complexities of being alive, a lesbian, and a feminist in America today. I wish for each of you the kind of challenge, argument, and critical support I have drawn upon, and for all of us, the kind of love we all deserve.

the david kopay story

from

DAVID KOPAY AND PERRY DEANE YOUNG
1977

I really wasn't prepared for the interview, but I also knew that was
why I was there. My story—and, through it, the story of thousands of
others still living the way I once thought I had to live—was about to
become public knowledge.

Why I did it is a question that seems to bother everybody but me.
I'm sure I don't have all the answers but I do know that it had to do
with images—the way people see athletes and the way people see
homosexuals. Of course I didn't have to talk about my sexual preference in public. Of course taking on any label is self-limiting and
wrong. But that's not the point. Because of my homosexuality I can't
get a job as a coach. Unless certain attitudes change there's no way
for me to function in this society doing what I want to do. If some of
us don't take on the oppressive labels and publicly prove them
wrong, we'll stay trapped by the stereotypes for the rest of our lives.

Basically I am an honest person—maybe that comes from my religious upbringing. It has seemed to me at times in the past that I was
lying just by walking down the street. People would see me and say,
"Hey, you look like an athlete. What do you do?" I would say I used
to play professional football. There would follow a lot of talk about
the Redskins and Packers and other teams I've played for. I could just
see their minds working on the same old stereotypes, which I think
are just as unfair to athletes as they are to homosexuals. Being a
homosexual does not mean you are a silly person; being an athlete
does not mean you are a dumb jock. Homosexuals, like athletes,
often have little more in common than coffee drinkers do.

I was caught between my own self-image and what I knew people
were thinking about me. I know I have always been homosexual. I

also know I am a very good athlete. While I was never any kind of superstar, I do have the credibility of having played ten years in the National Football League.

I kept making the teams year after year, although the coaches once told me I was too slow to make it as a running back. I loved playing. I think I was good for another two or three seasons after I was cut the last time. I loved being part of a team, part of a family. There was acceptance there based purely on what I could do. As long as I was able to play I never minded being relegated to the special teams or "suicide squads" sent in for punting, punt return, kickoff and kickoff return, field goals and extra points. I think it would be wrong for anybody to seize on some psychological interpretation of my enjoying those years on the special teams. It was not a case of the guilty homosexual relishing the extra punishment these squads took. In fact, I had no real choice. I either played on the special teams or not at all. But I was happy making my contribution even there.

Recently I've come to the conclusion that a lot of my extra drive came from the same forces that brought black athletes out of the ghettos to the forefront of professional sports. They were out to prove—among other things—that they were not inferior because of their race. I was out to prove that I was in no way less a man because I was homosexual. It is also true that during most of my athletic career the physical outlet of the game was a kind of replacement for sex in my life. My teammates nicknamed me "Psyche" because I would get so "psyched up" for the games. They also called me "Radar" because I could always find somebody to hit.

When Lynn Rosellini and I went over that first interview, the only thing I asked her to tone down were her comments about the University of Washington, where I had worked as an assistant coach one spring but was never asked back as a coach. I'd also been turned down when I applied for a job as a scout for the Seattle Seahawks.

I still look forward to my visits back to Seattle and the university. For the previous three years the annual Varsity-Alumni game in May had become my last chance actually to play the sport I devoted most of my life to. I played on the varsity team in 1962 in the first Varsity-Alumni game and—except for one year when I was in the Army Reserves—I have played in every game since then.

The game this year was to be in the new King Dome stadium and I wanted to be there. I began to worry for the first time that I might not be invited back to play. Most of my teammates knew about my homosexuality by then, but I didn't know what the coaches and university officials and fans would think of my public talk about it.

As Lynn had written it, the story implied that I should have been hired at the university but was not because of my homosexuality. If that was true I knew this prejudice wasn't restricted to the University of Washington. I was qualified to be a special teams coach or a backfield coach and I had applied for positions I knew were available on five different teams. Only Bart Starr of the Green Bay Packers acknowledged my application.

After telling about my problems getting a coaching job, the interview described my first sexual experience with another man. We were fraternity brothers and we loved each other. But we were always drunk when we had sex and the next day we could never talk about it.

I also talked about my brief marriage: "I loved her, but I was very mixed up. I'd gone through a very bad depression dealing with the problems of recognizing my sexual preference. And I kind of thought this was the way out of it." I did not mention that an analyst while I was under hypnosis had convinced me to get married. But the more time I spent on this doctor's couch—listening to him say I only liked women—the more I came to accept the fact that I truly preferred sex with men.

My apprehensions about the future came through in Lynn's interview: "Kopay worries what effect his disclosure will have on his business interests, his family and his friends. 'It's been such a difficult trip,' he says, 'and I'm sure it's just begun.'"

The next day the story was reprinted or quoted in nearly every major newspaper in the country. I put in a call to an old friend who had confessed to me about his homosexuality a few months earlier. He had been general manager for one of the NFL clubs. A man in his fifties now, he has never had sex with another person. But he finally acknowledged that his long association with football had everything to do with the sexual attraction he felt for men. The only difference between him and a lot of other coaches, owners, administrators in sports is that he is being honest about his feelings.

"How about letting me know when you're going to drop the next bomb," he said, laughing. He was nervous about my story—worried, I'm sure, about what it would mean for him and others who feel they have no choice but to stay secret about their sexual preference. But he was also very supportive of me and what I was doing—sharing, vicariously, in my liberation. Maybe what I am doing will help create some space so that people like my friend won't have to hide anymore.

My friend's laughter and support were in stark contrast to my parents' reaction. Nothing could have prepared them for what I did; nothing could have prepared me for their reaction. Apparently a reporter in Seattle had called them to get their reaction—and that was the first they knew of my talking publicly about homosexuality. I had told them four years before about my preference and they had never accepted it. That was why I hadn't called them before I did the interview. I knew they couldn't understand; I knew I had to make the decision on my own.

I had mentioned to them that I wanted to write a book someday and my mother would always say: "Over my dead body." I told myself that was more her rejection of homosexuality than it was of me. She had accepted the Catholic church's approach to sex and simply would not hear my explanations. She saw and still sees homosexuality as evil and disgusting—but, then, she sees all sex in the same way. She could only deal with it through the doctrines of the church: it is forbidden, therefore it does not exist.

When my mother called me, she was crying hysterically. "Why are you doing such a thing?" She said I had destroyed my older brother Tony's coaching career, that the reports about my homosexuality had kept him from getting the head coaching job at Oregon State. Tony had called them, saying he was a ruined man because of me.

I tried to reason with her. I said I hadn't destroyed Tony's opportunities. I said he was a very good coach and he would be judged on that basis, not on anything I had done. What's going on there, I told her, has a lot to do with why I decided to speak out. People think of homosexuality as some kind of curse. I knew it was a natural part of me—and always had been, even when I was dating Miss Washington and the Rose Bowl Queen. The problems I have experienced came from my confusion and fear over what other people would think of me as a homosexual.

"Mother," I said, "you know how hard I've tried to get back in football as a coach. Am I supposed to hide? Am I supposed to keep my mouth shut and allude to ladies everybody thinks I'm going out with? Do you want me to go ahead and lie like they want me to? That's not what I'm about."

She asked why I hadn't told them about the interview in advance. I said, "Mother, I've told you for so long and you haven't made any progress toward accepting it. You keep saying I'm not a homosexual and I know I am." "We can't even go outside the house," she said. I reminded her how friendly she and Dad were with a gay couple in the neighborhood. She said, "That's not my son." She also said they would have to put the house—where they have lived for more than twenty-five years—up for sale and move away.

I asked about Dad's reaction and she put him on the phone. "What the hell do you think you're doing? Who the hell do you think you are?" I said, "I know who I am." He said if I were there he would kill me. He said he never wanted to see me again. I couldn't talk any more. I was crying as I hung up the phone. It seemed my parents would never overcome the attitudes about sex that kept them from dealing with my homosexuality, attitudes, I knew, that had also always kept them from being more open and loving with each other.

Otherwise I was relieved and happy about most of the response to my interviews—first in the *Star* and then in other publications and on television. Even the negative reactions confirmed the importance of my speaking out. A columnist from Milwaukee wrote about a woman who said her son had my autograph and now she wanted him to tear it up. A man quoted in that column said he always thought I swished when I was running around end. I had to laugh at that one because the coaches were always yelling at me for not having enough nifty moves.

Mike Royko of Chicago wrote in his syndicated column about a wife's spoiling her husband's game by commenting on the homosexual aspects of the sport. Johnny Carson asked Joe Namath if all this were true about homosexuality among professional football players. Namath made a camp gesture of shock and wouldn't answer the question.

Lefty Driesell, basketball coach at the University of Maryland, called up and raved at Dave Burgin: "It is beyond my comprehension that a responsible sports editor could stoop to such trash when there are so many good things to write about in sports. What about the kids who read this stuff? They're easily influenced by what they read. What are they supposed to think? That to get publicity for playing sports you have to be queer?" Reacting to Driesell's words, Jane O'Reilly, a *Star* columnist who also writes for *New York* magazine, praised Lynn Rosellini for "extending the new humanism even to the sports pages . . . Human Being, properly marketed, could even replace the present image of Mythic Masculine Hero."

Mike McCormack, then head coach of the Philadelphia Eagles, was quoted as saying: "My reaction was one of sickness. I don't know first-hand of any homosexuality, and I don't know where it would fit in. I don't see any purpose to the article unless it was to get publicity for the girl." McCormack had been very friendly to me when he was an assistant coach and I was a player for the Washington Redskins. The other player quoted anonymously in the *Star* was one of McCormack's all-time favorite players. If McCormack did not know about the homosexuality or bisexuality of some of the outstanding players he has coached in Washington and in Philadelphia, he was the only man in the National Football League still ignorant of their names.

The letters to *The Washington Star* were overwhelmingly negative. The tone of most of them was that this subject should not even be in the newspapers—and certainly not on the sports pages. George Beveridge, the *Star's* ombudsman, responded to these letters by saying that the series only showed "that professional athletes are no less human beings in this regard than the rest of us, but that the blanket of secrecy surrounding the subject has helped to perpetuate situations within the male and female pro ranks that are both tragic and absurd."

Most of the other response, though, was positive. David Susskind (who once said he would send his son to a psychiatrist if he told him he was homosexual) was understanding and supportive of me when I appeared on his show, and so was Tom Snyder on the *Tomorrow* show. Snyder's show is normally taped at 8 P.M. for broadcast later that same night. The night of March 17, 1976, I sat waiting in the control room while Snyder interviewed Jimmy Carter for what was to have been only the first half of the show. As it neared the time when I was to be interviewed, Snyder interrogated Carter about laws against homosexuals as a sort of transition to my segment. By coincidence, that was a turning point in the campaign—Carter had just won the Illinois primary—so the candidate decided to stay the full hour and my portion wasn't taped until the next day. Carter was hardly what I would consider progressive in his responses to the questions. He said he was definitely against discrimination against homosexuals in employment and housing but he could not see any change in the federal laws where the employee might be a security risk because of his or her homosexuality. He offered that same old excuse for not changing the law. However, this was surely a rare time when a presidential candidate was even questioned on the subject.

A number of doctors, lawyers, professors and people in nearly every profession had announced their homosexuality and hadn't gotten nearly this much attention. I understood why I was being given this very privileged platform. I tried to speak from my own experience

in a way that would have some meaning to people in my own condition, but would also help to explain our lives to those who—out of
fear or ignorance—had caused us so much pain.

In the months that followed that first interview, I received several
hundred letters. Only three were negative; all three came from my
aunts. After an interview in *The Advocate,* my aunt Gerry Stifter
wrote: "If you have any explanation for this latest publicity stunt,
please give it to your mom and dad. Try to consider their difficulty in
understanding your position, especially when it is presented in this
manner. Perhaps you will be more selective in your avenues of publicity. I wish you no harm, Dave, quite the contrary. I send this
because of my love for your mom and dad and concern for your own
well being. I say my aspiration, 'Sacred Heart of Jesus, I place my
trust in thee/Sacred Heart of Jesus, protect our families,' which
includes you too. I send this with tears in my eyes, for I have always
held you in high regard. Sincerely, Aunt Gerry." The other two came
from an aunt who is a nun and another who has been principal of a
public school for twenty-five years.

All of the other letters I received were statements from the closet,
from people who felt trapped. They thanked me as they would a
friend for helping them. The letters were from all kinds of athletes
and from people in nearly every profession. Many of them said the
same things I would have said ten years earlier. One of my favorites
came from a young man in Delaware:

"You've got a lot of guts, buddy. My life's been torture until I saw
the articles in the *Star.* I thought I was losing my mind or something.
I've never had any trouble getting girl friends, but sometimes it feels
like an obligation. There're some girls sometimes I think I'm really in
love with, but down inside no girl has ever made me feel like I feel
about some buddies of mine.

"When I looked at what people told me were homosexuals, I
thought I'd be sick to my stomach. None of the guys I know are like
that. The people I was told were homosexual didn't make me feel
anything. They're not interested in the same things I am. I can't see
any of those people being part of my life. I've always kept everything
I've felt to myself. The only thing I've had to console me is that one
night a good friend of mine came over to my room one night after a
party. We slept together, and I knew from the way I felt it was the real
thing. But after that night it was months before he'd even say more
than hello to me. I was never more miserable in my life. I started
spending a lot of time with a couple girls to try to forget, but it wasn't

the same. I wondered if what had happened that night had just been some kind of accident. After reading those stories, I know it wasn't any accident. They showed me I wasn't losing my mind. Man, when I think what a long cruel joke it's been, I want to go out and cream somebody. There's probably a lot of guys in the same place I am who just haven't been saying what they feel. Thanks."

I mounted all those letters on paper and made a kind of "book of faith" out of them. Whenever I have any doubts about my decision to speak out, I turn to somebody else's story and feel reassured. Whatever my life is now, it's healthier than when I had to live with the gossip and the jokes and the lies about being masculine and being homosexual.

It has been a long and difficult journey for me. Sometimes I feel cheated for all the years I wasted in hiding. There were times when it seemed that the promise of "life, liberty and the pursuit of happiness" granted to other people would be denied me because of my sexual preference. There was a time when I felt that it would be the end of the world if people found out about my homosexuality. What I have found is that it's the beginning of a new world for me. This experience—both the highs and lows—has been like the emotions of a really good football game to me.

the hope speech

HARVEY MILK
March 10, 1978

my name is Harvey Milk and I'm here to recruit you.

I've been saving this one for years. It's a political joke. I can't help it—I've got to tell it. I've never been able to talk to this many political people before, so if I tell you nothing else you may be able to go home laughing a bit.

This ocean liner was going across the ocean and it sank. And there was one little piece of wood floating and three people swam to it and they realized only one person could hold onto it. So they had a little debate about which was the person. It so happened the three people were the Pope, the President, and Mayor Daley. The Pope said he was titular head of one of the great religions of the world and he was spiritual adviser to many, many millions and he went on and pontificated and they thought it was a good argument. Then the President said he was leader of the largest and most powerful nation of the world. What takes place in this country affects the whole world and they thought that was a good argument. And Mayor Daley said he was mayor of the backbone of the United States and what took place in Chicago affected the world, and what took place in the archdiocese of Chicago affected Catholicism. And they thought that was a good argument. So they did it the democratic way and voted. And Daley won, seven to two.

About six months ago, Anita Bryant in her speaking to God said that the drought in California was because of the gay people. On November 9, the day after I got elected, it started to rain. On the day I got sworn in, we walked to City Hall and it was kinda nice, and as soon as I said the word "I do," it started to rain again. It's been raining since then and the people of San Francisco figure the only way to stop it is to do a recall petition. That's a local joke.

So much for that. Why are we here? Why are gay people here? And what's happening? What's happening to me is the antithesis of what you read about in the papers and what you hear about on the radio. You hear about and read about this movement to the right. That we must band together and fight back this movement to the right. And I'm here to go ahead and say that what you hear and read is what they want you to think because it's not happening. The major media in this country has talked about the movement to the right so much that they've got even us thinking that way. Because they want the legislators to think that there is indeed a movement to the right and that the Congress and the legislators and the city councils will start to move to the right the way the major media want them. So they keep on talking about this move to the right.

So let's look at 1977 and see if there was indeed a move to the right. In 1977, gay people had their rights taken away from them in Miami. But you must remember that in the week before Miami and the week after that, the word homosexual or gay appeared in every single newspaper in this nation in articles both pro and con. In every radio station, in every TV station and every household. For the first time in the history of the world, everybody was talking about it, good or bad. Unless you have dialogue, unless you open the walls of dialogue, you can never reach to change people's opinion. In those two weeks, more good and bad, but *more* about the word homosexual and gay was written than probably in the history of mankind. Once you have dialogue starting, you know you can break down the prejudice. In 1977 we saw a dialogue start. In 1977, we saw a gay person elected in San Francisco. In 1977 we saw the state of Mississippi decriminalize marijuana. In 1977, we saw the convention of conventions in Houston. And I want to know where the movement to the right is happening.

What that is is a record of what happened last year. What we must do is make sure that 1978 continues the movement that is really happening that the media don't want you to know about, that is the movement to the left. It's up to CDC to put the pressures on Sacramento—not to just bring flowers to Sacramento—but to break down the walls and the barriers so the movement to the left continues and progress continues in the nation. We have before us coming up several issues we must speak out on. Probably the most important issue outside the Briggs—which we will come to—but we do know what will take place this June. We know there's an issue on the ballot called Jarvis-Gann. We hear the taxpayers talk about it on both sides. But what you don't hear is that it's probably the most racist issue on the ballot in a long time. In the city and county of San Francisco, if it passes and we indeed have to lay off people, who will they be? The last in, not the first in, and who are the last in but the minorities? Jarvis-Gann is a racist issue. We must address that issue. We must not talk away from it. We must not allow them to talk about the money it's going to save, because look at who's going to save the money and who's going to get hurt.

We also have another issue that we've started in some of the north counties and I hope in some of the south counties it continues. In San Francisco elections we're asking—at least we hope to ask—that the U.S. government put pressure on the closing of the South African consulate. That must happen. There is a major difference between an embassy in Washington which is a diplomatic bureau, and a consulate in major cities. A consulate is there for one reason only—to promote business, economic gains, tourism, investment. And every time you have business going to South Africa, you're promoting a regime that's offensive.

In the city of San Francisco, if everyone of 51 percent of that city were to go to South Africa, they would be treated as second-class citizens. That is an offense to the people of San Francisco and I hope all my colleagues up there will take every step we can to close down that consulate and hope that people in other parts of the state follow us in that lead. The battles must be started some place and CDC is the greatest place to start the battles.

I know we are pressed for time so I'm going to cover just one more little point. That is to understand why it is important that gay people run for office and that gay people get elected. I know there are many people in this room who are running for central committee who are gay. I encourage you. There's a major reason why. If my non-gay friends and supporters in this room understand it, they'll probably understand why I've run so often before I finally made it. Y'see right now, there's a controversy going on in this convention about the governor. Is he speaking out enough? Is he strong enough for gay rights? And there is a controversy and for us to say it is not would be foolish. Some people are satisfied and some people are not.

You see there is a major difference—and it remains a vital difference—between a friend and a gay person, a friend in office and a gay person in office. Gay people have been slandered nationwide. We've been tarred and we've been brushed with the picture of pornography. In Dade County, we were accused of child molestation. It's not enough anymore just to have friends represent us. No matter how good that friend may be.

The black community made up its mind to that a long time ago. That the myths against blacks can only be dispelled by electing black leaders, so the black community could be judged by the leaders and not by the myths or black criminals. The Spanish community must not be judged by Latin criminals or myths. The Asian community must not be judged by Asian criminals or myths. The Italian community should not be judged by the mafia, myths. And the time has come when the gay community must not be judged by our criminals and myths.

Like every other group, we must be judged by our leaders and by those who are themselves gay, those who are visible. For invisible, we remain in limbo—a myth, a person with no parents, no brothers, no sisters, no friends who are straight, no important positions in employment. A tenth of a nation supposedly composed of stereotypes and would-be seducers of children—and no offense meant to the stereotypes. But today, the black community is not judged by its friends, but by its black legislators and leaders. And we must give people the chance to judge us by our leaders and legislators. A gay person in office can set a tone, can command respect not only from the larger community, but from the young people in our own community who need both examples and hope.

The first gay people we elect must be strong. They must not be content to sit in the back of the bus. They must not be content to accept pablum. They must be above wheeling and dealing. They must be—for the good of all of us—independent, unbought. The anger and the frustrations that some of us feel is because we are misunderstood, and friends can't feel that anger and frustration. They can sense it in us, but they can't feel it. Because a friend has never gone through what is known as coming out. I will never forget what it was like coming out and having nobody to look up toward. I remember the lack of hope—and our friends can't fulfill that.

I can't forget the looks on faces of people who've lost hope. Be they gay, be they seniors, be they blacks looking for an almost-impossible job, be they Latins trying to explain their problems and aspirations in a tongue that's foreign to them. I personally will never forget that people are more important than buildings. I use the word "I" because I'm proud. I stand here tonight in front of my gay sisters, brothers and friends because I'm proud of you. I think it's time that we have many legislators who are gay and proud of that fact and do not have to remain in the closet. I think that a gay person, up-front, will not walk away from a responsibility and be afraid of being tossed out of office. After Dade County, I walked among the angry and the frustrated night after night and I looked at their faces. And in San Francisco, three days before Gay Pride Day, a person was killed just because he was gay. And that night, I walked among the sad and the frustrated at City Hall in San Francisco and later that night as they lit candles on Castro Street and stood in silence, reaching out for some symbolic thing that would give them hope. These were strong people, people whose faces I knew from the shop, the streets, meetings and people who I never saw before but I knew. They were strong, but even they needed hope.

And the young gay people in the Altoona, Pennsylvanias and the Richmond, Minnesotas who are coming out and hear Anita Bryant on television and her story. The only thing they have to look forward to is hope. And you have to give them hope. Hope for a better world, hope for a better tomorrow, hope for a better place to come to if the pressures at home are too great. Hope that all will be all right. Without hope, not only gays, but the blacks, the seniors, the handicapped, the us'es, the us'es will give up. And if you help elect to the central committee and other offices, more gay people, that gives a green light to all who feel disenfranchised, a green light to move forward. It means hope to a nation that has given up, because if a gay person makes it, the doors are open to everyone.

So if there is a message I have to give, it is that if I've found one overriding thing about my personal election, it's the fact that if a gay person can be elected, it's a green light. And you and you and you, you have to give people hope. Thank you very much.

the history of sexuality

MICHEL FOUCAULT

1976

for a long time, the story goes, we supported a Victorian regime, and we continue to be dominated by it even today. Thus the image of the imperial prude is emblazoned on our restrained, mute, and hypocritical sexuality.

At the beginning of the seventeenth century a certain frankness was still common, it would seem. Sexual practices had little need of secrecy; words were said without undue reticence, and things were done without too much concealment; one had a tolerant familiarity with the illicit. Codes regulating the coarse, the obscene, and the indecent were quite lax compared to those of the nineteenth century. It was a time of direct gestures, shameless discourse, and open transgressions, when anatomies were shown and intermingled at will, and knowing children hung about amid the laughter of adults: it was a period when bodies "made a display of themselves."

But twilight soon fell upon this bright day, followed by the monotonous nights of the Victorian bourgeoisie. Sexuality was carefully confined; it moved into the home. The conjugal family took custody of it and absorbed it into the serious function of reproduction. On the subject of sex, silence became the rule. The legitimate and procreative couple laid down the law. The couple imposed itself as model, enforced the norm, safeguarded the truth, and reserved the right to speak while retaining the principle of secrecy. A single locus of sexuality was acknowledged in social space as well as at the heart of every household, but it was a utilitarian and fertile one: the parents' bedroom. The rest had only to remain vague; proper demeanor avoided contact with other bodies, and verbal decency sanitized one's speech. And sterile behavior carried the taint of abnormality; if it insisted on making itself too visible, it would be designated accordingly and would have to pay the penalty.

Nothing that was not ordered in terms of generation or transfigured by it could expect sanction or protection. Nor did it merit a hearing. It would be driven out, denied, and reduced to silence. Not only did it not exist, it had no right to exist and would be made to disappear upon its least manifestation—whether in acts or in words. Everyone knew, for example, that children had no sex, which was why they were forbidden to talk about it, why one closed one's eyes and stopped one's ears whenever they came to show evidence to the contrary, and why a general and studied silence was imposed. These are the characteristic features attributed to repression, which serve to distinguish it from the prohibitions maintained by penal law: repression operated as a sentence to disappear, but also as an injunction to silence, an affirmation of nonexistence, and, by implication, an admission that there was nothing to say about such things, nothing to see, and nothing to know. Such was the hypocrisy of our bourgeois societies with its halting logic. It was forced to make a few concessions, however. If it were truly necessary to make room for illegitimate sexualities, it was reasoned, let them take their infernal mischief elsewhere: to a place where they could be reintegrated, if not in the circuits of production, at least in those of profit. The brothel and the mental hospital would be those places of tolerance: the prostitute, the client, and the pimp, together with the psychiatrist and his hysteric—those "other Victorians," as Steven Marcus would say—seem to have surreptitiously transferred the pleasures that are unspoken into the order of things that are counted. Words and gestures, quietly authorized, could be exchanged there at the going rate. Only in those places would untrammeled sex have a right to (safely insularized) forms of reality, and only to clandestine, circumscribed, and coded types of discourse. Everywhere else, modern puritanism imposed its triple edict of taboo, nonexistence, and silence.

But have we not liberated ourselves from those two long centuries in which the history of sexuality must be seen first of all as the chronicle of an increasing repression? Only to a slight extent, we are told. Perhaps some progress was made by Freud; but with such circumspection, such medical prudence, a scientific guarantee of innocuousness, and so many precautions in order to contain everything, with no fear of "overflow," in that safest and most discrete of spaces, between the couch and discourse: yet another round of whispering on a bed. And could things have been otherwise? We are informed that if repression has indeed been the fundamental link between power, knowledge, and sexuality since the classical age, it stands to reason that we will not be able to free ourselves from it except at a considerable cost: nothing less than a transgression of laws, a lifting of prohibitions, an irruption of speech, a reinstating of pleasure within reality, and a whole new economy in the mechanisms of power will be required. For the least glimmer of truth is conditioned by politics. Hence, one cannot hope to obtain the desired results simply from a medical practice, nor from a theoretical discourse, however rigorously pursued. Thus, one denounces Freud's conformism, the normalizing functions of psychoanalysis, the obvious timidity underlying Reich's vehemence, and all the effects of integration ensured by the "science" of sex and the barely equivocal practices of sexology.

This discourse on modern sexual repression holds up well, owing no doubt to how easy it is to uphold. A solemn historical and political guarantee protects it. By placing the advent of the age of repression in the seventeenth century, after hundreds of years of open spaces and free expression, one adjusts it to coincide with the development of capitalism: it becomes an integral part of the bourgeois order. The minor chronicle of sex and its trials is transposed into the ceremonious history of the modes of production; its trifling aspect fades from view. A principle of explanation emerges after the fact: if sex is so rigorously repressed, this is because it is incompatible with a general and intensive work imperative. At a time when labor capacity was being systematically exploited, how could this capacity be allowed to dissipate itself in pleasurable pursuits, except in those—reduced to a minimum—that enabled it to reproduce itself? Sex and its effects are perhaps not so easily deciphered; on the other hand, their repression, thus reconstructed, is easily analyzed. And the sexual cause—the demand for sexual freedom, but also for the knowledge to be gained from sex and the right to speak about it—becomes legitimately associated with the honor of a political cause: sex too is placed on the agenda for the future. A suspicious mind might wonder if taking so many precautions in order to give the history of sex such an impressive filiation does not bear traces of the same old prudishness: as if those valorizing correlations were necessary before such a discourse could be formulated or accepted.

But there may be another reason that makes it so gratifying for us to define the relationship between sex and power in terms of repression: something that one might call the speaker's benefit. If sex is repressed, that is, condemned to prohibition, nonexistence, and silence, then the mere fact that one is speaking about it has the appearance of a deliberate transgression. A person who holds forth in such language places himself to a certain extent outside the reach of power; he upsets established law; he somehow anticipates the coming freedom. This explains the solemnity with which one speaks of sex nowadays. When they had to allude to it, the first demographers and psychiatrists of the nineteenth century thought it advisable to excuse themselves for asking their readers to dwell on matters so trivial and base. But for decades now, we have found it difficult to speak on the subject without striking a different pose: we are conscious of defying established power, our tone of voice shows that we know we are being subversive, and we ardently conjure away the present and appeal to the future, whose day will be hastened by the contribution we believe we are making. Something that smacks of revolt, of promised freedom, of the coming age of a different law, slips easily into this discourse on sexual oppression. Some of the ancient functions of prophecy are reactivated therein. Tomorrow sex will be good again. Because this repression is affirmed, one can discreetly bring into coexistence concepts which the fear of ridicule or the bitterness of history prevents most of us from putting side by side: revolution and happiness; or revolution and a different body, one that is newer and more beautiful; or indeed, revolution and pleasure. What sustains our eagerness to speak of sex in terms of repression is doubtless this opportunity to speak out against the powers that be, to utter truths and promise bliss, to link together enlightenment, liberation, and manifold pleasures; to pronounce a discourse that combines the fervor of knowledge, the determination to change the laws, and the longing for the garden of earthly delights. This is perhaps what also explains the market value attributed not only to what is said about sexual repression, but also to the mere fact of lending an ear to those who would eliminate the effects of repression. Ours is, after all, the only civilization in which officials are paid to listen to all and sundry impart the secrets of their sex: as if the urge to talk about it, and the interest one hopes to arouse by doing so, have far surpassed the possibilities of being heard, so that some individuals have even offered their ears for hire.

But it appears to me that the essential thing is not this economic factor, but rather the existence in our era of a discourse in which sex, the revelation of truth, the overturning of global laws, the proclamation of a new day to come, and the promise of a certain felicity are

linked together. Today it is sex that serves as a support for the ancient
form—so familiar and important in the West—of preaching. A great
sexual sermon—which has had its subtle theologians and its popular
voices—has swept through our societies over the last decades; it has
chastised the old order, denounced hypocrisy, and praised the rights
of the immediate and the real; it has made people dream of a New
City. The Franciscans are called to mind. And we might wonder how
it is possible that the lyricism and religiosity that long accompanied
the revolutionary project have, in Western industrial societies, been
largely carried over to sex.

The notion of repressed sex is not, therefore, only a theoretical matter. The affirmation of a sexuality that has never been more rigorously
subjugated than during the age of the hypocritical, bustling, and
responsible bourgeoisie is coupled with the grandiloquence of a discourse purporting to reveal the truth about sex, modify its economy
within reality, subvert the law that governs it, and change its future.
The statement of oppression and the form of the sermon refer back to
one another; they are mutually reinforcing. To say that sex is not
repressed, or rather that the relationship between sex and power is not
characterized by repression, is to risk falling into a sterile paradox. It
not only runs counter to a well-accepted argument, it goes against the
whole economy and all the discursive "interests" that underlie this
argument.

This is the point at which I would like to situate the series of historical analyses that will follow, the present volume being at the same
time an introduction and a first attempt at an overview: it surveys a
few historically significant points and outlines certain theoretical
problems. Briefly, my aim is to examine the case of a society which
has been loudly castigating itself for its hypocrisy for more than a
century, which speaks verbosely of its own silence, takes great pains
to relate in detail the things it does not say, denounces the powers it
exercises, and promises to liberate itself from the very laws that have
made it function. I would like to explore not only these discourses
but also the will that sustains them and the strategic intention that
supports them. The question I would like to pose is not, Why are we
repressed? but rather, Why do we say, with so much passion and so
much resentment against our most recent past, against our present,
and against ourselves, that we are repressed? By what spiral did we
come to affirm that sex is negated? What led us to show, ostenta-
tiously, that sex is something we hide, to say it is something we
silence? And we do all this by formulating the matter in the most

explicit terms, by trying to reveal it in its most naked reality, by affirming it in the positivity of its power and its effects. It is certainly legitimate to ask why sex was associated with sin for such a long time—although it would remain to be discovered how this association was formed, and one would have to be careful not to state in a summary and hasty fashion that sex was "condemned"—but we must also ask why we burden ourselves today with so much guilt for having once made sex a sin. What paths have brought us to the point where we are "at fault" with respect to our own sex? And how have we come to be a civilization so peculiar as to tell itself that, through an abuse of power which has not ended, it has long "sinned" against sex? How does one account for the displacement which, while claiming to free us from the sinful nature of sex, taxes us with a great historical wrong which consists precisely in imagining that nature to be blameworthy and in drawing disastrous consequences from that belief?

It will be said that if so many people today affirm this repression, the reason is that it is historically evident. And if they speak of it so abundantly, as they have for such a long time now, this is because repression is so firmly anchored, having solid roots and reasons, and weighs so heavily on sex that more than one denunciation will be required in order to free ourselves from it; the job will be a long one. All the longer, no doubt, as it is in the nature of power—particularly the kind of power that operates in our society—to be repressive, and to be especially careful in repressing useless energies, the intensity of pleasures, and irregular modes of behavior. We must not be surprised, then, if the effects of liberation vis-à-vis this repressive power are so slow to manifest themselves; the effort to speak freely about sex and accept it in its reality is so alien to a historical sequence that has gone unbroken for a thousand years now, and so inimical to the intrinsic mechanisms of power, that it is bound to make little headway for a long time before succeeding in its mission.

One can raise three serious doubts concerning what I shall term the "repressive hypothesis." First doubt: Is sexual repression truly an established historical fact? Is what first comes into view—and consequently permits one to advance an initial hypothesis—really the accentuation or even the establishment of a regime of sexual repression beginning in the seventeenth century? This is a properly historical question. Second doubt: Do the workings of power, and in particular those mechanisms that are brought into play in societies such as ours, really belong primarily to the category of repression? Are prohibition, censorship, and denial truly the forms through which power is exercised in a general way, if not in every society, most certainly in our own? This is a historico-theoretical question. A third and final doubt: Did the critical discourse that addresses itself to repression come to act as a roadblock to a power mechanism that had operated unchallenged up to that point, or is it not in fact part of the same historical network as the thing it denounces (and doubtless misrepresents) by calling it "repression"? Was there really a historical rupture between the age of repression and the critical analysis of repression? This is a historico-political question. My purpose in introducing these three doubts is not merely to construct counterarguments that are symmetrical and contrary to those outlined above; it is not a matter of saying that sexuality, far from being repressed in capitalist and bourgeois societies, has on the contrary benefitted from a regime of unchanging liberty; nor is it a matter of saying that power in societies such as ours is more tolerant than repressive, and that the critique of repression, while it may give itself airs of a rupture with the past, actually forms part of a much older process and, depending on how one chooses to understand this process, will appear either as a new episode in the lessening of prohibitions, or as a more devious and discreet form of power.

The doubts I would like to oppose to the repressive hypothesis are aimed less at showing it to be mistaken than at putting it back within a general economy of discourses on sex in modern societies since the seventeenth century. Why has sexuality been so widely discussed, and what has been said about it? What were the effects of power generated by what was said? What are the links between these discourses, these effects of power, and the pleasures that were invested by them? What knowledge (*savoir*) was formed as a result of this linkage? The object, in short, is to define the regime of power-knowledge-pleasure that sustains the discourse on human sexuality in our part of the world. The central issue, then (at least in the first instance), is not to determine whether one says yes or no to sex, whether one formulates prohibitions or permissions, whether one asserts its importance or denies its effects, or whether one refines the words one uses to designate it; but to account for the fact that it is spoken about, to discover who does the speaking, the positions and viewpoints from which they speak, the institutions which prompt people to speak about it and which store and distribute the things that are said. What is at issue, briefly, is the over-all "discursive fact," the way in which sex is "put into discourse." Hence, too, my main concern will be to locate the forms of power, the channels it takes, and the discourses it permeates in order to reach the most tenuous and individual modes of behavior, the paths that give it access to the rare or scarcely perceivable forms of desire, how it penetrates and controls everyday pleasure—all this entailing effects that may be those of refusal, blockage, and invalidation, but also incitement and intensification: in short, the "polymorphous techniques of power." And finally, the essential aim will not be to determine whether these discursive productions and these effects of power lead one to formulate the truth about sex, or on the contrary falsehoods designed to conceal that truth, but rather to bring out the "will to knowledge" that serves as both their support and their instrument.

Let there be no misunderstanding: I do not claim that sex has not been prohibited or barred or masked or misapprehended since the classical age; nor do I even assert that it has suffered these things any less from that period on than before. I do not maintain that the prohibition of sex is a ruse; but it is a ruse to make prohibition into the basic and constitutive element from which one would be able to write the history of what has been said concerning sex starting from the modern epoch. All these negative elements—defenses, censorships, denials—which the repressive hypothesis groups together in one great central mechanism destined to say no, are doubtless only component parts that have a local and tactical role to play in a transformation into discourse, a technology of power, and a will to knowledge that are far from being reducible to the former.

In short, I would like to disengage my analysis from the privileges generally accorded the economy of scarcity and the principles of rarefaction, to search instead for instances of discursive production (which also administer silences, to be sure), of the production of power (which sometimes have the function of prohibiting), of the propagation of knowledge (which often cause mistaken beliefs or systematic misconceptions to circulate); I would like to write the history of these instances and their transformations. A first survey made from this viewpoint seems to indicate that since the end of the sixteenth century, the "putting into discourse of sex," far from undergoing a process of restriction, on the contrary has been subjected to a mechanism of increasing incitement; that the techniques of power exercised over sex have not obeyed a principle of rigorous selection, but rather one of dissemination and implantation of polymorphous sexualities; and that the will to knowledge has not come to a halt in the face of a taboo that must not be lifted, but has persisted in constituting—despite many mistakes, of course—a science of sexuality.

christianity, social tolerance, and homosexuality

JOHN BOSWELL
1980

"conclusions" may be too strong a term for the type of generalization or summary which can be made on the basis of this study; early treatments of any historical phenomena, no matter how thoroughly effected, must be regarded as provisional. Only a few themes emerge clearly from what has preceded. Roman society, at least in its urban centers, did not for the most part distinguish gay people from others and regarded homosexual interest and practice as an ordinary part of the range of human eroticism. The early Christian church does not appear to have opposed homosexual behavior per se. The most influential Christian literature was moot on the issue; no prominent writers seem to have considered homosexual attraction "unnatural," and those who objected to physical expression of homosexual feelings generally did so on the basis of considerations unrelated to the teachings of Jesus or his early followers. Hostility to gay people and their sexuality became noticable in the West during the period of the dissolution of the Roman state—i.e., from the third through the sixth centuries—due to factors which cannot be satisfactorily analyzed, but which probably included the disapearance of urban subcultures, increased governmental regulation of personal morality, and public pressure for asceticism in all sexual matters. Neither Christian society nor Christian theology as a whole evinced or supported any particular hostility to homosexuality, but both reflected and in the end retained positions adopted by some governments and theologians which could be used to derogate homosexual acts.

During the early Middle Ages gay people were as a consequence rarely visible. Manifestations of a distinctive subculture are almost wholly absent from this period, although many individual expressions of homosexual love, especially among clerics, survive. Moral theology through the twelfth century treated homosexuality as at worst comparable to heterosexual fornication but more often remained silent on the issue. Legal enactments were very rare and of dubious efficacy.

The revival of urban economies and city life notable by the eleventh century was accompanied by the reappearance of gay literature and other evidence of a substantial gay minority. Gay people were prominent, influential, and respected at many levels of society in most of Europe, and left a permanent mark on the cultural monuments of the age, both religious and secular. Homosexual passions became matters of public discussion and were celebrated in spiritual as well as carnal contexts. Opposition to gay sexuality appeared rarely and more as aesthetic partisanship than as moral censure; exceptions to this were ignored by religious and civic leaders.

Beginning roughly in the latter half of the twelfth century, however, a more virulent hostility appeared in popular literature and eventually spread to theological and legal writings as well. The causes of this change cannot be adequately explained, but they were probably closely related to the general increase in intolerance of minority groups apparent in ecclesiastical and secular institutions throughout the thirteenth and fourteenth centuries. Crusades against non-Christians and heretics, the expulsion of Jews from many areas of Europe, the rise of the Inquisition, efforts to stamp out sorcery and witchcraft, all testify to increasing intolerance of deviation from the standards of the majority, enforceable for the first time in the newly emerging corporate states of the High Middle Ages. This intolerance was both reflected in and perpetuated by its incorporation into theological, moral, and legal compilations of the later Middle Ages, many of which continued to influence European society for centuries.

Beyond these modest conclusions and the facts which support them, little can be asserted with confidence. The social topography of medieval Europe is so unexplored that the writer on this subject cannot hope to avoid leading his readers down many wrong paths or, occasionally, coming to a dead end. His comfort must subsist in the belief that he has at least posted landmarks where there were none before and opened the trails on which others will reach destinations far beyond his own furthest advance.

letter to ma

MERLE WOO

January, 1980

dear ma,

I was depressed over Christmas, and when New Year's rolled around, do you know what one of my resolves was? Not to come by and see you as much anymore. I had to ask myself why I get so down when I'm with you, my mother, who has focused so much of her life on me, who has endured so much; one who I am proud of and respect so deeply for simply surviving.

I suppose that one of the main reasons is that when I leave your house, your pretty little round white table in the dinette where we sit while you drink tea (with only three specks of Jasmine) and I smoke and drink coffee, I am down because I believe there are chasms between us. When you say, "I support you, honey, in everything you do except . . . except . . ." I know you mean except my speaking out and writing of my anger at all those things that have caused those chasms. When you say I shouldn't be so ashamed of Daddy, former gambler, retired clerk of a "gook suey" store, because of the time when I was six and saw him humiliated on Grant Avenue by two white cops, I know you haven't even been listening to me when I have repeatedly said that I am not ashamed of him, not you, not who we are. When you ask, "Are you so angry because you are unhappy?" I know that we are not talking to each other. Not with understanding, although many words have passed between us, many hours, many afternoons at that round table with Daddy out in the front room watching television, and drifting out every once in awhile to say "Still talking?" and getting more peanuts that are so bad for his health.

We talk and we talk and I feel frustrated by your censorship. I know it is unintentional and unconscious. But whatever I have told you about the classes I was teaching, or the stories I was working on, you've always forgotten within a month. Maybe you can't listen— because maybe when you look in my eyes, you will, as you've always done, sense more than what we're actually saying, and that makes you fearful. Do you see your repressed anger manifested in me? What doors would groan wide open if you heard my words with complete understanding? Are you afraid that your daughter is breaking out of our shackles, and into total anarchy? That your daughter has turned into a crazy woman who advocates not only equality for Third World people, for women, but for gays as well? Please don't shudder, Ma, when I speak of homosexuality. Until we can all present ourselves to the world in our completeness, as fully and beautifully as we see ourselves naked in our bedrooms, we are not free.

After what seems like hours of talking, I realize it is not talking at all, but the filling up of time with sounds that say, "I am your daughter, you are my mother, and we are keeping each other company and that is enough." But it is not enough because my life has been formed by your life. Together we have lived one hundred and eleven years in this country as yellow women, and it is not enough to enunciate words and words and words and then to have them only mean that we have been keeping each other company. I desperately want you to understand me and my work, Ma, to know what I am doing! When you distort what I say, like thinking I am against all "caucasians" or that I am ashamed of Dad, then I feel anger and more frustration and want to slash out, not at you, but at those external forces which keep us apart. What deepens the chasms between us are our different reactions to those forces. Yours has been one of silence, self-denial, self-effacement; you believing it is your fault that you never fully experienced self-pride and freedom of choice. But listen, Ma, only with a deliberate consciousness is my reaction different from yours.

When I look at you, there are images: images of you as a little ten-year-old Korean girl, being sent alone from Shanghai to the United States, in steerage with only one skimpy little dress, being sick and lonely on Angel Island for three months; then growing up in a "Home" run by white missionary women. Scrubbing floors on your hands and knees, hauling coal in heavy metal buckets up three flights of stairs, tending to the younger children, putting hot bricks on your cheeks to deaden the pain from the terrible toothaches you always had. Working all your life as maid, waitress, salesclerk, office worker, mother. But throughout there is an image of you as strong and courageous, and persevering: climbing out of windows to escape from the Home, then later, from an abusive first husband. There is so much more to these images than I can say, but I think you know what I mean. Escaping out of windows offered only temporary respites; surviving is an everyday chore. You gave me, physically, what you never had, but there was a spiritual, emotional legacy you passed down which was reinforced by society: self-contempt because of our race, our sex, our sexuality. For deeply ingrained in me, Ma, there has been that strong, compulsive force to sink into self-contempt, passivity, and despair. I am sure that my fifteen years of alcohol abuse have not been forgotten by either of us, nor my suicidal depressions.

Now, I know you are going to think that I hate and despise you for your self-hatred, for your isolation. But I don't. Because in spite of your withdrawal, in spite of your loneliness, you have not only survived, but been beside me in the worst of times when your company meant everything in the world to me. I just need more than that now, Ma. I have taken and taken from you in terms of needing you to mother me, to be by my side, and I need, now, to take from you two more things: understanding and support for who I am now and my work.

We are Asian American women and the reaction to our identity is what causes the chasms instead of connections. But do you realize, Ma, that I could never have reacted the way I have if you had not provided for me the opportunity to be free of the binds that have held you down, and to be in the process of self-affirmation? Because of your life, because of the physical security you have given me: my education, my full stomach, my clothed and starched back, my piano and dancing lessons—all those gifts you never received—I saw myself as having worth; now I begin to love myself more, see our potential, and fight for just that kind of social change that will affirm me, my race, my sex, my heritage. And while I affirm myself, Ma, I affirm you.

Today, I am satisfied to call myself either an Asian American Feminist or Yellow Feminist. The two terms are inseparable because race and sex are an integral part of me. This means that I am working with others to realize pride in culture and women and heritage (the heritage that is the exploited yellow immigrant: Daddy and you). Being a Yellow Feminist means being a community activist and a humanist. It does not mean "separatism," either by cutting myself off from

non-Asians or men. It does not mean retaining the same power structure and substituting women in positions of control held by men. It
does mean fighting the whites and the men who abuse us, straight-
jacket us and tape our mouths; it means changing the economic class
system and psychological forces (sexism, racism, and homophobia)
that really hurt all of us. And I do this, not in isolation, but in the
community.

We no longer can afford to stand back and watch while an insa-
tiable elite ravages and devours resources which are enough for all of
us. The obstacles are so huge and overwhelming that often I do
become cynical and want to give up. And if I were struggling alone, I
know I would never even attempt to put into action what I believe in
my heart, that (and this is primarily because of you, Ma) Yellow
Women are strong and have the potential to be powerful and effective leaders.

I can hear you asking now, "Well, what do you mean by 'social
change and leadership'? And how are you going to go about it?" To
begin with we must wipe out the circumstances that keep us down in
silence and self-effacement. Right now, my techniques are education
and writing. Yellow Feminist means being a core for change, and that
core means having the belief in our potential as human beings. I will
work with anyone, support anyone, who shares my sensibility, my
objectives. But there are barriers to unity: white women who are
racist, and Asian American men who are sexist. My very being
declares that those two groups do not share my complete sensibility. I
would be fragmented, mutilated, if I did not fight against racism and
sexism together.

And this is when the pain of the struggle hits home. How many
white women have taken on the responsibility to educate themselves
about Third World people, their history, their culture? How many
white women really think about the stereotypes they retain as truth
about women of color? But the perpetuation of dehumanizing
stereotypes is really very helpful for whites; they use them to justify
their giving us the lowest wages and all the work they don't want to
perform. Ma, how can we believe things are changing when as a
nurse's aide during World War II, you were given only the tasks of
changing the bed linen, removing bed pans, taking urine samples,
and then only three years ago as a retired volunteer worker in a local
hospital, white women gave themselves desk jobs and gave you, at
sixty-nine, the same work you did in 1943? Today you speak more
fondly of being a nurse's aide during World War II and how proud

you are of the fact that the Red Cross showed its appreciation for your service by giving you a diploma. Still in 1980, the injustices continue. I can give you so many examples of groups which are "feminist" in which women of color were given the usual least important tasks, the shitwork, and given no say in how that group is to be run. Needless to say, those Third World women, like you, dropped out, quit.

Working in writing and teaching, I have seen how white women condescend to Third World women because they reason that because of our oppression, which they know nothing about, we are behind them and their "progressive ideas" in the struggle for freedom. They don't even look at history! At the facts! How we as Asian American women have always been fighting for more than mere survival, but were never acknowledged because we were in our communities, invisible, but not inaccessible.

And I get so tired of being the instant resource for information on Asian American women. Being the token representative, going from class to class, group to group, bleeding for white women so they can have an easy answer—and then, and this is what really gets to me—they usually leave to never continue their education about us on their own.

To the racist white female professor who says, "If I have to watch everything I say I wouldn't say anything," I want to say, "Then get out of teaching."

To the white female poet who says, "Well, frankly, I believe that politics and poetry don't necessarily have to go together," I say, "Your little taste of white privilege has deluded you into thinking that you don't have to fight against sexism in this society. You are talking to me from your own isolation and your own racism. If you feel that you don't have to fight for me, that you don't have to speak out against capitalism, the exploitation of human and natural resources, then you in your silence, your inability to make connections, are siding with a system that will eventually get you, after it has gotten me. And if you think that's not a political stance, you're more than simply deluded, you're crazy!"

This is the same white voice that says, "I am writing about and looking for themes that are 'universal.'" Well, most of the time when "universal" is used, it is just a euphemism for "white": white themes, white significance, white culture. And denying minority groups their rightful place and time in U.S. history is simply racist.

Yes, Ma, I am mad. I carry the anger from my own experience and the anger you couldn't afford to express, and even that is often misinterpreted no matter how hard I try to be clear about my position. A white woman in my class said to me a couple of months ago, "I feel that Third World women hate me and that *they* are being racist; I'm being stereotyped, and I've never been part of the ruling class." I replied, "Please try to understand. Know our history. Know the racism of whites, how deep it goes. Know that we are becoming ever more intolerant of those people who let their ignorance be their excuse for their complacency, their liberalism, when this country (this world!) is going to hell in a handbasket. Try to understand that our distrust is from experience, and that our distrust is power*less*. Racism is an essential part of the status quo, power*ful*, and continues to keep us down. It is a rule taught to all of us from birth. Is it no wonder that we fear there are no exceptions?"

And as if the grief we go through working with white women weren't enough; so close to home, in our community, and so very painful, is the lack of support we get from some of our Asian American brothers. Here is a quote from a rather prominent male writer ranting on about a Yellow "sister":

> . . . I can only believe that such blatant sucking off of the identity is
> the work of a Chinese American woman, another Jade Snow Wong
> Pochahontas yellow. Pussywhipped again. Oh, damn, pussy-whipped
> again.

Chinese American woman: "another Jade Snow Wong Pochahontas yellow." According to him, Chinese American women sold out—are contemptuous of their culture, pathetically strain all their lives to be white, hate Asian American men, and so marry white men (the John Smiths)—or just like Pochahontas: we rescue white men while betraying our fathers; then marry white men, get baptized, and go to dear old England to become curiosities of the civilized world. Whew! Now, that's an indictment! (Of all women of color.) Some of the male writers in the Asian American community seem never to support us. They always expect us to support them, and you know what? We almost always do. Anti-Yellow men? Are they kidding? We go to their readings, buy and read and comment on their books, and try to keep up a dialogue. And they accuse us of betrayal, are resentful because we do readings together as Women, and so often do not come to our performances. And all the while we hurt because we are rejected by our brothers. The Pochahontas image used by a Chinese

American man points out a tragic truth: the white man and his ideology are still over us and between us. These men of color, with clear vision, fight the racism in white society, but have bought the white male definition of "masculinity": men only should take on the leadership in the community because the qualities of "originality, daring, physical courage, and creativity" are "traditionally masculine."[1]

Some Asian men don't seem to understand that by supporting Third World women and fighting sexism, they are helping themselves as well. I understand all too clearly how dehumanized Dad was in this country. To be a Chinese man in America is to be a victim of both racism and sexism. He was made to feel he was without strength, identity, and purpose. He was made to feel soft and weak, whose only job was to serve whites. Yes, Ma, at one time I was ashamed of him because I thought he was "womanly." When those two white cops said, "Hey, fat boy, where's our meat?" he left me standing there on Grant Avenue while he hurried over to his store to get it; they kept complaining, never satisfied, "That piece isn't good enough. What's the matter with you, fat boy? Don't you have respect? Don't wrap that meat in newspapers either; use the good stuff over there." I didn't know that he spent a year and a half on Angel Island; that we could never have our right names; that he lived in constant fear of being deported; that, like you, he worked two full-time jobs most of his life; that he was mocked and ridiculed because he speaks "broken English." And Ma, I was so ashamed after that experience when I was only six years old that I never held his hand again.

Today, as I write to you of all these memories, I feel even more deeply hurt when I realize how many people, how so many people, because of racism and sexism, fail to see what power we sacrifice by not joining hands.

But not all white women are racist, and not all Asian American men are sexist. And we choose to trust them, love and work with them. And there are visible changes. Real tangible, positive changes. The changes I love to see are those changes within ourselves.

Your grandchildren, my children, Emily and Paul. That makes three generations. Emily loves herself. Always has. There are shades of self-doubt but much less than in you or me. She says exactly what she thinks, most of the time, either in praise or in criticism of herself or others. And at sixteen she goes after whatever she wants, usually

---

[1] *AHEEEEE! An Anthology of Asian American Writers*, editors Frank Chin, Jeffrey Paul Chan, Lawson Fusao Inada, Shawn Wong (Howard University Press, 1974)

center stage. She trusts and loves people, regardless of race or sex (but, of course, she's cautious), loves her community and works in it, speaks up against racisim and sexism at school. Did you know that she got Zora Neale Hurston and Alice Walker on her reading list for a Southern Writers class when there were only white authors? That she insisted on changing a script done by an Asian American man when she saw that the depiction of the character she was playing was sexist? That she went to a California State House Conference to speak out for Third World students' needs?

And what about her little brother, Paul? Twelve years old. And remember, Ma? At one of our Saturday Night Family Dinners, how he lectured Ronnie (his uncle, yet!) about how he was a male chauvinist? Paul told me once how he knew he had to fight to be Asian American, and later he added that if it weren't for Emily and me, he wouldn't have to think about feminist stuff too. He says he can hardly enjoy a movie or TV program anymore because of the sexism. Or comic books. And he is very much aware of the different treatment he gets from adults: "You have to do everything right," he said to Emily, "and I can get away with almost anything."

Emily and Paul give us hope, Ma. Because they are proud of who they are, and they care so much about our culture and history. Emily was the first to write your biography because she knows how crucial it is to get our stories in writing.

Ma, I wish I knew the histories of the women in our family before you. I bet that would be quite a story. But that may be just as well, because I can say that *you* started something. Maybe you feel ambivalent or doubtful about it, but you did. Actually, you should be proud of what you've begun. I am. If my reaction to being a Yellow Woman is different than yours was, please know that that is not a judgment on you, a criticism or a denial of you, your worth. I have always supported you, and as the years pass, I think I begin to understand you more and more.

In the last few years, I have realized the value of Homework: I have studied the history of our people in this country. I cannot tell you how proud I am to be a Chinese/Korean American Woman. We have such a proud heritage, such a courageous tradition. I want to tell everyone about that, all the particulars that are left out in the schools. And the full awareness of being a woman makes me want to sing. And I do sing with other Asian Americans and women, Ma, anyone who will sing with me.

I feel now that I can begin to put our lives in a larger framework.

Ma, a larger framework! The outlines for us are time and blood, but today there is breadth possible through making connections with others involved in community struggle. In loving ourselves for who we are—American women of color—we can make a vision for the future where we are free to fulfill our human potential. This new framework will not support repression, hatred, exploitation and isolation, but will be a human and beautiful framework, created in a community, bonded not by color, sex or class, but by love and the common goal for the liberation of mind, heart, and spirit.

Ma, today, you are as beautiful and pure to me as the picture I have of you, as a little girl, under my dresser-glass.

I love you,
MERLE

letter to mama

ARMISTEAD MAUPIN
1980

dear mama,

I'm sorry it's taken me so long to write. Every time I try to write to you and Papa I realize I'm not saying the things that are in my heart. That would be O.K., if I loved you any less than I do, but you are still my parents and I am still your child.

I have friends who think I'm foolish to write this letter. I hope they're wrong. I hope their doubts are based on parents who loved and trusted them less than mine do. I hope especially that you'll see this as an act of love on my part, a sign of my continuing need to share my life with you.

I wouldn't have written, I guess, if you hadn't told me about your involvement in the Save Our Children campaign. That, more than anything, made it clear that my responsibility was to tell you the truth, that your own child is homosexual, and that I never needed saving from anything except the cruel and ignorant piety of people like Anita Bryant.

I'm sorry, Mama. Not for what I am, but for how you must feel at this moment. I know what that feeling is, for I felt it for most of my life. Revulsion, shame, disbelief—rejection through fear of something I knew, even as a child, was as basic to my nature as the color of my eyes.

No, Mama, I wasn't "recruited." No seasoned homosexual ever served as my mentor. But you know what? I wish someone had. I wish someone older than me and wiser than the people in Orlando had taken me aside and said, "You're all right, kid. You can grow up to be a doctor or a teacher just like anyone else. You're not crazy or sick or evil. You can succeed and be happy and find peace with friends—all kinds of friends—who don't give a damn *who* you go to bed with.

Most of all, though, you can love and be loved, without hating yourself for it."

But no one ever said that to me, Mama. I had to find it out on my own, with the help of the city that has become my home. I know this may be hard for you to believe, but San Francisco is full of men and women, both straight and gay, who don't consider sexuality in measuring the worth of another human being.

These aren't radicals or weirdos, Mama. They are shop clerks and bankers and little old ladies and people who nod and smile to you when you meet them on the bus. Their attitude is neither patronizing nor pitying. And their message is so simple: Yes, you are a person. Yes, I like you. Yes, it's all right for you to like me, too.

I know what you must be thinking now. You're asking yourself: What did we do wrong? How did we let this happen? Which one of us made him that way?

I can't answer that, Mama. In the long run, I guess I really don't care. All I know is this: If you and Papa are responsible for the way I am, then I thank you with all my heart, for it's the light and the joy of my life.

I know I can't tell you what it is to be gay. But I can tell you what it's not.

It's not hiding behind words, Mama. Like family and decency and Christianity. It's not fearing your body, or the pleasures that God made for it. It's not judging your neighbor, except when he's crass or unkind.

Being gay has taught me tolerance, compassion and humility. It has shown me the limitless possibilities of living. It has given me people whose passion and kindness and sensitivity have provided a constant source of strength.

It has brought me into the family of man, Mama, and I like it here. I *like* it.

There's not much else I can say, except that I'm the same Michael you've always known. You just know me better now. I have never consciously done anything to hurt you. I never will.

Please don't feel you have to answer this right away. It's enough for me to know that I no longer have to lie to the people who taught me to value the truth.

Mary Ann sends her love.

Everything is fine at 28 Barbary Lane.

Your loving son,
MICHAEL

pink triangle and yellow star

GORE VIDAL

1981

A few years ago on a trip to Paris, I read an intriguing review in *Le Monde* of a book called *Comme un Frère, Comme un Amant*, a study of "Male Homosexuality in the American Novel and Theatre from Herman Melville to James Baldwin," the work of one Georges-Michel Sarotte, a Sorbonne graduate and a visiting professor at the University of Massachusetts. I read the book, found it interesting; met the author, found him interesting. He told me that he was looking forward to the publication of his book in the United States by Anchor Press/Doubleday. What sort of response did I think he would have? I was touched by so much innocent good faith. There will be no reaction, I said, because no one outside of the so-called gay press will review your book. He was shocked. Wasn't the book serious? scholarly? with an extensive bibliography? I agreed that it was all those things; unfortunately, scholarly studies having to do with fags do not get reviewed in the United States (this was before the breakthrough of Yale's John Boswell, whose ferociously learned *Christianity, Social Tolerance and Homosexuality* obliged even the "homophobic" *New York Times* to review it intelligently). If Sarotte had written about the agony and wonder of being female and/or Jewish and/or divorced, he would have been extensively reviewed. Even a study of black literature might have got attention (Sarotte is beige), although blacks are currently something of a nonsubject in these last days of empire.

I don't think that Professor Sarotte believed me. I have not seen him since. I also have never seen a review of his book or of Roger Austen's *Playing the Game* (a remarkably detailed account of American writing on homosexuality) or of *The Homosexual as Hero in Contemporary Fiction* by Stephen Adams, reviewed at much length in

England and ignored here, or of a dozen other books that have been sent to me by writers who seem not to understand why an activity of more than casual interest to more than one-third of the male population of the United States warrants no serious discussion. That is to say, no serious *benign* discussion. All-out attacks on faggots are perennially fashionable in our better periodicals.

I am certain that the novel *Tricks* by Renaud Camus (recently translated for St. Martin's Press by Richard Howard, with a preface by Roland Barthes) will receive a perfunctory and hostile response out there in bookchat land. Yet in France, the book was treated as if it were actually literature, admittedly a somewhat moot activity nowadays. So I shall review *Tricks*. But first I think it worth bringing out in the open certain curious facts of our social and cultural life.

The American passion for categorizing has now managed to create two nonexistent categories—gay and straight. Either you are one or you are the other. But since everyone is a mixture of inclinations, the categories keep breaking down; and when they break down, the irrational takes over. You *have* to be one or the other. Although our mental therapists and writers for the better journals usually agree that those who prefer same-sex sex are not exactly criminals (in most of our states and under most circumstances they still are) or sinful or, officially, sick in the head, they must be, somehow, evil or inadequate or dangerous. The Roman Empire fell, didn't it? because of the fags?

Our therapists, journalists, and clergy are seldom very learned. They seem not to realize that most military societies on the rise tend to encourage same-sex activities for reasons that should be obvious to anyone who has not grown up ass-backward, as most Americans have. In the centuries of Rome's great military and political success, there was no differentiation between same-sexers and other-sexers; there was also a lot of crossing back and forth of the sort that those Americans who *do* enjoy inhabiting category-gay or category-straight find hard to deal with. Of the first twelve Roman emperors, only one was exclusively heterosexual. Since these twelve men were pretty tough cookies, rigorously trained as warriors, perhaps our sexual categories and stereotypes are—can it really be?—false. It was not until the sixth century of the empire that same-sex sex was proscribed by church and state. By then, of course, the barbarians were within the gates and the glory had fled.

Today, American evangelical Christians are busy trying to impose on the population at large their superstitions about sex and the sexes and the creation of the world. Given enough turbulence in the land, these natural fascists can be counted on to assist some sort of authoritarian—but never, never totalitarian—political movement. Divines from Santa Clara to Falls Church are particularly fearful of what they describe as the gay liberation movement's attempt to gain "special rights and privileges" when all that the same-sexers want is to be included, which they are not by law and custom, within the framework of the Fourteenth Amendment. The divine in Santa Clara believes that same-sexers should be killed. The divine in Falls Church believes that they should be denied equal rights under the law. Meanwhile, the redneck divines have been joined by a group of New York Jewish publicists who belong to what they proudly call "the new class" (*né arrivistes*), and these lively hucksters have now managed to raise fag-baiting to a level undreamed of in Falls Church—or even in Moscow.

In a letter to a friend, George Orwell wrote, "It is impossible to mention Jews in print, either favorably or unfavorably, without getting into trouble." But there are times when trouble had better be got into before mere trouble turns into catastrophe. Jews, blacks, and homosexualists are despised by the Christian and Communist majorities of East and West. Also, as a result of the invention of Israel, Jews can count on the hatred of the Islamic world. Since our own Christian majority looks to be getting ready for great adventures at home and abroad, I would suggest that the three despised minorities join forces in order not to be destroyed. This seems an obvious thing to do. Unfortunately, most Jews refuse to see any similarity between special situation and that of the same-sexers. At one level, the Jews are perfectly correct. A racial or religious or tribal identity is a kind of fact. Although sexual preference is an even more powerful fact, it is not one that creates any particular social or cultural or religious bond between those so-minded. Although Jews would doubtless be Jews if there was no anti-Semitism, same-sexers would think little or nothing at all about their preference if society ignored it. So there is a difference between the two estates. But there is no difference in the degree of hatred felt by the Christian majority for Christ-killers and Sodomites. In the German concentration camps, Jews wore yellow stars while homosexualists wore pink triangles. I was present when Christopher Isherwood tried to make this point to a young Jewish movie producer. "After all," said Isherwood, "Hitler killed six hundred thousand homosexuals." The young man was not impressed. "But Hitler killed six *million* Jews," he said sternly. "What are you?" asked Isherwood. "In real estate?"

Like it or not, Jews and homosexualists are in the same fragile boat, and one would have to be pretty obtuse not to see the common danger. But obtuseness is the name of the game among New York's new class. Elsewhere, I have described the shrill fag-baiting of Joseph Epstein, Norman Podhoretz, Alfred Kazin, and the Hilton Kramer Hotel. *Harper's* magazine and *Commentary* usually publish these pieces, though other periodicals are not above printing the odd expose of the latest homosexual conspiracy to turn the United States over to the Soviet Union or to structuralism or to Christian Dior. Although the new class's thoughts are never much in themselves, and they themselves are no more than spear carriers in the political and cultural life of the West, their prejudices and superstitions do register in a subliminal way, making mephitic the air of Manhattan if not of the Republic.

A case in point is that of Mrs. Norman Podhoretz, also known as Midge Decter (like Martha Ivers, *whisper* her name). In September of last year, Decter published a piece called "The Boys on the Beach" in her husband's magazine, *Commentary*. It is well worth examining in some detail because she has managed not only to come up with every known prejudice and superstition about same-sexers but also to make up some brand-new ones. For sheer vim and vigor, "The Boys on the Beach" outdoes its implicit model, *The Protocols of the Elders of Zion*.

Decter notes that when the "homosexual-rights movement first burst upon the scene," she was "more than a little astonished." Like so many new-class persons, she writes a stilted sort of genteel-gentile prose not unlike—but not very like, either—*The New Yorker* house style of the 1940s and 50s. She also writes with the authority and easy confidence of someone who knows that she is very well known indeed to those few who know her.

Decter tells us that twenty years ago, she got to know a lot of pansies at a resort called Fire Island Pines, where she and a number of other new-class persons used to make it during the summers. She estimates that 40 percent of the summer people were heterosexual; the rest were not. Yet the "denizens, homosexual and heterosexual alike, were predominantly professionals and people in soft marginal businesses—lawyers, advertising executives, psychotherapists, actors, editors, writers, publishers, etc." Keep this in mind. Our authoress does not.

Decter goes on to tell us that she is now amazed at the recent changes in the boys on the beach. Why have they become so politically militant—and so ill groomed? "What indeed has happened to the homosexual community I used to know—they who only a few short years ago [as opposed to those manly 370-day years] were characterized by nothing so much as a sweet, vain, pouting, girlish attention to the youth and beauty of their bodies?" Decter wrestles with this problem. She tells us how, in the old days, she did her very best to come to terms with her own normal dislike for these half-men—and half-women, too: "There were also homosexual women at the Pines, but they were, or seemed to be, far fewer in number. Nor, except for a marked tendency to hang out in the company of large and ferocious dogs, were they instantly recognizable as the men were." Well, if I were a dyke and a pair of Podhoretzes came waddling toward me on the beach, copies of Leviticus and Freud in hand, I'd get in touch with the nearest Alsatian dealer pronto.

Decter was disturbed by "the slender, seamless, elegant and utterly chic" clothes of the fairies. She also found it "a constant source of wonder" that when the fairies took off their clothes, "the largest number of homosexuals had hairless bodies. Chests, backs, arms, even legs were smooth and silky. . . . We were never able to determine just why there should be so definite a connection between what is nowadays called their sexual preference [previously known to right-thinking Jews as an abomination against Jehovah] and their smooth feminine skin. Was it a matter of hormones?" Here Decter betrays her essential modesty and lack of experience. In the no doubt privileged environment of her Midwestern youth, she could not have seen very many gentile males without their clothes on. If she had, she would have discovered that gentile men tend to be less hairy than Jews except, of course, when they are not. Because the Jews killed our Lord, they are forever marked with hair on their shoulders—something that no gentile man has on *his* shoulders except for John Travolta and a handful of other Italian-Americans from the Englewood, New Jersey, area.

It is startling that Decter has not yet learned that there is no hormonal difference between men who like sex with other men and those who like sex with women. She notes, "There is also such a thing as characteristic homosexual speech . . . it is something of an accent redolent of small towns in the Midwest whence so many homosexuals seemed to have migrated to the big city." Here one detects the disdain of the self-made New Yorker for the rural or small-town American. "Midwest" is often a code word for the flyovers, for the millions who do not really matter. But she is right in the sense that when a group chooses to live and work together, they do tend to sound and look alike. No matter how crowded and noisy a room, one can always detect the new-class person's nasal whine.

Every now and then, Decter does wonder if, perhaps, she is generalizing and whether this will "no doubt in itself seem to many of the uninitiated a bigoted formulation." Well, Midge, it does. But the spirit is upon her, and she cannot stop because "one cannot even begin to get at the truth about homosexuals without this kind of generalization. They are a group so readily distinguishable." Except of course, when they are not. It is one thing for a group of queens, in "soft, marginal" jobs, to "cavort," as she puts it, in a summer place and be "easily distinguishable" to her cold eye just as Jewish members of the new class are equally noticeable to the cold gentile eye. But it is quite another thing for those men and women who prefer same-sex sex to other-sex sex yet do not choose to be identified—and so are not. To begin to get at the truth about homosexuals, one must realize that the majority of those millions of Americans who prefer same-sex sex to other-sex sex are obliged, sometimes willingly and happily but often not, to marry and have children and to conform to the guidelines set down by the heterosexual dictatorship.

Decter would know nothing of this because in her "soft, marginal" world, she is not meant to know. She does remark upon the fairies at the Pines who did have wives and children: "They were for the most part charming and amusing fathers, rather like favorite uncles. And their wives . . . drank." This dramatic ellipsis is most Decterian.

She ticks off Susan Sontag for omitting to mention in the course of an essay on camp "that camp is of the essence of homosexual style, invented by homosexuals, and serving the purpose of domination by ridicule." The word "domination" is a characteristic new-class touch. The powerless are always obsessed by power. Decter seems unaware that all despised minorities are quick to make rather good jokes about themselves before the hostile majority does. Certainly Jewish humor, from the Book of Job (a laff-riot) to pre-*auteur* Woody Allen, is based on this.

Decter next does the ritual attack on Edward Albee and Tennessee Williams for presenting "what could only have been homosexual relationships as the deeper truth about love in our time." This is about as true as the late Maria Callas's conviction that you could always tell a Jew because he had a hump at the back of his neck— something Callas herself had in dromedarian spades.

Decter makes much of what she assumes to be the fags' mockery of the heterosexual men at the Pines: "Homosexuality paints them [heterosexuals] with the color of sheer entrapment," while the fags' "smooth and elegant exteriors, unmussed by traffic with the detritus of modern family existence, constituted a kind of sniggering reproach to their striving and harried straight brothers." Although I have never visited the Pines, I am pretty sure that I know the "soft marginal" types, both hetero and homo, that hung out there in the 1960s. One of the most noticeable characteristics of the self-ghettoized same-sexer is his perfect indifference to the world of the other-sexers. Although Decter's blood was always at the boil when contemplating these unnatural and immature half-men, they were, I would suspect, serenely unaware of her and her new-class cronies, solemnly worshipping at the shrine of The Family.

To hear Decter tell it, fags had nothing to complain of then, and they have nothing to complain of now: "Just to name the professions and industries in which they had, and still have, a significant presence is to define the boundaries of a certain kind of privilege: theatre, music, letters, dance, design, architecture, the visual arts, fashion at every level—from head, as it were, to foot, and from inception to retail—advertising, journalism, interior decoration, antique dealing, publishing . . . the list could go on." Yes. But these are all pretty "soft, marginal" occupations. And none is "dominated" by fags. Most male same-sexers are laborers, farmers, mechanics, small businessmen, schoolteachers, firemen, policemen, soldiers, sailors. Most female same-sexers are wives and mothers. In other words, they are like the rest of the population. But then it is hard for the new-class person to realize that Manhattan is not the world. Or as a somewhat alarmed Philip Rahv said to me after he had taken a drive across the United States, "My God! There are so many of them!" In theory, Rahv had always known that there were a couple of hundred million gentiles out there, but to see them, in the flesh, unnerved him. I told him that I was unnerved, too, particularly when they start showering in the Blood of the Lamb.

Decter does concede that homosexualists have probably not "established much of a presence in basic industry or government service or in such classic [new-classy?] professions as doctoring and lawyering but then for anyone acquainted with them as a group the thought suggests itself that few of them have ever made much effort in these directions." Plainly, the silly billies are too busy dressing up and dancing the hullygully to argue a case in court. Decter will be relieved to know that the percentage of same-sexers in the "classic" activities is almost as high, proportionately, as that of Jews. But a homosexualist in a key position at, let us say, the Department of Labor will be married and living under a good deal of strain because he could be fired if it is known that he likes to have sex with other men.

Decter knows that there have always been homosexual teachers, and she thinks that they should keep quiet about it. But if they keep quiet, they can be blackmailed or fired. Also, a point that would really distress her, a teacher known to be a same-sexer would be a splendid role model for those same-sexers that he—or she—is teaching. Decter would think this an unmitigated evil because men and women were created to breed; but, of course, it would be a perfect good because we have more babies than we know what to do with while we lack, notoriously, useful citizens at ease with themselves. That is what the row over the schools is all about.

Like most members of the new class, Decter accepts without question Freud's line (*Introductory Lectures on Psychoanalysis*) that "we actually describe a sexual activity as perverse if it has given up the aim of reproduction and pursues the attainment of pleasure as an aim independent of it." For Freud, perversion was any sexual activity involving "the abandonment of the reproductive function." Freud also deplored masturbation as a dangerous "primal affliction." So did Moses. But then it was Freud's curious task to try to create a rational, quasi-scientific basis for Mosaic law. The result has been not unlike the accomplishments of Freud's great contemporary, the ineffable and inexorable Mary Baker Eddy, whose First Church of Christ Scientist he was able to match with *his* First Temple of Moses Scientist.

Decter says that once faggots have "ensconced" themselves in certain professions or arts, "they themselves have engaged in a good deal of discriminatory practices against others. There are businesses and professions [which ones? She is congenitally short of data] in which it is less than easy for a straight, unless he makes the requisite gesture of propitiation to the homosexual in power, to get ahead." This, of course, was Hitler's original line about the Jews: they had taken over German medicine, teaching, law, journalism. Ruthlessly, they kept out gentiles; lecherously, they demanded sexual favors. "I simply want to reduce their numbers in these fields," Hitler told Prince Philip of Hesse. "I want them proportionate to their overall number in the population." This was the early solution; the final solution followed with equal logic.

In the 1950s, it was an article of faith in new-class circles that television had been taken over by the fags. Now I happen to have known most of the leading producers of that time and, of a dozen, the two who were interested in same-sex activities were both married to women who . . . did not drink. Neither man dared mix sex with business. Every now and then an actor would say that he had not got work because he had refused to put out for a faggot producer, but I doubt very much if there was ever any truth to what was to become a bright jack-o'-lantern in the McCarthy *Walpurgisnacht*.

When I was several thousand words into Decter's tirade, I suddenly realized that she does not know what homosexuality is. At some level she may have stumbled, by accident, on a truth that she would never have been able to comprehend in a rational way. Although to have sexual relations with a member of one's own sex is a common and natural activity (currently disapproved of by certain elements in this culture), there is no such thing as a homosexualist any more than there is such a thing as a heterosexualist. That is one of the reasons there has been so much difficulty with nomenclature. Despite John Boswell's attempts to give legitimacy to the word "gay," it is still a ridiculous word to use as a common identification for Frederick the Great, Franklin Pangborn and Eleanor Roosevelt. What makes some people prefer same-sex sex drives from whatever impulse or conditioning makes some people prefer other-sex sex. This is so plain that it seems impossible that our Mosaic-Pauline-Freudian society has not yet figured it out. But to ignore the absence of evidence is the basis of true faith.

Decter seems to think that yesteryear's chic and silly boys on the beach and today's socially militant fags are simply, to use her verb, "adopting" what she calls, in her tastefully appointed English, a lifestyle. On the other hand, "whatever disciplines it might entail, heterosexuality is not something adopted but something accepted. In woes — and they have of course nowhere been more exaggerated than in those areas of the culture consciously or unconsciously influenced by the propaganda of homosexuals — are experienced as the woes of life."

"Propaganda" — another key word. "Power." "Propitiation." "Domination." What *does* the new class dream of?

Decter now moves in the big artillery. Not only are fags silly and a nuisance but they are, in their unrelenting hatred of heterosexualists, given to depicting them in their plays and films and books as a bunch of klutzes, thereby causing truly good men and women to falter — even question — that warm, mature heterosexuality that is so necessary to keeping this country great while allowing new-class persons to make it materially.

Decter is in full cry. Fags are really imitation women. Decter persists in thinking that same-sexers are effeminate, swishy, girlish. It is true that a small percentage of homosexualists are indeed effeminate, just as there are effeminate heterosexualists. I don't know why this is so. No one knows why. Except Decter. She believes that this sort "of female imitation pointed neither to sympathy with nor flattery of the female principle." Yet queens of the sort she is writing about tend to get on very well with women. But Decter can only cope with two stereotypes: the boys on the beach, mincing about, and the drab political radicals of gay liberation. The millions of ordinary masculine types are unknown to her because they are not identifiable by voice or walk and, most important, because they have nothing in common with one another except the desire to have same-sex relations. Or, put the other way around, since Lyndon Johnson and Bertrand Russell were both heterosexualists, what character traits did *they* have in common? I should think none at all. So it is with the invisible millions—now becoming less invisible—of same-sexers.

But Decter knows her Freud, and reality may not intrude: "The desire to escape from the sexual reminder of birth and death, with its threat of paternity—that is, the displacement of oneself by others— was the main underlying desire that sent those Fire Island homosexuals into the arms of other men. Had it been the opposite desire—that is, the positive attraction to the manly—at least half the boutiques, etc.," would have closed. Decter should take a stroll down San Francisco's Castro Street, where members of the present generation of boys look like off-duty policemen or construction workers. They have embraced the manly. But Freud has spoken. Fags are fags because they adored their mothers and hated their poor, hard-working daddies. It is amazing the credence still given this unproven, unprovable thesis.

CURIOUSLY ENOUGH, AS I was writing these lines, expressing yet again the unacceptable obvious, I ran across Ralph Blumenthal's article in the *New York Times* (August 25), which used "unpublished letters and growing research into the hidden life of Sigmund Freud" to examine "Freud's reversal of his theory attributing neurosis in adults to sexual seduction in childhood." Despite the evidence given by his patients, Freud decided that their memories of molestation were "phantasies." He then appropriated from the high culture (a real act of hubris) Oedipus the King, and made him a complex. Freud was much criticized for this theory at the time — particularly by Sandor Ferenczi. Now, as we learn more about Freud (not to mention about the sexual habits of Victorian Vienna as reported in police records), his theory is again under attack. Drs. Milton Klein and David Tribich have written a paper titled "On Freud's Blindness." They have studied his case histories and observed how he ignored evidence, how "he looked to the child and only to the child, in uncovering the causes of psychopathology." Dr. Karl Menninger wrote Dr. Klein about these findings: "Why oh why couldn't Freud believe his own ears?" Dr. Menninger then noted, "Seventy-five per cent of the girls we accept at the Villages have been molested in childhood by an adult. And that's today in Kansas! I don't think Vienna in 1900 was any less sophisticated."

In the same week as Blumenthal's report on the discrediting of the Oedipus complex, researchers at the Kinsey Institute reported (*The Observer*, August 30) that after studying 979 homosexualists ("the largest sample of homosexuals — black and white, male and female — ever questioned in an academic study") and 477 heterosexualists, they came to the conclusion that family life has nothing to do with sexual preference. Apparently, "homosexuality is deep-rooted in childhood, may be biological in origin, and simply shows in more and more important ways as a child grows older. It is not a condition which therapy can reverse." Also, "homosexual feelings begin as much as three years before any sort of homosexual act, undermining theories that homosexuality is learned through experience." There goes the teacher as-seducer-and-perverter myth. Finally, "Psychoanalysts' theories about smothering mum and absent dad do not stand investigation. Patients may tend to believe that they are true because therapists subtly coach them in the appropriate memories of their family life."

SOME YEARS AGO, gay activists came to *Harper's*, where Decter was an editor, to demonstrate against an article by Joseph Epstein, who had announced, "If I had the power to do so, I would wish homosexuality off the face of the earth." Well, that's what Hitler had the power to do in Germany, and did — or tried to do. The confrontation at *Harper's* now provides Decter with her theme. She tells us that one of the demonstrators asked, "Are you aware of how many suicides you may be responsible for in the homosexual community?" I suspect that she is leaving out the context of this somewhat left-field *cri de coeur*. After all, homosexualists have more to fear from murder than suicide. I am sure that the actual conversation had to do with the sort of mischievous effect that Epstein's Hitlerian piece might have had on those fag-baiters who read it.

But Decter slyly zeroes in on the word "suicide." She then develops a most unusual thesis. Homosexualists hate themselves to such an extent that they wish to become extinct either through inviting murder or committing suicide. She notes that in a survey of San Francisco's homosexual men, half of them "claimed to have had sex with at least five hundred people." This "bespeaks the obliteration of all experience, if not, indeed, of oneself." Plainly Decter has a Mosaic paradigm forever in mind and any variation on it is abominable. Most men—homo or hetero—given the opportunity to have sex with 500 different people would do so, gladly; but most men are not going to be given the opportunity by a society that wants them safely married so that they will be docile workers and loyal consumers. It does not suit our rulers to have the proles tomcatting around the way that our rulers do. I can assure Decter that the thirty-fifth president went to bed with more than 500 women and that the well-known . . . but I must not give away the secrets of the old class or the newly-middle-class new class will go into shock.

Meanwhile, according to Decter, "many homosexuals are nowadays engaged in efforts at self-obliteration . . . there is the appalling rate of suicide among them." But the rate is not appreciably higher than that for the rest of the population. In any case, most who do commit—or contemplate—suicide do so because they cannot cope in a world where they are, to say the least, second-class citizens. But Decter is now entering uncharted country. She also has a point to make: "What is undeniable is the increasing longing among the homosexuals to do away with themselves—if not in the actual physical sense then at least spiritually—a longing whose chief emblem, among others, is the leather bars."

So Epstein will not be obliged to press that button in order to get rid of the fags. They will do it themselves. Decter ought to be pleased by this, but it is not in her nature to be pleased by anything that the same-sexers do. If they get married and have children and swear fealty to the family gods of the new class, their wives will . . . drink. If they live openly with one another, they have fled from woman and real life. If they pursue careers in the arts, heteros will have to be on guard against vicious covert assaults on heterosexual values. If they congregate in the fashion business the way that Jews do in psychiatry, they will employ only those heterosexuals who will put out for them.

Decter is appalled by the fag "takeover" of San Francisco. She tells us about the "ever deepening resentment of the San Francisco straight community at the homosexuals' defiant displays and power ['power'!] over this city," but five paragraphs later she contradicts herself: "Having to a very great extent overcome revulsion of common opinion, are they left with some kind of unappeased hunger that only their own feelings of hatefulness can now satisfy?"

There it is. *They are hateful.* They know it. That is why they want to eliminate themselves. "One thing is certain." Decter finds a lot of certainty around. "To become homosexual is a weighty act." She still has not got the point that one does not choose to have same-sex impulses; one simply has them, as everyone has, to a greater or lesser degree, other-sex impulses. To deny giving physical expression to those desires may be pleasing to Moses and Saint Paul and Freud, but these three rabbis are aberrant figures whose nomadic values are not those of the thousands of other tribes that live or have lived on the planet. Women's and gay liberation are simply small efforts to free men and women from this trio.

Decter writes, "Taking oneself out of the tides of ordinary mortal existence is not something one does from any longing to think oneself ordinary (but only following a different 'life-style')." I don't quite grasp this sentence. Let us move on to the next: "Gay Lib has been an effort to set the weight of that act at naught, to define homosexuality as nothing more than a casual option among options." Gay lib has done just the opposite. After all, people are what they are sexually not through "adoption" but because that is the way they are structured. Some people do shift about in the course of a life. Also, most of those with same-sex drives do indeed "adopt" the heterosexual life-style because they don't want to go to prison or to the madhouse or become unemployable. Obviously, there *is* an option but it is a hard one that ought not to be forced on any human being. After all, homosexuality is only important when made so by irrational opponents. In this, as in so much else, the Jewish situation is precisely the same.

Decter now gives us not a final solution so much as a final conclusion: "In accepting the movement's terms [hardly anyone has, by the way], heterosexuals have only raised to a nearly intolerable height the costs of the homosexuals' flight from normality." The flight, apparently, is deliberate, a matter of perverse choice, a misunderstanding of daddy, a passion for mummy, a fear of responsibility. Decter threads her clichés like Teclas on a string: "Faced with the accelerating round of drugs, S-M and suicide, can either the movement or its heterosexual sympathizers imagine they have done anyone a kindness?"

Although the kindness of strangers is much sought after, gay liberation has not got much support from anyone. Natural allies like the Jews are often virulent in their attacks. Blacks in their ghettos, Chicanos in their barrios, and rednecks in their pulpits also have been influenced by the same tribal taboos. That Jews and blacks and Chicanos and rednecks all contribute to the ranks of the same-sexers only increases the madness. But the world of the Decters is a world of perfect illogic.

Herewith the burden of "The Boys on the Beach": since homosexualists choose to be the way they are out of idle hatefulness, it has been a mistake to allow them to come out of the closet to the extent that they have, but now that they are out (which most are not), they will have no choice but to face up to their essential hatefulness and abnormality and so be driven to kill themselves with promiscuity, drugs, S-M and suicide. Not even the authors of *The Protocols of the Elders of Zion* ever suggested that the Jews, who were so hateful to them, were also hateful to themselves. So Decter has managed to go one step further than the Protocols' authors; she is indeed a virtuoso of hate, and thus do pogroms begin.

TRICKS IS THE story of an author—Renaud Camus himself—who has twenty-five sexual encounters in the course of six months. Each of these encounters involves a pick-up. Extrapolating from Camus's sexual vigor at the age of 35, I would suspect that he has already passed the 500 mark and so is completely obliterated as a human being. If he is, he still writes very well indeed. He seems to be having a good time, and he shows no sign of wanting to kill himself, but then that may be a front he's keeping up. I am sure that Decter will be able to tell just how close he is to OD'ing.

From his photograph, Camus appears to have a lot of hair on his chest. I don't know about the shoulders, as they are covered, modestly, with a shirt. Perhaps he is Jewish. Roland Barthes wrote an introduction to *Tricks*. For a time, Barthes was much admired in American academe. But then, a few years ago, Barthes began to write about his same-sexual activities; he is now mentioned a bit less than he was in the days before he came out, as they say.

Barthes notes that Camus's book is a "text that belongs to literature."

It is not pornographic. It is also not a Homosexual Novel in that there are no deep, anguished chats about homosexuality. In fact, the subject is never mentioned; it just is. Barthes remarks, "Homosexuality shocks less [well, he is—or was—French], but continues to be interesting; it is still at that stage of excitation where it provokes what might be called feats of discourse [see "The Boys on the Beach," no mean feat!]. Speaking of homosexuality permits those who aren't to show how open, liberal, and modern they are; and those who are to bear witness, to assume responsibility, to militate. Everyone gets busy, in different ways, whipping it up." You can say that again! And Barthes does. But with a nice variation. He makes the point that you are never allowed *not* to be categorized. But then, "say 'I am' and you will be socially saved." Hence the passion for the either/or.

Camus does not set out to give a panoramic view of homosexuality. He comments, in *his* preface, on the variety of homosexual expressions. Although there is no stigma attached to homosexuality in the French intellectual world where, presumably, there is no equivalent of the new class, the feeling among the lower classes is still intense, a memento of the now exhausted (in France) Roman Catholic Church's old dirty work ("I don't understand the French Catholics," said John Paul II). As a result, many "refuse to grant their tastes because they live in such circumstances, in such circles, that their desires are not only for themselves inadmissible but inconceivable, unspeakable."

It is hard to describe a book that is itself a description, and that is what *Tricks* is—a flat, matter-of-fact description of how the narrator meets the tricks, what each says to the other, where they go, how the rooms are furnished, and what the men do. One of the tricks is nuts; a number are very hairy—the narrator has a Decterian passion for the furry; there is a lot of anal and banal sex as well as oral and floral sex. *Frottage* flows. Most of the encounters take place in France, but there is one in Washington, D.C., with a black man. There is a good deal of comedy, in the Raymond Roussel manner.

Tricks will give ammunition to those new-class persons and redneck divines who find promiscuity every bit as abominable as same-sex relations. But that is the way men are when they are given freedom to go about their business unmolested. One current Arab ruler boasts of having ten sexual encounters a day, usually with different women. A diplomat who knows him says that he exaggerates, but not much. Of course, he is a Moslem.

The family, as we know it, is an economic, not a biological, unit. I

realize that this is startling news in this culture and at a time when
the economies of both East and West require that the nuclear family
be, simply, God. But our ancestors did not live as we do. They lived
in packs for hundreds of millennia before "history" began, a mere
5,000 years ago. Whatever social arrangements human society may
come up with in the future, it will have to be acknowledged that
those children who are needed should be rather more thoughtfully
brought up than they are today and that those adults who do not care
to be fathers or mothers should be let off the hook. This is beginning,
slowly, to dawn. Hence, the rising hysteria in the land. Hence, the
concerted effort to deny the human ordinariness of same-sexualists. A
recent attempt to portray such a person sympathetically on television
was abandoned when the Christers rose up in arms.

Although I would never suggest that Truman Capote's bright wit
and sweet charm as a television performer would not have easily
achieved for him his present stardom had he been a *hetero*sexualist, I
do know that if he had not existed in his present form, another would
have been run up on the old sewing machine because that sort of *persona* must be, for a whole nation, the stereotype of what a fag is.
Should some macho film star like Clint Eastwood, say, decide to
confess on television that he is really into same-sex sex, the cathode
tube would blow a fuse. That could never be allowed. That is all
wrong. That is how the Roman Empire fell.

There is not much *angst* in *Tricks.* No one commits suicide—but
there is one sad story. A militant leftist friend of Camus's was a
teacher in the south of France. He taught 14-year-old members of
that oldest of all the classes, the exploited laborer. One of his pupils
saw him in a fag bar and spread the word. The students began to torment what had been a favorite teacher. "These are little proles," he
tells Camus, "and Mediterranean besides—which means they're
obsessed by every possible macho myth, and by homosexuality as
well. It's all they can think about." One of the boys, an Arab, followed
him down the street, screaming "Faggot!" "It was as if he had finally
found someone onto whom he could project his resentment, someone he could hold in contempt with complete peace of mind."

This might explain the ferocity of the new class on the subject.
They know that should the bad times return, the Jews will be singled
out yet again. Meanwhile, like so many Max Naumanns (Naumann
as a German Jew who embraced Nazism), the new class passionately
supports our ruling class—from the Chase Manhattan Bank to the
Pentagon to the Op-Ed page of *The Wall Street Journal*—while hold-

ing in fierce contempt faggots, blacks (see Norman Podhoretz's "My Negro Problem and Ours," *Commentary*, February 1963), and the poor (see Midge Decter's "Looting and Liberal Racism," *Commentary*, September 1977). Since these Neo-Naumannites are going to be in the same gas chambers as the blacks and the faggots, I would suggest a cease-fire and a common front against the common enemy, whose kindly voice is that of Ronald Reagan and whose less than kindly mind is elsewhere in the boardrooms of the Republic.

from
how to have sex
in an epidemic

RICHARD BERKOWITZ AND MICHAEL CALLEN
1983

Should AIDS Patients Have Sex?

This is quite a controversial issue, but regardless of what one feels, the fact is that some men who have been diagnosed with AIDS are continuing to have sex. Of course, for some AIDS patients, sex is the furthest thing from their minds. But for other AIDS patients, sexual desire remains. Some are limiting the sexual contacts they have to other AIDS patients. Others are having sex only with their lovers. And some AIDS patients are continuing to have multiple sexual contacts.

AIDS patients are human beings and need affection and human contact. AIDS patients object to being treated like lepers and some end up taking this anger and frustration out to the baths and backrooms.

The issue of AIDS patients having sex must be viewed from two perspectives: the risk to the patient and the potential risk to his partner.

The one thing AIDS patients know for sure is that they are immune suppressed. This means they are more vulnerable to infections. In addition, if they *do* develop an infection, they know that they will have a more difficult time recovering. It is possible that sex is more of a danger to the AIDS patient than to his partner. Considering the risks to the patients themselves, multiple sexual contacts, particularly in settings such as the baths and backrooms where disease is rampant, is extremely unwise.

In terms of the risk to the partners of AIDS patients, we believe that the primary danger is the transmission of CMV. Of course, if you believe that there is a new virus which is the cause of AIDS, having sex with an AIDS patient might transmit such a new virus.

The decision of whether and how AIDS patients should have sex and the decisions of whether and how partners should have sex with AIDS patients are difficult ones to make. Each person must weigh the evidence, determine his own risk, and act accordingly. However, WE BELIEVE THAT AIDS PATIENTS HAVE AN ETHICAL OBLI-GATION TO ADVISE POTENTIAL PARTNERS OF THEIR HEALTH STATUS.

We believe that AIDS patients must allow their partners to make the the their own choice. There *are* gay men who are willing to take the necessary precautions designed to protect both partners' health. Obviously we believe that lovers of AIDS patients can continue having sex with AIDS patients if they exercise the precautions outlined in this paper. There are AIDS patients who are continuing to have "safe sex" and who are recovering from their immune suppression. And there are lovers who have continued to have sex safely with AIDS patients who are not showing signs of immune deficiency and who are not contracting CMV.

But apart from the issue of sex, the absence of firm evidence that AIDS can be transmitted by casual, non-sexual intimacy, we see no reason why hugging and affections should be discouraged or with-held.

Guilt, Morality and Sex Negativity

The AIDS crisis has forced many gay men to examine their lifestyles. It has also produced a lot of recommendations which are really misplaced morality masquerading as medical advice.

Gay men have always been criticized for having "too much sex" with "too many" different partners. Because the development of AIDS in gay men is obviously somehow connected with the amount and kind of sex we have, a lot of advice has focused on "reducing" the "number of different partners." Wherever we turn we are reminded of the joy of romance and dating by those who claim they are only concerned with our health.

In this age of AIDS, the advice most often given is that we should try to "cut down" on the number of different partners we have sex with and try to limit those partners we do have sex with to "healthy" men. This advice confuses many gay men. What is meant by "cut down"? Is it going to the baths once a month instead of once a week? Is it having two partners a night instead of four? And how can we determine whether or not a potential partner is "healthy" when there are many infections which don't have obvious symptoms? While having less sex will definitely reduce our chances for all STDs, it will certainly not eliminate them.

Advice which focuses only on *numbers* and which ignores ways to interrupt disease transmission is incomplete. For example, a gay man who is concerned with protecting his health may decide to "cut down" on the amount of sex he has by limiting himself to one different partner a month. At the end of the year, he will have had sex with 12 different partners. Few gay men would consider having 12 sex partners a year being "promiscuous," but this example illustrates the point that the issue isn't sex, it's disease. Since one out of every four of his 12 sexual partners was probably contagious for CMV (despite his best efforts to guess who was "healthy"), he will have been exposed to CMV 3 times that year—unless he limited which sexual acts he performed to ones which interrupt disease transmission.

If a concerned gay man makes the tremendous effort to change his sexual behavior by reducing the number of different partners, yet fails to modify what he does, chances are high that he will still often get sick. This has to be demoralizing. He may even feel that all his efforts have been useless and go back to his old patterns. Or he may respond by giving up sex completely.

But deciding to stop having sex because sex may lead to AIDS is not the same as deciding to stop smoking because smoking can cause cancer. Smoking is a habit, a luxury "vice." Sex is a natural and important human need. Although every individual will ultimately have to balance need and risk himself to do so will require that he have the information necessary to make informed changes.

And while we're on the subject, what's all this talk about "anonymous" sex being dangerous. Anonymity in itself has nothing to do with disease transmission.

If your partner introduces himself, he is no longer an anonymous partner. But if he is contagious for syphilis, you'll get syphilis. It's as simple as that.

A lot of this talk about "anonymous" sex being "bad" smacks of misplaced morality. This issue is disease—not sex.

One reason why anonymity can be dangerous is that when you don't know your partners, you may not be as cautious in protecting him from disease. We need a more precise vocabulary to talk about the various lifestyles we lead. When you are receiving advice about sex, it's very important to make sure that the advice is based on sound, scientific understanding of how diseases are transmitted. Don't be fooled just because the source of advice seems authoritative. Verify what you are told by talking to physicians and consulting other sources of information.

If we are to celebrate our gayness and get on with gay liberation, we must stay healthy. To stay healthy, we must realize that the issue isn't gayness or sex; the issue is simply disease.

Love

It came as quite a shock to us to find that we had written almost 40 pages on sex without mentioning the word "love" once. Truly, we have been revealed as products of the '70s.

It has become unfashionable to refer to sex a "lovemaking." Why might this be so?

If the sexual revolution that began in the '60's confirmed one thing it was that sex and affection—sex and love—are not necessarily the same thing. The concept of "recreational sex" has gained widespread acceptance.

At the same time, as the rising epidemics of STDs have demonstrated, there are certain unfortunate (and unforeseen?) side effects when love and affection become so separated from sex.

Without affection, it is less likely that you will care as much if you give your partners disease. During the '70s fantasy was encouraged. Sex with partners you did not know—and did not want to know—was justified as being personally meaningful even if it wasn't interpersonally so. Put another way, did gay male culture of the '70s encourage us to substitute the *fantasy* of the man we were holding for his reality?

Gay men are socialized as men first; our gay socialization comes later. From the day we are born we are trained as men to compete with other men. The challenge facing gay men in America is to figure out how to love someone you've been trained to "destroy."

The goal of gay male liberation must be to find ways in which love becomes possible despite continuing and often overwhelming pressure to compete and adopt adversary relationships with other men.

Gay male politics have historically suffered from fractionalism. Might this be a symptom of the competitiveness between males? And why has it been so difficult to involve gay men politically? Is it possible that all the great sex we've been having for the last decade has siphoned off our collective anger which might otherwise have been translated into social and political action?

The commercialization of urban gay male culture today offers us places to go and get sick and places to go and get treated. Too many gay men get together for only two reasons: to exploit each other and to be exploited.

Sex and "promiscuity" have become the dogma of gay male liberation. Have we modified the belief that we could dance our way to liberation into the belief that we could somehow fuck our way there? If sex is liberating, is more sex necessarily more liberating?

It has certainly become easier to fuck each other. But has it become any easier to love each other? Men *loving* men was the basis of gay male liberation, but we have now created "cultural institutions" in which love or even affection can be totally avoided.

If you love the person you are fucking with—*even for one night*—you will not want to make him sick:

Maybe affection is our best protection.

Hard question for hard times. But what happened to our great gay imaginations?

1,112 and counting _{from}

LARRY KRAMER

from the *New York Native* March, 1983

if this article doesn't scare the shit out of you, we're in real trouble. If this article doesn't rouse you to anger, fury, rage, and action, gay men may have no future on this earth. Our continued existence depends on just how angry you can get.

I am writing this as Larry Kramer, and I am speaking for myself, and my views are not to be attributed to Gay Men's Health Crisis.

I repeat: Our continued existence as gay men upon the face of this earth is at stake. Unless we fight for our lives, we shall die. In all the history of homosexuality we have never before been so close to death and extinction. Many of us are dying or already dead.

Before I tell you what we must do, let me tell you what is happening to us.

There are now 1,112 cases of serious Acquired Immune Deficiency Syndrome. When we first became worried, there were only 41. In only twenty-eight days, from January 13th to February 9th [1983], there were 164 new cases—and 73 more dead. The total death tally is now 418. Twenty percent of all cases were registered this January alone. There have been 195 dead in New York City from among 526 victims. Of all serious AIDS cases, 47.3 percent are in the New York metropolitan area.

These are the serious cases of AIDS, which means Kaposi's sarcoma, *Pneumocystis carinii* pneumonia, and other deadly infections. These numbers do not include the thousands of us walking around with what is also being called AIDS: various forms of swollen lymph glands and fatigues that doctors don't know what to label or what they might portend.

The rise in these numbers is terrifying. Whatever is spreading is now spreading faster as more and more people come down with AIDS.

And, for the first time in this epidemic, leading doctors and researchers are finally admitting they don't know what's going on. I find this terrifying too—as terrifying as the alarming rise in numbers. For the first time, doctors are saying out loud and up front, "I don't know."

For two years they weren't talking like this. For two years we've heard a different theory every few weeks. We grasped at the straws of possible cause: promiscuity, poppers, back rooms, the baths, rimming, fisting, anal intercourse, urine, semen, shit, saliva, sweat, blood, blacks, single virus, a new virus, repeated exposure to a virus, amoebas carrying a virus, drugs. Haiti, voodoo, Flagyl, constant bouts of amebiasis, hepatitis A and B, syphilis, gonorrhea.

I have talked with the leading doctors treating us. One said to me, "If I knew in 1981 what I know now, I would never have become involved with this disease." Another said, "The thing that upsets me the most in all of this is that at any given moment one of my patients is in the hospital and something is going on with him that I don't understand. And it's destroying me because there's some craziness going on in him that's destroying him." A third said to me, "I'm very depressed. A doctor's job is to make patients well. And I can't. Too many of my patients die."

After almost two years of an epidemic, there are still no answers. After almost two years of an epidemic, the cause of AIDS remains unknown. After almost two years of an epidemic, there is no cure.

Hospitals are now so filled with AIDS patients that there is often a waiting period of up to a month before admission, no matter how sick you are. And, once in, patients are now more and more being treated like lepers as hospital staffs become increasingly worried that AIDS is infectious.

Suicides are now being reported of men who would rather die than face such medical uncertainty, such uncertain therapies, such hospital treatment, and the appalling statistics that 86 percent of all serious AIDS cases die after three years' time.

If all of this had been happening to any other community for two long years, there would have been, long ago, such an outcry from that community and all its members that the government of this city and this country would not know what had hit them.

Why isn't every gay man in this city so scared shitless that he is screaming for action? Does every gay man in New York *want* to die?

Let's talk about a few things specifically.

Let's talk about which gay men get AIDS.

No matter what you've heard, there is no single profile for all AIDS victims. There are drug users and non-drug users. There are the truly promiscuous and the almost monogamous. There are reported cases of single-contact infection.

All it seems to take is the one wrong fuck. That's not promiscuity—that's bad luck.

• Let's talk about AIDS happening in straight people.

We have been hearing from the beginning of this epidemic that it was only a question of time before the straight community came down with AIDS, and when that happened AIDS would suddenly be high on all agendas for funding and research and then we would finally be looked after and all would then be well.

I myself thought, when AIDS occurred in the first baby, that would be the breakthrough point. It was. For one day the media paid an enormous amount of attention. And that was it, kids.

There have been no confirmed cases of AIDS in straight, white, non-intravenous-drug-using, middle-class Americans. The only confirmed straights struck down by AIDS are members of groups just as disenfranchised as gay men: intravenous drug users. Haitians, eleven hemophiliacs (up from eight), black and Hispanic babies, and wives or partners of IV drug users and bisexual men.

If there have been—and there may have been—any cases in straight, white, non-intravenous-drug-using, middle-class Americans, the Centers for Disease Control isn't telling anyone about them. When pressed, the CDC says there are "a number of cases that don't fall into any of the other categories." The CDC says it's impossible to fully investigate most of these "other category" cases; most of them are dead. The CDC also tends not to believe living, white, middle-class male victims when they say they're straight, or female victims when they say their husbands are straight and don't take drugs.

Why isn't AIDS happening to more straights? Maybe it's because gay men don't have sex with them.

Of all serious AIDS cases, 72.4 percent are in gay and bisexual men.

Let's talk about "surveillance."

The Centers for Disease Control is charged by our government to fully monitor all epidemics and unusual diseases.

To learn something from an epidemic, you have to keep records and statistics. Statistics come from interviewing victims and getting as much information from them as you can. Before they die. To get the best information, you have to ask the right questions.

There have been so many AIDS victims that the CDC is no longer able to get to them fast enough. It has given up. (The CDC also had been using a questionnaire that was fairly insensitive to the lives of gay men, and thus the data collected from its early study of us have been disputed by gay epidemiologists. The National Institutes of Health is also fielding a very naïve questionnaire.)

Important, vital case histories are now being lost because of this cessation of CDC interviewing. This is a woeful waste with as terrifying implications for us as the alarming rise in case numbers and doctors finally admitting they don't know what's going on. As each man dies, as one or both sets of men who had interacted with each other come down with AIDS, yet more information that might reveal patterns of transmissibility is not being monitored and collected and studied. We are being denied perhaps the easiest and fastest research tool available at this moment.

It will require at least $200,000 to prepare a new questionnaire to study the next important question that must be answered: *How* is AIDS being transmitted? (In which bodily fluids, by which sexual behaviours, in what social environments?)

For months the CDC has been asked to begin such preparations for continued surveillance. The CDC is stretched to its limits and is dreadfully underfunded for what it's being asked, in all areas, to do.

• Let's talk about various forms of treatment.

It is very difficult for a patient to find out which hospital to go to or which doctor to go to or which mode of treatment to attempt.

Hospitals and doctors are reluctant to reveal how well they're doing with each type of treatment. They may, if you press them, give you a general idea. Most will not show you their precise number of how many patients are doing well on what and how many failed to respond adequately.

Because of the ludicrous requirements of the medical journals, doctors are prohibited from revealing publicly the specific data they are gathering from their treatments of our bodies. Doctors and hospitals need money for research, and this money (from the National Institutes of Health, from cancer research funding organizations, from rich patrons) comes based on the performance of their work (i.e., their tabulations of their results of their treatment of our bodies); this performance is written up as "papers" that must be submitted to and accepted by such "distinguished" medical publications as the *New England Journal of Medicine*. Most of these "distinguished" publications, however, will not publish anything that has been spoken of, leaked, announced, or intimated publicly in advance. Even after acceptance, the doctors must hold their tongues until the article is actually published. Dr. Bijan Safai of Sloan-Kettering has been waiting over six months for the *New England Journal*, which has accepted his interferon study, to publish it. Until that happens, he is only permitted to speak in the most general terms of how interferon is or is not working.

Priorities in this area appear to be peculiarly out of kilter at this moment of life or death.

• Let's talk about hospitals.

Everybody's full up, fellows. No room in the inn.

Part of this is simply overcrowding. Part of this is cruel. Sloan-Kettering still enforces a regulation from pre-AIDS days that only one dermatology patient per week can be admitted to that hospital. (Karposi's sarcoma falls under dermatology at Sloan-Kettering.) But Sloan-Kettering is also the second-largest treatment center for AIDS patients in New York. You can be near death and still not get into Sloan-Kettering.

Additionally, Sloan-Kettering (and the Food and Drug Administration) require patients to receive their initial shots of interferon while they are hospitalized. A lot of men want to try interferon at Sloan-Kettering before they try chemotherapy elsewhere.

It's not hard to see why there is such a waiting list to get into Sloan-Kettering.

Most hospital staffs are still so badly educated about AIDS that they don't know much about it, except that they've heard it's infectious. (There still have been no cases in hospital staff or among the very doctors who have been treating AIDS victims for two years.) Hence, as I said earlier, AIDS patients are often treated like lepers.

For various reasons, I would not like to be a patient at the Veterans Administration Hospital on East 24th Street or at New York Hospital. (Incidents involving AIDS patients at these two hospitals have been reported in news stories in the *Native*.)

I believe it falls to this city's Department of Health, under Commissioner David Spencer, and the Health and Hospitals Corporation, under Commissioner Stanley Brezenoff, to educate this city, its citizens, and its hospital workers about all areas of a public health emergency. Well, they have done an appalling job of educating our citizens, our hospital workers, and even, in some instances, our doctors.

Almost everything this city knows about AIDS has come to it, in one way or another, through Gay Men's Health Crisis, and that includes television programs, magazine articles, radio commercials, newsletters, health-recommendation brochures, open forums, and sending speakers everywhere, including—when asked—into hospitals. If three out of four AIDS cases were occurring in straight men instead of gay men, you can bet all hospitals and staff would know what was happening. And it would be this city's Health Department and Health and Hospitals Corporation who would be telling them.

• Let's talk about what gay tax dollars are buying for gay men.

Now we're arriving at the truly scandalous.

For over a year and a half the National Institutes of Health has been "reviewing" which from among some $55 million worth of grant applications for AIDS research money it will eventually fund.

It's not even a question of NIH having to ask Congress for money. It's already there. Waiting. NIH has almost $8 million already appropriated that it has yet to release into usefulness.

There is no question that if this epidemic were happening to the straight, white, non-intravenous-drug-using middle class, that money would have been put into use almost two years ago, when the first alarming signs of this epidemic were noticed by Dr. Alvin Friedman-klen and Dr. Linda Laubenstein at New York University Hospital.

During the first *two weeks* of the Tylenol scare, the United States Government spent $10 million to find out what was happening.

Every hospital in New York that's involved in AIDS research has used up every bit of the money it could find for researching AIDS while waiting for NIH grants to come through. These hospitals have been working on AIDS for up to two years and are now desperate for replenishing funds. Important studies that began last year, such as Dr. Michael Lange's at St. Luke's Roosevelt, are now going under for lack of money. Important leads that were and are developing cannot be pursued. (For instance, few hospitals can afford plasma-pheresis machines, and few patients can afford this experimental treatment either, since few insurance policies will cover the $16,600 bill.) New York University Hospital, the largest treatment center for AIDS patients in the world, has had its grant application pending at NIH for a year and a half. Even if the application is successful, the earliest time that NYU could receive any money would be late summer.

The NIH would probably reply that it's foolish just to throw money away, that that hasn't worked before. And, NIH would say, if nobody knows what's happening, what's to study?

Any good administrator with half a brain could survey the entire AIDS mess and come up with twenty leads that merit further investigation. I could do so myself. In any research, in any investigation, you have to start somewhere. You can't just not start anywhere at all.

But then, AIDS is happening mostly to gay men, isn't it?

All of this is indeed ironic. For within AIDS, as most researchers have been trying to convey to the NIH, perhaps may reside the answer to the question of what it is that causes cancer itself. It straights had more brains, or were less bigoted 'against gays, they would see that, as with hepatitis B, gay men are again doing their suffering for them, revealing this disease to them. They can use us as guinea pigs to discover the cure for AIDS before it hits them, which most medical authorities are still convinced will be happening shortly in increasing numbers.

(As if it had not been malevolent enough, the NIH is now, for unspecified reasons, also turning away AIDS patients from its hospital in Bethesda, Maryland. The hospital, which had been treating anyone and everyone with AIDS free of charge, now will only take AIDS patients if they fit into their current investigating protocol. Whatever that is. The NIH publishers "papers," too.)

Gay men pay taxes just like everyone else. NIH money should be paying for our research just like everyone else's. We desperately need something from our government to save our lives, and we're not getting it.

• Let's talk about health insurance and welfare problems.

Many of the ways of treating AIDS are experimental, and many health insurance policies do not cover most of them. Blue Cross is particularly bad about accepting anything unusual.

Many serious victims of AIDS have been unable to qualify for increasing numbers of men unable to work and unable to claim welfare because AIDS is not on the list of qualifying disability illnesses. (Immune deficiency is an acceptable determining factor for welfare among children, but not adults. Figure that one out.) There are also increasing numbers of men unable to pay their rent, men thrown out on the street with nowhere to live and no money to live with, and men who have been asked by roommates to leave because of their illnesses. And men with serious AIDS are being fired from certain jobs.

The horror stories in this area, of those suddenly found destitute, of those facing this illness with insufficient insurance, continue to mount. (One man who'd had no success on other therapies was forced to beg from his friends the $16,600 he needed to try, as a last resort, plasmapheresis.)

• Finally, let's talk about our mayor, Ed Koch.

Our mayor, Ed Koch, appears to have chosen, for whatever reason, not to allow himself to be perceived by the non-gay world as visibly helping us in this emergency.

Repeated requests to meet with him have been denied us. Repeated attempts to have him make a very necessary public announcement about this crisis and public health emergency have been refused by his staff . . .

On October 28th, 1982, Mayor Koch was implored to make a public announcement about our emergency. If he had done so then, and if he was only to do so now, the following would be put into action:

1. The community at large would be alerted (you would be amazed at how many people, including gay men, still don't know enough about the AIDS danger).

2. Hospital staffs and public assistance offices would also be alerted and their education commenced.

3. The country, President Reagan, and the National Institutes of Health, as well as Congress, would be alerted, and these constitute the most important ears of all.

If the mayor doesn't think it's important enough to talk up AIDS, none of these people is going to, either.

The Mayor of New York has an enormous amount of power— when he wants to use it. When he wants to help his people. With the failure yet again of our civil rights bill, I'd guess our mayor doesn't want to use his power to help us.

With his silence on AIDS, the Mayor of New York is helping to kill us.

I AM SICK of our elected officials who in no way represent us. I am sick of our stupidity in believing candidates who promise us everything for our support and promptly forget us and insult us after we have given them our votes. Koch is the prime example, but not the only one. [Senator] Daniel Patrick Moynihan isn't looking very good at this moment, either. Moynihan was requested by gay leaders to publicly ask Margaret Heckler at her confirmation hearing for Secretary of Health and Human Services is she could be fair to gays in view of her voting record of definite anti-gay bias. (Among other horrors, she voted to retain the sodomy law in Washington, D.C., at Jerry Falwell's request.) Moynihan refused to ask this question, as he has refused to meet with us about AIDS, despite our repeated requests. Margaret Heckler will have important jurisdiction over the CDC, over the NIH, over the Public Health Service, over the Food and Drug Administration—indeed, over all areas of AIDS concerns. Thank you, Daniel Patrick Moynihan. I am sick of our not realizing we have enough votes to defeat these people, and I am sick of our not electing our own openly gay officials in the first place. Moynihan doesn't even have an openly gay person on his staff, and he represents the city with the largest gay population in America.

I am sick of closeted gay doctors who won't come out to help us fight to rectify any of what I'm writing about. Doctors—the very letters "M.D."—have enormous clout, particularly when they fight in groups. Can you imagine what gay doctors could accomplish, banded together in a network, petitioning local and federal governments, straight colleagues, and the American Medical Association. I am sick of the passivity or nonparticipation or half-hearted protestation of all the gay medical associations (American Physicians for Human Rights, Bay Area Physicians for Human Rights, Gay Psychiatrists of New York, etc., etc.), and particularly our own New York Physicians for Human Rights, a group of 175 of our gay doctors who have, as a group, done *nothing*. You can count on one hand the number of our doctors who have really worked for us.

I am sick of the *Advocate*, one of this country's largest gay publications, which has yet to quite acknowledge that there's anything going on. That newspaper's recent AIDS issue was to innocuous you'd have thought all we were going through was little worse than a rage of the latest designer flu. And their own associate editor, Brent Harris, died from AIDS. Figure that one out.

With the exception of the *New York Native* and a few, very few, other gay publications, the gay press has been useless. If we can't get our own papers and magazines to tell us what's really happening to us, and this negligence is added to the negligent non-interest of the straight press (*The New York Times* took a leisurely year and a half between its major pieces, and the *Village Voice* took a year and a half to write anything at all), how are we going to get the word around that we're dying? Gay men in smaller towns and cities everywhere must be educated, too. Has the *Times* or the *Advocate* told you that twenty-nine cases have been reported from Paris?

I am sick of gay men who won't support gay charities. Go give your bucks to straight charities, fellows, while we die. Gay Men's Health Crisis is going crazy trying to accomplish everything it does—printing and distributing hundreds of thousands of educational items, taking care of several hundred AIDS victims (some of them straight) in and out of hospitals, arranging community forums and speakers all over this country, getting media attention, fighting bad hospital care, on and on and on, fighting for you and us in two thousand ways, *and* trying to sell 17,600 circus tickets, too. Is the Red Cross doing this for you? Is the American Cancer Society? Your college alumni fund? The United Jewish Appeal? Catholic Charities? The United Way? The Lenox Hill Neighborhood Association, or any of the other fancy straight charities for which faggots put on black ties and dance at the Plaza? The National Gay Task Force—our only hope for national leadership, with its new and splendid leader, Virginia Apuzzo—which is spending more and more time fighting for the AIDS issue, is broke. Senior Action in a Gay Environment and Gay Men's Health Crisis are, within a few months, going to be without office space they can afford, and thus will be out on the street. The St. Mark's Clinic, held together by some of the few devoted gay doctors in this city who aren't interested in becoming rich, lives in constant terror of even higher rent and eviction. This community is desperate for the services these organizations are providing for it. And these organizations are all desperate for money, which is certainly not coming from straight people or President Reagan or Mayor Koch. (If every gay man within a 250-mile radius of Manhattan isn't in Madison Square Garden on the night of April 30th to help Gay Men's Health Crisis make enough money to get through the next horrible year of fighting against AIDS, I shall lose all hope that we have any future whatsoever.)

I am sick of closeted gays. It's 1983 already, guys, when are you going to come out? By 1984 you could be dead. Every gay man who is unable to come forward now and fight to save his own life is truly helping to kill the rest of us. There is only one thing that's going to save some of us, and this is *numbers* and pressure and our being perceived as united and a threat. As more and more of my friends die, I have less and less sympathy for men who are afraid their mommies will find out or afraid their bosses will find out or afraid their fellow doctors or professional associates will find out. Unless we can generate, visibly, numbers, masses, we are going to die.

I am sick of everyone in this community who tells me to stop creating a panic. How many of us have to die before *you* get scared off your ass and into action? Aren't 195 dead New Yorkers enough? Every straight person who is knowledgeable about the AIDS epidemic can't understand why gay men aren't marching on the White House. Over and over again I hear from them, "Why aren't you guys doing anything?" Every politician I have spoken to has said to me confidentially, "You guys aren't making enough noise. Bureaucracy only responds to pressure."

I am sick of people who say "it's no worse than statistics for smokers and lung cancer" or "considering how many homosexuals there are in the United States, AIDS is really statistically affecting only a very few." That would wash if there weren't 164 cases in twenty-eight days. That would wash if case numbers hadn't jumped from 41 to 1,112 in eighteen months. That would wash if cases in one city— New York—hadn't jumped to cases in fifteen countries and thirty-five states (up from thirty-four last week). That would wash if cases weren't coming in at more than four a day nationally and over two a day locally. That would wash if the mortality rate didn't start at 38 percent the first year of diagnosis and climb to a grotesque 86 percent after three years. Get your stupid heads out of the sand, you turkeys!

I am sick of guys who moan that giving up careless sex until this blows over is worse than death. How can they value life so little and cocks and asses so much? Come with me, guys, while I visit a few of our friends in Intensive Care at NYU. Notice the looks in their eyes, guys. They'd give up sex forever if you could promise them life.

I am sick of guys who think that all being gay means is sex in the first place. I am sick of guys who can only think with their cocks.

I am sick of "men" who say, "We've got to keep quiet or *they* will do such and such." *They* usually means the straight majority, the "Moral" Majority, or similarly perceived representatives of *them*. Okay, you "men"—be my guests: You can march off now to the gas chambers: just get right in line.

We shall always have enemies. Nothing we can ever do will remove them. Southern newspapers and Jerry Falwell's publications are already printing editorials proclaiming AIDS as God's deserved punishments on homosexuals. So what? Nasty words make poor little sissy pansy wilt and die?

And I am very sick and saddened by every gay man who does not get behind this issue totally and with commitment—to fight for his life.

I don't want to die. I can only assume you don't want to die. Can we fight together?

For the past few weeks, about fifty community leaders and organization representatives have been meeting at Beth Simchat Torah, the gay synagogue, to prepare action. We call ourselves the AIDS Network. We come from all areas of health concern: doctors, social workers, psychologists, psychiatrists, nurses; we come from Gay Men's Health Crisis, from the National Gay Health Education Foundation, from New York Physicians for Human Rights, the St. Mark's Clinic, the Gay Men's Health Project; we come from the gay synagogue, the Gay Men's Chorus, from the Greater Gotham Business Council, SAGE, Lambda Legal Defense, Gay Fathers, the Christopher Street Festival Committee, Dignity; Integrity; we are lawyers, actors, dancers, architects, writers, citizens; we come from many component organizations of the Gay and Lesbian Community Council.

We have a leader. Indeed, for the first time our community appears to have a true leader. Her name is Virginia Apuzzo, she is head of the National Gay Task Force, and, as I have said, so far she has proved to be magnificent.

The AIDS Network has sent a letter to Mayor Koch. It contains twelve points that are urged for his consideration and action.

This letter to Mayor Koch also contains the following paragraph:

> It must be stated at the outset that the gay community is growing increasingly aroused and concerned and angry. Should our avenues to the mayor of our city and the members of the Board of Estimate not be available, it is our feeling that the level of frustration is such that it will manifest itself in a manner heretofore not associated with this community and the gay population at large. It should be stated, too, at the outset, that as of February 25th, there were 526 cases of serious AIDS in New York's metropolitan area and 195 deaths (and 1,112 cases nationally and 418 deaths) and it is the sad and sorry fact that most gay men in our city now have close friends and lovers who have either been stricken with or died from this disease. It is against this background that this letter is addressed. It is this issue that has, ironically, united our community in a way not heretofore thought possible.

Further, a number of AIDS Network members have been studying civil disobedience with one of the experts from Dr. Martin Luther King's old team. We are learning how. Gay men are the strongest, toughest people I know. We are perhaps shortly to get an opportunity to show it.

I'm sick of hearing that Mayor Koch doesn't respond to pressures and threats from the disenfranchised, that he walks away from confrontations. Maybe he does. But we have *tried* to make contact with him, we are *dying*, so what other choice but confrontation has he left us?

I hope we don't have to conduct sit-ins or tie up traffic or get arrested. I hope our city and our country will start to do something to help start saving us. But it is time for us to be perceived for what we truly are: an angry community and a strong community, and therefore *a threat*. Such are the realities of politics. Nationally we are 24 million strong, which is more than there are Jews or blacks or Hispanics in this country.

I want to make a point about what happens if we *don't* get angry about AIDS. There are the obvious losses, of course: Little of what I've written about here is likely to be rectified with the speed necessary to help the growing number of victims. But something worse will happen, and is already happening. Increasingly, we are being *blamed* for AIDS, for this epidemic; we are being called its perpetrators, through our blood, through our "promiscuity," through just being the gay men so much of the rest of the world has learned to hate. We can point out until we are blue in the face that we are not the cause of AIDS but its victims, that AIDS has landed among us first, as it could have landed among them first. But other frightened populations are going to drown out these truths by playing on the worst bigoted fears of the straight world, and send the status of gays right back to the Dark Ages. Not all Jews are blamed for Meyer Lansky, Rabbis Bergman and Kahane, or for money-lending. All Chinese aren't blamed for the recent Seattle slaughters. But all gays are blamed for John Gacy, the North American Man/Boy Love Association, and AIDS.

Enough. I am told this is one of the longest articles the *Native* has ever run. I hope I have not been guilty of saying ineffectively in five thousand words what I could have said in five: we must fight to live.

I am angry and frustrated almost beyond the bound my skin and bones and body and brain can encompass. My sleep is tormented by nightmares and visions of lost friends, and my days are flooded by the tears of funerals and memorial services and seeing my sick friends. How many of us must die before *all* of us living fight back?

I know that unless I fight with every ounce of my energy I will hate myself. I hope, I pray, I implore you to feel the same.

I am going to close by doing what Dr. Ron Grossman did at

GMHC's second Open Forum last November at Julia Richman High School. He listed the names of the patients he had lost to AIDS. Here is a list of twenty dead men I knew:

> Nick Rock, Rick Wellikoff, Jack Nau, Shelly, Donald Krintzman, Jerry Green, Michael Maletta, Paul Graham, Toby, Harry Blumenthal, Stephen Sperry, Brian O'Hara, Barry, David, Jeffrey Croland, Z., David Jackson, Tony Rappa, Robert Christian, Ron Doud. And one more, who will be dead by the time these words appear in print. If we don't act immediately, then we face our approaching doom.

Volunteers Needed for Civil Disobedience

It is necessary that we have a pool of at least three thousand people who are prepared to participate in demonstrations of civil disobedience. Such demonstrations might include sit-ins or traffic tie-ups. All participants must be prepared to be arrested. I am asking every gay person and every gay organization to canvass all friends and members and make a count of the total number of people you can provide toward this pool of three thousand.

Let me know how many people you can be counted on providing. Just include the number of people; you don't have to send actual names—you keep that list yourself. And include your own phone numbers. *Start these lists now.*

la güera

CHERRÍE MORAGA
1979

It requires something more than personal experience to gain a philosophy or point of view from any specific event. It is the quality of
our response to the event and our capacity to enter into the lives of
others that help us to make their lives and experiences our own.
                                                    —EMMA GOLDMAN

I am the very well-educated daughter of a woman who, by the
standards in this country, would be considered largely illiterate. My
mother was born in Santa Paula, Southern California, at a time when
much of the central valley there was still farm land. Nearly thirty-five
years later, in 1948, she was the only daughter of six to marry an
anglo, my father.

I remember all of my mother's stories, probably much better than
she realizes. She is a fine story-teller, recalling every event of her life
with the vividness of the present, noting each detail right down to the
cut and color of her dress. I remember stories of her being pulled out
of school at the ages of five, seven, nine, and eleven to work in the
fields, along with her brothers and sisters; stories of her father drinking
away whatever small profit she was able to make for the family; of her
going the long way home to avoid meeting him on the street, stagger-
ing toward the same destination. I remember stories of my mother
lying about her age in order to get a job as a hat-check girl at Agua
Caliente Racetrack in Tijuana. At fourteen, she was the main support
of the family. I can still see her walking home alone at 3 a.m., only to
turn all of her salary and tips over to her mother, who was pregnant
again.

The stories continue through the war years and on: walnut crack-ing factories, the Voit Rubber factory, and then the computer boom. I remember my mother doing piecework for the electronics plant in our neighborhood. In the late evening, she would sit in front of the T.V. set, wrapping copper wires into the backs of circuit boards, talk-ing about "keeping up with the younger girls." By that time she was already in her mid-fifties.

Meanwhile, I was college-prep in school. After classes, I would go with my mother to fill out job applications for her, or write checks for her at the supermarket. We would have the scenario all worked out ahead of time. My mother would sign the check before we'd get to the store. Then, as we'd approach the checkstand, she would say— within earshot of the cashier—"oh honey, you go 'head and make out the check," as if she couldn't be bothered with such an insignificant detail. No one asked any questions.

I was educated, and wore it with a keen sense of pride and satisfac-tion, my head propped up with the knowledge, from my mother, that my life would be easier than hers. I was educated; but more than this, I was "la güera"—fair-skinned. Born with the features of my Chicana mother, but the skin of my Anglo father, I had it made.

No one ever quite told me this (that light was right), but I knew that being light was something valued in my family (who were all Chicano, with the exception of my father). In fact, everything about my upbring-ing (at least what occurred on a conscious level) attempted to bleach me of what color I did have. Although my mother was fluent in it, I was never taught much Spanish at home. I picked up what I did learn from school and from over-heard snatches of conversation among my rela-tives and mother. She often called other lower-income Mexicans "braceros," or "wet-backs," referring to herself and family as "a different class of people." And yet, the real story was that my family, too, had been poor (some still are) and farmworkers. My mother can remember this in her blood as if it were yesterday. But this is something she would like to forget (and rightfully), for to her, on a basic economic level, being Chicana meant being "less." It was through my mother's desire to protect her children from poverty and illiteracy that we became "anglocized"; the more effectively we could pass in the white world, the better guaranteed our future.

From all of this, I experience, daily, a huge disparity between what I was born into and what I was to grow up to become. Because, (as Goldman suggests) these stories my mother told me crept under my "güera" skin. I had no choice but to enter into the life of my mother.

I had no choice. I took her life into my heart, but managed to keep a lid on it as long as I feigned being the happy, upwardly mobile heterosexual.

When I finally lifted the lid to my lesbianism, a profound connection with my mother reawakened in me. It wasn't until I acknowledged and confronted my own lesbianism in the flesh, that my heartfelt identification with and empathy for my mother's oppression—due to being poor, uneducated, and Chicana—was realized. My lesbianism is the avenue through which I have learned the most about silence and oppression, and it continues to be the most tactile reminder to me that we are not free human beings.

You see, one follows the other. I had known for years that I was a lesbian, had felt it in my bones, had ached with the knowledge, gone crazed with the knowledge, wallowed in the silence of it. Silence *is* like starvation. Don't be fooled. It's nothing short of that, and felt most sharply when one has had a full belly most of her life. When we are not physically starving, we have the luxury to realize psychic and emotional starvation. It is from this starvation that other starvations can be recognized—if one is willing to take the risk of making the connection—if one is willing to be responsible to the result of the connection. For me, the connection is an inevitable one.

What I am saying is that the joys of looking like a white girl ain't so great since I realized I could be beaten on the street for being a dyke. If my sister's being beaten because she's Black, it's pretty much the same principle. We're both getting beaten any way you look at it. The connection is blatant; and in the case of my own family, the difference in the privileges attached to looking white instead of brown are merely a generation apart. In this country, lesbianism is a poverty—as is being brown, as is being a woman, as is being just plain poor. The danger lies in ranking the oppressions. *The danger lies in failing to acknowledge the specificity of the oppression.* The danger lies in attempting to deal oppression purely from a theoretical base. Without an emotional, heartfelt grappling with the source of our own oppression, without naming the enemy within ourselves and outside of us, no authentic, non-hierarchical connection among oppressed groups can take place.

When the going gets rough, will we abandon our so-called comrades in a flurry of racist/heterosexist/what-have-you panic? To whose camp, then, should the lesbian of color retreat? Her very presence violates the ranking and abstraction of oppression. Do we merely live hand to mouth? Do we merely struggle with the "ism" that's sitting on top of our heads?

The answer is: yes, I think first we do; and we must do so thoroughly and deeply. But to fail to move out from there will only isolate us in our own oppression—will only insulate, rather than radicalize us.

To illustrate: a gay white male friend of mine once confided to me that he continued to feel that, on some level, I didn't trust him because he was male; that he felt, really, if it ever came down to a "battle of the sexes," I might kill him. I admitted that I might very well. He wanted to understand the source of my distrust. I responded, "You're not a woman. Be a woman for a day. Imagine being a woman." He confessed that the thought terrified him because, to him, being a woman meant being raped by men. He *had* felt raped by men; he wanted to forget what that meant. What grew from that discussion was the realization that in order for him to create an authentic alliance with me, he must deal with the primary source of his own sense of oppression. He must, first, emotionally come to terms with what it feels like to be a victim. If he—or anyone—were to truly do this, it would be impossible to discount the oppression of others, except by again forgetting how we have been hurt.

And yet, oppressed groups are forgetting all the time. There are instances of this in the rising Black middle class, and certainly an obvious trend of such "capitalist-unconsciousness" among white gay men. Because to remember may mean giving up whatever privileges we have managed to squeeze out of this society by virtue of our gender, race, class, or sexuality.

Within the women's movement, the connections among women of different backgrounds and sexual orientations have been fragile, at best. I think this phenomenon is indicative of our failure to seriously address ourselves to some very frightening questions: How have I internalized my own oppression? How have I oppressed? Instead, we have let rhetoric do the job of poetry. Even the word "oppression" has lost its power. We need a new language, better words that can more closely describe women's fear of and resistance to one another; words that will not always come out sounding like dogma.

What prompted me in the first place to work on an anthology by radical women of color was a deep sense that I had a valuable insight to contribute, by virtue of my birthright and my background. And yet, I don't really understand first-hand what it feels like being shitted on for being brown. I understand much more about the joys of it—being Chicana and having family are synonymous for me. What I know about loving, singing, crying, telling stories, speaking with my heart and hands, even having a sense of my own soul comes from the love of my mother, aunts, cousins . . .

But at the age of twenty-seven, it is frightening to acknowledge that I have internalized a racism and classism, where the object of oppression is not only someone *outside* my skin, but the someone *inside* my skin. In fact, to a large degree, the real battle with such oppression, for all of us, begins under the skin. I have had to confront the fact that much of what I value about being Chicana, about my family, has been subverted by anglo culture and my own cooperation with it. This realization did not occur to me overnight. For example, it wasn't until long after my graduation from the private college I'd attended in Los Angeles, that I realized the major reason for my total alienation from and fear of my classmates was rooted in class and culture.

Three years after graduation, in an apple orchard in Sonoma, a friend of mine (who comes from an Italian-Irish working-class family) says to me, "Cherrie, no wonder you felt like such a nut in school. Most of the people there were white and rich." It was true. All along I had felt the difference, but not until I had put the words "class" and "race" to the experience, did my feelings make any sense. For years, I had berated myself for not being as "free" as my classmates. I completely bought that they simply had more guts than I did—to rebel against their parents and run around the country hitch-hiking, reading books and studying "art." They had enough privilege to be atheists, for chrissake. There was no one around filling in the disparity for me between their parents, who were Hollywood filmmakers, and my parents, who wouldn't know the name of a filmmaker if their lives depended on it (and precisely because their lives didn't depend on it, they couldn't be bothered). But I knew nothing about "privilege" then. White was right. Period. I could pass. If I got educated enough, there would never be no telling.

Three years after that, I had a similar revelation. In a letter to a friend, I wrote:

> I went to a concert where Ntosake Shange was reading. There, everything exploded for me. She was speaking in a language that I knew—in the deepest parts of me—existed, and that I ignored in my own feminist studies and even in my own writing. What Ntosake caught in me is the realization that in my development as a poet, I have, in many ways, denied the voice of my own brown mother—the brown in me. I have acclimated to the sound of a

> white language which, as my father represents it, does not speak to
> the emotions in my poems—emotions which stem from the love of
> my mother.
>
> The reading was agitating. Made me uncomfortable. Threw me
> into a week-long terror of how deeply I was affected. I felt that I had
> to start all over again. That I turned only to the perceptions of white
> middle-class women to speak for me and all women. I am shocked
> by my own ignorance.

Sitting in that auditorium chair was the first time I had realized to
the core of me that for years I had disowned the language I knew
best—ignored the words and rhythms that were the closest to me.
The sounds of my mother and aunts gossiping—half in English, half
in Spanish—while drinking cerveza in the kitchen. And the
hands—I had cut off the hands in my poems. But not in conversation; still the hands could not be kept down. Still they insisted on
moving.

The reading had forced me to remember that I knew things from
my roots. But to remember puts me up against what I don't know.
Shange's reading agitated me because she spoke with power about a
world that is both alien and common to me: "the capacity to enter
into the lives of others." But you can't just take the goods and run. I
knew that then, sitting in the Oakland auditorium (as I know in my
poetry), that the only thing worth writing about is what seems to be
unknown and, therefore, fearful.

The "unknown" is often depicted in racist literature as the "darkness" within a person. Similarly, sexist writers will refer to fear in
the form of the vagina, calling it "the orifice of death." In contrast,
it is a pleasure to read works such as Maxine Hong Kingston's
Woman Warrior, where fear and alienation are depicted as "the
white ghosts." And yet, the bulk of literature in this country rein-
forces the myth that what is dark and female is evil. Consequently,
each of us—whether dark, female, or both—has in some way *internalized* this oppressive imagery. What the oppressor often succeeds
in doing is simply *externalizing* his fears, projecting them into the
bodies of women, Asians, gays, disabled folks, whoever seems most
"other."

    call me
    roach and presumptuous

nightmare on your white pillow
your itch to destroy
the indestructible
part of yourself

—AUDRE LORDE[3]

But it is not really difference the oppressor fears so much as similarity. He fears he will discover in himself the same aches, the same longings as those of the people he has shitted on. He fears the immobilization threatened by his own incipient guilt. He fears he will have to change his life once he has seen himself in the bodies of the people he has called different. He fears the hatred, anger, and vengeance of those he has hurt.

This is the oppressor's nightmare, but it is not exclusive to him. We women have a similar nightmare, for each of us in some way has been both oppressed and the oppressor. We are afraid to look at how we have failed each other. We are afraid to see how we have taken the values of our oppressor into our hearts and turned them against ourselves and one another. We are afraid to admit how deeply "the man's" words have been ingrained in us.

To assess the damage is a dangerous act. I think of how, even as a feminist lesbian, I have so wanted to ignore my own homophobia, my own hatred of myself for being queer. I have not wanted to admit that my deepest personal sense of myself has not quite "caught up" with my "woman-identified" politics. I have been afraid to criticize lesbian writers who choose to "skip over" these issues in the name of feminism. In 1979, we talk of "old gay" and "butch and femme" roles as if they were ancient history. We toss them aside as merely patriarchal notions. And yet, the truth of the matter is that I have sometimes taken society's fear and hatred of lesbians to bed with me. I have sometimes hated my lover for loving me. I have sometimes felt "not women enough" for her. I have sometimes felt "not man enough." For a lesbian trying to survive in a heterosexist society, there is no easy way around these emotions. Similarly, in a white-dominated world, there is little getting around racism and our own internalization of it. It's always there, embodied in someone we least expect to rub up against.

[3]From "The Brown Menace or Poem to the Survival of Roaches," *The New York Head Shop and Museum* (Detroit: Broadside, 1974), p. 48.

When we do rub up against this person, *there* then is the challenge. *There* then is the opportunity to look at the nightmare within us. But we usually shrink from such a challenge.

Time and time again, I have observed that the usual response among white women's groups when the "racism issue" comes up is to deny the difference. I have heard comments like, "Well, we're open to *all* women; why don't they (women of color) come? You can only do so much . . ." But there is seldom any analysis of how the very nature and structure of the group itself may be founded on racist or classist assumptions. More importantly, so often the women seem to feel no loss, no lack, no absence when women of color are not involved; therefore, there is little desire to change the situation. This has hurt me deeply. I have come to believe that the only reason women of a privileged class will dare to look at *how* it is that *they* oppress, is when they've come to know the meaning of their own oppression. And understand that the oppression of others hurts them personally.

The other side of the story is that women of color and white working-class women often shrink from challenging white middle-class women. It is much easier to rank oppressions and set up a hierarchy, rather than take responsibility for changing our own lives. We have failed to demand that white women, particularly those that claim to be speaking for all women, be accountable for their racism.

The dialogue has simply not gone deep enough.

In conclusion, I have had to look critically at my claim to color, at a time when, among white feminist ranks, it is a "politically correct" (and sometimes peripherally advantageous) assertion to make. I must acknowledge the fact that, physically, I have had a *choice* about making that claim, in contrast to women who have not had such a choice, and have been abused for their color. I must reckon with the fact that for most of my life, by virtue of the very fact that I am white-looking, I identified with and aspired toward white values, and that I rode the wave of that Southern California privilege as far as conscience would let me.

Well, now I feel both bleached and beached. I feel angry about this—the years when I refused to recognize privilege, both when it worked against me, and when I worked it, ignorantly, at the expense of others. These are not settled issues. This is why this work feels so risky to me. It continues to be discovery. It has brought me into contact with women who invariably know a hell of a lot more than I do about racism, as experienced in the flesh, as revealed in the flesh of their writing.

I think: what is my responsibility to my roots: both white and brown, Spanish-speaking and English? I am a woman with a foot in both worlds. I refuse the split. I feel the necessity for dialogue. Sometimes I feel it urgently.

But one voice is not enough, nor two, although this is where dialogue begins. It is essential that feminists confront their fear of and resistance to each other, because without this, there *will* be no bread on the table. Simply, we will not survive. If we could make this connection in our heart of hearts, that if we are serious about a revolution—better—if we seriously believe there should be joy in our lives (real joy, not just "good times"), then we need one another. We women need each other. Because my/your solitary, self-asserting "go-for-the-throat-of-fear" power is not enough. The real power, as you and I well know, is collective. I can't afford to be afraid of you, nor you of me. If it takes head-on collisions, let's do it. This polite timidity is killing us.

As Lorde suggests in the passage I cited earlier, it is looking to the nightmare that the dream is found. There, the survivor emerges to insist on a future, a vision, yes, born out of what is dark and female. The feminist movement must be a movement of such survivors, a movement with a future.

i am your sister: black women organizing across sexualities

AUDRE LORDE

1985

whenever I come to Medgar Evers College I always feel a thrill of anticipation and delight because it feels like coming home, like talking to family, having a chance to speak about things that are very important to me with people who matter the most. And this is particularly true whenever I talk at the Women's Center. But, as with all families, we sometimes find it difficult to deal constructively with the genuine differences between us and to recognize that unity does not require that we be identical to each other. Black women are not one great vat of homogenized chocolate milk. We have many different faces, and we do not have to become each other in order to work together.

It is not easy for me to speak here with you as a Black Lesbian feminist recognizing that some of the ways in which I identify myself make it difficult for you to hear me. But meeting across difference always requires mutual stretching and until you *can* hear me as a Black Lesbian feminist, our strengths will not be truly available to each other as Black women.

Because I feel it is urgent that we not waste each other's resources, that we recognize each sister on her own terms so that we may better work together toward our mutual survival, I speak here about heterosexism and homophobia, two grave barriers to organizing among Black women. And so that we have a common language between us, I would like to define some of the terms I use. HETEROSEXISM: A belief in the inherent superiority of one form of loving over all others and thereby the right to dominance. HOMOPHOBIA: A terror surrounding feelings of love for members of the same sex and thereby a hatred of those feelings in others.

In the 1960's, when liberal white people decided that they didn't want to appear racist, they wore dashikis, and danced Black, and ate Black, and even married Black, but they did not want to feel Black or even think Black, so they never even questioned the textures of their daily living (why should flesh-colored bandaids always be pink) and then they always wondered "why are those Black folks always taking offense so easily at the least little thing? Some of our best friends are Black . . ."

Well, it is not necessary for some of your best friends to be Lesbian, although some of them probably are, no doubt. But it is necessary for you to stop oppressing me through false judgment. I do not want you to ignore my identity, nor do I want you to make it an insurmountable barrier between our sharing of strengths.

When I say I am a Black feminist, I mean I recognize that my power as well as my primary oppressions come as a result of my Blackness as well as my womanness, and therefore my struggles on both these fronts are inseparable.

When I say I am a Black Lesbian, I mean I am a woman whose primary focus of loving, physical as well as emotional, is directed to women. It does not mean I hate men. Far from it. The harshest attacks I have ever heard against Black men come from those women who are intimately bound to them and cannot free themselves from a subservient and silent position. I would never presume to speak about Black men the way I have heard some of my straight sisters talk about the men they are attached to. And of course that concerns me, because it reflects a situation of non-communication in the heterosexual Black community that is far more truly threatening than the existence of Black Lesbians.

What does this have to do with Black women organizing?

I have heard it said—usually behind my back—that Black Lesbians are not normal. But what is normal in this deranged society by which we are all trapped? I remember, and so do many of you, when being Black was considered NOT NORMAL, when they talked about us in whispers, tried to paint us, lynch us, bleach us, ignore us, pretend we did not exist. We called that racism.

I have heard it said that Black Lesbians are a threat to the Black family. But when 50% of children born to Black women are born out of wedlock, and 30% of all Black families are headed by women without husbands, we need to broaden and redefine what we mean by family.

I have heard it said that Black Lesbians will mean the death of the race. Yet Black Lesbians bear children in exactly the same way other women bear children, and a Lesbian household is simply another kind of family. Ask my son and daughter.

The terror of Black Lesbians is buried in that deep inner place where we have been taught to fear all difference—to kill it or ignore it. Be assured—loving women is not a communicable disease. You don't catch it like the common cold. Yet the one accusation that seems to render even the most vocal straight Black woman totally silent and ineffective is the suggestion that she might be a Black Lesbian.

If someone says you're Russian and you know you're not, you don't collapse into stunned silence. Even if someone calls you a bigamist, or a childbeater, and you know you're not, you don't crumple into bits. You say it's not true, and keep on printing the posters. But let anyone, particularly a Black man, accuse a straight Black woman of being a Black Lesbian, and right away that sister becomes immobilized, as if that is the most horrible thing she could be, and must at all costs be proven false. That is homophobia. It is a waste of woman energy, and it puts a terrible weapon into the hands of your enemies to be used against you to silence you, to keep you docile and in line. It also serves to keep us isolated and apart.

I have heard it said that Black Lesbians are not political, that we have not been and are not involved in the struggles of Black people. But when I taught Black and Puerto Rican students writing at City College in the SEEK program in the 60s I was a Black Lesbian. I was a Black Lesbian when I helped organize and fight for the Black Studies Department of John Jay College. And because I was 15 years younger then and less sure of myself, at one crucial moment I yielded to pressures that said I should step back for a Black man even though I knew him to be a serious error of choice, and I did, and he was. But I was a Black Lesbian then.

When my girl friends and I went out in the car one July 4th night after fireworks with cans of white spray paint and our kids asleep in the back of the car, one of us staying behind to keep the motor running and watch the kids while the other two worked our way down the suburban New Jersey street, spraying white paint over the black jockey statues and their little red jackets too, we were Lesbians.

When I drove through the Mississippi delta to Jackson in 1968 with a group of Black students from Tougaloo, another car full of redneck kids trying to bump us off the road all the way back into town, I was a Black Lesbian.

When I weened my daughter in 1963 to go to Washington in August to work in the coffee tents along with Lena Horne, making coffee for the marshalls because that was what most Black women did in the 1963 March on Washington, I was a Black Lesbian.

When I taught a poetry workshop at Tougaloo, a small Black college in Mississippi, where white rowdies shot up the edge of campus every night, and I felt the joy of seeing young Black poets find their voices and power through words in our mutual growth, I was a Black Lesbian. And there are strong Black poets today who date their growth and awareness from those workshops.

When Yoli and I cooked curried chicken and beans and rice and took our extra blankets and pillows up the hill to the striking students occupying buildings at City College in 1969, demanding open admissions and the right to an education, I was a Black Lesbian. When I walked through the midnight hallways of Lehman College that same year, carrying Midol and Kotex pads for the young Black radical women taking part in the action, and we tried to persuade them that their place in the revolution was not ten paces behind Black men, that spreading their legs to the guys on the tables in the cafeteria was not a revolutionary act no matter what the brothers said, I was a Black Lesbian. When I picketed for Welfare Mothers' Rights, and against the enforced sterilization of young Black girls, when I fought institutionalized racism in the New York City schools, I was a Black Lesbian.

But you did not know it, because we did not identify ourselves, so now you can still say that Black Lesbians and gay men have nothing to do with the struggles of the Black Nation.

And I am not alone.

When you read the words of Langston Hughes you are reading the words of a Black gay man. When you read the words of Alice Dunbar-Nelson and Angelina Weld Grimké, poets of the Harlem Renaissance, you are reading the words of Black Lesbians. When you listen to the life-affirming voice of Bessie Smith and Ma Rainey, you are hearing Black Lesbian women. When you see the plays and read the words of Lorraine Hansberry, you are reading the words of a woman who loved women deeply.

Today, some of the most active and engaged members of "Art Against Apartheid" which is making visible and immediate our cultural responsibilities against the tragedy of South Africa are Lesbians and gay men. We have organizations such as the National Coalition of Black Lesbians and Gays, Dykes Against Racism Everywhere, and

Men of All Colors Together, all of whom are committed to and engaged in anti-racist activity.

Homophobia and heterosexism mean you allow yourselves to be robbed of the sisterhood and strength of Black Lesbian women because you are afraid of being called a Lesbian yourself. Yet we share so many concerns as Black women, so much work to be done. The urgency of the destruction of our Black children and the theft of young Black minds are joint urgencies. Black children shot down or doped up on the streets of our cities are priorities for all of us. The fact of Black women's blood flowing with grim regularity in the streets and living rooms of Black communities is not a Black Lesbian rumor. It is sad statistical fact. The fact that there is a widening and dangerous lack of communication around our differences between Black women and men is not a Black Lesbian plot. It is a fact that becomes starkly clarified as we see our young people becoming more and more uncaring of each other. Young Black boys believing that they can define their manhood between a sixth grade girl's legs, growing up believing that Black women and girls are the fitting target for their justifiable furies rather than the racist structures grinding us all into dust, these are not Black Lesbian myths. These are sad realities of Black communities today and of immediate concern to us all. We cannot afford to waste each other's energies in our common battles.

What does homophobia mean? It means that high-powered Black women are told it is not safe to attend a Conference on the Status of Women in Nairobi simply because we are Lesbians. It means that in a political action, you rob yourselves of the vital insight and energies of political women such as Betty Powell and Barbara Smith and Gwendolyn Rogers and Raymina Mays and Robin Christian and Yvonne Flowers. It means another instance of the divide and conquer routine.

How do we organize around our differences, neither denying them nor blowing them up out of proportion?

The first step is an effort of will on your part. Try to remember, to keep certain facts in mind. Black Lesbians are not apolitical. We have been a part of every freedom struggle within this country. Black Lesbians are not a threat to the Black family. Many of us have families of our own. We are not white, and we are not a disease. We are women who love women. This does not mean we are going to assault your daughters in an alley on Nostrand Avenue. It does not mean we are about to attack you if we pay you a compliment on your dress. It does not mean we only think about sex, any more than you only think about sex.

Even if you *do* believe any of these stereotypes about Black Lesbians, begin to practice *acting* like you don't believe them. Just as racist stereotypes are the problem of the white people who believe them, so also are homophobic stereotypes the problem of the heterosexuals who believe them. In other words, those stereotypes are yours to solve, not mine, and they are a terrible and wasteful barrier to our working together. I am not your enemy. We do not have to become each other's unique experiences and insights in order to share what we have learned through our particular battles for survival as Black women . . .

There was a poster in the 60s that was very popular: HE'S NOT BLACK, HE'S MY BROTHER! It used to infuriate me because it implied that the two were mutually exclusive—"he" couldn't be both brother and Black. Well, I do not want to be tolerated, nor misnamed. I want to be recognized.

I am a Black Lesbian, and I *am* your sister.

i dissent

JUSTICE HARRY BLACKMUN
1986

in 1985, in Bowers V. Hardwick the Supreme Court upheld a Georgia state law forbidding sodomy. Below is Justice Harry Blackmun's dissent.

JUSTICE BLACKMUN, with whom JUSTICE BRENNAN, JUSTICE MARSHALL, and JUSTICE STEVENS join, dissenting.

This case is no more about "a fundamental right to engage in homosexual sodomy," as the Court purports to declare, *ante*, at 191, than *Stanley* v. *Georgia*, was about a fundamental right to watch obscene movies, or *Katz* v. *United States*, was about a fundamental right to place interstate bets from a telephone booth. Rather, this case is about "the most comprehensive of rights and the right most valued by civilized men," namely, "the right to be let alone." *Olmstead* v. *United States* (Brandeis, J., dissenting).

The statute at issue, Ga. Code Ann. § 16-6-2 (1984), denies individuals the right to decide for themselves whether to engage in particular forms of private, consensual sexual activity. The Court concludes that § 16-6-2 is valid essentially because "the laws of . . . many States . . . still make such conduct illegal and have done so for a very long time." *Ante*, at 190. But the fact that the moral judgments expressed by statutes like § 16-6-2 may be " 'natural and familar . . . ought not to conclude our judgment upon the question whether statutes embodying them conflict with the Constitution of the United States.' " *Roe* v. *Wade*, quoting *Lochner* v. *New York* (Holmes, J., dissenting). Like Justice Holmes, I believe that "[i]t is revolting to have no better reason for a rule of law than that so it was laid down in the time of Henry IV. It is still more revolting if the grounds upon which it was laid down have vanished long since, and the rule simply persists from blind imitation of the past." Holmes, The Path of the Law, Harv. L. Rev. I believe we must analyze respondent Hardwick's claim in the light of the values that underlie the constitutional right to privacy. If that right means anything, it means that, before Georgia can prosecute its citizens for making choices about the most intimate aspects of their lives, it must do more than assert that the choice they have made is an " 'abominable crime not fit to be named among Christians.' " Herring v. State.

I

In its haste to reverse the Court of Appeals and hold that the Constitution does not "confe[r] a fundamental right upon homosexuals to engage in sodomy," ante, at 190, the Court relegates the actual statute being challenged to a footnote and ignores the procedural posture of the case before it. A fair reading of the statute and of the complaint clearly reveals that the majority has distorted the question this case presents.

First, the Court's almost obsessive focus on homosexual activity is particularly hard to justify in light of the broad language Georgia has used. Unlike the Court, the Georgia Legislature has not proceeded on the assumption that homosexuals are so different from other citizens that their lives may be controlled in a way that would not be tolerated if it limited the choices of those other citizens. Rather, Georgia has provided that "[a] person commits the offense of sodomy when he performs or submits to any sexual act involving the sex organs of one person and the mouth or anus of another." The sex or status of the persons who engage in the act is irrelevant as a matter of state law. In fact, to the extent I can discern a legislative purpose for Georgia's 1968 enactment of § 16-6-2, that purpose seems to have been to broaden the coverage of the law to reach heterosexual as well as homosexual activity.[1] I therefore see no basis for the Court's decision to treat this case as an "as applied" challenge to § 16-6-2, or for Georgia's attempt, both in its brief and at oral argument, to defend § 16-6-2 solely on the grounds that it prohibits homosexual activity. Michael Hardwick's standing may rest in significant part on Georgia's apparent willingness to enforce against homosexuals a law it seems not to have any desire to

[1]Until 1968, Georgia defined sodomy as "the carnal knowledge and connection against the order of nature, by man with man, or in the same unnatural manner with woman." Ga. Crim. Code § 26-5901 (1933). In Thompson v. Aldredge, the Georgia Supreme Court held that § 26-5901 did not prohibit lesbian activity. And in Riley v. Garrett, the Georgia Supreme Court held that § 26-5901 did not prohibit heterosexual cunnilingus. Georgia passed the act-specific statute currently in force "perhaps in response to the restrictive court decisions such as Riley."

enforce against heterosexuals. But his claim that § 16-6-2 involves an unconstitutional intrusion into his privacy and his right of intimate association does not depend in any way on his sexual orientation.

Second, I disagree with the Court's refusal to consider whether § 16-6-2 runs afoul of the Eighth or Ninth Amendments or the Equal Protection Clause of the Fourteenth Amendment. Respondent's complaint expressly invoked the Ninth Amendment, see App. 6, and he relied heavily before this Court on *Griswold* v. *Connecticut*, which identifies that Amendment as one of the specific constitutional provisions giving "life and substance" to our understanding of privacy. More importantly, the procedural posture of the case requires that we affirm the Court of Appeals' judgment if there is *any* ground on which respondent may be entitled to relief. This case is before us on petitioner's motion to dismiss for failure to state a claim. See App. 17. It is a well-settled principle of law that "a complaint should not be dismissed merely because a plaintiff's allegations do not support the particular legal theory he advances, for the court is under a duty to examine the complaint to determine if the allegations provide for relief on any possible theory." Thus, even if respondent did not advance claims based on the Eighth or Ninth Amendments, or on the Equal Protection Clause, his complaint should not be dismissed if any of those provisions could entitle him to relief. I need not reach either the Eighth Amendment or the Equal Protection Clause issues because I believe that Hardwick has stated a cognizable claim that § 16-6-2 interferes with constitutionally protected interests in privacy and freedom of intimate association. But neither the Eighth Amendment nor the Equal Protection Clause is so clearly irrelevant that a claim resting on either provision should be peremptorily dismissed.[2] The Court's

---

[2]In *Robinson* v. *California*, the Court held that the Eighth Amendment barred convicting a defendant due to his "status" as a narcotics addict, since that condition was "apparently an illness which may be contracted innocently or involuntarily." In *Powell* v. *Texas*, where the Court refused to extend *Robinson* to punishment of public drunkenness by a chronic alcoholic, one of the factors relied on by JUSTICE MARSHALL, in writing the plurality opinion, was that Texas had not "attempted to regulate appellant's behavior in the privacy of his own home." JUSTICE WHITE wrote separately:
"Analysis of this difficult case is not advanced by preoccupation with the label 'condition.' In *Robinson* the Court dealt with 'a statute which makes the "status" of narcotic addiction a criminal offense. . . .' By precluding criminal conviction for such a 'status' the Court was dealing with a condition brought about by acts remote in time from the application of the criminal sanctions contemplated, a condition which was relatively permanent in duration, and a condition of great magnitude and significance in terms of human behavior and values. . . . If it were necessary to distinguish between 'acts' and 'conditions' for purposes of the Eighth Amendment, I would adhere to the concept of 'condition' implicit in the opinion in *Robinson*. . . . The proper subject of inquiry is whether volitional acts brought about the 'condition' and whether those acts are sufficiently proximate to the 'condition' for it to be permissible to impose penal sanctions on the 'condition.' "

cramped reading of the issue before it makes for a short opinion, but it does little to make for a persuasive one.

II

"Our cases long have recognized that the Constitution embodies a promise that a certain private sphere of individual liberty will be kept largely beyond the reach of government." *Thornburgh* v. *American College of Obstetricians & Gynecologists.* In construing the right to privacy, the Court has proceeded along two somewhat distinct, albeit complementary, lines. First, it has recognized a privacy interest with reference to certain *decisions* that are properly for the individual to make. Second, it has recognized a privacy interest with reference to certain *places* without regard for the particular activities in which the individuals who occupy them are engaged. The case before us implicates both the decisional and the spatial aspects of the right to privacy.

A

The Court concludes today that none of our prior cases dealing with various decisions that individuals are entitled to make free of governmental interference "bears any resemblance to the claimed constitutional right of homosexuals to engage in acts of sodomy that is asserted in this case." While it is true that these cases may be characterized by their connection to protection of the family, the Court's conclusion that they extend no further than this boundary ignores the warning in *Moore* v. *East Cleveland* (plurality opinion), against

---

Despite historical views of homosexuality, it is no longer viewed by mental health professionals as a "disease" or disorder. But, obviously, neither is it simply a matter of deliberate personal election. Homosexual orientation may well form part of the very fiber of an individual's personality. Consequently, under JUSTICE WHITE's analysis in *Powell*, the Eighth Amendment may pose a constitutional barrier to sending an individual to prison for acting on that attraction regardless of the circumstances. An individual's ability to make constitutionally protected "decisions concerning sexual relations," *Carey* v. *Population Services International*, (POWELL, J., concurring in part and concurring in judgment), is rendered empty indeed if he or she is given no real choice but a life without any physical intimacy.

With respect to the Equal Protection Clause's applicability to § 16-6-2, I note that Georgia's exclusive stress before this Court on its interest in prosecuting homosexual activity despite the gender-neutral terms of the statute may raise serious questions of discriminatory enforcement, questions that cannot be disposed of before this Court on a motion to dismiss. The legislature having decided that the sex of the participants is irrelevant to the legality of the acts, I do not see why the State can defend § 16-6-2 on the ground that individuals singled out for prosecution are of the same sex as their partners. Thus, under the circumstances of this case, a claim under the Equal Protection Clause may well be available without having to reach the more controversial question whether homosexuals are a suspect class.

"clos[ing] our eyes to the basic reasons why certain rights associated with the family have been accorded shelter under the Fourteenth Amendment's Due Process Clause." We protect those rights not because they contribute, in some direct and material way, to the general public welfare, but because they form so central a part of an individual's life. "[T]he concept of privacy embodies the 'moral fact that a person belongs to himself and not others nor to society as a whole.'" *Thornburgh* v. *American College of Obstetricians & Gynecologists* (STEVENS, J., concurring), quoting Fried, Correspondence, Phil. & Pub. Affairs. And so we protect the decision whether to marry precisely because marriage "is an association that promotes a way of life, not causes; a harmony in living, not political faiths; a bilateral loyalty, not commercial or social projects." *Griswold* v. *Connecticut.* We protect the decision whether to have a child because parenthood alters so dramatically an individual's self-definition, not because of demographic considerations or the Bible's command to be fruitful and multiply. And we protect the family because it contributes so powerfully to the happiness of individuals, not because of a preference for stereotypical households. The Court recognized in *Roberts.* v. United States Jaycees, that the "ability independently to define one's identity that is central to any concept of liberty" cannot truly be exercised in a vacuum; we all depend on the "emotional enrichment from close ties with others." *Ibid.*

Only the most willful blindness could obscure the fact that sexual intimacy is "a sensitive, key relationship of human existence, central to family life, community welfare, and the development of human personality," *Paris Adult Theatre I* v. *Slaton.* The fact that individuals define themselves in a significant way through their intimate sexual relationships with others suggests, in a Nation as diverse as ours, that there may be many "right" ways of conducting those relationships, and that much of the richness of a relationship will come from the freedom an individual has to *choose* the form and nature of these intensely personal bonds.

In a variety of circumstances we have recognized that a necessary corollary of giving individuals freedom to choose how to conduct their lives is acceptance of the fact that different individuals will make different choices. For example, in holding that the clearly important state interest in public education should give way to a competing claim by the Amish to the effect that extended formal schooling threatened their way of life, the Court declared: "There can be no assumption that today's majority is 'right' and the Amish and others like them are 'wrong.' A way of life that is odd or even erratic but interferes with no rights or interests of others is not to be condemned because it is different." *Wisconsin* v. *Yoder.* The Court claims that its decision today merely refuses to recognize a fundamental right to engage in homosexual sodomy; what the Court really has refused to recognize is the fundamental interest all individuals have in controlling the nature of their intimate associations with others.

B

The behavior for which Hardwick faces prosecution occurred in his own home, a place to which the Fourth Amendment attaches special significance. The Court's treatment of this aspect of the case is symptomatic of its overall refusal to consider the broad principles that have informed our treatment of privacy in specific cases. Just as the right to privacy is more than the mere aggregation of a number of entitlements to engage in specific behavior, so too, protecting the physical integrity of the home is more than merely a means of protecting specific activities that often take place there. Even when our understanding of the contours of the right to privacy depends on "reference to a 'place,' " *Katz* v. *United States* (Harlan, J., concurring), "the essence of a Fourth Amendment violation is 'not the breaking of [a person's] doors, and the rummaging of his drawers,' but rather is 'the invasion of his indefeasible right of personal security, personal liberty and private property.' " *California* v. *Ciraolo* (POWELL, J., dissenting), quoting *Boyd* v. *United States.*

The Court's interpretation of the pivotal case of *Stanley* v. *Georgia,* is entirely unconvincing. *Stanley* held that Georgia's undoubted power to punish the public distribution of constitutionally unprotected, obscene material did not permit the State to punish the private possession of such material. According to the majority here, *Stanley* relied entirely on the First Amendment, and thus, it is claimed, sheds no light on cases not involving printed materials. But that is not what *Stanley* said. Rather, the *Stanley* Court anchored its holding in the Fourth Amendment's special protection for the individual in his home:

> " 'The makers of our Constitution undertook to secure conditions
> favorable to the pursuit of happiness. They recognized the signifi-
> cance of man's spiritual nature, of his feelings and of his intellect.
> They knew that only a part of the pain, pleasure and satisfactions of

life are to be found in material things. They sought to protect
Americans in their beliefs, their thoughts, their emotions and their
sensations.'
"These are the rights that appellant is asserting in the case before us.
He is asserting the right to read or observe what he pleases—the right to
satisfy his intellectual and emotional needs in the privacy of his own
home." quoting *Olmstead* v. *United States* (Brandeis, J., dissenting).

The central place that *Stanley* gives Justice Brandeis' dissent in
Olmstead, a case raising *no* First Amendment claim, shows that
Stanley rested as much on the Court's understanding of the Fourth
Amendment as it did on the First. Indeed, in *Paris Adult Theatre I*
v. *Slaton*, the Court suggested that reliance on the Fourth Amendment not only supported the Court's outcome in *Stanley* but actually was *necessary* to it: "If obscene material unprotected by the
First Amendment in itself carried with it a 'penumbra' of constitutionally protected privacy, this Court would not have found it necessary to decide *Stanley* on the narrow basis of the 'privacy of the
home,' which was hardly more than a reaffirmation that 'a man's
home is his castle.'" "The right of the people to be secure in
their . . . houses," expressly guaranteed by the Fourth Amendment,
is perhaps the most "textual" of the various constitutional provisions
that inform our understanding of the right to privacy, and thus I
cannot agree with the Court's statement that "[t]he right pressed
upon us here has no . . . support in the text of the Constitution."
Indeed, the right of an individual to conduct intimate relationships
in the intimacy of his or her own home seems to me to be the heart
of the Constitution's protection of privacy.

III

The Court's failure to comprehend the magnitude of the liberty
interests at stake in this case leads it to slight the question whether
petitioner, on behalf of the State, has justified Georgia's infringe-
ment on these interests. I believe that neither of the two general justifications for § 16-6-2 that petitioner has advanced warrants
dismissing respondent's challenge for failure to state a claim.

First, petitioner asserts that the acts made criminal by the statute
may have serious adverse consequences for "the general public
health and welfare," such as spreading communicable diseases or
fostering other criminal activity. Brief for Petitioner 37. Inasmuch

as this case was dismissed by the District Court on the pleadings, it is not surprising that the record before us is barren of any evidence to support petitioner's claim.[3] In light of the state of the record, I see no justification for the Court's attempt to equate the private, consensual sexual activity at issue here with the "possession in the home of drugs, firearms, or stolen goods," *ante*, to which *Stanley* refused to extend its protection. None of the behavior so mentioned in *Stanley* can properly be viewed as "[v]ictimless," *ante* drugs and weapons are inherently dangerous, and for property to be "stolen," someone must have been wrongfully deprived of it. Nothing in the record before the Court provides any justification for finding the activity forbidden by § 16-6-2 to be physically dangerous, either to the persons engaged in it or to others.[4]

The core of petitioner's defense of § 16-6-2, however, is that respondent and others who engage in the conduct prohibited by § 16-6-2 interfere with Georgia's exercise of the " 'right of the Nation and of the States to maintain a decent society,' " *Paris Adult Theatre I* v. *Slaton*, quoting *Jacobellis* v. *Ohio*. (Warren, C. J., dissenting). Essentially, petitioner argues, and the Court agrees, that the fact that

[3]Even if a court faced with a challenge to § 16-6-2 were to apply simple rational-basis scrutiny to the statute, Georgia would be required to show an actual connection between the forbidden acts and the ill effects it seeks to prevent. The connection between the acts prohibited by § 16-6-2 and the harms identified by petitioner in his brief before this Court is a subject of hot dispute, hardly amenable to dismissal under Federal Rule of Civil Procedure 12(b)(6). Compare, *e. g.*, Brief for Petitioner 36–37 and Brief for David Robinson, Jr., as *Amicus Curiae* 23–28, on the one hand, with *People* v. *Onofre*. Brief for the Attorney General of the State of New York, joined by the Attorney General of the State of California, as *Amici Curiae* 11–14; and Brief for the American Psychological Association and American Public Health Association as *Amici Curiae* 19–27, on the other.

[4]Although I do not think it necessary to decide today issues that are not even remotely before us, it does seem to me that a court could find simple, analytically sound distinctions between certain private, consensual sexual conduct, on the one hand, and adultery and incest (the only two vaguely specific "sexual crimes" to which the majority points, *ante*,) on the other. For example, marriage, in addition to its spiritual aspects, is a civil contract that entitles the contracting parties to a variety of governmentally provided benefits. A State might define the contractual commitment necessary to become eligible for these benefits to include a commitment of fidelity and then punish individuals for breaching that contract. Moreover, a State might conclude that adultery is likely to injure third persons, in particular, spouses and children of persons who engage in extramarital affairs. With respect to incest, a court might well agree with respondent that the nature of familial relationships renders true consent to incestuous activity sufficiently problematical that a blanket prohibition of such activity is warranted. Notably, the Court makes no effort to explain why it has chosen to group private, consensual homosexual activity with adultery and incest rather than with private, consensual heterosexual activity by unmarried persons or, indeed, with oral or anal sex within marriage.

the acts described in § 16-6-2 "for hundreds of years, if not thousands, have been uniformly condemned as immoral" is a sufficient reason to permit a State to ban them today. Brief for Petitioner 19.

I cannot agree that either the length of time a majority has held its convictions or the passions with which it defends them can withdraw legislation from this Court's scrutiny.[5] As Justice Jackson wrote so eloquently for the Court in *West Virginia Board of Education* v. *Barnette*, "we apply the limitations of the Constitution with no fear that freedom to be intellectually and spiritually diverse or even contrary will disintegrate the social organization. . . . [F]reedom to differ is not limited to things that do not matter much. That would be a mere shadow of freedom. The test of its substance is the right to differ as to things that touch the heart of the existing order." It is precisely because the issue raised by this case touches the heart of what makes individuals what they are that we should be especially sensitive to the rights of those whose choices upset the majority.

The assertion that "traditional Judeo-Christian values proscribe" the conduct involved, Brief for Petitioner 20, cannot provide an adequate justification for § 16-6-2. That certain, but by no means all, religious groups condemn the behavior at issue gives the State no license to impose their judgments on the entire citizenry. The legitimacy of secular legislation depends instead on whether the State can advance some justification for its law beyond its conformity to religious doctrine. Thus, far from buttressing his case, petitioner's invocation of Leviticus, Romans, St. Thomas Aquinas, and sodomy's heretical status during the Middle Ages undermines his

[5]The parallel between *Loving* v. Virginia and this case is almost uncanny. There, too, the State relied on a religious justification for its law. Compare 388 U. S., at 3 (quoting trial court's statement that "Almighty God created the races white, black, yellow, malay and red, and he placed them on separate continents. . . . The fact that he separated the races shows that he did not intend for the races to mix"), with Brief for Petitioner 20–21 (relying on the Old and New Testaments and the writings of St. Thomas Aquinas to show that "traditional Judeo-Christian values proscribe such conduct"). There, too, defenders of the challenged statute relied heavily on the fact that when the Fourteenth Amendment was ratified, most of the States had similar prohibitions. Compare Brief for Appellee in *Loving* v. *Virginia*, O. T. 1966, No. 395, pp. 28–29, with *ante*, at 192–194, and n. 6. There, too, at the time the case came before the Court, many of the States still had criminal statutes concerning the conduct at issue. Compare 388 U. S., at 6, n. 5 (noting that 16 States still outlawed interracial marriage), with *ante*, at 193–194 (noting that 24 States and the District of Columbia have sodomy statutes). Yet the Court held, not only that the invidious racism of Virginia's law violated the Equal Protection Clause, but also that the law deprived the Lovings of due process by denying them the "freedom of choice to marry" that had "long been recognized as one of the vital personal rights essential to the orderly pursuit of happiness by free men." *Id.*

suggestion that § 16-6-2 represents a legitimate use of secular coer-
cive power.[6] A State can no more punish private behavior because
of religious intolerance than it can punish such behavior because
of racial animus. "The Constitution cannot control such prejudices, but neither can it tolerate them. Private biases may be outside the reach of the law, but the law cannot, directly or indirectly,
give them effect." *Palmore v. Sidoti*. No matter how uncomfortable
a certain group may make the majority of this Court, we have held
that "[m]ere public intolerance or animosity cannot constitutionally justify the deprivation of a person's physical liberty." *O'Connor
v. Donaldson*.

Nor can § 16-6-2 be justified as a "morally neutral" exercise of
Georgia's power to "protect the public environment," *Paris Adult
Theatre I*. Certainly, some private behavior can affect the fabric of
society as a whole. Reasonable people may differ about whether particular sexual acts are moral or immoral, but "we have ample evidence for believing that people will not abandon morality, will not
think any better of murder, cruelty and dishonesty, merely because
some private sexual practice which they abominate is not punished
by the law." H. L. A. Hart, Immorality and Treason, reprinted in
The Law as Literature. Petitioner and the Court fail to see the difference between laws that protect public sensibilities and those that
enforce private morality. Statutes banning public sexual activity are
entirely consistent with protecting the individual's liberty interest in
decisions concerning sexual relations: the same recognition that
those decisions are intensely private which justifies protecting them
from governmental interference can justify protecting individuals
from unwilling exposure to the sexual activities of others. But the
mere fact that intimate behavior may be punished when it takes
place in public cannot dictate how States can regulate intimate
behavior that occurs in intimate places. See *Paris Adult Theatre I*.
("marital intercourse on a street corner or a theater stage" can be

---

[6]The theological nature of the origin of Anglo-American antisodomy statutes is patent. It was
not until 1533 that sodomy was made a secular offense in England. 25 Hen. VIII, ch. 6. Until
that time, the offense was, in Sir James Stephen's words, "merely ecclesiastical." 2J. Stephen, A
History of the Criminal Law of England 429–430 (1883). Pollock and Maitland similarly
observed that "[t]he crime against nature . . . was so closely connected with heresy that the vulgar had but one name for both." 2 F. Pollock & F. Maitland, The History of English Law 554
(1895). The transfer of jurisdiction over prosecutions for sodomy to the secular courts seems
primarily due to the alteration of ecclesiastical jurisdiction attendant on England's break with
the Roman Catholic Church, rather than to any new understanding of the sovereign's interest
in preventing or punishing the behavior involved. Cf. 6 E. Coke, Institutes, ch. 10 (4th ed.
1797).

forbidden despite the constitutional protection identified in *Griswold* v. *Connecticut*).[7]

This case involves no real interference with the rights of others, for the mere knowledge that other individuals do not adhere to one's value system cannot be a legally cognizable interest, let alone an interest that can justify invading the houses, hearts, and minds of citizens who choose to live their lives differently.

IV

It took but three years for the Court to see the error in its analysis in *Minersville School District* v. *Gobitis*, and to recognize that the threat to national cohesion posed by a refusal to salute the flag was vastly outweighed by the threat to those same values posed by compelling such a salute. I can only hope that here, too, the Court soon will reconsider its analysis and conclude that depriving individuals of the right to choose for themselves how to conduct their intimate relationships poses a far greater threat to the values most deeply rooted in our Nation's history than tolerance of nonconformity could ever do. Because I think the Court today betrays those values, I dissent.

---

[7]At oral argument a suggestion appeared that, while the Fourth Amendment's special protection of the home might prevent the State from enforcing § 16-6-2 against individuals who engage in consensual sexual activity there, that protection would not make the statute invalid. The suggestion misses the point entirely. If the law is not invalid, then the police *can* invade the home to enforce it, provided, of course, that they obtain a determination of probable cause from a neutral magistrate. One of the reasons for the Court's holding in *Griswold* v. *Connecticut*, was precisely the possibility, and repugnancy, of permitting searches to obtain evidence regarding the use of contraceptives. Permitting the kinds of searches that might be necessary to obtain evidence of the sexual activity banned by § 16-6-2 seems no less intrusive, or repugnant.

fear of going home: homophobia

GLORIA ANZALDUA
1987

for the lesbian of color, the ultimate rebellion she can make against her native culture is through her sexual behavior. She goes against two moral prohibitions: sexuality and homosexuality. Being lesbian and raised Catholic, indoctrinated as straight, I *made the choice to be queer* (for some it is genetically inherent). It's an interesting path, one that continually slips in and out of the white, the Catholic, the Mexican, the indigenous, the instincts. In and out of my head. It makes for *loqueria*, the crazies. It is a path of knowledge—one of knowing (and of learning) the history of oppression of our *raza*. It is a way of balancing, of mitigating duality.

In a New England college where I taught, the presence of a few lesbians threw the more conservative heterosexual students and faculty into a panic. The two lesbian students and we two lesbian instructors met with them to discuss their fears. One of the students said, "I thought homophobia meant fear of going home after a residency."

And I thought, how apt. Fear of going home. And of not being taken in. We're afraid of being abandoned by the mother, the culture, *la Raza*, for being unacceptable, faulty, damaged. Most of us unconsciously believe that if we reveal this unacceptable aspect of the self our mother/culture/race will totally reject us. To avoid rejection, some of us conform to the values of the culture, push the unacceptable parts into the shadows. Which leaves only one fear—that we will be found out and that the Shadow-Beast will break out of its cage. Some of us take another route. We try to make ourselves conscious of the Shadow-Beast, stare at the sexual lust and lust for power and destruction we see on its face, discern among its features the undershadow that the reigning order of heterosexual males project on our Beast. Yet still others of us take it another step: we try to waken the Shadow-Beast inside us. Not many jump at the chance to confront the Shadow-Beast in the mirror without flinching at her lidless serpent eyes, her cold clammy moist hand dragging us underground, fangs barred and hissing. How does one put feathers on this particular serpent? But a few of us have been lucky—on the face of the Shadow-Beast we have seen not lust but tenderness; on its face we have uncovered the lie.

how to bring your kids up gay

EVE KOSOFSKY SEDGWICK

1989

in the summer of 1989, the United States Department of Health and Human Services released a study entitled *Report of the Secretary's Task Force on Youth Suicide*. Written in response to the apparently burgeoning epidemic of suicides and suicide attempts by children and adolescents in the United States, the 110-page report contained a section analyzing the situation of gay and lesbian youth. It concluded that because "gay youth face a hostile and condemning environment, verbal and physical abuse, and rejection and isolation from families and peers," young gays and lesbians are two to three times more likely than other young people to attempt and to commit suicide. The report recommends, modestly enough, an "end [to] discrimination against youths on the basis of such characteristics as . . . sexual orientation."

On October 13, 1989, Dr. Louis W. Sullivan, Secretary of the Department of Health and Human Services, repudiated this section of the report—impugning not its accuracy, but, it seems, its very existence. In a written statement Sullivan said, "[T]he views expressed in the paper entitled 'Gay Male and Lesbian Youth Suicide' do not in any way represent my personal beliefs or the policy of this Department. I am strongly committed to advancing traditional family values. . . . In my opinion, the views expressed in the paper run contrary to that aim.

It's always open season on gay kids. What professor who cares for her students' survival and dignity can fail to be impressed and frightened by the unaccustomed, perhaps impossible responsibilities that devolve on faculty as a result of the homophobia uniformly enjoined on, for example, teachers in the primary and secondary levels of public school—who are subject to being fired, not only for being visibly gay, but, whatever their sexuality, for providing any intimation that homosexual desires, identities, cultures, adults, children, or adolescents have a right to expression or existence?

And where, in all this, is psychoanalysis? Where are the "helping professions"? In this discussion of institutions, I mean to ask not about Freud and the possibly spacious affordances of the mother-texts, but about psychoanalysis and psychiatry as they are functioning in the United States today. I am especially interested in revisionist psychoanalysis, including ego-psychology, and in developments following on the American Psychiatric Association's much-publicized 1973 decision to drop the pathologizing diagnosis of homosexuality from its next Diagnostic and Statistical Manual (DSM-III). What is likely to be the fate of children brought under the influence of psychoanalysis and psychiatry today, post-DSM-III, on account of anxieties about their sexuality?

The monographic literature on the subject is, to begin with, as far as I can tell, exclusively about boys. A representative example of this revisionist, ego-based psychoanalytic theory would be Richard C. Friedman's *Male Homosexuality: A Contemporary Psychoanalytic Perspective*, published by Yale in 1988. (A sort of companion-volume, though by a nonpsychoanalyst psychiatrist, is Richard Green's *The "Sissy Boy Syndrome" and the Development of Homosexuality* [1987], also from Yale.) Friedman's book, which lavishly acknowledges his wife and children, is strongly marked by his sympathetic involvement with the 1973 depathologizing movement. It contains several visibly admiring histories of gay men, many of them encountered in nontherapeutic contexts. These include "Luke, a forty-five-year-old career army officer and a life-long exclusively homosexual man" (152); and Tim, who was "burly, strong, and could work side by side with anyone at the most strenuous jobs": "gregarious and likeable," "an excellent athlete," Tim was "captain of [his high-school] wrestling team and editor of the school newspaper" (206–7). Bob, another "well-integrated individual," "had regular sexual activity with a few different partners but never cruised or visited gay bars or baths. He did not belong to a gay organization. As an adult, Bob had had a stable, productive work history. He had loyal, caring, durable friendships with both men and women" (92–93). Friedman also, by way of comparison, gives an example of a *hetero*sexual man with what he considers a highly integrated personality, who happens to be a combat jet pilot: "Fit and trim, in his late twenties, he had the quietly commanding style of an effective decision maker" (86).

Is a pattern emerging? Revisionist analysts seem prepared to like some gay men, but the healthy homosexual is (a) one who is already grown up and (b) acts masculine. In fact Friedman correlates, in so many words, adult gay male effeminacy with "global character pathology" and what he calls "the lower part of the psychostructural spectrum" (93). In the obligatory paragraphs of his book concerning "the question of when behavioral deviation from a defined norm should be considered psychopathology," Friedman makes explicit that while "clinical concepts are often somewhat imprecise and admittedly fail to do justice to the rich variability of human behavior," a certain baseline concept of pathology will be maintained in his study; and that baseline will be drawn in a very particular place. "The distinction between nonconformists and people with psychopathology is usually clear enough during childhood. Extremely and chronically effeminate boys, for example, should be understood as falling into the latter category" (32–33).

"For example," "extremely and chronically effeminate boys"—this is the subject that haunts revisionist psychoanalysis. The same DSM-III that, published in 1980, was the first that did not contain an entry for "homosexuality," was also the first that *did* contain a new diagnosis, numbered (for insurance purposes) 302.60: "Gender Identity Disorder of Childhood." Nominally gender-neutral, this diagnosis is actually highly differential between boys and girls: a girl gets this pathologizing label only in the rare case of asserting that she actually is anatomically male (e.g., "that she has, or will grow, a penis"); while a boy can be treated for Gender Identity Disorder of Childhood if he merely asserts "that it would be better not to have a penis"—*or*, alternatively, if he displays a "preoccupation with female stereotypical activities as manifested by a preference for either cross-dressing or simulating female attire, or by a compelling desire to participate in the games and pastimes of girls." While the decision to remove "homosexuality" from DSM-III was highly polemicized and public, accomplished only under intense pressure from gay activists outside the profession, the addition to DSM-III of the "Gender Identity Disorder of Childhood" appears to have attracted no outside attention at all—nor even to have been perceived as part of the same conceptual shift. Indeed, the gay movement has never been quick to attend to issues concerning effeminate boys. There is a discreditable reason for this in the marginal or stigmatized position to which even adult men who are effeminate have often been relegated in the movement. A more understandable reason than effeminophobia, however, is the conceptual need of the gay movement to interrupt a long tradition of viewing gender and sexuality as continuous and collapsible cate-gories—a tradition of assuming that anyone, male or female, who desires a man must by definition be feminine; and that anyone, male or female, who desires a woman must by the same token be mascu-line. That one woman, *as a woman*, might desire another; that one man, *as a man*, might desire another: the indispensable need to make these powerful, subversive assertions has seemed, perhaps, to require a relative deemphasis of the links between gay adults and gender-nonconforming children. To begin to theorize gender and sexuality as distinct though intimately entangled axes of analysis has been, indeed, a great advance of recent lesbian and gay thought.

There is a danger, however, that that advance may leave the effem-inate boy once more in the position of the haunting abject—this time the haunting abject of gay thought itself. This is an especially horrifying thought if—as many studies launched from many different theoretical and political positions have suggested—for any given adult gay man, wherever he may be at present on a scale of self-perceived or socially ascribed masculinity (ranging from extremely masculine to extremely feminine), the likelihood is disproportion-ately high that he will have a childhood history of self-perceived effeminacy, femininity, or nonmasculinity. In this case the eclipse of the effeminate boy from adult gay discourse would represent more than a damaging theoretical gap; it would represent a node of anni-hilating homophobic, gynephobic, and pedophobic hatred internal-ized and made central to gay-affirmative analysis. The effeminate boy would come to function as the open secret of many politicized adult gay men.

One of the most interesting aspects—and by interesting I mean cautionary—of the new psychoanalytic developments is that they are based on *precisely* the theoretical move of distinguishing gender from sexuality. This is how it happens that the *de*pathologization of an atyp-ical sexual object-choice can be yoked to the *new* pathologization of an atypical gender identification. Integrating the gender-constructivist research of, for example, John Money and Robert Stoller, research that many have taken (though perhaps wrongly) as having potential for feminist uses, this work posits the very early consolidation of some-thing called Core Gender Identity—one's basal sense of being male or female—as a separate stage prior to, even conceivably independent of, any crystallization of sexual fantasy or sexual object-choice. Gender Disorder of Childhood is seen as a pathology involving the Core Gender Identity (failure to develop a CGI consistent with one's biological sex); sexual object-choice, on the other hand, is unbundled from this Core Gender Identity through a reasonably space-making series of two-phase narrative moves. Under the pressure, ironically, of having to show how gay adults whom he considers well-integrated personalities do sometimes evolve from children seen as the very definition of psychopathology, Friedman unpacks several developmental steps that have often otherwise been seen as rigidly unitary.

One serious problem with this way of distinguishing between gender and sexuality is that, while denaturalizing sexual object-choice, it radically *re*naturalizes gender. All ego-psychology is prone, in the first place, to structuring developmental narrative around a none-too-dialectical trope of progressive *consolidation* of self. To place a very early core-gender determinant (however little biologized it may be) at the very center of that process of consolidation seems to mean, essentially, that for a nontranssexual person with a penis, nothing can ever be assimilated to the self through this process of consolidation unless it can be assimilated *as masculinity*. For even the most feminine-self-identified boys, Friedman uses the phrases "sense of masculine self-regard" (245), "masculine competency" (20), and "self-evaluation as appropriately masculine" (244) as synonyms for any self-esteem and, ultimately, for any *self*. As he describes the interactive process that leads to any ego-consolidation in a boy:

> Boys measure themselves in relation to others whom they estimate to be similar. [For Friedman, this means only men and other boys.] Similarity of self-assessment depends on consensual validation. The others must agree that the boy is and will remain similar to them. The boy must also view both groups of males (peers and older men) as appropriate for idealization. Not only must he be like them in some ways, he must want to be like them in others. They in turn must want him to be like them. Unconsciously, they must have the capacity to identify with him. This naturally occurring [!] fit between the male social world and the boy's inner object world is the juvenile phase-specific counterpoint to the preoedipal child's relationship with the mother. (237)

The reason effeminate boys turn out gay, according to this account, is that other men don't validate them as masculine. There is a persistent, wistful fantasy in this book: "One cannot help but wonder how these [prehomosexual boys] would have developed if the males they idealized had had a more flexible and abstract sense of masculine competency" (20). For Friedman, the increasing flexibility in what kinds of attributes or activities *can* be processed as masculine, with increasing maturity, seems fully to account for the fact that so many "gender-disturbed" (pathologically effeminate) little boys manage to grow up into "healthy" (masculine) men, albeit after the phase where their sexuality has differentiated as gay.

Or rather, it *almost* fully accounts for it. There is a residue of mystery, resurfacing at several points in the book, about why most gay men turn out so resilient—about how they even survive—given the profound initial deficit of "masculine self-regard" characteristic of many proto-gay childhoods, and the late and relatively superficial remediation of it that comes with increasing maturity. Given that "the virulence and chronicity of [social] stress [against it] puts homosexuality in a unique position in the human behavioral repertoire," how does one account for "the fact that severe, persistent morbidity does not occur more frequently" among gay adolescents (205)? Friedman essentially throws up his hands at these moments. "A number of possible explanations arise, but one seems particularly likely to me: namely, that homosexuality is associated with some psychological mechanism, not understood or even studied to date, that protects the individual from diverse psychiatric disorders" (236). It "might include mechanisms influencing ego resiliency, growth potential, and the capacity to form intimate relationships" (205). And "it is possible that, for reasons that have not yet been well described, [gender-disturbed boys'] mechanisms for coping with anguish and adversity are unusually effective" (201).

These are huge blank spaces to be left in what purports to be a developmental account of proto-gay children. But given that egosyntonic consolidation for a boy can come only in the form of masculinity, given that masculinity can be conferred only by men (20), and given that femininity, in a person with a penis, can represent nothing but deficit and disorder, the one explanation that could *never* be broached is that these mysterious skills of survival, filiation, and resistance could derive from a secure identification with the resource-richness of a mother. Mothers, indeed, have nothing to contribute to this process of masculine validation, and women are reduced in the light of its urgency to a null set: any involvement in it by a woman is overinvolvement; any protectiveness is overprotectiveness; and, for instance, mothers "proud of their sons' nonviolent qualities" are manifesting unmistakable "family pathology" (193).

For both Friedman and Green, then, the first, imperative developmental task of a male child or his parents and caretakers is to get a properly male Core Gender Identity in place, as a basis for further and perhaps more flexible explorations of what it may be to *be* masculine—that is, for a male person, to be *human*. Friedman is rather equivocal about whether this masculine CGI necessarily entails any particular content, or whether it is an almost purely formal, preconditional differentiation that, once firmly in place, can cover an almost infinite range of behaviors and attitudes. He certainly does not see a necessary connection between masculinity and any scapegoating of male homosexuality; since ego-psychology treats the development of male heterosexuality as nonproblematical after adolescence, as not involving the suppression of any homosexual or bisexual possibility (263–67), and therefore as completely unimplicated with homosexual panic (178), it seems merely an unfortunate, perhaps rectifiable misunderstanding that for a proto-gay child to identify "masculinely" might involve his identification with his own erasure.

The renaturalization and enforcement of gender assignment are not the worst news about the new psychiatry of gay acceptance, however. The worst is that it not only fails to offer, but seems conceptually incapable of offering, even the slightest resistance to the wish endemic in the culture surrounding and supporting it: the wish that gay people *not exist*. There are many people in the worlds we inhabit, and these psychiatrists are unmistakably among them, who have a strong interest in the dignified treatment of any gay people who may happen already to exist. But the number of persons or institutions by whom the existence of gay people is treated as a precious desideratum, a needed condition of life, is small. The presiding asymmetry of value assignment between hetero and homo goes unchallenged everywhere: advice on how to help your kids turn out gay, not to mention your students, your parishioners, your therapy clients, or your military subordinates, is less ubiquitous than you might think. On the other hand, the scope of institutions whose programmatic undertaking is to prevent the development of gay people is unimaginably large. There is no major institutionalized discourse that offers a firm resistance to that undertaking: in the United States, at any rate, most sites of the state, the military, education, law, penal institutions, the church, medicine, and mass culture enforce it all but unquestioningly, and with little hesitation at even the recourse to invasive violence.

The books cited above, and the associated therapeutic strategies and institutions, are not about invasive violence. What they are about is a train of squalid lies. The overarching lie is that they are predicated on anything but the therapists' disavowed desire for a nongay outcome. Friedman, for instance, speculates wistfully that—with proper therapeutic intervention—the sexual orientation of one gay man whom he describes as quite healthy might conceivably (not have *been changed* but) "have shifted *on its own*" (Friedman's italics): a speculation, he artlessly remarks, "not value-laden with regard to sexual orientation" (212). Green's book, composed largely of interview transcripts, is a tissue of his lies to children about their parents' motives for bringing them in for therapy. (It was "not to prevent you from becoming homosexual," he tells one young man who had been subjected to behavior modification, "it was because you were unhappy" [318]; but later on the very same page, he unselfconsciously confirms to his trusted reader that "parents of sons who entered therapy were . . . worried that the cross-gender behavior portended problems with later sexuality.") He encourages predominantly gay young men to "reassure" their parents that they are "bisexual" ("Tell him just enough so he feels better" [207]), and to consider favorably the option of marrying and keeping their wives in the dark about their sexual activities (205). He lies to himself and to us in encouraging patients to lie to him. For instance, in a series of interviews with Kyle, the boy subjected to behavioral therapy, Green reports him as saying that he is unusually withdrawn—"I suppose I've been overly sensitive when guys look at me or something ever since I can remember, you know, after my mom told me why I have to go to UCLA because they were afraid I'd turn into a homosexual" (307); as saying that homosexuality "is pretty bad, and I don't think they should be around to influence children. . . . I don't think they should be hurt by society or anything like that—especially in New York. You have them who are into leather and stuff like that. I mean, I think that is really sick, and I think that maybe they should be put away" (307); as saying that he wants to commit violence on men who look at him (307); and as saying that if he had a child like himself, he "would take him where he would be helped" (317). The very image of serene self-acceptance?

Green's summary:

> Opponents of therapy have argued that intervention underscores
> the child's "deviance," renders him ashamed of who he is, and

makes him suppress his "true self." Data on psychological tests do
not support this contention; nor does the content of clinical interviews. The boys look back favorably on treatment. They would
endorse such intervention if they were the father of a "feminine"
boy. Their reason is to reduce childhood conflict and social stigma.
Therapy with these boys appeared to accomplish this. (319)

Consistent with this, Green is obscenely eager to convince parents
that their hatred and rage at their effeminate sons really is only a
desire to protect them from peer-group cruelty—even when the parents name *their own* feelings as hatred and rage (391–92). Even when
fully one-quarter of parents of gay sons are *so* interested in protecting
them from social cruelty that, when the boys fail to change, their parents kick them out on the street, Green is withering about mothers
who display any tolerance of their sons' cross-gender behavior
(373–75). In fact, his bottom-line identifications as a clinician actually seem to lie with the enforcing peer group: he refers approvingly
at one point to "therapy, be it formal (delivered by paid professionals)
or informal (delivered by the peer group and the larger society via
teasing and sex-role standards)" (388).

Referring blandly on one page to "psychological intervention directed
at increasing [effeminate boys'] comfort with being male" (259), Friedman says much more candidly on the next page: "[T]he rights of parents to oversee the development of children is a long-established
principle. Who is to dictate that parents may not try to raise their children in a manner that maximizes the possibility of a heterosexual outcome?" (260). Who indeed—if the members of this profession can't
stop seeing the prevention of gay people as an ethical use of their skills?

Even outside of the mental health professions and within more
authentically gay-affirmative discourses, the theoretical space for supporting gay development is, as I've pointed out in the introduction to
Epistemology of the Closet, narrow. Constructivist arguments have
tended to keep hands off the experience of gay and protogay kids. For gay
and gay-loving people, even though the space of cultural malleability is
the only conceivable theater for our effective politics, every step of this
constructivist nature/culture argument holds danger: the danger of the
difficulty of intervening in the seemingly natural trajectory from identifying a place of cultural malleability, to inventing an ethical or therapeutic mandate for cultural manipulation, to the overarching, hygienic
Western fantasy of a world without any more homosexuals in it.

That's one set of dangers, and it is as against them, as I've argued, that essentialist and biologizing understandings of sexual identity accrue a certain gravity. Conceptualizing an unalterably *homosexual body* seems to offer resistance to the social-engineering momentum apparently built into every one of the human sciences of the West, and that resistance can reassure profoundly. At the same time, however, in the postmodern era it is becoming increasingly problematical to assume that grounding an identity in biology or "essential nature" is a stable way of insulating it from societal interference. If anything, the gestalt of assumptions that undergird nature/nurture debates may be in process of direct reversal. Increasingly it is the conjecture that a particular trait is genetically or biologically based, *not* that it is "only cultural," that seems to trigger an estrus of manipulative fantasy in the technological institutions of the culture. A relative depressiveness about the efficacy of social engineering techniques, a high mania about biological control: the Cartesian bipolar psychosis that always underlay the nature/nurture debates has switched its polar assignments without surrendering a bit of its hold over the collective life. And in this unstable context, the dependence on a specified *homosexual body* to offer resistance to any gay-eradicating momentum is tremblingly vulnerable. AIDS, although it is used to proffer every single day to the news-consuming public the crystallized vision of a world after the homosexual, could never by itself bring about such a world. What whets these fantasies more dangerously, because more blandly, is the presentation, often in ostensibly or authentically gay-affirmative contexts, of biologically based "explanations" for deviant behavior that are absolutely invariably couched in terms of "excess," "deficiency," or "imbalance"—whether in the hormones, in the genetic material, or, as is currently fashionable, in the fetal endocrine environment. If I had ever, in any medium, seen any researcher or popularizer refer even once to any supposed gay-producing circumstance as the *proper* hormone balance, or the *conducive* endocrine environment, for gay generation, I would be less chilled by the breezes of all this technological confidence. As things are, a medicalized dream of the prevention of gay bodies seems to be the less visible, far more respectable underside of the AIDS-fueled public dream of their extirpation.

In this unstable balance of assumptions between nature and culture, at any rate, under the overarching, relatively unchallenged aegis of a culture's desire that gay people *not be*, there is no unthreatened, unthreatening theoretical home for a concept of gay and lesbian origins. What the books I have been discussing, and the institutions to which they are attached, demonstrate is that the wish for the dignified treatment of already gay people is necessarily destined to turn into either trivializing apologetics or, much worse, a silkily camouflaged complicity in oppression—in the absence of a strong, explicit, *erotically invested* affirmation of some people's felt desire or need that there be gay people in the immediate world.

untitled

DAVID WOJNAROWICZ
1990

one day this kid will get larger. One day this kid will come to know something that causes a sensation equivalent to the separation of the earth from its axis. One day this kid will reach a point where he senses a division that isn't mathematical. One day this kid will feel something stir in his heart and throat and mouth. One day this kid will find something in his mind and body and soul that makes him hungry. One day this kid will do something that causes men who wear the uniforms of priests and rabbis, men who inhabit certain stone buildings, to call for his death. One day politicians will enact legislation against this kid. One day families will give false information to their children and each child will pass that information down generationally to their families and that information will be designed to make existence intolerable for this kid. One day this kid will begin to experience all this activity in his environment and that activity and information will compel him to commit suicide or submit to danger in hopes of being murdered or submit to silence and invisibility. Or one day this kid will talk. When he begins to talk, men who develop a fear of this kid will attempt to silence him with strangling, fists, prison, suffocation, rape, intimidation, drugging, ropes, guns, laws, menace, roving gangs, bottles, knives, religion, decapitation, and immolation by fire. Doctors will pronounce this kid curable as if his brain were a virus. This kid will lose his constitutional rights against the government's invasion of his privacy. This kid will be faced with electro-shock, drugs, and conditioning therapies in laboratories tended by psychologists and research scientists. He will be subject to loss of home, civil rights, jobs, and all conceivable freedoms. All this will begin to happen in one or two years when he discovers he desires to place his naked body on the naked body of another boy.

a coming-out letter and a response

MARVIN LIEBMAN AND WILLIAM F. BUCKLEY, JR.
July 17, 1970

Following is a condensed version of a letter sent by Marvin Liebman to National Review *editor in chief William F. Buckley Jr. The text is from a manuscript edited by Buckley. The final revised text was not available when* The ADVOCATE *went to press.*

dear bill:

We've known each other for almost 35 years now, and ten years ago you served as my godfather when I entered the Catholic church. Though the subject never arose, you and Pat, among my oldest friends, must have known that I'm gay. It never seemed to matter.

But it does matter to many "movement" conservatives—this question of who is, who is not gay; and they wonder whether homosexuals are a menace to society. Just as, too often, there has been an undercurrent of anti-Semitism among even some mainstream conservatives, there has always been an element of homophobia among us. In many years of service to The Cause, I've sat in rooms where people we both know—brilliant, thoughtful, kind people—have said, without any sense of shame, vulgar and cruel things about people who through no fault of their own happen to be different in their sexuality.

I am almost 67 years old. For more than half of my lifetime I have been engaged in, and indeed helped to organize and maintain, the conservative and anticommunist cause. All the time I labored in the conservative vineyard, I was gay.

This was not my choice! The term "sexual preference" is deceptive. It is how I was born, how God decreed that I should be. As with most gay men of my generation, I kept it secret as best I could. It was probably not a secret to those who knew me well—my beloved friends and family—but no one Spoke Its Name. I now regret all those years of compliant silence.

Why have I chosen this moment to go public with that part of my life that had been so private for all those years? Because I fear that our cause might sink back into the ooze in which so much of it rested in pre-NR days. In that dark age, the American right was heavily, perhaps dominantly, made up of bigots: anti-Semites, anti-Catholics, the KKK, rednecks, Know-Nothings, a sorry lot of public hucksters and religious medicine men. I think there is general agreement that it wasn't until the founding of this publication that the modern conservative movement was granted light and form.

I was privileged to be a part of the enterprise from its earliest days, together with such great men as Whittaker Chambers, Frank Meyer, James Burnham, Russell Kirk, Brent Bozell—all of them. This effort, combined with the groups we founded, resulted in the eight-year reign of Ronald Reagan.

Now times are changing. There is no longer the anticommunist cement to hold the edifice together. The great enterprise, in which so much time has been invested, is in danger of sinking back to an aggregation of bigotries.

I've watched as some of our conservative brethren, employing the direct-mail medium I helped pioneer, use Robert Mapplethorpe's bad taste and the NEA's poor judgment to rile small donors, provoking them with a vision of a homosexual vanguard intent on forcing sadomasochistic images into every schoolroom. I have been appalled to read in newsletters by conservative leaders that George Bush, by inviting a gay leader to a White House ceremony, is caving in to "the homosexual lobby." I was outraged to see a spokesman for one of the more prominent conservative foundations quoted as saying that the fear of contracting AIDS in hospitals treating AIDS patients could well give rise to forcible euthanasia.

The conservative movement must reject the bigots and the hypocrites and provide a base for gays as well as others. The politics of inclusion is the model by which what we achieved with Ronald Reagan can continue and flourish without the anticommunist and the antitax movements as sustaining elements. Conservatives need to remind themselves that gay men and women, almost always residing in the closet, were among those who helped in the founding, nurturing, and maintaining of the movement. They should be welcomed based on common beliefs and without regard to our response to different sexual stimuli.

One day the conservative movement will recognize that there are gays among us who have advanced our cause. They should not be victims of small-mindedness, prejudice, fear, or cynicism. That day may be a long way off, and I sometimes think the trend is in the opposite direction. *National Review* could have an important role here, once again guiding conservatives toward the more enlightened path. I pray that it will.

As ever, your friend
MARVIN LIEBMAN

Following is the text of a draft version of Buckley's response to Liebman. The final revised text was not available when The ADVOCATE *went to press.*

dear marvin:

I hope you will believe me when I say that I understand the pain you have felt. Certainly I honor your decision to raise publicly the points you raise. My affection and respect for you are indelibly recorded here and there, in many ways, in many places.

But you too must realize what are the implications of what you ask. Namely, that the Judeo-Christian tradition, which is aligned with, no less, one way of life, become indifferent to another way of life.

There is, of course, argument on the question whether homosexuality is in all cases congenital. But let us assume that this is so and then ask, Is it reasonable to expect the larger community to cease to think of the activity of homosexuals as unnatural, whatever its etiology?

The social question becomes. How, exercising toleration and charity, ought the traditional community to treat that minority? Ought considerations of charity entirely swamp us, causing us to submerge convictions having to do with that which we deem to be normal and healthy?

It is a vexed and vexing subject, and your poignant letter serves to remind us of the pain we often inflict, sometimes unintentionally, sometimes sadistically. It is wholesome that we should be reproached for causing that pain and useful to be reminded that we need to redouble the effort on the one hand to understand, even as we must be true to ourselves in maintaining convictions rooted, in our opinion, in theological and moral truths. You help us to remember that a gay person overhearing relaxed chatter meanspirited in its references to gays suffers. Suffers just as much as an unidentifiably Jewish or Catholic human being would suffer on hearing invidious locker-room talk about their ethnic or religious affiliations.

I close by saying that *National Review* will not be scarred by thoughtless gay bashing, let alone be animated by such practices. I qualify this only by acknowledging that humor (if wholesomely motivated) is as irresistible to us as it is to you. You are absolutely correct in saying that gays should be welcome as partners in efforts to mint sound public policies; not correct, in my judgment, in concluding that such a partnership presupposes the repeal of convictions that are more, much more, than mere accretions of bigotry.

You remain, always, my dear friend and my brother in combat.

WFB

letter to jerry falwell

MEL WHITE
1991

dear jerry,

In 1986 and 1987, when I was ghostwriting your autobiography, *Strength for the Journey*, there was no reason for us to talk about me or about my life story. Your publisher, Simon and Schuster, and your agent, Irving Lazar, had hired me to do a job and I did it. You never asked me about my political beliefs or my personal values. And though we came from two rather different worlds, I liked you immediately and I appreciated your frankness, your sense of humor, and your loyalty to friends and family. For your friendship and for the clients you have sent me, I am grateful.

But in the past few years, Jerry, it has become more and more painful for me not to share with you my own personal journey. Now, in light of your October 1991 letter against homosexuality and homosexuals, I can no longer remain silent.

I am gay. For the past eight years (which include all the time I've been in your employment) I have been in a loving, monogamous relationship with another gay man. I am a member of a Metropolitan Community Church congregation (the only Christian denomination that is truly open to gay and lesbian people) and a member of Evangelicals Concerned (a national Bible study and prayer movement of gay and lesbian evangelical Christians).

I came close to sharing this part of my own story with you one night in a hotel suite in Washington, D.C., when we were celebrating the successful release of your autobiography. During that conversation you admitted that the church needed to do much more to help those who suffered from AIDS, and you confided that one of your own close friends was a gay man in a long-term relationship with another gay man. "I'm not going to put him in a corner," you said quietly, "if he doesn't put me in one."

You seemed compassionate and understanding that night. Then, today, I received a copy of the October 1991 fund-raising letter describing me and millions of men and women like me as "perverts" who "unashamedly flaunt their perversion." The letter declares "homosexuality a sin." It warns that "our nation has become a modern day Sodom and Gomorra" and that you have decided to speak out against this "perversion" for the purpose of "moral decency and traditional family values."

Jerry, I am hoping that staff or agency "ghostwriters" wrote that letter and that you didn't have time to read it before it was signed and mailed on your behalf. Did they realize the immediate and long-term impact of its cloud of misinformation, half-truth, and hyperbole? Did they understand the confusion and the suffering that it helps cause in the lives of American families who have gay or lesbian members? Did they know that the letter's misleading statements fuel bigotry, hatred, and violence?

Closer home, did anyone consider the tragic consequences of that letter in the lives of the people who see you as their spiritual guide? Certainly you know that in the Thomas Road Baptist Church, in Liberty University, and in the audience of the "Old Time Gospel Hour," there are thousands of Christians struggling with this issue. Did anyone think about the confusion, the anguish, and the despair that the letter's simplistic, judgmental, and erroneous position creates for them and for their families?

I know personally what it means to be a victim of this uninformed and noncompassionate "Christian" position on homosexuality. I went through twenty-five years of Christian counseling and "ex-gay therapy" including electric shock to try to overcome my sexual and affectional orientation. Finally, feeling abandoned by God, by the church, and by society, I longed to end my life.

Now, looking back, I can see that God was there, all the time, in the midst of my suffering, leading me to a remnant of faithful, well-informed Christians who had the courage to speak the truth whatever it cost them.

My most helpful counselor was fired from Fuller Seminary (where I was a professor for fourteen years) because she dared to tell the truth about homosexuality and the false claims that the "ex-gay" movement makes. And though telling the truth cost her

her academic position, she saved a lot of lives and ministries in the process.

If you are really trying to educate the nation about homosexuality as the letter states, you owe it to yourself to look more closely at the scientific, sociological, ethical, and biblical data that is now available to us. The letter mailed in your name was tragically uninformed and dangerously inflammatory in the process. What a wonderful thing it could be if you really took this issue seriously and tried to deal with it lovingly, thoughtfully, and in the spirit of Christian truth.

Jerry, we are called by Christ to bear witness to the truth, and yet the October 1991 letter is based on lies. We gay people are not "perverts" nor "degenerates" as the letter claims. My homosexuality is as much at the heart of what it means to be Mel White as your heterosexuality is at the heart of what it means to be Jerry Falwell. The wide array of intimacy and relational needs that you and your wife, Macel, meet for each other are only met for us in same-sex relationships. If you really want to help end promiscuity, tell the truth. We need you to honor and support our relationships, not oppose and condemn them.

The letter also lies when it claims that we gay and lesbian people are a menace to this nation. In fact, we are your fellow pastors, deacons, church musicians, and people in the pew. We write and arrange the songs you sing. We are your studio technicians and members of your staff. We are doctors and scientists, secretaries and clerks. We even write your books.

We are not a threat to the American family, either. We are committed to the family. Millions of us have raised wonderful families of our own. We have adopted the unwanted and the unloved and proved to be faithful, loving parents by anyone's standards.

And we certainly pose no danger to your children. Most child molestation cases are heterosexual. You know that. The truth is we have taught and nurtured your children in schools and Sunday schools without your ever knowing that we are gay.

Most of us gay and lesbian people are just normal folk who try our best to live respectable, productive lives in spite of the hatred and the condemnation heaped upon us.

We didn't choose our sexual orientation, Jerry, and no matter how hard we try, we cannot change it. There is no trustworthy, long-term evidence that sexual "reorientation" or a lifetime of celibacy is possible for tens of millions of gay and lesbian people. What brings us health is the realization that our sexuality, too, is a gift from God.

And to lead a whole, productive life we have to quit struggling against God's gift and learn to lead our lives as responsible gay and lesbian Christians.

Almost every day, I speak with gays and lesbians who are struggling to survive the waves of hatred and self-hatred generated by Christians who write letters like your letter of October 1991, or who make similar statements in sermons, on talk shows, and in interviews. Is it any wonder that gays and lesbians have finally run out of patience and are taking to the streets to protest the prejudice and the bigotry?

In your recent contact with the Act-Up demonstration in Los Angeles, it must have been terrible to realize how many people felt hatred toward you and your position. With the memories still fresh in your mind of those fearful moments in the Hotel Roosevelt kitchen, let me help you understand the bigotry and the violence we face every day, not just on the streets but in our homes, on our jobs, and even in our churches.

Every year, thousands of innocent gay and lesbian people face physical and psychological assault. Dozens are murdered. Tens of thousands are rejected by their families, fired from their jobs, and kicked out of their homes or apartments. Three times I have had rocks or bottles thrown at me from passing cars simply because I was walking with friends near a gay church or restaurant. Fundamentalist Christian extremists hound and harass us, carrying hateful signs and shouting profane and demeaning accusations in the name of "Christian love."

I know that every group has its zealots, and I thank you for stating clearly in your letter that "the majority of gay persons are not violent." But Jerry, we have reasons to demonstrate. And the letter issued in your name, using the same old, tired lies to whip up more bigotry and more hatred against us makes you a primary target for our demonstrations.

Is it any wonder that we are protesting Governor Wilson's veto of AB101, a measure that would have protected gays and lesbians from being fired simply because of their sexual orientation? Think about it. Even though you have praised my Christian commitment and my writing skills, would you hire me or recommend me again now that you know I am gay? Don't you find it ironic that if I had made my sexual orientation known, I could not have served the church faithfully these thirty years as pastor, professor, author, filmmaker, and television producer?

At this moment when hysteria and misinformation about gay and lesbian people threaten our most important public and private institutions, you could become a great healing agent. Wise counsel about homosexuality could lead to reconciliation in the family, in the church, and in the nation. Telling the truth that gay and lesbian people are a responsible and productive force in the church and throughout society could lead to understanding where misunderstanding and hatred now grow.

Jerry, I am also worried about the motives behind your letter. I remember clearly in one of our interviews that you described a noisy confrontation you once had with "radical activist gays" in San Francisco. "They played right into my hands," you said to me. "Those poor, dumb fairy demonstrators gave me the best media coverage I've ever had. If they weren't out there, I'd have to invent them."

Whatever motives caused the letter to be written, antihomosexuality is not an appropriate issue for fund-raising. Too many lives are damaged or destroyed in the process. On behalf of myself and other Christian gays and lesbians in Lynchburg and around the world, please, before you speak or write again about this issue, could we meet face-to-face to talk about the consequences?

> I make this proposal, Jerry. Will you meet with me—anytime or anyplace at your convenience—so that I can share with you the other side of the story? I appeal to you as a fellow Christian believer in the name of our Lord, Jesus, who said: "If thy brother do ought against thee, go and tell him between thee and him alone" (Matthew 18:15). I am glad to volunteer my time and travel to serve you. Do what you want with the information I could bring, but please hear it!

Lyla, my wife for twenty-five years of this painful journey, is eager to join in our discussion. As a heterosexual woman, wife, and mother, Lyla knows firsthand what it costs the families and friends of gays and lesbians to go on loving and supporting them when everyone else turns away. Her wisdom and counsel would serve us both well.

Maybe Macel, too, would like to be included in our conversation. Wherever and whenever it takes place, I am confident that in a open, loving dialogue we will both grow in our understanding of the issues and in our determination to contribute to the healing of the Christian church and of the nation.

Sincerely,
MEL WHITE

the gay moment

ANDREW KOPKIND

1993

the gay moment is unavoidable. It fills the media, charges politics, saturates popular and elite culture. It is the stuff of everyday conversation and public discourse. Not for thirty years has a class of Americans endured the peculiar pain and exhilaration of having their civil rights and moral worth—their very humanness—debated at every level of public life. Lesbians and gay men today wake up to headlines alternately disputing their claim to equality under the law, supporting their right to family status, denying their desire, affirming their social identity. They fall asleep to TV talk shows where generals call them perverts, liberals plead for tolerance and politicians weigh their votes. "Gay invisibility," the social enforcement of the sexual closet, is hardly the problem anymore. Overexposure is becoming hazardous.

While gays organize what may be the biggest march on Washington ever, set for April 25, Congress ponders the pros and cons of granting gays first-class citizenship, in the civilian order as well as the military. Courts consider the legality of discrimination against the last community in the country officially excluded from constitutional protection. Senator Edward Kennedy and Representative Henry Waxman hope to introduce a new national lesbian and gay civil rights bill soon. But until that passes—certainly not for many years—the ruling federal precedent is the notorious decision by retiring Supreme Court Justice Byron White in the 1986 *Bowers v. Hardwick* case, in which he invoked the entire Judeo-Christian tradition of patriarchy and homophobia to deny gay people the rights all other Americans enjoy. Newspapers censor pro-gay comic strips, television stations ban gay programs, schools proscribe gay-positive materials, church hierarchs forbid gay people from preaching (and parading), state electorates revoke existing anti-discrimination laws and outlaw passage of new ones, and bullies on streets of every city beat and bash gays and lesbians with escalating hatred. Some 1,900 incidents of anti-gay violence were reported in 1992. Except for a small number of enlightened workplaces in college towns and the big cities of both coasts, American institutions make it dangerous or impossible for millions of gays to leave their closets and lead integrated, fulfilling lives. In schools everywhere young gay pupils are routinely taunted and worse, and a third of all youthful suicides are gay-related (according to a government report never disseminated by the Bush Administration). Across the country, gay cavaliers must prepare to joust with Christian roundheads for the right to protect their young sisters and brothers.

But it is the contradictions rather than the cruelties of sexual struggle that define the moment. Despite the difficulties, most gays would agree that life as a homosexual is better now than ever before in American history. The Reverend Al Carmines's hopeful but unconvincing post-Stonewall song, "I'm Gay and I'm Proud" now reflects a widespread reality. Responding to the rigidity of the old order, younger gay men and "baby dykes" have created a queer culture that is rapidly reconfiguring American values, redesigning sensibilities and remodelling politics. The gay movement, broadly construed, is *the* movement of the moment. Devastated by a plague that threatens the very existence of their community, gay men have converted horror and grief into creative energy and purpose. AIDS has given a new sense of solidarity to lesbians and gay men who for years have often pursued separate agendas.

Suddenly, "out" gays inhabit high and mid-level positions in journalism and publishing, law, academia, medicine and psychiatry, the arts and creative professions. They have made it not only possible but comfortable and natural for younger lesbians and gay men to come out at the entry level. More out gays are in public office throughout the land, at least up to the sub-Cabinet level of the federal government. A quarter of a century of gay and lesbian political action has produced, *inter alia*, the first pro-gay White House — despite distressing backsliding. Gay couples are winning recognition as legal families by some city governments and a few corporations (*The Nation* is one), although valuable benefits have been extended to only a small number of registrants. And a complex infrastructure of activist, educational and professional organizations give gay life a formidable institutional base and contribute to the general appreciation of "gay power." Morley Safer was not way over the top when he suggested to his *60 Minutes* audience recently that it "face up to the gay nineties."

Suddenly, it seems, gay faces adorn the covers of major magazines; Broadway is bursting with gay plays; big book awards go to gay authors; even Hollywood is developing movies with gay themes; and gay people of every age and social stratum are shattering their closets with explosive force. "Queer theory"—also known as lesbian and gay studies—is explored by scholars and students at hundreds of colleges.

In the realm of pop music alone, stars such as k.d. lang and Elton John have come out; the late Freddie Mercury (of Queen) was outed after he died of AIDS, while others, such as Pete Townshend (of The Who) and Kurt Cobain (of Nirvana), have more or less matter-of-factly talked about bisexual times of their lives. Madonna, the premier sex symbol of the decade, is graphic about her own Sapphic activities. More important, her videos have shown same-sex couples in intimate poses—a crucially legitimizing image for the MTV generation. Prince exudes androgyny, and what more can be said about Michael Jackson in that department? Only Brooke Shields knows for sure. Perhaps the most consequential gay moment in music was a single line in the new Garth Brooks country hit "We Shall Be Free," which instructs the Nashville nation to be accepting of same-sex love. Brooks, who outsells everyone else in music these days, told Barbara Walters that he wrote it in support of his lesbian sister. *Newsweek* devoted an entire page to the song and the "turmoil" it has engendered among the hee-haw set.

Nor is a *tour d'horizon* of the gay moment complete without a mention of *The Crying Game*, the most successful mainstream movie to deal frankly with a straight/gay relationship—with full frontal nudity. Never in the history of film has a single penis shot grossed so much: $54 million at this writing.

While the arrival of the gay moment is unmistakable, its provenance and history are ambiguous and debatable. There is a feeling prevalent in the lesbian and gay community that Bill Clinton's groundbreaking pro-gay campaign and election made all the difference in the world. Jeffrey Schmalz began an important state-of-the-gays article in *The New York Times Magazine* last fall with an account of Clinton's long friendship with David Mixner, an influential, openly gay consultant and fundraiser, and how that relationship led to Clinton's stand.

The two first met, Mixner says, at a 1969 reunion for people who had worked on Eugene McCarthy's presidential campaign the year before. Mixner was still in the closet; Clinton was heading to Oxford. In time, Clinton returned to Arkansas and became a politician; Mixner went to California and became a political consultant. He came out—to the world and to his old friend Bill—in the mid-1970s, and immersed himself in gay politics. In 1978 he ran the successful campaign to defeat the Briggs Initiative, which would have effectively barred gays from teaching in the state's public schools. (His most important ally in that struggle was, of all people, Ronald Reagan, who had recently retired as governor to run, again, for the presidency. Mixner got one of Reagan's top gubernatorial aides, a gay man who had become a department store executive, to sensitize his former boss to the issue.)

Mixner kept in contact with Bill and Hillary and, by his account, instructed the couple in the elements of gay oppression and liberation. Mixner was on the Clinton presidential bus from day one, served as the campaign's co-chair in California and as a senior adviser to the candidate nationally. He also helped bring huge pots of gay money to the campaign and to position Clinton to win in excess of 75 percent of the gay vote, a crucial component of the Democratic totals in big cities where gays are concentrated. The Human Rights Campaign Fund and the Victory Fund, the two leading gay money-raising groups in Washington, estimate that $3.5 million was contributed to Clinton; perhaps three to four times that was given to all political campaigns.

But it was the crisis engendered by the military's anti-gay policies and the many challenges by lesbians and gays in the service that set the stage for Clinton's stance on homosexuals' rights. And it was Paul Tsongas who, in a manner of speaking, brought Clinton out on the issue. Campaigning in frigid Iowa before the caucuses there, Tsongas was asked by a reporter at an airport stop whether the candidate favored letting gays into the military. "Everybody's in, nobody's out," Tsongas replied, in a phrase he would often use. Soon, all the other Democratic candidates would second Tsongas's motion. Clinton, who was plummeting in New Hampshire after the Gennifer Flowers story broke, could not afford to give Tsongas an advantage with the liberal Democrats who work hard and vote often in the early primaries, and he added his support for lifting the ban.

Clinton's national strategy, however, had targeted the "Reagan Democrats," those middle- and lower-middle-class white suburbanites, including many Catholics and churchgoing Protestants, who would respond to progressive class issues (such as tax "fairness") but not liberal social issues (such as affirmative action for minorities and civil rights for gays). Accordingly, Clinton remained mute on the military ban and other gay issues (except AIDS, which has its built-in escape clause) until the end of May, just before the California primary, when he gave an extraordinary speech to an absolutely delirious gay audience at the Palace Theater in Los Angeles.

Flanked by Mixner and an array of gay notables, Clinton reiterated his promise to reverse the military's ban, and in the course of citing a Defense Department study that supported such a move, all but outed the high-profile Pentagon "spokesperson who himself was said to be gay" who released it to the press. He promised to put gays in government jobs, to start a "Manhattan Project" crash program to combat AIDS, to appoint an AIDS czar, and to "make a major speech on AIDS to a non-traditional group of Americans," presumably gays, who had never been so addressed by Reagan or Bush. Clinton choked with emotion as he praised the gay and lesbian community for its courageous and committed work against AIDS.

A videotape was shot, of course, and it quickly made the rounds of gay activists as well as Republican "opposition researchers," who never quite got up the gumption to use it against Clinton in the campaign. Clinton asked Bob Hattoy, another gay friend and early campaign adviser, who has AIDS, to speak at the Democratic National Convention—but about AIDS, not gay rights. Clinton argued with Hattoy, Mixner and other gays on his staff up until the last minute before his acceptance speech about whether to include *the word* "gay" in his text. Reports filtered onto the convention floor: it's in, it's out, it's back in. At length, Clinton used the g-word, in the predictable litany of diverse groups he would include in his Administration. But that was practically the last time he initiated a discussion of gay issues in his campaign. In fact, when he spoke in Oregon in October he pointedly failed even to mention the battle then in progress around a virulently anti-gay ballot referendum.

As the political campaign progressed, it dawned on many gay and lesbian activists that from now on every Democratic candidate for President would be pro-gay. The reason that Mike Dukakis was so bad on gay issues in 1988 and Bill Clinton was good enough in 1992 had less to do with their characters or their ideologies than with their personal histories. For Dukakis, as for most straights and gays of the 1950s generation, the sexual closet was a reassuring structure of social architecture. He had close gay associates—indeed, one of the top men in his 1988 campaign was out in certain corners of the gay community—but none of them were open about their identity.

Openness has enormous power in the politics of personal relationships. Straight friends and relatives of gays have to confront truths about themselves and their social environment that they have long denied. Clinton, boomer child of the sixties, when Stonewall broke open the closet, had mixed easily with gays for years. More than that, he must deal all the time with openly gay journalists, politicians, lobbyists and advisers. For the better part of a year Clinton travelled day and night with *Newsweek* reporter Mark Miller, who was preparing the Clinton story for the magazine's special issue that would detail "how the candidate won." Miller, who is gay, did not hide his interest in gay issues, and Clinton apparently responded earnestly.

It was Miller who also pressed Clinton, at his first televised press conference in March, to admit that he would consider segregation of gays in the military. Miller seemed to be barely restraining his anger at Clinton's apparent betrayal of his own promise to end discrimination in the service, and it could be that if Miller had not been there the issue would have been blurred or buried. Even the presence of gay people in an office, a classroom, a legislative hall or a city room changes the political dynamics. Within hours after the press conference, Mixner and Hattoy were denouncing their friend the President with exceptional vehemence. Meetings were hastily called at the White House and in New York, where millionaire contributors explicitly threatened Democratic National Chairman David Wilhelm with a financial boycott of the party if Clinton didn't recant on segregation.

It is doubtful that Clinton knew from the start how immensely complex lifting the ban would become. But he should have. He reiterated his campaign pledge on the morning after his election, in response to a reporter's question. A brief but intense firestorm followed, and then seemed to subside. But according to a White House source, machinations continued below sea level. The Joint Chiefs and top Pentagon brass were unhappy at the prospect of admitting homosexuals into the service, but they were equally concerned about losing power in what they feared would be an instinctively anti-military Administration. They worried about budget cuts, cancellation of weapons systems and the organization of congressional forces hostile to the Pentagon.

The generals had apparently tried to stop Clinton before the election by pitching the gays in the military issue to Bush, but for some reason—perhaps because of the backlash to the gay-bashing that went on at the GOP convention in August—the Bushies passed. But soon after Les Aspin was chosen as Secretary of Defense, the brass began working with him to undermine the expected executive order on gays, and in the process stake out a perimeter around their own turf.

Clinton did not "stack" the ban-lifting order with those on the abortion counselling "gag rule," on fetal-tissue research and on experimentation with the abortifacient RU-486, all of which he issued two days after taking the oath of office. If he had, he might have outflanked the opposition—a tactic endorsed by some gay activists, *The New York Times* and others who wanted to see the ban lifted. Instead, he did the worst thing, which was to talk about lifting the ban, but not do it.

Over the weekend after the inauguration, a kind of quiet military coup was leveraged, with the gay ban as the lever. Morton Halperin, then an adviser to Aspin (he has since been nominated assistant secretary of defense for democracy and human rights), prepared a memo, which he also leaked to the press, predicting dire consequences in Congress if the ban was lifted. He recommended postponing the order until summer. The week's delay also allowed the Christian right around the country to mount an impressive anti-gay letter-writing campaign to representatives in Washington. Right-wing talk-show jocks were out in force on the issue. But the consequences were in a sense predetermined by the Pentagon, which, with Aspin's compliance, had been lobbying key legislators to form the pro-military bloc the Joint Chiefs wanted. Halperin had served on Richard Nixon's National Security Council and had suddenly turned civil libertarian after he found out Henry Kissinger tapped his telephone. In recent years he headed the Washington office of the ACLU, where he worked on cases of gay people harassed and cashiered by the military. He was close to and completely trusted by lesbian and gay activists. During "the week" when the expected executive order seemed to slip away, Halperin's role was crucial, but estimations of his effect on events differ according to one's sense of political possibility. A gay lawyer who is still fighting to lift the ban is convinced of Halperin's loyalty to the cause, and believes he had to orchestrate a delay to have a chance of winning the issue. But there is the smell of sell-out in the air. A gay Democratic source says, ruefully, "Mort's no friend of ours." By doing the bidding of the Joint

Chiefs and congressional conservatives, Halperin undercut the potential strength of a Clinton *coup de foudre,* and made it all the more likely the hearings and negotiations would produce a defeat for gay rights in the guise of a "compromise" that would reinforce the military closet and keep things pretty much as they were. (Halperin declined to talk about the issue.)

For most gay people, the military ban was not the issue of choice. As one former "gayocrat" who left gay politics in Washington rather than devote all his time to fighting the ban said, "Why should I spend my life getting queers the right to kill or be killed? The best thing about being gay was that you *didn't* have to go in the army."

But it was the issue of opportunity. For as far as gays have come, they cannot yet completely determine the order of their own social agenda. There is also a serious disjunction between the gayocracy and the millions of lesbians and gays around the country who have quite different needs and demands from the fundraisers and check-writers who are the active participants in gay politics. There is no real nation-wide gay organization of activists similar to the great movements for civil rights, women's liberation and radical social change that blossomed in the 1960s and soon after. The National Gay and Lesbian Task Force claims a membership of 26,000, and it performs many useful services, such as its national campaign to counter the homophobic right and to win validation for lesbian and gay families. But for the most part membership means annual giving. ACT UP around the country has been able to muster several thousand shock troops for demonstrations and civil disobedience, but there is no national coordination and, besides, it is not specifically a gay organization. Queer Nation, which was formed on the ACT UP model to deal militantly with gay issues, is small and decentralized, and riven with dissension where it still exists. There are hundreds of new organizations formed by gays in professions, and lesbian and gay groups now thrive on many college campuses. All of them contribute to the moment, but not one has assumed a leading role.

AIDS has had a painfully paradoxical effect on the movement. At the same time that it ravaged the gay male community in institutional as well as personal terms, it has unquestionably contributed to the visibility of gay people against the social background. AIDS contains many tragedies, but first and still foremost it is a catastrophe for gay men in America. What is happening is the destruction of an affectional community very much like an ethnic or national community. Half the gay men in San Francisco are said to be infected with

HIV, and the numbers in New York and other big cities are stagger-
ing; there is nothing yet to keep most of them from dying. Clinton
has dithered in launching his "Manhattan Project" for AIDS. Ever
fearful of the right, he refused to reverse the Reagan/Bush order
excluding people with HIV from immigrating. As of mid-April he
had still not appointed an AIDS czar, even though he had indicated
it would be a first order of business. He has included full funding for
the Ryan White Act programs to help care for people with AIDS and
for education to prevent its spread, but the sum of appropriations for
that and AIDS research is nowhere near what the crisis demands.

But again the contradictions intrude. Clinton is failing to live up
to his promises, but at least he talked about the issues. Now homosexuality is—by presidential directive—a positive qualification for an
Administration job. Gays in Washington are finding Administration
jobs for themselves and other gays, but they are also trying to convince closeted gays (in the super-closeted capital) that coming out
would help, not hurt, the chances of getting hired.

Donna Shalala, Secretary of Health and Human Services, had
been "outed," without supporting evidence, by students at the University of Wisconsin, where she was chancellor. According to an
Administration official, she was asked many times during the transition, by co-chair Warren Christopher and others, whether the rumors
were true. Moreover, the Clintonites repeatedly tried to assure her
that it was okay to be gay, and they would support her coming out. "It
began to sound like a *Seinfeld* shtick," one Washington insider told
me. When the press repeated the rumor, Shalala made a statement:
"Have I lived an alternative lifestyle? The answer is no." That ended
it for the White House, but lesbians and gays were upset. "Lifestyle"
is *their* word, not ours. Homosexuality is an orientation or an identity,
never a lifestyle.

What has changed the climate in America is the long experience of
gay struggle, the necessary means having been, first, coming out, and
second, making a scene. Sometimes it is personal witness, other
times political action, and overall it is the creation of a cultural community based on sexual identity. The ascension of gay people to positions of authority in key sectors of society has made a huge difference
in the weather. The prerequisite for their influence is being out—
which is why the destruction of the closet is the most vital issue of gay
life, beyond any act of censorship or exclusion. It is also the reason
that "outing" has become such a charged political question.

Every opinion survey shows that people who say they have a gay friend or family member are twice or three times as likely to support gay rights than are those who say they know no gay people. What the surveys don't report is the opinion of people who know out gays. None of the political victories, the cultural successes achieved by gays in the past short period of time, would have been possible if closets were shut.

The military establishment, schools, churches all understand the importance of the closet in maintaining institutional order. That is why the services never cared a damn about gays who did not proclaim their identity, by word or deed. It is why school superintendents have lived for centuries with lesbian and gay teachers, but panic when anyone comes out. It is why churches countenance lesbian nuns and gay priests and ministers as long as they lie about themselves.

Andrew Sullivan, the gay neoconservative editor of *The New Republic*, wrote recently in *The New York Times* that dropping the military ban on gays would be a deeply conservative act, in that gays who join up would be, by definition, patriotic and traditionalist. That may be true in the particular, but in general and historical terms, nothing could be more radical than upsetting the sexual apple cart. As Randy Shilts asserts in his study of gays in the service, *Conduct Unbecoming*, "The presence of gay men [in the military] . . . calls into question everything that manhood is supposed to mean." And homophobia — like its blood relations, racism, misogyny and anti-Semitism — is an ideology that rationalizes the oppressive uses of male power. When cruel and self-hating homophobes such as J. Edgar Hoover and Roy Cohn are outed, even posthumously, the power system is shaken.

The counterpower of coming out has given the gay movement primary this year in the unfinished civil rights revolution. It's more than appropriate that the NAACP has decided to participate in the April 25 march on Washington, along with every major civil liberties and civil rights organization in the country. Labor unions, which have not been particularly supportive of the gay movement, are also sending busloads of marchers. Modern American feminism has a natural affinity with gay liberation: the latter was, in a sense, born of the former. The two have not always been on the best of terms, but increasingly, adherents of both movements understand how closely allied are their ideologies, how similar their enemies and how important their coalition. The kind of broad "rainbow" coalition now developing was unthinkable only a few years ago.

But the gay nineties is not only about civil rights, tolerance and legitimacy. What started tumbling out of the closets at the time of Stonewall is profoundly altering the way we all live, form families, think about and act towards one another, manage our health and well-being and understand the very meaning of identity. All the cross-currents of present-day liberation struggles are subsumed in the gay struggle. The gay moment is in some ways similar to the moment that other communities have experienced in the nation's past, but it is also something more, because sexual identity is in crisis throughout the population, and gay people—at once the most conspicuous subjects and objects of the crisis—have been forced to invent a complete cosmology to grasp it. No one says the changes will come easily. But it's just possible that a small and despised sexual minority will change America forever.

April 15, 1993, THE NATION

open letter to the christian coalition

ELIZABETH BIRCH
1995

dear Members of the Christian Coalition: An Open Letter was not my first choice as a way of reaching you. I would have preferred speaking to all of you directly, and in a setting where you would be most comfortable. That was my motivation, some weeks ago, when I asked your executive director, Ralph Reed, for the opportunity to address the Christian Coalition's "Road to Victory" Conference. It is still my motivation today. And it is supported by a single, strong belief that the time has come for us to speak to each other rather than past each other. It took Mr. Reed very little time to reject my request. Perhaps he misunderstood my motivation. But I can assure you that what has driven my request is this: I believe in the power of the word and the value of honest communication. During my years of work as a litigator at a major corporation, I was often amazed at what simple, fresh and truthful conversation could accomplish. And what is true in the corporate setting is also true, I'm convinced, in our communities. If we could learn to speak and listen to each other with integrity, the consequences might shock us. Although your podium was not available to me, I am grateful for those who have come today and will give me "the benefit of the doubt" and be willing to consider what I have to say. I will be pleased if you are able to hear me without prejudging either the message or the messenger. And I will be hopeful, most of all, if you respond by joining me in finding new ways to speak with honesty not only about one another, but also to one another. If I am confident in anything at all, it is this: our communities have more in common than we care to imagine. This is not to deny the many differences. But out of our sheer humanity comes some common ground. Although the stereotype would have us believe otherwise, there are many conservative Americans within the nation's gay and lesbian communities. What's more, there are hundreds of thousands of Christians among us—Christians of all traditions, including those represented in the Christian Coalition. And, like it or not, we are part of your family. And you are part of our community. We are neighbors and colleagues, business associates and friends. More intimately still, you are fathers of sons who are gay and mothers of daughters who are lesbians. I know many of your children very, very well. I work with them. I worry with them. And I rejoice that they are part of our community. Part of what I want you to know is that many of your children who are gay and lesbian are gifted and strong. Some are famous; most of them are not. But many are heroic in the way they have conquered barriers to their own self-respect and the courage with which they've set out to serve a higher good. All were created by God. And you have every right to be proud of each of them. I begin by noting the worthiness of the gays and lesbians in your family and our community for a reason: it's hard to communicate with people we do not respect. And the character of prejudice, of stereotype, of demagoguery, is to tear down the respect others might otherwise enjoy in public, even the respect they would hold for themselves in private. By taking away respectability, rhetorically as well as legally, we justify the belief that they are not quite human, not quite worthy, not quite deserving of our time, or our attention, or our concern. And that is, sadly, what many of your children and colleagues and neighbors who are gay and lesbian have feared is the intent of the Christian Coalition. If it were true, of course, it would be not only regrettable, but terribly hypocritical; it would not be worthy of the true ideals and values based in love at the core of what we call "Christian." The reason I have launched this conversation is to ask that you join me in a common demonstration that this is not true. I make my appeal as an individual, as Elizabeth Birch, and also as the executive director of the Human Rights Campaign Fund, America's largest policy organization for gay men and lesbian women. This is such a basic appeal—to human communication and common decency—that I do not even know how to distinguish between what is personal and what is professional. But my appeal is sincere. I am convinced that if we cannot find ways to respect one another as human beings, and therefore to respect one another's rights, we will do great damage not only to each other, but also to those we say we represent. I recognize that it is not easy for us to speak charitably to each other. I have read fundraising letters in which people like me are assigned labels which summon up the ugliest of dehumanizing stereotypes. Anonymous writers have hidden under the title of "Concerned

Christian" to condemn me with the fires of God and to call on all of you to deny me an equal opportunity to participate in the whole range of American life. I have heard of political agendas calling not merely for the defeat of those I represent, but for our eradication. Such expressions of hatred do not, can not, beget a spirit of trust. Nor do they pass the test of either truthfulness or courage. They bear false witness in boldface type. And I believe that they must embarrass those who, like me, heard of another gospel—even the simple gospel taught me as a child in Sunday School. I would not ask that you, as members of a Christian group, or as supporters of a conservative political cause, set aside either your basic beliefs or your historic commitments. The churches which many of you represent—Baptist, for example, and Pentecostal—were also the churches I attended as a young woman. In those days, I heard sermons about justice and sang songs about forgiveness. My greatest hope is not that you will give up your faith, but that it will work among all of us. Neither of us should forsake our fundamental convictions. But we could hold those convictions with a humility that allows room for the lives of others; neither of us may be the sole possessors of truth on every given issue. And we could express our convictions in words that are, if not affectionate, and if not even kind, then at least decent, civil, humane. We need not demonize each other simply because we disagree. I came to my task in the campaign for human rights with this conviction: if we, in the name of civil rights, slander you, we have failed our own ideals, as surely as any Christian who slanders us in the name of God has failed the ideals of Scripture. Some of those who asked me to serve at HRCF may believe that I am naive, that it is foolish to appeal to "the enemy" for common decency, let alone to ask for trusting conversations. But those who wonder about my ideals may not know my childhood. I am an American, born on American soil, but raised in Canada throughout my formative years. Even from a distance—perhaps especially from a distance—the American ideal and the centuries-old American dream captured my imagination and my spirit. When I saw America, I saw responsible freedom being exercised everywhere from the picket line to the voting booth. When I learned of the values rooted at the heart of the American Spirit, I felt undying hope. That hope is also rooted in the Judeo-Christian tradition of this nation. From my vantage point on the Canadian prairies, the promise of America tugged at my soul. I could fight it, but I could not win, and America quite literally won my heart. More remarkable still, all this happened during my adolescence, when we are most subject to peer pressure, and in the 1960's during the height of Canadian nationalism. It was, in those days, as daring to publicly acknowledge your love for America as it was to come out of the closet as a lesbian. But I could not hide my affection for my homeland, even though I saw its obvious failings and short-comings. I believed then, and I believe no less staunchly today, that no other nation in the world offers all its citizens such promises of fairness and equality, principles that are equally reflected in the Christian tradition and the American Constitution. What surprised me when I first became active in America's gay and lesbian communities was that, in this idealism about America, I was not alone. Gay men were beaten with baseball bats, and they went off to find justice, confident that the American ideal would protect them. Lesbians were fired from their jobs, and they said to one another, "We'll be protected by the law." So keen was confidence in the American hope that it took the gay and lesbian communities decades to conclude, regretfully, that civil rights are as likely to be withheld as granted, despite the Constitution; and that true believers are as likely to engage in cruel discrimination as in compassion, even in the name of Christ. Many of us in this community have a long history with the church. Gay men I have loved deeply and lesbians I've known well have talked long into the night about their love for God and for God's church. For some of them, the church had provided the one message of hope they knew as children. The promise of good news was seized gladly by adolescents who did not understand why they were different, or what that difference would mean.

For some, the deepest agony of life is not that they risk physical abuse or that they will never gain their civil rights, but that they have felt the judgment of an institution on which they staked their lives: the church. What they long for most is what they once believed was theirs as a birthright: the knowledge that they are God's children, and that they can come home. And it is not only those of us who are gay or lesbian who have suffered on the doorstep of some congregations. Parents, fearing what others at church might whisper, choose to deny the reality that their son is gay or their daughter is a lesbian. Brothers and sisters suffer an unhealthy, and unwarranted, and un-Christian shame. They bear a burden that cripples their faith, based on a fear that cripples us all. This means, I think, that we are still a long way from realizing the ideal of America as a land of hope and promise, from achieving the goal of religion as a healing force that unites us, from discovering that human beings are, simply by virtue of being human beings, deserving of respect and common decency. And so, I have come today—in person, bearing this letter, and in writing to those who will only receive it—to make three simple, sincere appeals to those of you who are members of the Christian Coalition. The first appeal is this: please make integrity a watchword for the campaigns you launch. We all struggle to be people of integrity, especially when we campaign for funds. But the fact that we are tempted by money is no excuse. We need to commit ourselves to a higher moral ground. I do not know when the first direct-mail letter was issued in your name that defamed gay men and abused gay women, that described us as less than human and certainly unworthy of trust. Neither do I know when people discovered that the richest financial return came from letters that depicted gays and lesbians with intentionally dishonest images. But I do know—and I must believe that you know too—that this is dishonest, this is wrong. I can hardly imagine that a money machine is being operated in your name, spinning out exaggerations as if they were truths, and that you do not see it. But perhaps you do not. In which case, I ask that you hear my second appeal: I ask that, as individuals, you talk to those of us who are gay or lesbian, rather than succumb to the temptation to either avoid us at all cost, as if we are not a part of your community, or to rant at us, as if we are not worthy of quiet conversation. We are, all of us and those we represent, human beings. As Americans, you will have your political candidates; we will have ours. But we could, both of us, ask that our candidates speak the truth to establish their right to leadership, rather than abuse the truth in the interest of one evening's headline. We may work for different outcomes in the elections, but we can engage in an ethic of basic respect and decency. Finally, I appeal to you as people who passionately uphold the value of the family. You have brothers and sons who have not heard a word of family affection since the day they summoned the courage to tell the simple truth. You have sisters and daughters who have given up believing that you mean it when you say, "The family is the basic unit of society," or even, "God loves you, and so do I." Above all the other hopes with which I've come to you hovers this one: that some member of the Christian Coalition will call some member of the Human Rights Campaign Fund and say, "It's been a long time, son"—or, "I'm missing you, my daughter"—and before the conversation ends, someone will hear the heartfelt words, "Come home. Let's talk to each other." In that hope, I appeal to each of you.

romer, governor of colorado, et al. v. evans, et al.

JUSTICE ANTHONY KENNEDY
May 20, 1996

after various Colorado municipalities passed ordinances banning discrimination based on sexual orientation in housing, employment, education, public accommodations, health and welfare services, and other transactions and activities, Colorado voters adopted by statewide referendum -Amendment 2- to the State Constitution, which precludes all legislative, executive, or judicial action at any level of state or local government designed to protect the status of persons based on their "homosexual, lesbian or bisexual orientation, conduct, practices or relationships." Respondents, who include aggrieved homosexuals and municipalities, commenced this litigation in state court against petitioner state parties to declare Amendment 2 invalid and enjoin its enforcement. The trial court's grant of a preliminary injunction was sustained by the Colorado Supreme Court, which held that Amendment 2 was subject to strict scrutiny under the Equal Protection Clause of the Fourteenth Amendment because it infringed the fundamental right of gays and lesbians to participate in the political process. On remand, the trial court found that the Amendment failed to satisfy strict scrutiny. It enjoined Amendment 2's enforcement, and the State Supreme Court affirmed.

Held: Amendment 2 violates the Equal Protection Clause. Pp. 4–14.

(a) The State's principal argument that Amendment 2 puts gays and lesbians in the same position as all other persons by denying them special rights is rejected as implausible. The extent of the change in legal status effected by this law is evident from the authoritative construction of Colorado's Supreme Court-which establishes that the amendment's immediate effect is to repeal all existing statutes, regulations, ordinances, and policies of state and local entities barring discrimination based on sexual orientation, and that its ultimate effect is to prohibit any governmental entity from adopting similar, or more protective, measures in the future absent state constitutional amendment-and from a review of the terms, structure, and operation of the ordinances that would be repealsed and prohibited by Amendment 2. Even if, as the State contends, homosexuals can find protection in laws and policies of general application, Amendment 2 goes well beyond merely depriving them of special rights. It imposes a broad disability upon those persons alone, forbidding them, but no others, to seek specific legal protection from injuries caused by discrimination in a wide range of public and private transactions. Pp. 4–9.

(b) In order to reconcile the Fourteenth Amendment's promise that no person shall be denied equal protection with the practical reality that most legislation classifies for one purpose or another, the Court has stated that it will uphold a law that neither burdens a fundamental right nor targets a suspect class so long as the legislative classification bears a rational relation to some independent and legitimate legislative end. See, e.g., Heller v. Doe, 509 U. S. 312, 319–320. Amendment 2 fails, indeed defies, even this conventional inquiry. First, the amendment is at once too narrow and too broad, identifying persons by a single trait and then denying them the possibility of protection across the board. This disqualification of a class of persons from the right to obtain specific protection from the law is unprecedented and is itself a denial of equal protection in the most literal sense. Second, the sheer breadth of Amendment 2, which makes a general announcement that gays and lesbians shall not have any particular protections from the law, is so far removed from the reasons offered for it, i.e., respect for other citizens' freedom of association, particularly landlords or employers who have personal or religious objections to homosexuality, and the State's interest in conserving resources to fight discrimination against other groups, that the amendment cannot be explained by reference to those reasons; the Amendment raises the inevitable inference that it is born of animosity toward the class that it affects. Amendment 2 cannot be said to be directed to an identifiable legitimate purpose or discrete objective. It is a status-based classification of persons undertaken for its own sake, something the Equal Protection Clause does not permit. Pp. 9–14.

882 P. 2d 1335, affirmed.

Kennedy, J., delivered the opinion of the Court, in which Stevens, O'Connor, Souter, Ginsburg, and Breyer, JJ., joined. Scalia, J., filed a dissenting opinion, in which Rehnquist, C. J., and Thomas, J., joined.

Justice Kennedy delivered the opinion of the Court.

One century ago, the first Justice Harlan admonished this Court that the Constitution -neither knows nor tolerates classes among citizens.- Plessy v. Ferguson, 163 U. S. 537, 559 (1896) (dissenting opinion). Unheeded then, those words now are understood to state a commitment to the law's neutrality where the rights of persons are at stake. The Equal Protection Clause enforces this principle and today requires us to hold invalid a provision of Colorado's Constitution.

I

Amendment 2 repeals these ordinances to the extent they prohibit discrimination on the basis of -homosexual, lesbian or bisexual orientation, conduct, practices or relationships.-

II

The State's principal argument in defense of Amendment 2 is that it puts gays and lesbians in the same position as all other persons. So, the State says, the measure does no more than deny homosexuals special rights. This reading of the amendment's language is implausible. We rely not upon our own interpretation of the amendment but upon the authoritative construction of Colorado's Supreme Court. The state court, deeming it unnecessary to determine the full extent of the amendment's reach, found it invalid even on a modest reading of its implications. The critical discussion of the amendment, set out in Evans I, is as follows:

The immediate objective of Amendment 2 is, at a minimum, to repeal existing statues, regulations, ordinances, and policies of state and local entities that barred discrimination based on sexual orientation.

Metropolitan State College of Denver prohibits college sponsored social clubs from discriminating in membership on the basis of sexual orientation and Colorado State University has an antidiscrimination policy which encompasses sexual orientation.

The 'ultimate effect' of Amendment 2 is to prohibit any governmental entity from adopting similar, or more protective statutes, regulations, ordinances, or policies in the future unless the state constitution is first amended to permit such measures.

Sweeping and comprehensive is the change in legal status effected by this law. So much is evident from the ordinances that the Colorado Supreme Court declared would be void by operation of Amendment 2. Homosexuals, by state decree, are put in a solitary class with respect to transactions and relations in both the private and governmental spheres. The amendment withdraws from homosexuals, but no others, specific legal protection from the injuries caused by discrimination, and it forbids reinstatement of these laws and policies.

The change that Amendment 2 works in the legal status of gays and lesbians in the private sphere is far-reaching, both on its own terms and when considered in light of the structure and operation of modern anti-discrimination laws. That structure is well illustrated by contemporary statutes and ordinances prohibiting discrimination by providers of public accomodations. -At common law, innkeepers, smiths, and others who 'made profession of a public employment,' were prohibited from refusing, without good reason, to serve a customer.- Hurley v. Irish-American Gay, Lesbian and Bisexual Group of Boston, Inc. The duty was a general one and did not specify protection for particular groups. The common law rules, however, proved insufficient in many instances, and it was settled early that the Fourteenth Amendment did not give Congress a general power to prohibit discrimination in public accomodations, Civil Rights Cases. In consequence, most States have chosen to counter discrimination by enacting detailed statutory schemes.

Colorado's state and municipal laws typify this emerging tradition of statutory protection and follow a consistent pattern. The laws first enumerate the persons or entities subject to a duty not to discriminate. The list goes well beyond the entities covered by the common law. The Boulder ordinance, for example, has a comprehensive definition of entities deemed places of -public accomodation.- They include -any place of business engaged in any sales to the general public and any place that offers services, facilities, privileges, or advantages to the general public or that receives financial support through solicitation of the general public or through governmental subsidy of any kind.- The Denver ordinance is of similar breadth, applying, for example, to hotels, restaurants, hospitals, dental clinics, theaters, banks, common carriers, travel and insurance agencies, and -shops and stores dealing with goods or services of any kind,-

These statutes and ordinances also depart from the common law by enumerating the groups or persons within their ambit of protection.

Enumeration is the essential device used to make the duty not to discriminate concrete and to provide guidance for those who must comply. In following this approach, Colorado's state and local governments have not limited anti-discrimination laws to groups that have so far been given the protection of heightened equal protection scrutiny under our cases. Rather, they set forth an extensive catalogue of traits which cannot be the basis for discrimination, including age, military status, marital status, pregnancy, parenthood, custody of a minor child, political affiliation, physical or mental disability of an individual or of his or her associates—and, in recent times, sexual orientation.

Amendment 2 bars homosexuals from securing protection against the injuries that these public-accomodations laws address. That in itself is a severe consequence, but there is more. Amendment 2, in addition, nullifies specific legal protections for this targeted class in all transactions in housing, sale or real estate, insurance, health and welfare services, private education, and employment.

Not confined to the private sphere, Amendment 2 also operates to repeal and forbid all laws or policies providing specific protection for gays or lesbians from discrimination by every level of Colorado government. The State Supreme Court cited two examples of protections in the governmental sphere that are now rescinded and may not be reintroduced. The first is Colorado Executive Order, which forbids employment discrimination against -'all state employees, classified and exempt' on the basis of sexual orientation.- Also repealed, and now forbidden, are -various provisions prohibiting discrimination based on sexual orientation at state colleges.- The repeal of these measures and the prohibition against their future reenactment demonstrates that Amendment 2 has the same force and effect in Colorado's governmental sector as it does elsewhere and that it applies to policies as well as ordinary legislation.

Amendment 2's reach may not be limited to specific laws passed for the benefit of gays and lesbians. It is a fair, if not necessary, inference from the broad language of the amendment that it deprives gays and lesbians even of the protection of general laws and policies that prohibit arbitrary discrimination in governmental and private settings. At some point in the systematic administration of these laws, an official must determine whether homosexuality is an arbitrary and thus forbidden basis for decision. Yet a decision to that effect would itself amount to a policy prohibiting discrimination on the basis of homosexuality, and so would appear to be no more valid under

Amendment 2 than the specific prohibitions against discrimination the state court held invalid.

If this consequence follows from Amendment 2, as its broad language suggests, it would compound the constitutional difficulties the law creates. The state court did not decide whether the amendment has this effect, however, and neither need we. In the course of rejecting the argument that Amendment 2 is intended to conserve resources to fight discrimination against suspect classes, the Colorado Supreme Court made the limited observation that the amendment is not intended to affect many anti-discrimination laws protecting non-suspect classes. In our view that does not resolve the issue. In any event, even if, as we doubt, homosexuals could find some safe harbor in laws of general application, we cannot accept the view that Amendment 2's prohibition on specific legal protections does no more than deprive homosexuals of special rights. To the contrary, the amendment imposes a special disability upon those persons alone. Homosexuals are forbidden the safeguards that others enjoy or may seek without constraint. They can obtain specific protection against discrimination only by enlisting the citizenry of Colorado to amend the state constitution or perhaps, on the State's view, by trying to pass helpful laws of general applicability. This is so no matter how local or discrete the harm, no matter how public and widespread the injury. We find nothing special in the protections Amendment 2 withholds. These are protections taken for granted by most people either because they already have them or do not need them; these are protections against exclusion from an almost limitless number of transactions and endeavors that constitute ordinary civic life in a free society.

III

The Fourteenth Amendment's promise that no person shall be denied the equal protection of the laws must co-exist with the practical necessity that most legislation classifies for one purpose or another, with resulting disadvantage to various groups or persons. We have attempted to reconcile the principle with the reality by stating that, if a law neither burdens a fundamental right nor targets a suspect class, we will uphold the legislative classification so long as it bears a rational relation to some legitimate end.

Amendment 2 fails, indeed defies, even this conventional inquiry. First, the amendment has the peculiar property of imposing a broad and undifferentiated disability on a single named group, an exceptional and, as we shall explain, invalid form of legislation. Second, its sheer breadth is so discontinuous with the reasons offered for it that the amendment seems inexplicable by anything but animus toward the class that it affects; it lacks a rational relationship to legitimate state interests.

Taking the first point, even in the ordinary equal protection case calling for the most deferential of standards, we insist on knowing the relation between the classification adopted and the object to be attained. The search for the link between classification and objective gives substance to the Equal Protection Clause; it provides guidance and discipline for the legislature, which is entitled to know what sorts of laws it can pass; and it marks the limits of our own authority. In the ordinary case, a law will be sustained if it can be said to advance a legitimate government interest, even if the law seems unwise or works to the disadvantage of a particular group, or if the rationale for it seems tenuous. The laws challenged in the cases just cited were narrow enough in scope and grounded in a sufficient factual context for us to ascertain that there existed some relation between the classification and the purpose it served. By requiring that the classification bear a rational relationship to an independent and legitimate legislative end, we ensure that classifications are not drawn for the purpose of disadvantaging the group burdened by the law.

Amendment 2 confounds this normal process of judicial review. It is at once too narrow and too broad. It identifies persons by a single trait and then denies them protection across the board. The resulting disqualification of a class of persons from the right to seek specific protection from the law is unprecedented in our jurisprudence. The absence of precedent for Amendment 2 is itself instructive; - [d]iscriminations of an unusual character especially suggest careful consideration to determine whether they are obnoxious to the constitutional provision.- Louisville Gas & Elec. Co. v. Coleman.

It is not within our constitutional tradition to enact laws of this sort. Central both to the idea of the rule of law and to our own Constitution's guarantee of equal protection is the principle that government and each of its parts remain open on impartial terms to all who seek its assistance. -'Equal protection of the laws is not achieved through indiscriminate imposition of inequalities.'- Sweatt v. Painter (quoting Shelley v. Kraemer). Respect for this principle explains why laws singling out a certain class of citizens for disfavored legal status or general hardships are rare. A law declaring that in general it shall be more difficult for one group of citizens than for all others to seek aid from the government is itself a denial of equal protection of the laws in the most literal sense. -The guaranty of 'equal protection of the laws is a pledge of the protection of equal laws.'- Skinner v. Oklahoma ex rel. Williamson (quoting Yick Wo v. Hopkins).

Davis v. Beason, not cited by the parties but relied upon by the dissent, is not evidence that Amendment 2 is within our constitutional tradition, and any reliance upon it as authority for sustaining the amendment is misplaced. In Davis, the Court approved an Idaho territorial statute denying Mormons, polygamists, and advocates of polygamy the right to vote and to hold office because, as the Court construed the statute, it -simply excludes from the privilege of voting, or of holding any office of honor, trust or profit, those who have been convicted of certain offences, and those who advocate a practical resistance to the laws of the Territory and justify and approve the commission of crimes forbidden by it.- Id. To the extent Davis held that persons advocating a certain practice may be denied the right to vote, it is no longer good law. To the extent it held that the groups designated in the statute may be deprived of the right to vote because of their status, its ruling could not stand without surviving strict scrutiny, a most doubtful outcome. To the extent Davis held that a convicted felon may be denied the right to vote, its holding is not implicated by our decision and is unexceptionable.

A second and related point is that laws of the kind now before us raise the inevitable inference that the disadvantage imposed is born of animosity toward the class of persons affected. -[I]f the constitutional conception of 'equal protection of the laws' means anything, it must at the very least mean that a bare . . . desire to harm a politically unpopular group cannot constitute a legitimate governmental interest.- Department of Agriculture v. Moreno. Even laws enacted for broad and ambitious purposes often can be explained by reference to legitimate public policies which justify the incidental disadvantages they impose on certain persons. Amendment 2, however, in making a general announcement that gays and lesbians shall not have any particular protections from the law, inflicts on them immediate, continuing, and real injuries that outrun and belie any legitimate justifications that may be claimed for it. We conclude that, in addition to the far-reaching deficiencies of Amendment 2 that we have noted, the principles it offends, in another sense, are conventional and venerable; a law must bear a rational relationship to a legitimate governmental purpose, and Amendment 2 does not.

The primary rationale the State offers for Amendment 2 is respect for other citizens' freedom of association, and in particular the liberties of landlords or employers who have personal or religious objections to homosexuality. Colorado also cites its interest in conserving resources to fight discrimination against other groups. The breadth of the Amendment is so far removed from these particular justifications that we find it impossible to credit them. We cannot say that Amendment 2 is directed to any identifiable legitimate purpose or discrete objective. It is a status-based enactment divorced from any factual context from which we could discern a relationship to legitimate state interests; it is a classification of persons undertaken for its own sake, something the Equal Protection Clause does not permit. - [C]lass legislation . . . [is] obnoxious to the prohibitions of the Fourteenth Amendment. . . . - Civil Rights Cases.

We must conclude that Amendment 2 classifies homosexuals not to further a proper legislative end but to make them unequal to everyone else. This Colorado cannot do. A State cannot so deem a class of persons a stranger to its laws. Amendment 2 violates the Equal Protection Clause, and the judgment of the Supreme Court of Colorado is affirmed.

It is so ordered.

the liberation of pleasure

MICHAEL BRONSKI
1998

to the dominant culture, organized around the containment of pleasure, homosexuality has come to represent unrestrained pleasure. While other minority cultures are experienced as threatening by the dominant culture—in part because of the way they manifest pleasure—homosexuality has come to symbolize pleasure itself. And it is the dominant culture's conflicted relationship to pleasure that has created a paradoxical, even contradictory, response to a more visible gay culture and to the concurrent movement for gay rights.

In the three decades since the Stonewall Riots, the dominant culture has continued to enjoy and learn from gay culture. Yet as gay culture has become more accepted by the dominant culture, the fight for gay civil rights has engendered a different response. Although some basic civil rights and antidiscrimination protections have been secured for gay people, there has been an enormous backlash against the drive for gay rights. This backlash, while an inextricable part of the culture of resentment, is directly related to the increased acceptance and visibility of gay and lesbian culture. Rather than paving the way for an acceptance of gay rights, a wider acceptance of gay culture has, ironically, reinforced in the dominant culture a determined antipathy to the idea of full citizenship for gay people.

This is, in part, a fearful reaction to the direct challenge posed to the social order by a highly organized political campaign. But this simple backlash reaction is only a partial explanation. The strength of the support this backlash has elicited is indicative of its emotional power for heterosexuals. While individual antigay political campaigns waged by the right may be mounted or funded by specific political groups, they have the tacit approval of the majority of Americans. The swift passage of the Defense of Marriage Act in 1996 by an astounding majority of legislators, and its enormous popular approval rating, show the depth and fervor of Americans' approval for legally limiting the rights of gay people.

The gay rights movement is a threat to the social and political structures that maintain heterosexuality as a dominant social institution. Yet even when civil rights or antidiscrimination laws are passed (usually by slim margins), they do not necessarily change, or even challenge, deep-seated prejudices and fears. Ultimately, the threat posed by gay rights activism is—despite the enormous efforts of conservatives that go into countering it—a fragile one.

The threat posed by gay culture and art is, on the other hand, far more complex and potent. Gay culture engenders ambivalent emotions in heterosexuals about pleasure, sexuality, and personal autonomy. Caught between the longing for more freedom and the fear of breaking from the comforting, if repressive, restraints of civilization, heterosexuals are often profoundly troubled by their disparate reactions to gay culture and need to find a way to mitigate them. Because an outright rejection of gay culture would deprive heterosexuals of pleasures they want, they have to find another solution.

Refusing to grant homosexuals full citizenship, basic civil liberties, or minimal respect for their personal and sexual integrity is a primary way for heterosexuals to feel more comfortable in their enjoyment of gay culture. Individual heterosexuals don't have to invent this dynamic personally; it is offered to them—already formulated in explicitly political language—by conservative politicians and political groups. Right-wing campaigns that claim gay rights are special rights, or that seek to prohibit the "promotion" of homosexuality in schools or public life, are engineered not only to regulate public displays of homosexuality but to provide constituents (as well as potential converts) with a simple resolution of their own ambivalence toward gay culture.

So deep is this ambivalence that even mainstream and liberal political and social groups employ variations of it. The desire to avoid or down-play gay concerns and sexuality is at the root of much liberal policy. The Defense Department's "don't ask, don't tell" military policy, which acknowledged the existence of gay people in the armed services and then instituted an official method of closeting them is a clear example of this thinking. This kinder, gentler version of the closet underlies a wide range of liberal political positions: the lack of sustained support for gay teachers and gay curricula in middle and high schools, the media's outrage over "outing" and their use of "privacy" to reinforce the closet, the prioritization of other minority groups' rights as "more important" than gay rights, the repackaging of homosexuals as socially productive consumers, and the constant promotion in the media of a "good image" of gay people—that is, not visibly gay, political, angry, or openly sexual. Many of these variations of the closet are subsumed under the larger social tenets of decent or tasteful behavior that, while ostensibly calling for "good manners" or "civility," actually implement the invisibilization of homosexuality.

The fight to gain equal rights for homosexuals is a vital one that will not only make U.S. democracy more just, but will help fulfill the idealistic dream of America as a land of freedom for everyone. But this project cannot happen in a vacuum. Just as the repeal of Jim Crow laws and the enactment of civil rights legislation did not eradicate racism, the repeal of antigay laws and the passing of equal protection and nondiscrimination legislation for homosexuals will not bring about freedom for gay people. Changing or enacting a law will not change heterosexuals' hearts and minds or speak to their deepest fears.

Traditional western political theory views culture and politics as separate entities, having little to do with one another. The reality is that they are intimately connected, and in the struggle for gay freedom they are inseparable. Complete freedom for gay people will only happen when the repression of sexuality and pleasure, now perceived to be the bulwark of civilization, is replaced by more humane visions of freedom and sexuality, pleasure and responsibility.

This process has been happening—slowly and painstakingly—for centuries. It is evident in the struggles of women to find autonomy and freedom, and in the rebellions by women and men against stifling gender roles. It is evident in the emergence of a new understanding of the importance of sexuality and the self that has emerged in the last one hundred years. It is evident in changing attitudes about children and sexuality and in the nascent changes occurring in the restructuring of traditional arrangements of, and sometimes the very idea of, the family.

Paradoxically, the freedom of gay people will only come when heterosexuals reject "civilization" to seek and realize more freedom in their own lives. Until now many of the profound changes in the defining paradigms of society have come, largely, through the influence of gay culture. This is what has made it a beacon of freedom and a decisive threat.

It will never be possible for gay people to assimilate, because civilization—as it is now defined and structured—does not, cannot, admit the value and worth of homosexuality. This negates the argument that gay people will achieve full rights as citizens when they begin to act like heterosexuals. The reality is that only when those in the dominant culture realize that *they* are better off acting like gay people will the world change and be a better, safer, and more pleasurable place for everyone.

"We are your worst fear. We are your best fantasy" is as valid today as it was in 1971. But it is not a solution. The truth is that fears and fantasies are terrible—even destructive—means of organizing civilization. In the end, the freedom of gay people will signal the beginning of freedom for heterosexuals as well. Only after freedom and sexuality are valued and prioritized by the dominant culture will we all be able to live lives that are not only fully human, but also filled with pleasure.

j'accuse!

GORE VIDAL

1998

a political decision was made some 20 years ago by a rightwing
money-raiser and political operator, Richard Viguerie, that henceforth the far right would not only raise vast sums of money, which
they had been doing from tax-free "church" donations and foundations, but they must now use that money effectively to defeat any
politician who might not sufficiently worship flag and fetus, in whose
sign they mean to conquer.

Despite millions of dollars raised and spent, these subversives
failed to capture the House of Representatives until 1994, when,
thanks to President Clinton's political ineptitude, they were able to
shift enough of the flat rocks of the republic to provide the Republican Party with a truly weird, squirming majority of nonrepresentative
(let us hope) representatives. Meanwhile, according to the Viguerie
blueprint of 1979, they are careful to avoid actual politics (there is, as
yet, no foreseeable majority to repeal the 13th Amendment) in favor
of what they call "hot buttons," which means sex and drugs or both.
Just press the hot button, and you can destroy your opponent by
revealing his sex life, real or imagined—it makes no difference if you
have the hard-soft cash to buy time for a TV ad or to finance something like Gary Bauer's Family Research Council, where gays are
compassionately demonized for having made a "a bad choice" in the
cafeteria of sexual delights when, with a bit of therapy or prayer, they
could change and become as wretched as those sad straights, half of
whom are doomed to undergo divorce, battles over child custody,
and charges of overpopulating the planet (if only from me) while
glumly submitting, if in office—if oval-shaped—to the eager, if
incompetent (the navy blue dress!), blowjobs from crazed fans.

This year's hot button, impeachment, is now too hot for even Newt G. to press, at least preelection. That leaves the children of mud only the fag villain, a permanent fixture in the America psyche, where every eve is Halloween.

The tragedy in Wyoming has now cast a bright light on the Christian right. Predictably, liberals have wrung their hands. But easily the most chilling sight in years on TV was Wyoming's hard-eyed governor, Jim Geringer, saying that he hoped "we would not use Matt to further our agenda [sic]." But we must further one if good is ever to come from the ooze and the slime where Matt's death came from.

I propose a class action of interested and concerned organizations and individuals. Since it is bad law that has made our republic so safe a place for hate to fester in, I suggest that only at law can there be the war *they* want and a victory that a sane society must win. Sen. Trent Lott recently denounced homosexuality as an illness akin to "alcoholism and kleptomania" (two popular pastimes of Congress). Simultaneously Bauer's Family Research Council began its hate-campaign ads on TV, condemning those men and women who made "bad choices" sexually, as if choice were any more involved than the color of one's eyes or the degree of mental sickness—or crass opportunism—as expressed by Lott and Bauer.

I believe that as the highest-ranking member of the U.S. Senate, Mr. Lott should be charged with incitement to violence and to murder, specifically in the case of Matthew Shepard, and that Mr. Bauer and others who have indulged in the same reckless demonizing of millions of Americans be equally charged.

Amnesty International recently reported that the United States is the most barbarous of first-world countries in the treatment of its citizens by its government. If so, then the Tree of Liberty . . . I trust that all of you know the rest of Mr. Jefferson's sentence.

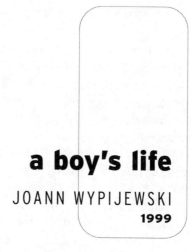

a boy's life

JOANN WYPIJEWSKI
1999

"When I think of how fragile men are," a dominatrix once said to me, "I feel so much pity. All that fear, all that self-mutilation, just to be 'men.' When I heard that those guys in Laramie took Matthew Shepard's shoes, I was so creeped out. I mean, shoes are so symbolic — 'walk a mile in my shoes' and all that. Why did they take his shoes?"

From the beginning there was something too awfully iconic about the case. Matthew Shepard, young, small, gay, a college boy in the cowboy town of Laramie, Wyoming, a kid who, his father says, didn't know how to make a fist until he was thirteen, lured out of a bar by two "rednecks" ("trailer trash," "drop-outs," every tabloid term has been applied), hijacked to a lonely spot outside of town, strung up like a scarecrow on a buck fence, bludgeoned beyond recognition, and left to die without his shoes, his ring, his wallet, or the $20 inside it. With that mix of real and fanciful detail, it has been called a trophy killing, a hate crime, a sacrifice. Press crews who had never before and have not since lingered over gruesome murders of homosexuals came out in force, reporting their brush with a bigotry so poisonous it could scarcely be imagined. County Attorney Cal Rerucha says death by injection is the just response. At the site where Shepard was murdered, in a field of prairie grass and sagebrush within eyeshot of suburban houses, a cross has been laid out in pink limestone rocks. In crotches of the killing fence, two stones have been placed; one bears the word "love"; the other, "forgive." The poignancy of those messages has been transmitted out and beyond via television; it is somewhat diminished if one knows that the stones were put there by a journalist, whose article about the murder for *Vanity Fair* was called "The Crucifixion of Matthew Shepard."

Torture is more easily imagined when masked in iconography but no better understood. Perhaps it all will become clear in October, when one of the accused, Aaron McKinney, goes on trial for kidnapping, aggravated robbery, and capital murder (his companion, Russell Henderson, pled guilty on April 5 and avoided death with two consecutive life terms), but it seems unlikely. "The story" passed into myth even before the trials had been set, and at this point fact, rumor, politics, protective cover, and jailhouse braggadocio are so entangled that the truth may be elusive even to the protagonists.

What is known, though somehow elided, is that in the most literal definition of the word, Matthew Shepard was not crucified. His hands were not outstretched, as has been suggested by all manner of media since October 7, 1998, when the twenty-one-year-old University of Wyoming student was discovered near death, but rather tied behind him as if in handcuffs, lashed to a pole four inches off the ground. His head propped on the lowest fence rail, his legs extending out to the east, he was lying almost flat on his back when Deputy Reggie Fluty of the Albany County Sheriff's Department found him at 6:22 P.M., eighteen hours, it's believed, after he was assaulted. It was Shepard's diminutive aspect—Fluty thought he was thirteen—and the horrid condition of his face and heard, mangled by eighteen blows from a three-pound Smith & Wesson .357 magnum, that most compelled her attention.

Shepard had encountered McKinney and Henderson, both also twenty-one, at the Fireside Bar on October 6. They exchanged words that no one heard, then left the bar and got into a truck belonging to McKinney's father. There Shepard was robbed and hit repeatedly. Out by the fence came the fatal beating. Shepard must have been kicked too, because he was bruised between his legs and elsewhere. Amid the blows he cried, "Please don't." He was left alive but unconscious, as McKinney and Henderson headed for an address they'd got out of him. En route they ran into two local punks out puncturing tires, Emiliano Morales and Jeremy Herrera, and started a fight. McKinney cracked Morales's head open with the same gun he'd used on Shepard, coating the weapon with still more blood. Herrera then whacked McKinney's head with a stick. Police arrived, grabbed Henderson (he and McKinney had run in different directions), and found the truck, the gun, Shepard's shoes and credit card. Police wouldn't put the crimes together until later, so Henderson was cited for interference with a peace officer and released. Henderson then drove to Cheyenne with his girlfriend, Chasity Pasley; and McKinney's girlfriend, Kristen LeAnn Price (both later charged as accessories after the fact), to dispose of his bloody clothes. McKinney, dazed from the gash in his head, stayed home in bed, and Price hid Shepard's wallet in the dirty diaper of her and McKinney's infant son, Cameron. Six days later, on October 12, Shepard died.

Those are the facts as disclosed by court records and McKinney's confession. (He has pleaded not guilty.) In response, the Equality State—which enfranchised women long before anyplace else, which struck sodomy laws from the books in 1977—has disowned McKinney and Henderson as monsters. So has the rest of the country.

And yet McKinney and Henderson appear to be young men of common prejudices, far more devastatingly human than is comfortable to consider. They acquired the gun a few days before the murder in a trade for $100 in methamphetamine—crank, speed, crystal meth—the drug of choice among white rural youth, cheaper than cocaine and more long-lasting, more relentless in its accelerating effects, more widely used in Wyoming, per capita, than in any state in the country. McKinney, says the friend who traded him for it, desired the gun for its badass beauty eight-inch barrel, fine tooling, "the Dirty Harry thing." The trade occurred while these three fellows and their girlfriends were on a meth binge. Before it was over they would smoke or snort maybe $2,000 worth of the drug. By the time they met Matthew Shepard, says the friend, who saw them that day, McKinney and Henderson were on the fifth day of that binge. They had not slept, he says, since before October 2, payday, when the partying had begun.

Those unreported facts-to the extent that anything can be factually determined in Laramie these days, with everyone involved in the case under a gag order[1]-may tell more about the crime, more about the everyday life of hate and hurt and heterosexual culture than all the quasi-religious characterizations of Matthew's passion, death, and resurrection as patron saint of hatecrime legislation. It's just possible that Matthew Shepard didn't die because he was gay; he died because Aaron McKinney and Russell Henderson are straight.

"If you're telling your feelings, you're kind of a wuss." Brent Jones, a heterosexual who went to high school with McKinney and Henderson, was guiding me through the psychic terrain of a boy's life.

"So what do you do when things hurt?"

"That's why God created whiskey, don't you think? You get drunker than a pig and hope it drains away—or you go home and cry."

"Is that true for most guys, do you think?"

"Yeah, pretty much."

"So secretly you're all wusses, and you know you're wusses, but you can't let anyone know, even though you all know you know."

"You could say that."

"Can you talk to girls about this stuff?" "Unless you know this is the one—like, you're going to get married, and then you're in so deep you can't help yourself—but if not, if you think she might break up with you, then no, because she might tell someone, and then it gets around, and then everyone thinks you're a wuss. And you don't want people to think you're a wuss, unless you are a wuss, and then you know you're a wuss, and then it doesn't matter."

Among the weighty files on the proceedings against McKinney and Henderson in the Albany County Courthouse is a curious reference. The state had charged, as an "aggravating factor" in the murder, that "the defendant[s] knew or should have known that the victim was suffering from a physical or mental disability." The court threw this out; Judge Jeffrey Donnell, who presided over Henderson's case, told me he assumed it referred to Shepard's size (five foot two, 105 pounds) but was legally irrelevant whatever its intent. In a sense, it is sociologically irrelevant as well whether the prosecution regarded Shepard as crippled more by sexuality or size, since by either measure he was, in the vernacular of Laramie's straight youth, a wuss.

Wussitude haunts a boy's every move. It must have haunted Aaron McKinney most of his life. McKinney, too, is a little thing—not as little as Shepard, but at about five foot six, 145 pounds, he doesn't cut a formidable figure. George Markle, who roomed with him after they both dropped out of high school, describes McKinney as having "tiny arms, a tiny, tiny chest, no definition in his body." He affected a gangsta style-droopy jeans, baggy shirt, Raiders jacket, gold chains, gold on all his fingers. He'd ape hip-hop street talk, but "he couldn't get it going if he tried." His nickname was Dopey, both for his over-sized ears and for his reputation as a serious drug dealer and user. His shoulder bears a tattoo of the Disney character pouring a giant can of beer on his mother's grave, an appropriation of a common rapper's homage to a fallen brother: "Pour a forty ounce on my homey's grave."

The prosecution contends that Shepard was lured out of the bar as if on a sexual promise. County public defender Wyatt Skaggs says that neither Henderson nor McKinney ever asserted that they came on to Shepard. And in his confession, McKinney said Shepard "did not hit on or make advances toward" him and Henderson according to Sheriff's Detective Sgt. Rob DeBree. Perhaps McKinney said something different when he came home that night and wept in the arms of

Kristen Price, or perhaps, presuming homophobia to be an acceptable alibi, she thought she was helping him when she told the press that he and Henderson "just wanted to beat [Shepard] up bad enough to teach him a lesson not to come on to straight people." But once at the Albany County Detention Center, McKinney seemed to take up the pose of fag-basher as a point of pride. At least five prisoners awaiting trial or sentencing have asked their lawyers if the things he's said to them might be leveraged to their own advantage. "Being a verry [sic] drunk homofobick [sic] I flipped out and began to pistol whip the fag with my gun," McKinney wrote in a letter to another inmate's wife. He didn't mean to kill Shepard, he wrote; he was turning to leave him, tied to the fence but still conscious, when Matthew "mouthed off to the point that I became angry enough to strike him more with my gun." Even then, he insists, his attitude toward homosexuals is not particularly venomous and the murder was unintentional.

McKinney's mother was a nurse; she died as a result of a botched operation when Aaron was sixteen. Markle says there was a kind of shrine to her in his house, but Aaron rarely spoke of her, and then only superficially and only when he was high: "He was always happy then. Once, on mushrooms, he said that if he would slide backward down a hill, he could see his mom in heaven." According to probate records, McKinney got $98,268.02 in a settlement of the wrongful-death lawsuit his stepfather brought against the doctors and the hospital. "After he got the money, he had a lot of friends," Markle told me. He bought cars and cracked them up, bought drugs and became an instant figure in town. He was engaged at one point—"she got the drugs, he got the sex; I guess it worked out for a while"—until the girl found a more attractive connection. "He wasn't a babe magnet," Brent Jones says. He might make a good first impression—he's funny, I was told, though no one could quite explain how—but he couldn't keep that up. Women were bitches and hos, just like other men, who might also be called fag, wuss, queer, sissie, girly man, woman, the standard straight-boy arsenal, which McKinney employed indiscriminately, says Markle, "about as much as anybody-you know, joking around—he never mentioned anything about hating gays." He talked about marrying Price, who is eighteen, but according to more than one person who was acquainted with them, he wasn't faithful and didn't seem even to like her much.

He loves his son, I'm told. And what else? Blank. What did he talk about? Blank. What did he fear? Blank. Who is he? None of the boys can really say. Interior life is unexplored territory, even when it's their own. Exterior life, well, "Actually, when he wasn't high he was kind of a geek," says a guy who's done drugs with him since high school. "He wasn't the sharpest tool in the shed. He always wanted to seem bigger, badder, and tougher than anybody," says Jones, a strongly built fellow who first noticed McKinney when the latter hit him from behind. "He usually didn't pick on anyone bigger than him. He could never do it alone, and he couldn't do it toe-to-toe." Markle says nothing much mattered to McKinney in picking a fight, except that if he started to lose, his friends would honor the rule they had among themselves and come in to save him.

A stock media image of McKinney and Henderson in this tragedy has them counting out quarters and dimes with dirty fingers to buy a pitcher of beer at the Fireside. It is meant to indicate their distance from Shepard, who had clean hands and paid for his Heinekens with bills, and to offer some class perspective on the cheap. They were poor, they were losers, they lived in trailers, for God's sake! McKinney, as it happens, didn't live in a trailer, though he had when he was younger—a nice double one with his stepfather, until recently program director at KRQU radio. His natural father is a long-haul truck driver whom he was heard to call "Daddy" only a few years ago, and in Aaron's childhood the family lived on Palomino Drive in the Imperial Heights subdivision. As teenagers he and his friends would drink and get high in the field behind it—"quite the hangout," according to Markle—where McKinney had played as a boy and where he would later leave Shepard to die.

Henderson spent most of his childhood in the warmly appointed ranch house where his grandmother runs a day care and to which his late grandfather would repair after work at the post office. At the time of the murder, Russell lived with Pasley, a UW art student, now serving fifteen to twenty-four months, in a trailer court no uglier than most in Laramie and with the same kinds of late-model cars, trucks, and four-wheel-drive vehicles parked outside, the same proportion of people pulling in and out wearing ties or nice coats or everyday workers' clothes, and probably the same type of modest but comfortable interiors as in the ones I visited. No matter, in the monumental condescension of the press, "trailer" always means failure, always connotes "trash," and, however much it's wrapped up in socioculturoeconomico froufrou, always insinuates the same thing: What can you expect from trash?

McKinney and Henderson were workers. At the end of the day they had dirty hands, just like countless working men who head to the bars at quitting time. Dirt is symbolic only if manual labor is, and manual laborers usually find their symbolism elsewhere. The pair had drunk two pitchers of beer at the Library bar before going to the Fireside; no one remembers anything about them at the Library, presumably because they paid in dollars. Maybe they resented a college boy's clean hands and patent-leather loafers and moneyed confidence; they wouldn't have been the only people in town who do, though acquaintances ascribe no such sentiments to them. UW is a state school, the only university in Wyoming. It stands aloof from the town, but no more than usual. Poll a classroom, and about a fifth of the students are from Laramie, and half say their parents are manual workers. Shepard, originally from Casper but schooled abroad because his father is in the oil business, didn't need a job; Pasley, like most students, did. There's nothing unique here about the injuries of class. In a month at Laramie Valley Roofing, McKinney and Henderson each would gross around $1,200, roughly $7.50 an hour. With rent payments of $370 and $340, respectively, they were like a lot of people in Laramie, where the median household income is $26,000, the average monthly rent is $439, and the average family works two jobs, maybe more.

It's said that McKinney squandered the entire hundred grand from his mother's settlement, and in his application for a public defender he listed $0 in assets. Before moving to his last address, he and his family briefly lived rent-free in a converted indoor stable with no shower, no stove, no refrigerator, and, in some rooms, a cloth ceiling and cloth walls. But everyone I spoke with who was openly familiar with him through drugs was skeptical about the poverty story. To finance his recreation, I was told by the guy tweaking with him in the days before the murder, McKinney would often be fronted an "eight ball" of meth (three grams, an eighth of anounce, street price about $300; for him, wholesale, sometimes as low as $100), keep two grams for himself, double the amount of the remaining powder by cutting it with vitamin B, sell that, and have $200 and enough crank to keep two people awake for practically a week before he'd even paid a cent. At one point a few years ago, according to a friend now monitored by an ankle bracelet, McKinney was buying an eight ball every few days.

Maybe he miscalculated the costs of his binge in that first week in October. A few days before Shepard would be tied to the fence, McKinney and Henderson walked into the Mini-Mart where George Markle works, and, in an agitated state, McKinney shouted that Markle owed him $4,000 and that he needed it. Years earlier, Aaron had bought George a used Chevy S-10 low-rider truck. First it was called a gift, then a loan, then no one talked about it much, Markle says, and after the friendship broke, he didn't intend to pay anything back. That day in the Mini-Mart, Aaron threatened to kill George. He had threatened him once or twice before within the last few weeks, always with Henderson silently in tow. Markle told his boss, but neither of them thought too much of it. "I'm gonna kill you"—it was just Aaron pretending to be big and bad. It was the way he talked; like when he first came into the Mini-Mart and, seeing George, exclaimed, "Oh, look at that—it's my favorite little bitch, my favorite little whore."

"Things are good enough for me to stay for now," Elam Timothy, a writer, gardener, and handyman, was telling me just before we decided what his pseudonym would be. "I have a relationship, I'm out at work and to as many people as I care to be—but I'm not looking through rose-colored glasses. They're demonizing those boys so they don't have to look at themselves. Yes, this could have happened anywhere, but it didn't. Can we please look at it? That whole 'live and let live' myth. In my mind that boils down to one sentence: If I don't tell you I'm a fag, you won't beat the crap out of me."

"Have you ever been hurt or threatened here?"

"No."

"Do you know anyone who has been?"

"No, but I don't know many gay men either."

"So what is it that's dangerous?"

"What's scary is just hearing people use the word 'faggot' all the time. It makes me feel like a pig at a weenie roast. Danger isn't palpable, but I keep myself in safe pockets. I wouldn't expect to find safety in the Cowboy [bar], but Coal Creek [coffeehouse], yeah, that's safe."

Laramie was founded on sex and the railroad, in that order. Women created the region's first service industry, and soon after the town's establishment, in 1868, it was associated with some thirty saloons, gambling houses, and brothels. Before any of that, it was associated with death. Around 1817, a French Canadian trapper named Jacques LaRamie was working these parts with his mates. As the story goes, he was young and handsome, and in winter decided to take his beaver traps upstream on what is now either the Big or the Little Laramie River. In spring he failed to return, and Indians told his erstwhile companions that he'd been killed by other natives and stuffed under the ice of a beaver pond. His headstone thus became the plains, a mountain range, two rivers, a fort, a county, a railroad terminal, and, ultimately, the city.

From the foothills of the Laramie Range, the high prairie where the city is situated stretches out, scored by steel tracks and pocked by late-model houses defiant of the city's already shaggy boundaries. From the right vantage point those are obscured, and all that's in sight is the plain and, to the west, the Snowy Range and what, against reason, seems like infinity. People may swoon about Wyoming's mountains and river valleys, but the power is all in the wind, which has shaped the plains like a pair of enormous hands playing in a sandbox of soft soil and red clay, massaging the earth into fine over- lapping layers and fluid hollows. Such subtlety is merely the profit of aeons. Over spring break a student from the university left his truck out in an open field while the winds blew thirty, forty miles an hour; within two weeks, the windward side of the truck had been sand- blasted down to bare metal.

Laramie, a pleasant place of liberal inclination and some 27,000 people, is not a railroad town anymore. Freight lines rush through but are marginal to the city's economy. It's not a sex town either, though in the history-charmed buildings abutting the rail yard along 1st Street shopkeepers will happily show off narrow cubicles in an upstairs flat, or a slotted box in a side door, where nighttime ladies deposited their earnings under the madam's gaze and key, their work organized as on a sharecrop, with ledgered debt always exceeding income. Carol Bow- ers, an archivist at the university's American Heritage Center, recounts a history in which the town elders seesawed between plans for eradication and regulation, usually recognizing the superior bene- fits of the latter. (In one nineteenth-century city record, all but $20 out of $240 in fines and fees collected one month came from prosti- tutes.) So the women were harassed, corralled, controlled by periodic raids, punished for any venture into legitimate civic life by threats to their licenses—but tolerated. "The town didn't want them to go away," Bowers says. "The town wanted them to be invisible."

A hundred years later, sex is almost totally in the closet. Only the truck stops off I-80 are worked, by mobile squads of women or by men, who also work the rest stops. For every other unspoken desire there's The Fort, a rambling warehouse south of town that has sur- vived Cal Rerucha's tireless efforts at suppression. There men, mostly men, stop in (all classes and tendencies, all night on weekends), nervous and chatty—about a practical joke or a bachelor party or the wife—before surveying the aisles, then scuttling to the checkout with a strap—on dildo or a Miss Perfection "port-a-pussy" or a sexual ban- quet of videos. A tall, lean man of the muscular outdoors type crouches before a display and comes away with the Sauna Action Pump, guaranteed to improve an erection beyond any natural capac- ity. Now and then one man is followed five minutes later by another, under the red light and into the video booths in back.

In the best of times, sex is playground to the imagination, the place where what is need not be what it seems, where strength and weakness swap clothes, and the thin cry, "This is who I am, this is who I dream of being—don't hurt me" seeks its voice. Laramie happens now to be associated with sex in the worst of times, sex boxed and squared in the unexamined terms of the "natural" course of things or the unexamined terms of "identity." Many in town are irritated by this association and by all the talk of hate since the murder attracted national attention. McKinney and Henderson, it's said, are "not Laramie." Before his death, Shepard was surely "not Laramie" either, if only because he took risks that other gay men in town might not have. Laramie, it's said, is not censorious about sex, homo or hetero We're just tight-lipped. We don't go there. We believe "live and let live"—and it's certainly not hateful, just as most of the country is not, just as, perhaps, even McKinney and Henderson are not. If they all were, everything would be much simpler.

Hatred is like pornography—hard to define, but you know it when you see it. On the morning before Russell Henderson pleaded guilty, the Reverend Fred Phelps of Topeka, Kansas, brought his flock to the county courthouse with signs declaring GOD HATES FAGS, FAG GOD=RECTUM, PHIL 3:19, SAVE THE GERBILS. Phelps cited as his guide for most of this (the Bible has nothing to say about gerbils) such scriptural passages as Leviticus 18:22, "Thou shalt not lie with mankind, as with womankind: it is abomination." I asked if he also subscribes to Moses' suggestion a bit further on in Leviticus 20:13, "If a man also lie with mankind, as he lieth with a woman, . . . they shall surely be put to death." He said he thought all civil law should be based on biblical code, but "it's never going to happen. I'm a pragmatist, a visionary."

"So, if you could, though, you would execute homosexuals?"

"I wouldn't execute them. The government would execute them."

His only audience were police, press, and a ring of angels—counterprotesters dressed in white robes, their great wings sweeping up before his gaudy placards. The next day the university's student newspaper covered the day's events, running in enlarged type the observation of freshman Kristen Allen that "they have no business using the Bible verses out of context. God hates the sin but loves the sinner." On campus, where Phelps later moved his protest, onlookers expressed disgust at his message and invoked "tolerance."

Before it came to signify the highest state to which straight society could aspire, tolerance was something one had for a bad job or a bad smell or a nightmare relative who visited once a year. In its new guise, tolerance means straight people know of gay men and women, but there is no recognizable gay life, no clubs except a tiny one on campus, no bars or restaurants or bookstores flying the rainbow flag. It means the university might institute a Matthew Shepard Chair in Civil Liberties but has no antidiscrimination policy that applies to homosexuals and no employee benefit policy that extends to domestic partners.* It means the public school curriculum does not say teachers must "avoid planning curriculum promoting perversion, homosexuality, contraception, promiscuity and abortion as healthy lifestyle choices" the policy in Lincoln County, Wyoming—but it also does not include "homosexuality" among vocabulary terms for sex-ed classes at any grade level and mentions the word only once, for eight grade, under "Topics to be Discussed . . . particularly as they relate to [sexually transmitted diseases]." It means a father tells his lesbian daughter, "If you have to do this you should do it in the closet," and the mother tells her, "Let's just pretend I don't know, okay?" It means her brother "tries to be as supportive as he can be—and he is but if a man hit on him, he'd beat the shit out of him. He wouldn't beat up someone for another reason, and he thinks that's an accomplishment and it is." It means Chasity Pasley's mother won her custody battle over the charge that as a lesbian she was unfit, but her children had to call her partner "Aunt." It means if you're gay and out and attend a company party with your boyfriend, the sense in the room is "We know you're gay and that's okay, but do you have to bring your boyfriend?" It means Fred Dahl, the straight head of UW's Survey Research Center, accepts the university's expression of outrage over Shepard's murder but tells a social work master's candidate named Shannon Bell that her project to poll Wyoming residents on their attitudes toward homosexuality might amount to harrasment of straight people, and anyway, "one good rodeo season and Wyoming will be back to normal."

In a graduate-class discussion right after Shepard was found, the high-minded talk was all of tolerance as students challenged a woman who had said she abhorred violence but still . . . homosexuality, it's immoral. Amid the chatter, a cowboy who'd been silent said plainly, "The issue isn't tolerance. We don't need to learn tolerance; we need to learn love."

There may be, as the song goes, a thin line between love and hate, but, however many twists it takes, it is life's defining line. And people like Phelps are no more responsible for it than pop music is responsible for the murders at Columbine High School. What keeps that line so strong, like strands of the clothesline used to tie Matthew Shepard's wrists, are all the little things of a culture, mostly unnoticed and unremarked, like the way in which the simplest show of affection is a decision about safety, like the way in which a man entwined with a woman is the stuff of everyday commerce but a man expressing vulnerability is equivalent to a quaint notion of virginity—you save it for marriage.

"Masks are no longer as protective as they used to be," John Scagliotti, the maker of *Before (and now After) Stonewall*, was telling me. "If you're gay, no longer can you hide, because straight people watch TV, and they see how people hide. And also this has changed straight culture, so all the little things you do might make you question whether you're straight, or straight enough. Your own suspicions are suspicious.

"It gets even more complicated now that all these things that represent maleness are very attractive to both gay and straight men. The downside of this, in a way, is that straight male bonding, and male bonding in general, especially in rural places, is going to be a very confused thing. Already at gyms, eighteen-year-olds don't take showers anymore—or if they do, they take all their things in with them, like modest little girls. You're confused, you're eighteen, and you really like this guy; he's your best buddy, and you'd rather spend all your time with him than with this girl. And you are straight, but now you're worried too."

The Henderson trial was to have begun on the first Tuesday after Easter. At the Harvest Foursquare full-gospel church that Sunday, people wore name tags and expressed a serene camaraderie. Then they sent the children downstairs to play while the "illustrated sermon"—a dramatization of Christ's Passion and death—took place. It was a stunning performance, beginning with the Jesus character racked with sorrow in the Garden of Gethsemane. The narrator said Jesus suffered like any man. Then he said, departing from the script, "Every time I see an image of a feminine Jesus, it makes my blood boil. Jesus wasn't a weakling. Jesus was a man. If Jesus was here today, he could take on any man in this room." Later, when the Jesus character was tied to a post, flogged by two men-soldiers who took "sensual pleasure" in every fall of the whip, the narrator said, "Jesus didn't cry out for mercy . . . Jesus was a man. Jesus was a man's man." The Jesus character writhed in agony. After he stumbled offstage with the cross, and the only sounds were his moans amid the pounding of nails, the narrator described the tender caress of the hands now ripped by sharp iron. In the congregation, men as well as women were moved to weeping. By the end, they were all singing, swaying, proclaiming their weakness before the Lord.

Time was when "a man's man" could mean only one thing, and in the romance of the West, that meant cowboys. In reality, Laramie is as contradictory as anything liberated from caricature, but in symbolism its outward identity remains hitched to the cowboy. Wild Willie's Cowboy Bar anchors one corner downtown; a few feet away is The Rancher. Farther up the same street is the Ranger Lounge and Motel; down another, the legendary Buckhorn Bar, with its mirror scarred by a bullet hole, its motionless zoo of elk and deer and pronghorned antelope, bobcat and beaver and buffalo, a two-headed foal, a twinset of boar. Around the corner stands the Cowboy Saloon, with its tableau of locomotives and thundering horses, lightning storms and lassos, portraits of grand old men who'd graced the town in history (Buffalo Bill Cody) and in dreams (Clint Eastwood). A wall inside the courthouse bears a silhouette of a bronco buster, whose figure has also appeared on Wyoming license plates since 1936. The university's symbol is the rodeo rider; its sports teams, the Cowboys and Cowgirls; its paper, the *Branding Iron*; its mascot, Pistol Pete; and its recruiting slogan, "It's in our nature."

For the men of Laramie who didn't grow up on a ranch riding horses and roping cattle—that is, most of them—the cowboy cult appears to be as natural as the antlers affixed to a female elk's head hanging on a wall at the Buckhorn. It all seems to fit, until you look closer and realize that this buck is actually Bambi's mother butched up. For those who did grow up to be cowboys, the rituals and vestments may be just as they were for their fathers and grandfathers-like going to the dance hall on a Saturday night, scrubbed and polished and wearing one's best hat and boots, but the meanings have changed, or at least got more complicated. In a different setting, the waves of men kicking it up to "Cotton Eye Joe" at the Cowboy Saloon would be high camp, just as the beautiful, guileless cowboy explaining the rodeo to me, undulating in a pantomime of the art of bull riding, could as easily have been auditioning for a spot with The Village People.

Camp still flies under the radar of straight Laramie: heterosexuals didn't wink when the golden anniversary commemorative booklet of the university union featured a sailor flanked by two gamesome cowboys, circa the 1940s, with the caption "Come alongside cowboys . . . let me tell you a sea story . . ." But the rodeo rider doesn't need to know he's a gay icon for such things to tinge his identity, any more than he needs to know he's a Western icon. He grows up on a ranch but takes a degree in civil engineering, forsaking the land but not the culture. His children then trade in the heels and pointy toes for something else, or they affect the look but with a suspect authenticity. Their grandfathers' world is still theirs as well, but now only in nostalgia.

The cowboy was not part of Wyoming's conscious image until after he had ceased to exist in the form later to be romanticized. In 1889, the governor's appeals for statehood contained none of the heroic references advertised on the front of the Cowboy Saloon; instead, he imagined Wyoming as a magnet for industrial capital, a dream that would not be fully abandoned by state planners until 1997. As detailed by Frieda Knobloch, a UW professor of American Studies, the state's history in this regard can be read as a continual longing to be what it is not: anticipation that vast oil and mineral reserves would issue forth factory towns like those in the East; then advancement of the Wild West as a tourist attraction just as the enclosure of the open range was complete. Central to the latter project were artists from the East—Frederic Remington, Owen Wister—whose work was financed or seized upon by local promoters. By 1922 the governor was urging citizens to put on "four-gallon hats" for the benefit of Eastern experience-seekers at the state's Frontier Days celebration. In 1939, even as the Department of Commerce and Industry was lobbying investors with forecasts of a manufacturing dawn, its head man was again reminding locals to dress up as cowboys to "give our guests what they want."

Perhaps some in Laramie bridled so at the presence of the national press on the Shepard case not only out of their own defensiveness and justified outrage at reporters' arrogance—jamming the door when Henderson's grandmother declined to comment, blustering over being barred from the courtroom even though they never reserved seats, mistaking cottonwoods for oaks—but also because of some deep vibrations of that old tradition of outside gawking and self-exploitation. A heterosexual lawyer named Tony Lopez chatted with me for a long time but nevertheless let me know, "This is home, and you're an uninvited guest."

Now in front of the small ranches on the edge of Laramie, the third vehicle might be a school bus, which the rancher drives to make $300, $400 a month in the off-season. No small spread survives just on cattle; in fewer than ten years the price of a calf has fallen from well over a dollar to sixty cents a pound. The profit margin for these ranches, never fantastic, according to Brett Moline, the University Agricultural Cooperative Extension educator for Albany County, is now "squeezed so tight one financial mistake can be enough to wipe you out." Most ranch owners are in their late fifties or early sixties; younger ones have either inherited the land or are carrying so much debt from buying that they won't be in business long. Without a lot of money to live on and huge assets all tied up in land, the only way to realize the value of what they have is to sell it-usually to housing developers or to out-of-state gentility, who might pay three times the land's worth to set up what Moline calls their "ranchette."

Wyoming, with 480,000 people, still has the lowest population density in the country, and where there's space there is a kind of freedom. The state has no income tax, no motorcycle-helmet law, no law against openly carrying a gun, no open-container law on the interstates (meaning you can drink without worry unless you're drunk); there's a seat-belt law, but it's not enforced (police take $5 off the fine for another violation-say, speeding-if you're buckled up); until last year children didn't have to go to school before the age of seven and didn't have to stay in school past the eight grade; unless there's a weapon involved, Laramie police say they prefer wrestling a suspect to the ground to other kinds of force, and in ten years they have killed only one civilian.

"This is the last frontier," says Laramie police officer Mike Ernst, with a curl in his voice. After the university, the government is the biggest employer, and after the bars, the most striking commercial establishments are bookstores and restaurants and, near UW, the fast-food strip. On the fringes of town rise some enormous houses, and elsewhere some people have no running water or refrigeration, so the soup kitchen substitutes peanut butter for meat in takeaway lunches in summer. Most, though, live in bungalows in town, trailers and suburban houses a bit farther out. Except for Mountain Cement and the sawmills, there's little manufacturing work, mostly only retail and service jobs, maid work at the motels, short-order cooking and rig washing out at the truck stops, telemarketing for the hippie kids, and temp work from construction to computers, but none of that pays more than $8 an hour.

McKinney and Henderson were roofers. Construction has a short season in Wyoming, intensifying even normally intense work. An eight-hour day can stretch into ten or twelve hours of fitting a shingle, banging a hammer, fitting and banging and banging bent over, on a grade, on your knees-bang, bang, bang. "I hurt a lot every day. I'm only twenty-one," Brent Jones told me. "My back shouldn't hurt." Jones works for a competing roofing company. "It's not bad if you use a nail gun, but if you use a hammer-eight hours of that and you can't even turn a doorknob . . . You just work through the pain. Sometimes you take a bunch of Advil. You go to bed at night and just pray that when you wake up you don't hurt so much."

Sometimes you drink "booze, the cause of and answer to all of life's problems," in Jones's crisp phrase. Drinking is a pleasure in its own way in Laramie and a curse in all of the usual ways. Officer Ernst said that if alcohol somehow disappeared, Laramie wouldn't need three quarters of its police force. *The Boomerang*: a daily police blotter is dominated by DUI and "domestic disturbance" calls, and not by coincidence. News of murder is rare, but it's ugly. In the year before Matthew Shepard was killed, fifteen-year-old Daphne Sulk was found naked in the snow, dead from seventeen stab wounds; eight-year-old Kristin Lamb, while away visiting her grandparents in the town of Powell, was kidnapped, raped, and thrown into the garbage in a duffel bag. No one calls those hate crimes. Just as six years ago no one called it a hate crime when the body of a gay UW professor, Steve Heyman, was found dumped by the side of a road in Colorado. Law enforcement and university administrators alike simply forgot that murder. After hearing of Shepard's beating, State Senator Craig Thomas declared, "It's the most violent, barbaric thing I've ever heard of happening in Wyoming."

There are 14,869 women in Albany County, according to the 1990 census, and 1,059 extra men. Stefani Farris at the SAFE Project, a haven and advocacy center for people who've been abused or sexually assaulted, said she thought "people in this town would be spinning if they knew how many times women were beaten by a husband or boyfriend." The state recorded 163 incidents of domestic violence in the county in 1997, nine rapes, and ninety-nine aggravated assaults. In its 1997–98 report, though, SAFE records 3,958 phone calls, almost all from women, reporting battering, stalking, sexual assault, and other physical or emotional hurts, almost all committed by men. It notes 1,569 face-to-face sessions; 1,118 individuals served; 164 individuals sheltered for 2,225 total days. SAFE can't spend much time analyzing perpetrators, Farris explained. "When you see that women are being battered, their children are being abused, their pets are being killed, you see a woman who comes in and we've seen three other women before come in who were in the same situation with the same guy—it's hard to have any sympathy for what the man went through."

The court remands some batterers to the ADAM Program at the Southeast Wyoming Mental Health Center for reeducation, but the project's director, Ed Majors, says that all he can deal with is behavior.

"I can't find a dime for services, [so] the deep issues are still not addressed. If you eat chocolate and use Clearasil, you're still going to have problems."

Such as?

"When it's fear or hurt, which is typically the primary emotion at work, when you can't say, I'm scared shitless,' most hurt and fear will come out in the only vehicle men are allowed. It comes out crooked. It looks like anger, it's expressed as anger, but it isn't."

"Here's a joke for you," an amiable guy offered: "What do you get when you play a country song backward? You get your car back, you get your dog back, you get your house back, you get your wife back . . . "Here's another one: You can have sex with a sheep in Wyoming, just don't tie the shepherd to the fence . . . Oh, God, now you're gonna think I'm an inbred redneck asshole."

There was no trial for Russell Henderson in the end, so what drama his story could arouse had to be fit into one early-April hearing. According to his testimony, Henderson had disagreed when McKinney suggested robbing Shepard, but when they all left the bar, McKinney said drive, and he drove. McKinney said go past Wal-Mart, and he proceeded; stop the car, and he stopped; get the rope, and he got it; tie his hands, and he tied them. Henderson never hit Shepard, he said. "I told him [McKinney] to stop hitting him, that I think he's had enough." McKinney, in this account, then hit Henderson, who retreated into the truck. Finally, again McKinney said drive, and Henderson drove.

Henderson offered nothing more. How is it that Shepard left the bar with them? Why did they beat him? Why were they going to 7th Street—supposedly to rob Shepard's house—when he lived on 12th? Why did they fight with Morales and Herrera? When Henderson and Pasley and Price drove to Cheyenne to throw away the bloody clothes, why didn't they take McKinney and little Cameron with them and keep on going? Such questions have to wait for McKinney.

At the hearing Henderson looked like a man numb from combat as Cal Rerucha and Wyatt Skaggs—men whose names appear on court documents involving Henderson since childhood went through the legal motions, as Judy Shepard told the court of Matthew's sweetness and ambition, of his mounting achievements, of the horror of his last days, and the depth of her loss; as Henderson's grandmother, Lucy Thompson, the woman who raised him, told of his own sweetness and disappointments, of his expectations for his GEDs, of the inexplicability of his actions and the breadth of her grief. When Russell told the

Shepards, "There is not a moment that goes by that I don't see what happened that night," he spoke as one does of a bad dream half-remembered, hopeless to resurrect the rest. When Mrs. Shepard told him, "At times, I don't think you're worthy of an acknowledgment of your existence," he did not flinch. In a proceeding marked by sobs and tears suppressed, the only figure who flinched less was Mr. Shepard.

Henderson was transferred to the Wyoming State Penitentiary. The word around town, originating with a prison guard, was that the inmates had held an auction, or perhaps it was a lottery, for his services and those of McKinney. Prosecutor Rerucha says he expects the only time Henderson will leave the pen is as a corpse for burial. Only death would have been a harsher sentence. The tumbrels are rolling for McKinney.

It should be easier for the state to cast McKinney's trial as a contest between good and evil: to caricature Shepard as a child-saint, because to think of him as a man evokes a sexual experience no one wants to know; and to caricature McKinney as a devil-man, because to think of him as Laramie's, or anyone's, child sits harder on the conscience. In this respect, Henderson's was the more difficult case, because from the beginning he emerged as that stock character in the country's rerun violent drama—a quiet boy, kept to himself, "the most American kid you can get," in the words of his landlord.

Judy Shepard told *Vanity Fair*, "I believe there are people who have no souls," and others have told me they believe some people are just "born bad," but Russell Henderson was born like any child of a young mother in bad trouble—premature, sickly, poisoned by the alcohol in her blood. Cindy Dixon was nineteen when she had Russell, and, as Wyatt Skaggs remembers, "she was the sweetest, most considerate, loving person when she wasn't drinking; when she was drinking, she was abusive, obnoxious, every single adjective you could think of for an intoxicated person." On January 3, 1999, at forty, she was found dead in the snow about eight and a half miles from town. Early reports had her somehow losing her way after leaving the bars on foot, in light clothing, on a night so frigid and blustery that Elam Timothy and his boyfriend turned back while driving on the road where she'd be found. The death was later determined a homicide: Dixon was bruised, her underwear torn, there was evidence of semen; and now a Florida man, Dennis Menefee, is on trial for her murder. Somehow the fact that Russell lost a mother—and Mrs. Thompson, a daughter through another murder, a sex crime, never counted for much in all the stories about Laramie.

"I don't like my place in this town," Henderson said to an old girlfriend, Shaundra Arcuby, not long before Shepard's murder. "Part of it," she said, "had to do with his mom and what people said about her. The thing about this town is that who you are is kind of set in stone. It's not that easy to remake yourself."

Shaundra fell in love with Russell when they both were in high school (he a sophomore, she a senior) and worked at Taco Bell. She was confused about an old boyfriend, who was bullying her to get back with him. "Do what makes you happy," Russell said. "That was the winning point with me," she recalled. "Someone's giving me an ultimatum and someone's telling me to be happy, there was no question what I'd choose." They'd hang out, watch movies; he always came to the door, spoke to her mom. He made her tapes: Pearl Jam, The Violent Femmes. They went to her prom; friends thought they'd get married. Then she dumped him: "I was the first female in my family to graduate high school and not be pregnant," she said. "I just couldn't think of marriage. It scared me, so I ran away." Not long after, she'd get married, disastrously, and then divorce.

Most of the guys who knew McKinney in high school didn't know Henderson—"he was a little too good." He collected comic books and baseball cards, loved Scouting, even beyond making Eagle Scout. He pumped gas, fiddled with an old Corvair. He played soccer-the "fag sport," as it's known. He had fantasies of being a doctor but was headed for Wyoming Technical Institute for mechanics until he was told, days before he was to celebrate high school graduation, that he wouldn't get a diploma because he'd missed a paper. He was prayerful in the Mormon tradition. About homosexuality, Lucy Thompson says, he believed "everyone has a right to their own free agency." Until he was fifteen he helped Lucy with the dialysis machine that kept his beloved grandfather alive, and watched as his life drained away. Bill Thompson never let on how he suffered. Neither did Russell. "He never ever talked about the hurt that was inside him," Lucy told me. "He'd say, 'That's okay, Grandma; don't worry, Grandma.'" She told the court, "When my husband and his grandfather passed away, so did a part of Russell."

Brent Jones remembers Henderson as "kind of an asshole," less of a troublemaker than McKinney but "his elevator didn't go to the top floor either." He had some juvie trouble. A judge once told Cindy Dixon she'd have to choose between Russell and her boyfriend. She was not in good shape that day and said, "Oh, that's easy," with an approving gesture toward the boyfriend.

It's said that over the past forty years Lucy Thompson has raised half the kids in Laramie. She is a woman of profound serenity. Russell was in his grandparents' care from his birth to the age of five, when they thought he should be in the nuclear family. Cindy was married then, with two little girls. Three and a half years later the Thompsons again got custody. In the intervening period, Russell took a physical and emotional battering from his mother's partners. Years of police reports follow Cindy's own familiarity with violence. Once Russell told his grandparents about a harrowing beating he had watched his mother endure. Why didn't he call them? "When that happens, I just freeze, and when I do something about it, I just get retaliation," Lucy remembers him saying.

The standard description of Henderson is that "he was a follower." At work, though, he was the leader, says Joe Lemus of Laramie Valley Roofing. Both boys are nice, friendly people. Sure, they'd talk fag, wuss, sissy, Lemus says. "In grade school, you call people fat, stupid. When you get older, this is just what you say; it's like calling someone a retard." Everybody does it, even college kids (one of whom scratched KILL THEM under the title of the UW library's copy of *How to Make the World a Better Place for Gays and Lesbians*), even the straight-boy cub reporter at *The Boomerang* who helped cover the case before becoming an intern at *Rolling Stone*. According to police accounts, when McKinney and Henderson came upon Morales and Herrera, it was Henderson who called them "fucking bitches." "Why the fuck are you calling us bitches?" Morales answered, and McKinney hit him from behind. Police Commander David O'Malley testified that in questioning Henderson about the fight, Officer Flint Waters said if police found someone with a bullet they'd have more to talk to him about: "Mr. Henderson laughed and said, 'I guarantee that you wouldn't find anybody with a bullet in them.' "

Lemus says that in the period leading up to the murder Henderson was downhearted; Chasity had cheated on him. McKinney was excited; he'd just bought a gun. They were working between eight and eleven hours a day. Henderson had recently turned twenty-one and was eager to go to a bar. It was new for him, though I'm told he was not a stranger to drink and had his own sources for crank as well. When he was younger, a doctor had told him that because of the circumstances of his birth, alcohol (and presumably drugs) could affect him very badly. His grandfather asked Russell if he understood what that meant. "Deeper than you think," he answered, gesturing to his mother's photograph.

"Certain things make sense only if you're out of your mind," a knowing woman told me. "On meth, you would know what you were doing, but in that moment it doesn't matter. We used to have the rankest, most foul sex when we were on dope. Men don't get erections too well on speed, so already that's bad, but then there's the two-hour blow job, because when you start something, you just have to finish, only you can't finish because he won't get an erection and he won't have an orgasm, and you'd really like to stop, but you just can't."

Maybe Wyatt Skaggs is right when he says "drugs were not involved in this case," or maybe he's just being lawyerly. Rumors abound about what set that night in motion—love triangles, revenge, a mob-style debt collection. Reality is usually less baroque. Matthew Shepard smoked pot and had at least tried methamphetamine; McKinney dealt drugs and used them with Henderson; they all had a mutual acquaintance who regularly carries a police scanner, whose feigned ignorance about drugs could be matched only by an extraterrestrial, and whom every drug user I met recognizes as a link in the trade. Those things are not rumors but maybe just coincidence. And maybe Skaggs is more right when he adds, "That's not to say [meth] couldn't have been used sometime before; you don't need to take it that night to feel the effects." McKinney and Henderson never were tested for drugs, but then police say that one of the beauties of meth for the user is that there's no sure test for it.

History is one long quest for relief through chemicals, more powerful substitutes for endorphins, released when you cry so hard you run out of tears. But it is difficult to imagine a more unappetizing recipe for relief than methamphetamine. It is made from ephedrine or pseudoephedrine, extracted from over-the-counter cold and asthma medicines, then cooked up with any of a variety of agents—lye, battery acid, iodine, lantern fuel, antifreeze. A former user says it tastes like fake crab "sea legs" marinated in cat piss, but its medicinal benefits, especially for its large constituency of construction workers, is that "nothing hurts anymore; you're wide awake; you seem to accomplish what you set out to accomplish. Only later do you understand that you've been up for two days"—and that, depending on how much you smoke or snort or shoot, euphoria morphs into hallucination, which morphs into paranoia, which morphs into God knows what.

According to the state's Methamphetamine Initiative, Wyoming's eighth-graders use meth at a higher rate than twelfth-graders nationwide, and among juvenile offenders in its correctional institutions in 1997 at least 50 percent had a history of meth use. Albany County is not one of the state's top three target zones, but drug sources in Laramie volunteer that meth is everywhere. Maybe McKinney is lying and maybe he's not when he says Shepard "mouthed off," prompting him to the fatal frenzy of violence, but one crank-head told me that he once almost wasted someone just for saying hi. "You're so paranoid, you think, 'Why is he saying hi?' Does he know something? Is he a cop?" And maybe all the meth users I met were lying or wrong or putting me on in saying they immediately took the murder for a meth crime because it was all too stupid and, except for one heinous detail, all too recognizable.

None of this is a defense for what happened, but it all complicates the singular picture of hate crime. Why did they kill him? "That was the meth talking," I was told. But why did they pick on him to begin with? "Because he was a fag." So why do you think they didn't kill him because he was gay? "They were regular guys, and then they beat up the Mexicans." And, anyway, "what kind of a man beats the shit out of a wussy guy?"

Ask around for impressions of Matthew Shepard and you find as many characters as there are speakers: a charming boy, always smiling and happy; a suicidal depressive who mixed street drugs and alcohol with Effexor and Klonopin; a good listener who treated everyone with respect; "a pompous, arrogant little dick" who condescended to those who served him; a bright kid who wanted to change the world; a kid you'd swear was mentally defective; a generous person; a flasher of money; a good tipper; a lousy tipper; a sexual seeker; a naif; a man freaked by his HIV status or at peace with it; a "counterphobic" who courted risk rather than live in fear; a boy who, his father said, "liked to compete against himself," entering races he couldn't win and swimming contests he'd finish "dead last by the length of the pool" just to prove he could do it; a boy never quite sure of his father's approval; a gay man; a faggot; a human being. Any one of those Matthew Shepards could have been set up for death; the only constant is that he'd still be dead, and McKinney and Henderson would still be responsible. Gay men are killed horribly everywhere in this country, more than thirty just since Shepard—one of them, in Richmond, Virginia, beheaded. Gay and straight, male and female, some 40,000 individuals have been murdered since Shepard; the only constant is that they are dead, and that most of their killers are straight and most of them are men.

Among those who advocate hate-crime laws, it's always the sexuality of the victim that's front and center, not the sexuality of the criminal or the everyday, undifferentiated violence he took to extremity. Among the tolerance peddlers, it's always the "lifestyle" of the gay guy, never the "lifestyle" of the straight guy or the culture of compulsory heterosexuality. Even among those who argue that the victim's sexuality is irrelevant—that Shepard died just because a robbery went bad or just because McKinney and Henderson were crazy on crank—the suggestion is that the crime is somehow less awful once homophobia is removed, and what is brewing inside the boys bears less attention. "The news has already taken this up and blew it totally out of proportion because it involved a homosexual," McKinney's father told the press. Eighteen blows with a .357 magnum—murder happens.

A few years ago during an exercise at Laramie High School, students were asked to list the five best things about being a boy or a girl. The boys' list noted no breasts, no period, no pregnancy, and one other scourge of femininity that the guidance counselor who told me this story had been too stunned to remember. I was at the school, flipping through yearbooks, noticing that the class of '96, Henderson's class, had identified its number two "pet peeve" as "skinny wimps who complain about jocks." The previous day, Dylan Klebold and Eric Harris had killed their classmates in Littleton, Colorado, 140 miles away. Through that crime ran a thread from every high-profile school shooting over the past two years. Springfield, Pearl, Paducah, Jonesboro, Conyers—every one of those boy murderers or would-be murderers had been taunted as a wuss, a fag, a loser, or had been rejected by a girl, or was lonely and withdrawn, or had written harrowing stories of mayhem and slaying. Two of them had killed their pets. All of it, like the meanness of the jocks some of them despised, was regarded as just boy play—Oh, Fluffy's in the trash can? Boys will be boys. And by the logic of the culture, it was just boy play, like McKinney's brawling, like Henderson's admonition out by the fence, "I think he's had enough." Only when it turned to murder did it register, and for that there's punishment, prison, the death penalty, more violence.

For any of these boys—for any boy, for that matter—what does it take to pass as a man? At Henderson's hearing, Judy Shepard memorialized the number of languages Matthew spoke, the friends he'd had and books he'd read, the countries he'd traveled, the promise life held. As she spoke the courtroom heaved with her agony. But in the story writ large, it's almost as if Matthew's death counted for more than it might have if he had been just a wuss, a fag, her son; if he had been found in a ramble, with his pants down, with a trick (as have so many murdered gay men, whose cases have never been exploited by presidents to win points or by big, polite gay groups to raise dollars); if he had been killed simply because he was tiny and weak; if anything about the murder or its aftermath had forced a consideration of sex and freedom, instead of only tolerance and hate.

Since Shepard's death, the talk is all of hate crime laws. But as Rita Addessa of the Lesbian and Gay Task Force in Philadelphia, who nevertheless supports such laws, admits, they "will have no impact whatsoever on addressing the causes of anti-gay violence." They matter only to the dead or the maimed, for even if Wyoming were to become the twenty-third state with a hate-crime law including anti-gay violence, and even if a federal law were to pass, the little Matt and Matty Shepards of America would still grow up learning their place, because for them in all but eleven states discrimination is legal, and everywhere equality under the law is a myth. It's said that hate crime laws symbolize a society's values. If that is true, it means gay people are recognized only in suffering, and straight people are off the hook. It means Shepard may stand for every homosexual, but McKinney and Henderson stand just for themselves. It means nothing for life and, because its only practical function is to stiffen penalties, everything for death.

In her interview with *Vanity Fair*, Judy Shepard said she thought that her son would probably approve of the death penalty if he could know this case, if it had been his friend and not himself beaten at the fence. And in her conclusion at the hearing, she told Henderson, "My hopes for you are simple. I hope you never experience a day or night without feeling the terror, the humiliation, the helplessness, the hopelessness my son felt that night." Not just that night. As a gay man in America, Shepard must have sensed all of those things just around the corner, and not just in violence, not just in blood. Looking back on Henderson's biography, and on McKinney's, I wonder if, in different measure, they aren't already too well acquainted with such things; if perhaps the injuries of terror and humiliation aren't already too well spread around in this season of punishment and revenge.

"If a guy at a bar made some kind of overture to you, what would you do?"

"It depends on who's around. If I'm with a girl, I'd be worried about what she thinks, because, as I said, everything a man does is in some way connected to a woman, whether he wants to admit it or not. Do I look queer? Will she tell other girls?

"If my friends were around and they'd laugh and shit, I might have to threaten him.

"If I'm alone and he just wants to buy me a beer, then okay, I'm straight, you're gay—hey, you can buy me a beer."

[1]The order prohibits lawyers, witnesses, local, state and federal law-enforcement officers, et al. from discussing the case. McKinney's friend says he was visited by black-suited agents of

the Alcohol, Tobacco and Firearms Department shortly after McKinney and Henderson were arrested, and told them this story. Before it passed into his hands, says McKinney's friend, the gun had been stolen, which is consistent with court records. Henderson's grandmother says she noticed nothing unusual about Russell when he visited her on October 5. McKinney's friend and the other drug users, ex-users, or dealers in Laramie spoke with me on condition of anonymity.

*UW president Philip Dubois told me that the university has such an antidiscrimination policy, but as of July 1999 sexual orientation was still not included as a protected category in the university's official Equal Employment Opportunity/Affirmative Action Statement approved by the trustees. Nor does it appear in the antidiscrimination provisions for student admissions. Only these formal statements of policy have the force of law, says the ACLU's Marv Johnson.

letter from an american mom

SHARON UNDERWOOD

2000

For the *Valley News* (White River Junction, VT/Hanover, NH)

As the mother of a gay son, I've seen firsthand how cruel and misguided people can be.

Many letters have been sent to the *Valley News* concerning the homosexual menace in Vermont. I am the mother of a gay son and I've taken enough from you good people.

I'm tired of your foolish rhetoric about the "homosexual agenda" and your allegations that accepting homosexuality is the same thing as advocating sex with children. You are cruel and ignorant. You have been robbing me of the joys of motherhood ever since my children were tiny.

My firstborn son started suffering at the hands of the moral little thugs from your moral, upright families from the time he was in the first grade. He was physically and verbally abused from first grade straight through high school because he was perceived to be gay.

He never professed to be gay or had any association with anything gay, but he had the misfortune not to walk or have gestures like the other boys. He was called "fag" incessantly, starting when he was 6.

In high school, while your children were doing what kids that age should be doing, mine labored over a suicide note, drafting and redrafting it to be sure his family knew how much he loved them. My sobbing 17-year-old tore the heart out of me as he choked out that he just couldn't bear to continue living any longer, that he didn't want to be gay and that he couldn't face a life without dignity.

You have the audacity to talk about protecting families and children from the homosexual menace, while you yourselves tear apart families and drive children to despair. I don't know why my son is gay, but I do know that God didn't put him, and millions like him, on this Earth to give you someone to abuse. God gave you brains so that you could think, and it's about time you started doing that.

At the core of all your misguided beliefs is the belief that this could never happen to you, that there is some kind of subculture out there that people have chosen to join. The fact is that if it can happen to my family, it can happen to yours, and you won't get to choose. Whether it is genetic or whether something occurs during a critical time of fetal development, I don't know. I can only tell you with an absolute certainty that it is inborn.

If you want to tout your own morality, you'd best come up with something more substantive than your heterosexuality. You did nothing to earn it; it was given to you. If you disagree, I would be interested in hearing your story, because my own heterosexuality was a blessing I received with no effort whatsoever on my part. It is so woven into the very soul of me that nothing could ever change it. For those of you who reduce sexual orientation to a simple choice, a character issue, a bad habit or something that can be changed by a 10-step program, I'm puzzled. Are you saying that your own sexual orientation is nothing more than something you have chosen, that you could change it at will? If that's not the case, then why would you suggest that someone else can?

A popular theme in your letters is that Vermont has been infiltrated by outsiders. Both sides of my family have lived in Vermont for generations. I am heart and soul a Vermonter, so I'll thank you to stop saying that you are speaking for "true Vermonters."

You invoke the memory of the brave people who have fought on the battlefield for this great country, saying that they didn't give their lives so that the "homosexual agenda" could tear down the principles they died defending. My 83-year-old father fought in some of the most horrific battles of World War II, was wounded and awarded the Purple Heart.

He shakes his head in sadness at the life his grandson has had to live. He says he fought alongside homosexuals in those battles, that they did their part and bothered no one. One of his best friends in the service was gay, and he never knew it until the end, and when he did find out, it mattered not at all. That wasn't the measure of the man.

You religious folk just can't bear the thought that as my son emerges from the hell that was his childhood he might like to find a lifelong companion and have a measure of happiness. It offends your sensibilities that he should request the right to visit that companion in the hospital, to make medical decisions for him or to benefit from tax laws governing inheritance.

How dare he? you say. These outrageous requests would threaten the very existence of your family, would undermine the sanctity of marriage.

You use religion to abdicate your responsibility to be thinking human beings. There are vast numbers of religious people who find your attitudes repugnant. God is not for the privileged majority, and God knows my son has committed no sin.

The deep-thinking author of a letter to the April 12 *Valley News* who lectures about homosexual sin and tells us about "those of us who have been blessed with the benefits of a religious upbringing" asks: "What ever happened to the idea of striving . . . to be better human beings than we are?"

Indeed, sir, what ever happened to that?

• Sharon Underwood lives in White River Junction, Vt.

credits

every effort has been made to identify and give proper credit to copyright holders. Grateful acknowledgment is made to the following for permission to reprint previously published material:

in America: A Subjective Approach. Copyright © 1951 by Donald Webster Cory. Reprinted with the permission of Ayer Company Publishers.

Robert Duncan, "The Homosexual in Society" from *Selected Prose*. Copyright © 1968 by Robert Duncan. Reprinted with the permission of New Directions Publishing Corporation.

Havelock Ellis, "Sexual Inversion" from *Psychology of Sex*. Copyright © 1933 by Havelock Ellis. Reprinted with the permission of Harcourt, Inc.

Michel Foucault, excerpt from *The History of Sexuality*, Volume I: An Introduction, translated by Robert Hurley (New York: Pantheon, 1978). Copyright © 1978 by Random House, Inc. Reprinted with the permission of Georges Borchardt, Inc

Sigmund Freud, "Letter to an American Mother" Reprinted with the permission of Sigmund Freud Copyrights.

Paul Goodman, "The Politics of Being Queer" from *Nature Heals: The Psychological Essays of Paul Goodman*, edited by Taylor Stoehr (Highland, NY: Gesalt Journal Press, 1991). This essay contains Paul Goodman, "We Have a Crazy Love Affair" from *Hawkweed: Poems* (New York: Random House, 1967). Copyright © 1967 by Paul Goodman. All reprinted with the permission of Mrs. Sally Goodman.

Alfred C. Kinsey, Wardell P. Pomeroy, and Clyde E. Martin, "Homosexual Play" from *Sexual Behavior in the Human Male* (Bloomington: Indiana University Press, 1998). Reprinted with the permission of The Kinsey Institute for Research in Sex, Gender, and Reproduction.

David Kopay and Perry Deane Young, Chapter 4 from *The David Kopay Story*. Copyright © 1977 by David Kopay and Perry Deane Young. Reprinted with the permission of Don Congdon Associates, Inc.

Andrew Kopkind, "The Gay Moment" from *The Thirty Years' War: Dispatches and Diversions of a Radical Journalist, 1965-1994*. Originally published in The Nation (January 13, 1994). Copyright © 1995. Reprinted with the permission of Verso.

Larry Kramer, excerpt from "1,112 and Counting" from *Reports from the Holocaust: The Making of an AIDS Activist*. Originally collected in New York Native (March 1983). Copyright © 1983, 1989 by Larry Kramer. Reprinted with the permission of St. Martin=s Press, LLC and the author.

Marvin Liebman and William F. Buckley Jr., "A Coming-Out Letter and a Response" from *The Advocate* (1990). Reprinted with the permission of the Estate of Marvin Liebman and William F. Buckley Jr.

Audre Lorde, excerpt from *I Am Your Sister: Black Women Organizing Across Sexualities* Copyright © 1985 by Audre Lorde. Reprinted with the permission of Kitchen Table: Women of Color Press.

Norman Mailer, "Advertisement for 'The Homosexual Villain'" and "The Homosexual Villain" from *Advertisements for Myself*. Copyright © 1959 and renewed 1987 by Norman Mailer. Reprinted with the permission of Harvard University Press.

Armistead Maupin, "Letter to Mama" from *More Tales of the City*. Copyright © 1980 by Armistead Maupin. Reprinted with the permission of HarperCollins Publishers, Inc.